T X

Reinventing the Museum

To my graduate students in the

Department of Museum Studies

John F. Kennedy University

1986–1997

Reinventing the Museum

Historical and Contemporary Perspectives on the Paradigm Shift

EDITED BY GAIL ANDERSON

A Division of
ROWMAN & LITTLEFIELD PUBLISHERS, INC.
Walnut Creek • *Lanham* • *New York* • *Toronto* • *Oxford*

ALTAMIRA PRESS
A division of Rowman & Littlefield Publishers, Inc.
1630 North Main Street, #367
Walnut Creek, CA 94596
www.altamirapress.com

Rowman & Littlefield Publishers, Inc.
A wholly owned subsidary of The Rowman & Littlefield Publishing Group, Inc.
4501 Forbes Boulevard, Suite 200
Lanham, MD 20706

PO Box 317
Oxford
OX2 9RU, UK

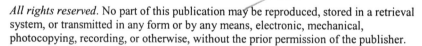

British Library Cataloguing in Publication Information Available

Library of Congress Cataloging-in-Publication Data
Reinventing the museum : historical and contemporary perspectives on the paradigm
shift / edited by Gail Anderson.
   p. cm.
  Includes bibliographical references.
  ISBN 0-7591-0169-8 (hardcover : alk. paper) — ISBN 0-7591-0170-1 (pbk. : alk.
paper)
  1. Museums—Philosophy. 2. Museums—Social aspects. 3. Museums—
Historiography. 4. Cultural property—Protection. I. Anderson, Gail, 1954– II. Title.
  AM7.R435 2004
  069—dc22
                                      2003017987

Printed in the United States of America

10394

Contents

Preface

Reinventing the Museum: Historical and Contemporary Perspectives on the Paradigm Shift endeavors to document the conversation that has been taking place since the early 1900s within the museum community about the evolving role of museums and their operations—what I call the *reinvention* of the museum.

HOW THIS BOOK WAS BUILT AND HOW TO USE IT

Organization

This anthology is organized into five parts that relate to the key areas of change in museums. The introduction frames the book with a discussion about the broad concept of reinvention and the main areas of museum operations that have been most affected. The primary sections align with a philosophical hierarchy that is intended to trace and elucidate the changing paradigm for museums. Each part has an introduction that relates the discussion to the reinvention concept and then sets the stage for the articles that follow. Each introduction outlines the predominant shift in thinking relative to the particular component of museum operations, with a brief statement about each author and the focus and emphasis of each article.

In Part I on the role of museums, the essays appear in chronological order and are designed to capture the historical evolution of thinking about the changing role of the museum and create a foundation for the rest of the book. The next three parts contribute essential discussions about the role of the public as central to the survival of a museum, the role of exhibitions and programs as the primary vehicles for serving the public, and the role of the collections cared for by museums. Part V addresses the need for sound leadership as the key ingredient for enabling museums to reach their greatest potential. The chapters in Parts II through V represent some of the best contemporary thinking about these particular aspects of museum operations. The first chapter in each section either frames the historical development of the particular topic area or provides an introduction to the section, and the remaining chapters highlight some of the most significant breakthroughs or best current thinking on that particular topic.

Essay Selection

The selected works address the paradigm shift in museums from a fieldwide perspective. Benchmark essays as well as representative pieces from recent literature were identified in a process that unfolded over two years, with many articles and book chapters reviewed and considered. One goal was to select pieces that corresponded to primary aspects of museum philosophy and operations such as governance, mission, management, curatorial concerns, collection care, education and public programs, exhibitions, visitor studies, marketing, and law and ethics. A second goal was to select works that captured the essence of the dialogue about each of those areas from a philosophical or issue-based perspective rather than from a how-to perspective.

The common threads among the chapters in this book are a recognition of and belief in:

- the centrality of the mission to all aspects of museum management and activities;
- the role of museums as educational institutions;
- the importance of informed, sensitive, and enlightened leadership at all levels to further the work of museums in a responsible, meaningful, and relevant way;
- the primary responsibility of museum leadership to fulfill its social contract by serving and reflecting diverse people and communities in all ways;
- the importance of averting complacency by engaging in ongoing evaluation; looking beyond the walls of the institution to understand communities, trends, changing demographics, and the marketplace; and undertaking strategies to assure that museums remain relevant to their communities while operating in a responsive and responsible manner;
- the legal and ethical behavior of trustees, staff, and volunteers, as set forth by international, federal, and state laws and currently accepted professional standards, in service to the museum and its role in the community.

The chapters demonstrate clear writing and sound reasoning, and they make reference to the evolution and issues of the museum profession. A deliberate effort was made to present a broad cross-section of the leading thinkers in the industry. For that reason, most authors are represented only once with the exception of the prolific author and contemporary museum critic, Stephen Weil. A balance of male and female perspectives, and diversity in background and expertise, was also sought. All authors represented are committed to the vitality of museums as cultural and educational institutions in society and in many cases are lobbying for substantial change, as the reader will discover.

Each chapter has qualities that transcend variations in museum type, size, and location. An early decision was made not to select essays with a heavy emphasis on any particular type of museum. Likewise, trying to cover the content issues represented in our diverse museum community was deemed unrealistic since it is as broad as the body of knowledge itself. While some of the chapters do reveal leanings toward one area of specialization or another, it was felt that the overriding qualities of the pieces pointed toward inclusion in the book. The editor's interest in cultural history and anthropology may be evident to the reader, but the goal was to be as evenhanded as possible in selecting a range of perspectives.

In the end, the overarching goal was to build a book that was circumspect in content and useful to trustees, volunteers, museum students, and professionals—whether seasoned, midcareer, or newcomer.

Recommendations to the Reader

Reinventing the Museum: Historical and Contemporary Perspectives on the Paradigm Shift has many intended uses that include the following:

- *outlining the historical evolution and dialogue about the museum* as an institution over the past century in order to understand the roots of contemporary issues and the future of museums;
- *identifying museum leaders* in the field who have made and continue to make significant contributions to our understanding and thinking about museums;
- *providing fodder for discussion and dialogue* among staff members, trustees, and students about the issues affecting museums;
- *providing a basic review of the literature* for students and professors of museum studies while stimulating dialogue about the evolving issues in the field.

In recognition of the many excellent essays that could not be included in this anthology, the reader is encouraged to seek out other related books and articles. It is also recommended that references about museum techniques be consulted to complement the philosophical approach presented here. At the end of each part is a list of suggested additional readings, and at the end of the book is a more extensive, although still select, bibliography. Finally, museum professionals need to continue the dialogue in the field and contribute to the literature on museums; they should be encouraged to write and to challenge the museum community with new insights and perspectives.

ACKNOWLEDGMENTS

In many ways, this book started taking shape when my tenure as chair of the Department of Museum Studies at John F. Kennedy University began early in 1986. It is only fitting first to thank all of the museum professionals represented in this volume.

Their thoughtful writing and perspectives have been instrumental in shaping the current thinking about museums. I am most grateful for their tenacity and efforts to push the field forward.

Several colleagues played a key role in reviewing the book at different stages in its development. In particular, I want to thank Stephen Weil for his feedback on the book in its early stages—he continues to inspire me with his wisdom and perspective on museums. A special thanks to Greta Brunschwyler for her candid advice and encouragement that led to the framework used for this book. With deep gratitude and appreciation to Elaine Heumann Gurian and Kathleen McLean for critiquing the book and providing me with invaluable insight about ways to improve it.

I want to thank Mitch Allen, who twisted my arm to tackle this project in the first place, and Susan Walters, who has been patiently nudging me and encouraging me during the long process of building this book. I can't imagine tackling this book with any other editor or publisher. Susan, you have been a joy to work with from start to finish.

Cheryl Kessler and Aubrey Wilder devoted and volunteered their time over a two-year period from the beginning to the conclusion of developing this anthology. Thank you for your tireless effort from conducting research, maintaining project records, attending numerous work sessions, reading endlessly, and participating in the ongoing review and critique of articles for inclusion. Aubrey, thank you for taking on the laborious task of securing copyright, and Cheryl, a special thanks for your editing feedback and, finally, reading the entire book from beginning to end to check for coherence. Simply put, this book would not have happened without the two of you.

A special thanks to Jennifer Rose and Danika McKenna for their unwavering patience and assistance during the laborious copyediting check of the book.

And to my family: John and Maya, your patience, love, and support have made undertaking this project possible. Maya, thank you for giving up some of our time together so that I could work on this project. John, thank you for standing by me throughout the long process of creating this book.

Introduction: Reinventing the Museum

Throughout the last century, museum leaders have been influencing the transformation of the museum and its role in society. During this time, every aspect of museum operations has at one point or another been placed under the microscope and examined for its clarity of focus and function relative to furthering the role of the museum as a cultural and educational institution within the greater fabric of society. The museum is no longer sacred or untouchable; rather, the museum is open to scrutiny, from within its walls and from an increasingly discriminating public. The process of rethinking the museum has brought intense examination of values and assumptions, the scope and nature of services offered, the focus and approach to leadership and management, and the relationship between museums and the people they wish to serve—the public. This examination of fundamental assumptions about museum operations has facilitated a dramatic paradigm shift in the way museum professionals, and some members of the public, regard museums.

The last century of self-examination—reinventing the museum—symbolizes the general movement of dismantling the museum as an ivory tower of exclusivity and toward the construction of a more socially responsive cultural institution in service to the public. While the seeds of change were sown by forward-looking thinkers like John Cotton Dana, it has taken almost a century of debate and discussion for the museum profession to embrace some of the core tenets espoused by Dana. The evolving dialogue and general acceptance of the new ideology within a much broader segment of the museum profession indicates that the paradigm shift from collection-driven institutions to visitor-centered museums has really taken hold. Policy statements and program initiatives advanced by our national museum associations reinforce this. But, as with any shift in thinking, each museum and museum professional interprets and applies new perspectives in ways unique to their own specific institutional resource capabilities or leadership style. At the heart of the reinvention of the museum is the desire by museum professionals to position the museum to be relevant and to provide the most good in society.

The parallel terms in table 1 capture the essence of the trends in the paradigm shift. This list of terms was developed over nearly three decades of working with museum leaders and listening to conversations about the changing role of muse-

Table 1   Reinventing the Museum

Traditional Museum		Reinvented Museum
Governance		
Mission as document	. . . .	Mission driven
Elitist	. . . .	Equitable
Exclusive	. . . .	Inclusive
Reactive	. . . .	Proactive
Ethnocentric	. . . .	Multicultural
Internal focus	. . . .	External focus
Singular vision	. . . .	Shared vision
Single visionary leader	. . . .	Shared leadership
Top-down management	. . . .	Bottom-up management
Assumed value	. . . .	Earned value
Good intentions	. . . .	Public accountability
Social activity	. . . .	Social responsibility
Paternal	. . . .	Mutual respect and stewardship
Managing	. . . .	Governing
Institutional Priorities		
Management	. . . .	Leadership
Various activities	. . . .	Mission-related activities
Collection driven	. . . .	Audience focused
Limited representation	. . . .	Broad representation
Internally based	. . . .	Community based
Open to the public	. . . .	Visitor oriented
Business as usual	. . . .	Institutional assessment
Voice of authority	. . . .	Multiple viewpoints
Focused on past	. . . .	Relevant and forward looking
Management Strategies		
Inwardly driven	. . . .	Responsive to visitor needs
Isolated and insular	. . . .	Participant in marketplace
Selling	. . . .	Marketing
Assumptions about audiences	. . . .	Knowledge about audiences
Hierarchical structure	. . . .	Learning organization
Unilateral decision making	. . . .	Shared decision making
Compartmentalized goals	. . . .	Holistic, shared goals
Cautious	. . . .	Informed risk taker
Fund development	. . . .	Entrepreneurial
Individual work	. . . .	Teamwork
Static role	. . . .	Strategic positioning
Communication Style		
Privileged information	. . . .	Open communication
Suppressed differences	. . . .	Welcomed differences
Debate/discussion	. . . .	Dialogue
One-way communication	. . . .	Two-way communication
Keeper of knowledge	. . . .	Exchange of knowledge
Protective	. . . .	Welcoming

Note: This chart was adapted from Museum Mission Statements: Building a Distinct Identity, edited and written by Gail Anderson and published by the American Association of Museums Technical Information Service in 1998.

ums. The terms on the left depict the assumptions and values that describe traditional museums and their view of their role. The terms on the right illustrate the characteristics typical of the reinvented museum. Please note that the term *traditional* is not intended to be pejorative but is rather a term for reference in this particular dialogue.

Within every institution, a useful dialogue can unfold about where the museum currently stands in the continuum between the traditional museum and the reinvented museum and where it wishes to be. Such a dialogue may point to a need to revisit the mission or shape a new vision in order to embrace the institution's greatest potential within today's complex marketplace. In the process of self-examination, the reinvented museum is likely to modify some traditions and retire others. In its most dramatic iteration, the conversation may cause a museum to overhaul the institution systematically at all levels of operation. Each museum will determine which aspects of its operation to retain and which new strategies to adopt, while charting a path that is realistic and appropriate.

Strong leadership is critical for leading a museum through any degree of institutional change, and visionary leadership is essential for leading a museum through fundamental change. Visionary leaders display a blend of talents that include undertaking institutional analysis while building consensus with stakeholders about a shared vision for the future of the institution. A visionary leader is masterful at communicating with diverse constituents while inspiring board, staff, and volunteers to work toward a more vital institution. Such a leader builds a rapport with the community, works in a healthy partnership with trustees to foster optimal functioning of the board, acknowledges the talents of staff and nurtures professional growth, and genuinely inspires and acknowledges the contributions of volunteers. In the end, significant change simply will not happen without a united, enlightened board in partnership with a visionary director.

It can be liberating for stakeholders to understand that change tends to unfold in stages. First an awareness of need must occur, followed by an acceptance of the need for change by stakeholders, then the exploration of different strategies for implementing change, and, finally, the adoption of an agreed-on approach for moving forward. Acceptance of the need to change may well be the biggest barrier to overcome. Without acceptance of the need to change, individuals or groups can become obstacles to advancing a new agenda and will dramatically slow progress. It is equally important to understand that fundamental change does not happen quickly; rather, it tends to unfold in layers that can span a year at the minimum and more likely several. Time is needed for such a shift to fully take hold and be embraced by all the internal stakeholders, as well as the immediate community and the public at large.

What does the reinvented museum look like? The following brief discussions illustrate some of the characteristics of the reinvented museum as listed in table 1.

GOVERNANCE

A governing body (board of trustees) for a museum is the oversight and leadership group responsible for the proper and ethical care of a museum's resources in support of fulfilling its public service mission. The role of the governing body is critical: An effective board of trustees can enable a museum to move forward and fulfill its role in the community, or an ineffectual board may impede the growth of a museum, cause it to function at a level far below its full potential, or even jeopardize its future. Leaving behind the elitist club image of boards, the reinvented board strives to diversify its membership in order to serve its community and fulfill its mission more effectively. The focused and enlightened board of trustees uses the mission statement as a core management tool for making decisions and guiding the work of the museum. The role of a trustee is clear and focused on shaping policies to guide the museum's work; upholding legal, ethical, and professional standards; and assuring prudent financial management and adequate resources to support the museum. Boards require enlightened leadership and members who understand not only the range of issues and complexities unique to museum governance in contemporary times but also the difference between their role and the role of implementation that is delegated to staff.

The enlightened board understands that it is accountable to the public and has a social responsibility to further the work of the museum in the public interest. The reinvented board takes actions that are in the best interests of the museum and its community—actions that offer the best potential for gaining public support through attendance, participation, and financial contributions. Board and staff understand that earning public trust is the ongoing endeavor and goal of the entire museum.

INSTITUTIONAL PRIORITIES

Institutional priorities in the reinvented museum support and advance the mission. The positioning of the visitor, education, and public service as the central focus embodies the most significant shift in institutional priorities for museums. Collections—historically viewed as the center of museum activities—have moved toward a supporting role that advances the educational impact of the museum. The collection holdings are no longer viewed as the primary measure of value for a museum; rather, the relevant and effective role of the museum in service to its public has become the core measuring stick. This sea change has shifted the sensibilities and ideology of some museums. The debate and dialogue continues with many museum professionals subscribing to these concepts, while some do not.

As museum priorities change over time, museum leaders will have to make difficult decisions while aiming to assure a stable, relevant organization that fulfills its responsibilities to the public. Institutional priorities are typically a blend of steps to strengthen the infrastructure of the museum (internal stability) balanced with delivering public services (external role). The ongoing tension of balancing the less visible inner workings of a museum with the more evident public engagement and activities can be challenging. Developing an appropriate organizational infrastructure is essential to supporting the board, staff, and volunteers in their efforts to raise financial support, build collections, and implement effective and appropriate public programs. Substantial change can occur with the greatest impact when the right infrastructure suits the new agenda.

The growing role of the public has a profound impact on museum operations. Frequently, the public is invited into the conversation about the future of the museum and about the shaping of exhibitions, programs, collections, and other activities. The visitor is regarded as both customer and guest, to be served with the goal of achieving visitor satisfaction and building a broader constituency. Offering effective visitor services is a more recent trend. In the past, just having the doors well guarded and open for business was considered adequate. Today, museum leaders know that understanding visitors' comforts, interests, and needs as well as engaging in market research are considered essential when making decisions and setting priorities.

The museum's role is a delicate balancing act—responding to the public's needs, while simultaneously challenging them with new ideas and interpretations. In the reinvented museum, voices of diverse cultures are visible throughout—in exhibitions; in the makeup of staff, volunteers, and trustees; and in policies that deepen the role of the museum in a way relevant to its entire community.

MANAGEMENT STRATEGIES

Management strategies are just that—strategic—and grounded in an understanding of the potential of museums in today's complex world. With clear roles and responsibilities for trustees, staff, and volunteers; well-defined mission, values, and vision; and a long-term plan, management strategies should be holistic and well integrated. Some management practices, once viewed as the purview of the corporate world, are now understood to be ingredients for enabling the museum to survive and achieve its mission. In the reinvented museum, philosophy translates into practice, and practice reflects philosophy, values, and mission.

In the reinvented museum, assumptions are scrutinized and questioned regularly. Regular evaluation of museum operations and public services provides ongoing feedback that keeps the museum on course and responsive to the external environment. Staff understands how their role advances the mission and adds value to the work of the museum. Decision-making processes reflect institutional values with an understood accountability for actions taken. A museum's position in the cultural life of the community is not taken for granted, and continuously looking beyond the walls of the institution is an accepted and encouraged mode of operation. Understanding the challenges of the marketplace is not an option but rather an essential ingredient for informed decision making. There are no isolated silos of operation. Instead, a holistic and interrelated mode of operation exists. All elements of museum operation support each other and contribute to the advancement of the mission. Thus, the reinvented museum is well managed, and it has a clear identity and public image, as well as the ability to implement the appropriate strategies to ensure a healthy and viable institution.

COMMUNICATION STYLE

Effective communication and mutual respect among trustees, staff, and volunteers are critical to a museum's ability to be effective. Key stakeholders need to understand all parts of the whole and how each individual, no matter his or her role, enables the institution to move forward. For example, understanding the importance of conservation cannot be the privileged domain of the conservator alone. Conservation needs to be understood within the full context of museum operations and its significant role in the responsible care of collections in support of the mission.

Sharing information within the organization is essential for staff and volunteers to understand and support institutional decisions and to participate in appropriate responses to financial pressures. The reinvented museum creates an open organizational culture with support for individual successes and risk taking. Along the path, implementing change means remaining open to disagreements and shifting to a dialogue format in which mutual understanding is more important than winning the argument. Acceptance, trust, and mutual respect are at the heart of the reinvented museum's organizational culture.

Internal communication is only part of the story for museums because their fundamental role is as a communicator with the external world. The traditional communication ideology of the museum has been to see the museum as the holder of knowledge and truth with a responsibility to exercise one-way communication *to* the public. In the reinvented museum, communication *between* museum and public is exemplified by a mutually respectful relationship; the ideology of two-way communication *with* the public creates a more responsive interchange of ideas, supplanting the older approach.

The meshing of internal and external communication is perhaps most apparent in the reinvented museum's approach to exhibit development. An audience advocate on the staff works with community members to represent the needs of the exhibit's target audience. They help facilitate a dialogue among the curator or exhibit developer, the designers, and the community that merges concerns and messages into a product that is more effective as a result of shared responsibility, joint planning, and exhibition development.

CONCLUSION

The paradigm shift discussed here and detailed in table 1 represents a continuum of change that started over a century ago and has moved us toward the contemporary museum. The dialogue continues in the museum community and will continue in the years ahead as new external pressures and new challenges continually stir museum leaders to reflect on and reassess their work. Keeping the dialogue alive on the local, regional, national, and international levels keeps the ongoing process of revitalization alive and helps avoid stagnation.

The reinvented museum is not formulaic, nor is it one-size-fits-all. The reinvented museum is a living, evolving model with the potential to maximize its impact. What is discussed here is the core of the model now—a model that will continue to reinvent itself in the years ahead.

Calling on the museum field to reexamine itself is one thing; initiating and leading change in an institution is quite another. Leading an institution through fundamental change requires strong, persistent, visionary leadership. Institutional change takes time, and it takes leaders who are willing to dig deep into the institution's history, values, and organizational culture to understand potential barriers and create consensus about a future vision and the steps to achieving that vision. Institutional change is a complex challenge. Leading change requires a thoughtful, sensitive, and tireless effort to address issues as they arise and as the institution evolves. To succeed, leadership is needed throughout the organization and most critically at the trustee and executive director levels. The strength and health of the executive director–board partnership is the barometer for institutional success in the reinvention process.

The discourse that unfolds in *Reinventing the Museum: Historical and Contemporary Perspectives on the Paradigm Shift* reveals the diverse levels and foci of the evolution of the museum over the past century from the perspective of some of its most vocal and gifted leaders. When considering the relevance of John Cotton Dana's "The Gloom of the Museum," written almost ninety years ago, it becomes clear how long it has taken for some of his ideas and challenges to be internalized. In today's museum community, some museums elect to remain unchanged and run the risk of becoming anachronistic. Others continue to question assumptions and motives in an effort to remain fresh in a dynamic world. There are lessons to be learned from both. The challenge is for museum leaders to be alert, questioning, and committed to the ongoing challenge of making museums a relevant and integral part of civic life.

THE ROLE OF THE MUSEUM: THE CHALLENGE TO REMAIN RELEVANT

The challenge for museums to remain relevant in society is an ongoing process of assessment that has occupied many museum leaders for years. The process is both external and internal—that is, given the external environment and contemporary issues (external) and the museum's capabilities and available resources (internal), what role should the museum assume or what services can the museum offer that will satisfy needs in the competitive marketplace? Of course, it is more complicated than that because a range of elements influences what is relevant for each museum. The evolving interests and needs of the public and immediate community; the institution's history of undertaking change; the mission of the museum; its leaders— past, present and future; and the museum's current role in its immediate community are just a few. The interplay of these elements is a part of what determines the vitality of a museum and its relevance to its community.

The process of assessing the external environment is an essential precursor to understanding what pressing issues and matters affect our communities and the public and, as a result, our museums. Having a grasp on emerging trends can also be useful in determining which aspects of the external environment require the attention of museum leadership. Obviously, to try to respond to the whole spectrum of societal ills or the constant ebb and flow of issues present in our immediate world is unrealistic, but to ignore them is foolish and risky. Visionary leaders have developed the ability to strike a balance between assessing the impact of external trends and examining their institution's capability to remain strategically positioned in the marketplace. This constant process of engaging in an external assessment and internal critique can help a museum remain in touch with and responsive to the specific issues of the external environment and thus position itself to remain relevant to its constituents.

The articles in this part capture the evolution of thinking about the role of museums over the past one hundred years. Presented in chronological order, these articles convey some of the milestones in the dialogue about museums and their role in society. The goal is to highlight the best discussions of the past century rather than to select the best pieces for each decade.

It is appropriate that John Cotton Dana, the innovative director of The Newark Museum in the early 1900s, introduces this part. Dana, recognized by museum professionals as a museum pioneer, has been often credited for his conviction to publicly challenge museums about their then-current practices of serving an elite group of patrons and not serving the broader public. In one of his most noteworthy articles, "The Gloom of the Museum," written in 1917 and a part of his *The New Museum Series*, Dana encouraged museum leaders to take their message to the greater community and to examine new methods for reaching a broader public, including dismantling an exclusive attitude about who should benefit from museums. He was a revolutionary spokesperson in his own right, and today he is still regarded as one of the most visionary museum leaders in recent times.

Theodore Low, a museum educator at the Metropolitan Museum of Art and another widely acknowledged contributor to the national discourse, was commissioned by the American Association of Museums (AAM) to write about museums. In his seminal piece "What Is the Museum?" written in 1942 while the world was at war, Low makes the case that the primary role of museums is as an educational institution contributing to society. He launched a discussion that has dominated professional literature and conferences for decades in which he argues for recognizing the museum as a vital educational resource along with schools and universities—as an institution rather than the role of a department within the museum.

Fast-forward to the 1970s. On the heels of the civil rights movement of the 1960s, the protests against the Vietnam War, and the growing role of television and the media, new voices were being heard in fundamental opposition to the establishment. Then just a few years later, Watergate pushed the door of public scrutiny and accountability wide open, alerting civic leaders that actions taken must be carefully measured in anticipation of public review and comment. This reality has remained a part of the fabric of life in the United States and for museums as well. The remaining articles in this part depict and outline some of the heated debates and issues that surfaced in the final decades of the twentieth century.

In her 1970 article, "A Twelve Point Program for Museum Renewal," Alma Wittlin outlines a compelling list of issues that continued to plague museums—some of the same issues raised by Dana years earlier, including the issue of a museum's isolation from the public. Yet she pushes the discussion to a new level, challenging museum leaders to examine honestly their motivations for decisions and to accept the fact that the actions of museums are not benign in a complex cultural world. It is interesting to note that her piece was published the same year the American Association of Museums Accreditation Program was launched.

The 1970s launched a new chapter in the development of museum professionalism as achieving new industry standards and expanding professional training took center stage in the museum community's national dialogue. Given the social tenor of this period, it is not surprising that in 1971, Duncan Cameron, the director emeritus of the Glenbow-Alberta Institute, wrote his piece, "The Museum, Temple or Forum," in which he frames the debate: Are museums to be places for reverence and worship of the object or places where the public gathers to debate, to consider issues of the day and the consequences of human actions? At the time, many museum leaders felt they had to choose. Today, many museums elect to embrace both.

By the 1990s, museum professionals began to publish articles and books at a more substantial rate than in decades past. One article, "Rethinking the Museum: An Emerging New Paradigm," written in 1990 by Stephen Weil, now an emeritus senior scholar at the Smithsonian Center for Education and Museum Studies, crystallizes much of the discussion of the prior decades about the shift in the primary functions of museums. Weil traces the evolution of the museum industry's definition of purpose for museums—from museum as primary collector to museum as educator in service to the public. Weil, one of the most prolific writers on museums and their issues, has for decades helped museum leaders look at their decisions and actions with new candor and more accountability.

Michael Ames, a well-known anthropologist and museologist and a former director and professor at the Museum of Anthropology, University of British Columbia, examines museums from an anthropological point of view—studying the often-peculiar habits and assumptions made by museums. In his 1992 article "Museums in the Age of Deconstruction," Ames slowly deconstructs the actions and attitudes of museums to illustrate how museums have approached the interpretation and voices of other cultures in museums. He illustrates, through carefully selected examples, how museums use and impose museological and anthropological approaches when interpreting and exhibiting cultures past and present within the culture of museums. Not uncommon is the resulting culture clash between their institutions and their respective publics and communities.

While the civil rights movement figured prominently in the national media from the 1960s onward, racism and equity did not enter the national dialogue in the museum community more fully until the late 1980s. Amalia Mesa-Bains, a MacArthur Foundation Fellow, professor, and champion of the Chicano artist movement, eloquently unveils the impact of a colonial paradigm in a world of multiple voices and diverse communities—a world in which most of those communities are not represented in museums. In her 1992 article "The Real Multiculturalism: A Struggle for Authority and Power," Mesa-Bains reveals how racial and societal inequities have played out within the walls of museums.

Edmund Barry Gaither, the longtime executive director of the Museum of the National Center of Afro-American Artists in Boston and a cofounder of the African American Museums Association, contributed his perspective to the milestone 1992 publication, *Museums and Communities: The Politics of Public Culture.* In his article,

"Hey! That's Mine: Thoughts on Pluralism and America," Gaither addresses the issue of power—the power of objects as reflections of self-identity and sources of personal validation—the thread of national consciousness absent for so many people
of color in our nation's museums, collections, and exhibitions. Gaither, credited for
reminding the museum industry of its "social contract" with the public, has been a
voice for underserved communities for many decades.

Although not reprinted here, readers should keep in mind that at the same time
the Mesa-Bains and Gaither articles were published, the American Association of
Museums formally adopted the policy paper *Excellence and Equity: Museums and
the Public Dimension.* This policy paper was created under the leadership of Joel
Bloom, then president of AAM who launched the initiative, and Bonnie Pitman, the
founder of EdCom, a standing professional committee on education for AAM, and
now the deputy director of the Dallas Museum of Art, who chaired the committee
of museum professionals that shaped this policy. This document, a clarion call to
the profession, emphasized the necessity for equity in all aspects of museums and
heralded the primary role of museums as educational institutions.

Closing out Part I is a 1999 article from *Daedalus* by Harold Skramstad, the president emeritus of the Henry Ford Museum and Greenfield Village in Dearborn,
Michigan, a former commissioner for the AAM Accreditation Commission, and
now a consultant. In "An Agenda for American Museums in the Twenty-First Century," Skramstad reframes the discussion of relevance as he points to the need for
museums to engender trust, openness, and connectedness with the communities
they serve. The seeds of Dana's comments a century earlier are placed in the contemporary context of the challenges facing museums at the beginning of the
twenty-first century.

The Gloom of the Museum

John Cotton Dana

PROLOGUE

Today, museums of art are built to keep objects of art, and objects of art are bought to be kept in museums. As the objects seem to do their work if they are safely kept, and as museums seem to serve their purpose if they safely keep the objects, the whole thing is as useful in the splendid isolation of a distant park as in the center of the life of the community which possesses it.

Tomorrow, objects of art will be bought to give pleasure, to make manners seem more important, to promote skill, to exalt handwork, and to increase the zest of life by adding to it new interests; and these objects being bought for use will be put where the most people can most handily use them: in a museum planned for making the best use of all it contains, and placed where a majority of its community can quickly and easily visit it.

PART I: HOW THE ARTS HAVE BEEN INDUCED TO FLOURISH

The story of an art epoch in the life history of a people seems to resolve itself into something like this:

Character and circumstances lead the people into conquest. It may sound better, though it means the same, to say that character and circumstances bring out a few men of genius who lead and rule the people and take them on to conquest. The conquest means wealth, and this is true whether the conquest be of other peoples by leadership and force of arms, or of the land's natural resources and of methods of producing and using power.

Always a few gain most of the wealth and hold most of the power. The conquest being somewhat well assured, these few have leisure. They search for occupations

---

John Cotton Dana (1856–1929), a prolific writer and librarian, was the founding director of The Newark Museum in Newark, New Jersey, and widely recognized as one of the pioneer museum thinkers of the last century. "The Gloom of the Museum" written by Dana in 1917 was part of *The New Museum Series*, a series of small booklets that addressed issues pertinent to museums. It is reprinted here by permission of The Newark Museum Association/The American Association of Museums.

and things and indulgences which may give them pleasure. Whatever else these occupations, objects, and indulgences may be, they must be such as the common people cannot have; for the rich and ruling class must always keep itself distinct from
the lower classes in its pleasures and pastimes, just as it always did in its leadership
in war and government. These distinctive recreations and diversions and admired
objects of the powerful and rich have always been of about the same character. War
is first choice; if not war of the higher kind in which is involved the existence of the
tribe, family, city, dukedom, principality, kingdom, or nation over which the rich
and powerful in question rule, then a war of petty conquest, mean in itself, but permitting some braggadocio, keeping up the clan spirit and exalting the ruling class.
Lacking a vigorous and dangerous war on battlefields to engage all their activities,
the rulers have often turned to hunting—to hunting in a form which nature, or special laws, or the rules of the game make somewhat dangerous; for if it does not at
least seem dangerous, those who engage in it will not appear brave to the lower
classes. The form of hunting chosen is usually one which is quite inaccessible to the
poor and weak. Big game near home, and better still at a good distance; falconry, the
right to use falcons being easily restricted to the few; fox hunting on horseback; dangerous athletic sports; and latterly automobiling, ballooning, and flying—these have
all had or shall have their vogue.

Another obvious method of distinguishing their life from that of the common
people has been the possession of distinctive residences beyond all need in size,
number, cost, and adornment. It is through these residences that the rich and powerful have chiefly been led to become patrons of the arts. The wish to make full use
of the religious habits of the ruled has often led the rich to build and adorn
churches; and always, of course, the need of expensive and peculiar dress has been
an occasion for calling in the aid of artisans of certain kinds. The study of literature,
language, history, and the fine arts has also often been a recreating of the rich,
though usually these studies have been pursued by proxy. As unusual native ability
has almost always been one of the essentials to success in acquiring wealth and
power, it is not strange that an occasional member of the class of the ruling rich has
shown marked ability in letters and the arts, or at least in appreciation of them. But
pursuit of art and letters has usually ended with little more than such a patronage
of them as would bring in return ample adulation, a reputation for learning, and
glorification in history.

Comparative security, then, after a series of profitable wars, finds the rich and
powerful compelled to engage in expensive sports, to build large and expensive residences, and to decorate them and to adorn elaborately their own persons that there
may be no lack of distinctions between themselves and the common people. The demand for architects, painters, sculptors, gold and silversmiths, ironworkers, and artisans of all kinds thus at once arises; and a demand also for teachers, poets, orators,
and historians to make a pretense of love of learning.

It is worth noting here that in former days these workers produced without the intervention of machinery; that the rich have usually been ready to adopt the older methods in art productions if for any reason they were inaccessible to the poor; and that today admiration for the handmade is largely born of a desire to have something which, being unique in its kind, will impart a little of the old leisure-class exclusiveness to its owner.

The patronage of the arts, with the consequent development thereof, has varied in extent in the rise to wealth and leisure of the leaders among different peoples, as circumstances dictated, but its origin seems always to have been about the same. Whenever this patronage has appeared—whenever, that is, the demand for objects of art has arisen—the supply has been forthcoming.

Fashion among the rich has sometimes prevented the results of this patronage of art from showing themselves very plainly in the country of the rich. In our day, for example, the fashion is to import from abroad and to say that good artwork cannot be produced at home; so we have a Barbizon painting factory in Paris, makers of antiques in Italy, and a digging up of gone-by utensils and furniture in all European and Asiatic countries. These old things cost more in the first place, the tariff makes them more expensive still, and their ownership gives considerable of the ruling-class distinction. Were it to become the fashion to patronize American designers and craftsmen in all lines and to give artists and architects a free hand instead of insisting on conformity to the ancient ways as interpreted by the ignorant rich, we would have a larger art demand in America; the supply would raise prices and wages; art study would be encouraged; more men of genius, skill, and training would come here from abroad; and we would begin our own renaissance.

Those who know Mr. Veblen's delightful book on "The Theory of the Leisure Class" will see that I have borrowed from him in my statement about the character of the diversions and the conspicuous waste of the rich.

But our renaissance does not come. We have an aristocracy based on wealth, with accompanying power. This aristocracy feels the same need that aristocracies have always felt of acquiring ancient, rare, and costly objects that the possession of them may mark them as superior to the poor and weak. They find that the easiest way to acquire such objects is not to cause them to be produced by artists and artisans of their own country—America—but, as already noted, to purchase them in older countries. What had already given distinction to their owners in France, Italy, England, and Germany is seen at once to be peculiarly well fitted to give a like distinction here. Hence the products of our own people are definitely held in no esteem as honorific possessions. Art in America does not flourish.

I have used the foregoing remarks, taken from a paper published in the *Independent* seven years ago, as a preface to the essay which follows on the gloom of the museum in the hope that they will make still more self-evident the statements in the latter concerning the origin of American museums of art. The kinds of objects—ancient, costly, and imported—that the rich feel they must buy to give themselves a desired distinction are inevitably the kinds that they, as patrons and directors of museums, cause those museums to acquire. Veritably, most of our great museums look with open scorn on the products of American artists and artisans.

The peculiar sanctity of oil paint on canvas has been graciously extended in some small degree to New World products, and our great museums occasionally buy, more often receive as gifts, and still more often receive as loans for exhibition the works of American painters. But most of our richer museums of art, that in Chicago being a notable exception, follow the dictates of the rich. They very evidently do not think it is the proper function of a museum of art to promote, foster, or patronize American talent.

The new museum, for the development of which this series is designed, will hold that its first duty is to discover talent and encourage its development here at home.

The rich and powerful collect foreign things and insist that foreign things only shall be enshrined in the museum they patronize. The poor follow the rich in this thinking. The attempt to modify this state of affairs is not one that is full of hope. But the growing habit of cities to maintain their own museums will surely tend to democratize them; and if, in the beginnings of the museums that are now coming into existence, the suggestions for making them immediately and definitely useful to their founders and patrons—the public—which we find today so widely approved among museum workers are quite generally adopted, the day will soon come when many public museums will look upon the promotion of American art as one of their most important functions.

PART II: THE GLOOM OF THE MUSEUM, WITH SUGGESTIONS FOR REMOVING IT

Prefatory Note

The art of museum construction, acquisition, and management is in its infancy. No one can say with authority how that art will be developed in the next few years. But on this much at least the public may congratulate itself: that museum authorities now feel that their respective establishments should be, above all things, attractive in a sane and homely way to the public which owns them.

Art museums of necessity have the faults of their ancestry, and these faults are so obvious that even a layman like myself may see them, and the plain statement of such of them as a layman dares to say he sees may help to move the intelligent part of the public to set to work to correct them.

Throughout this discussion I have art museums almost solely in mind.

How Museums Came to Be So Gloomily Beautiful

One need visit only a few of the older museums of art and archaeology in Europe to understand why most American museums of the same subjects are so ineffective.

In Europe, these older museums have objects of great importance to students of art, of history in general, of the history of art, of social development, and of the history of invention and discovery. Large groups of these objects were first collected many years ago by wealthy and powerful individuals: princes, kings, emperors, and members of the nobility. These collectors were usually entirely selfish in their acquisition, rarely looking beyond their own personal pleasure or the aggrandizement of their immediate families. They collected that they might possess, not that they might use, or that others might use, the things collected for the pleasure and advancement of the world at large.

As the idea of general welfare crept into and modified the government of any given country, the ruling powers of that country in many cases confiscated or purchased these collected treasures, added other purchases and gifts to them, made them so-called public collections, and deposited them for safekeeping in national and municipal buildings. These buildings were for the most part erected for other purposes than the reception and proper display of works of art and archaeology. This fact usually made it possible to install collections in them only under such conditions of space and light as prevented either logical or artistic arrangement and made both casual observation and careful study of most of the objects a burden instead of pleasure.

As the collections were of very great value—consisting usually of originals which no money could replace, which should therefore be guarded with the utmost care—the first thought in regard to them was their preservation; their utilization being a secondary and rather remote affair.

Why Museum Buildings Are Temples and Palaces

The character of the buildings which, as time went on, were here and there erected to house these collections of priceless originals, was determined by several factors. As most of the collections had found their first homes in the palaces of rulers or members of the nobility, it was quite naturally concluded that their new homes should also be in the style of the local palace or royal residences. As the things collected were objects of art, it seemed obvious that they should be housed in artistic buildings, and as for several centuries it has been difficult for architects or those having power over art collections to conceive of an artistic building save in terms of Greek or Renaissance architecture, nearly all special museum buildings imitated either the Greek temple or the Italian palace.

In Europe, therefore, we find museums to be either old buildings of the royal palace type or later constructions copying the palace or the Greek temple; containing priceless originals in all lines of art, craftsmanship, and archaeology; arranged as the characters of the several buildings compel; guarded with extreme care; dutifully visited by serious-minded tourists; and used sparingly by a small number of special students.

New America Copies the Old Europe, of Course

This, roughly speaking, was the museum idea as it embodied itself in Europe when the subject of museums began a few decades ago to be taken up seriously in America. It was inevitable that the first wish of all our museum enthusiasts should be to produce imitations of the European institutions. Those institutions were, in most cases, long established and greatly admired, and they furnished the only illustrations of the museum idea.

Moreover, collections more or less well suited to form the beginnings of art museums had been made here, after the European manner, by a few of the rich; some of these had fallen by gift or will to public use, accompanied not infrequently by the requirement that they be permanently housed in art buildings which were inevitably fashioned after the European type.

The promoters of art museums in America had no choice in the matter. The approved examples of Europe, the precedents already established in America in accordance with those examples, the unanimous votes of architects and trustees on what it is that makes a building a fit home for works of art, and the voice of so much of the general public as had ever seen or heard of European museums—all these factors united to complete the erection here of the kind of museum building which now oppresses us.

Why Museums Are Way Off in the Woods

The prevalence of the European idea of a museum determined not only the character of our museum buildings but also their location. As they must be works of art, and as temples and palaces need open space about them to display their excellences, and as space in the centers of towns is quite expensive, donors, architects, trustees, and city fathers all agreed that the art museum building should be set apart from the city proper, preferably in a park with open space about it. Distance from the center of population and the difficulty most citizens would encounter did they attempt to see the museum's contents were given no weight in comparison with the obvious advantages of display of the building's outer charms.

The Museum of Religious Gloom

A city may with perfect propriety set itself to the task of making a collection of rare and ancient original products of man's craftsmanship, spending, for example, $10,000 for a piece of tapestry, $100,000 for a painting, $30,000 for a marble statue, $20,000 for a piece of porcelain, and so on; it may add to these by gift and may place them all in a one-story, poorly lighted, marble, fireproof building set in a park remote from the city's center. But it ought to do this with a full comprehension of the fact that, while it is in so doing establishing a "Museum of Art" in the sense in which that phrase is most often used today, it is not forming an institution which will either entertain or instruct the community to an extent at all commensurate with its cost. In such an establishment the city will have an "art museum" of the kind which the citizen points out with pride to visiting friends; which appears in the advertising pamphlets of the local boards of trade; which is the recipient of an occasional painting or other work of art from a local art patron; which some strangers and a few resident women and children occasionally use to produce in themselves the maximum of fatigue with the minimum of pleasure; which will offer through the opening of loan collections a few opportunities each winter for society to display itself and demonstrate its keen aesthetic interests.

Rarity and High Price Make Things More Beautiful

The European examples which were so disastrous in their effect on the character and location of our museum buildings had an unfortunate influence also on the character and arrangement of their contents.

In the order of events in Europe, as already noted, one country after another and one city after another came into the possession of treasures of art and archaeology—priceless originals—which it was the duty of the authorities to preserve with the utmost care. Our own art museum enthusiasts, imitating their predecessors, sought also to form collections of unique and costly objects. A delusion like that which everywhere possesses the art novice as to the relative value of real oil paintings, however atrocious, and colored lithographic reproductions of paintings, however excellent, possessed those who made private art collections and those who selected and purchased objects for our museums. Art museum objects were not chosen for their beauty or for the help they might give in developing good taste in the community, but for their rarity, their likeness to objects found in European museums, and for their cost.

The older collections on the continent are naturally largely historical and archaeological. This seemed sufficient reason for making our collections of the same kind.

The wish to form collections which should illustrate the development of this or that special form of art also influenced greatly the character of our early museums.

But the wish to make them, like their European models, include a large number of things peculiar, unique, not copies, not obtainable by others, and costly, was probably the chief factor in making our museums mausoleums of curios.

The objects acquired being rare and costly, it was inevitable that they should be very carefully safeguarded, placed where they could be seen only (and that not very adequately), and never handled and examined closely.

American Museums Today

That this rough outline of recent museum history in America is fairly correct is amply demonstrated by present-day American museums themselves. They are usually housed in buildings fashioned to look like Greek temples or Renaissance palaces, which are very poorly adapted to the proper installation of collections and very rarely well planned for growth. These buildings are set apart from the city whose citizens they are built to serve, often in remote parks. The objects in them are very largely second-rate original artworks, usually with large additions of things historical or archaeological of little art value. Many of the buildings are so expensive to administer and to light and to heat that the managers can keep them open to the public only a small part of the hours when the public can best visit them. They are visited by few, that few being made up largely of strangers passing through the city; and the objects displayed are used for practical, everyday purposes and are looked to for suggestions applying to daily life by a very small number of persons, and by them very rarely.

Museum Failures Are Not Chargeable to Specific Persons

It may be said that if this development of American art museums into remote palaces and temples—filled with objects not closely associated with the life of the people who are asked to get pleasure and profit from them, and so arranged and administered as to make them seem still more remote—it may be said that if this development has been as natural and inevitable as has been suggested, then no one can be charged with responsibility for the fact, and not much can be done to correct the error.

It would indeed be difficult to lay the burden of this unfortunate line of development on the shoulders of any persons who may be specifically named. It would be difficult also to correct the mistake already made. No one, for example, would quite dare to suggest (taking up the point only of location) to the citizens of Boston, New York, Buffalo, and Cincinnati that they can much better afford, in the long run, to move their museums into the centers of daily movement of population and thereby secure a tenfold enlargement of their use and influence, than they can to go on paying large sums for their maintenance in relative idleness where they are now.

And it would be idle to attempt to persuade architects and trustees and a public, bound to accept the architectural conventions of their time, that when they use the outward presentations of one-story buildings designed for housing gods in a perpetual twilight as the peripheries of well-lighted and convenient and easily warmed and controlled spaces for the display of precious objects to thousands of visitors, they show a certain magnificent courage, but not good architectural traits, not originality, and not common sense.

But, in spite of the depressing influence of fashion and of the architectural paralysis induced by the classic burden in these matters, one may hope that all museums hereafter built need not conform to the old ideas, and that some of the museums already in existence can be so modified as to be far more useful and influential than they are today.

The Art of Museum Making in Its Infancy

The art of making museums which will be largely used by those who pay for them and will please and profit all who visit them is in its infancy. No one ventures to describe definitely the ideal American art museum. A few suggestions may at least provoke helpful discussion.

Museums Should Be Central

An art museum should be so located that it may be reached by a maximum number of persons with a minimum expenditure of time and money. It should be near the center of the city which maintains it—not its population center but its rapid transit center—and as near as possible also to its more important railway stations that strangers may visit it quickly and cheaply.

It may be said that a collection of art objects properly housed in a beautiful building gains somewhat in dignity and importance and in its power to influence beneficially those who visit it if it is set apart a little from the city's center of strenuous commercial and material life; holds itself somewhat aloof, as it were; detaches itself from the crowd; and seems to care to speak only to those whose desire for its teachings is strong enough to lead them to make some sacrifice of time and money to enjoy them.

The suggestion is a specious one. This theory of the fitness of remoteness is born of pride and satisfaction in the location and character of museums as they are. The buildings are remote and are religious or autocratic or aristocratic in style; their administrators, perhaps in part because of this very aloofness and sacrosanct environment, are inclined to look upon themselves as high priests of a peculiar cult, who may treat the casual visitor with tolerance only when he comes to worship rather than to look with open eyes and to criticize freely; and the trustees are prone to think more of their view of the proper museum atmosphere than of museum patronage, more of preservation than of utilization.

This same theory as to the preciosity which remoteness may confer, applied to art in general and carried to its logical conclusions, would forbid the expenditure of public funds or private gifts on the beautifying of streets or bridges or public buildings. Under its application, one might say that a commercial city should be built in the coldest, baldest possible style, and that beautiful façades of homes, office buildings, and factories should be erected as façades only in remote parks and boulevards, there to be solemnly visited and viewed by those who truly care to exalt their souls and purify their intellects.

The Museum Building: Some of Its Obvious Qualities

The museum building located in the city's center should satisfy the fundamental conditions of all good architecture: It should be large enough for its purpose; it should be constructed of the materials, proper in its day, which are best adapted to its form and size; it should be in harmony with its surroundings; and it should be as beautiful as the highest technique and the best taste of the time can make it.

A building of steel and concrete in a modern American city is not made an appropriate home of the fine arts by placing on its front the façade of one or the façades of half a dozen Greek temples or of 15th-century Italian palaces. It is impossible to believe that the best Greek architects, if they were the masters in good taste we suppose them to have been, would have continued to make their buildings look as though they were built of columns of stone, with huge girders and crossbeams of the same material, long after they had learned to use steel and concrete in construction.

In time we shall learn to insist that great public buildings like libraries and museums be erected as such and not as imitations of structures developed for quite other purposes, in other cities, in other times, and under limitations as to material and method by which we are no longer bound.

A modern museum building for an American city is a distinct problem in arrangement and a difficult one not to be solved by the adoption for its exterior of a type, however beautiful, which in origin and development never bore the slightest relation to the subject of museums.

It may be said that the contents of art museums are in part priceless, cannot be replaced, must be so housed as to make their destruction by fire impossible, and that, therefore, the only safe location for a museum is in a park, far from all other buildings. In reply it may be said that the high value put on many of the objects in art museums is largely fictitious, born of the rivalry of rich collectors and even of rich museums in their search for objects of honorable uniqueness; that a few students could truly feel their loss; but that as instruments of human enlightenment and happiness they are by no means priceless. Next, it may be noted that it is doubtful if any art museum authorities have yet erected a remote building on the contents of which they can get fire insurance rates as low as they could get them on the same contents housed in a fireproof building in the center of their city. There are risks in remoteness as well as safeguards. It should also be said that if a city wants a warehouse for the storage of art treasures, build it by all means; but do not encumber it with the fine, open spaces of a public park. But if it wants an institution of the newer museum type, something from which can be derived pleasure, surely, and profit if the gods permit, then let that be built where it can be easily made use of, in the city's center.

In a great city the museum building could properly be several, perhaps many, stories high, and if open space about it were quite impossible for financial reasons, light could be had from courts. Nearly all rooms would then be lighted from one side, as nearly all exhibition, study, and lecture rooms should be.

The Vast Extent of Museum Collections Leads to Obscurity

The objects gathered in art museums will continue to include the works of men's hands in all materials, for all purposes, of all countries, and for all time. Students of every form of art will continue to ask that museums include not only the products of that art when it was at the highest point of its development, but also its products in every stage of its growth and of its decline. Museums—that is, some of the large museums at least—must continue to be not only museums of many arts, but also of the histories of those arts, and therefore of archaeology and of ethnology.

But as time goes on, many collections, thus expanding naturally into other fields than that of art, will become unwieldy, overloaded with objects of interest only to the very special student, mere confusing masses of seemingly unrelated objects to the ordinary visitor. They will lose all effectiveness in what should be their special field—that of suggesting to the observer that a certain refinement of daily life is worth all it costs—and, to the would-be promoter of this refinement, that certain special methods in this, that, and the other field have been successful once and may be successful again. That is to say, art museum collections continually tend to lose the power of doing that which they were designed to do, which is to say to us that manners and feelings are important parts of life. For the objects which have to do with age-long gropings after good things will always tend to become so numerous as to hide the good things themselves.

The Undue Reverence for Oil Paint

The extreme veneration now paid by museum authorities to great paintings will surely become weaker as the possibilities of a museum's influence become better understood. Painting in oil upon canvas is not a craft that makes a strong appeal to the average man, save through the stories it tells. Its value, after all, is almost entirely pictorial. As mere pictures—which is all that they are to the average observer of ordinary intelligence, plus the interest born of their age, their history, and their cost—they each year suffer more and more from the competition of other pictures not done in oil on canvas, found in posters, in journals and newspapers, and in the cinema. In due course the oil painting will take its place in museums with other products of men's hands simply as one of the many things of high beauty and great suggestiveness produced in perfection only by men of special talent who have been able to master a difficult technique.

This fact will in time be recognized and acted upon: that the oil painting has no such close relation to the development of good taste and refinement as have countless objects of daily use. The genius and skill which have gone into the adornment and perfecting of familiar household objects will then receive the same recognition as do now the genius and skill of the painter in oils. Paintings will no longer be given an undue share of space, and on them will be expended no undue share of the museum's annual income. It is doubtful if any single change in the general principles of art museum management will do as much to enhance museum influence as will this placing of the oil painting in its proper relation with other objects.

The Subordination of Painting and the Promotion of Applied Art

If oil paintings are put in the subordinate place in which they belong, the average art museum will have much more room for the display of objects which have quite a direct bearing on the daily life of those who support it, visit either the main buildings or its branches, and make use of its collections. One need not be specific; the museum will show by originals or replicas what has been done by other people to make more convenient and attractive all the things that we use and wear and see day by day, from shoes to signposts and from table knives to hat pins. As the museum gives more space and more attention to these things, it will quite inevitably also display the objects in which its own city is particularly interested. It will have no absurd fear that it will be commercialized and debased if it shows what is being done today in the field of applied art in its own city and in other parts of the world. It will take no shame from the fact that it is handling and installing and displaying articles made by machinery for actual daily use by mere living people. One of the grotesqueries of expertness in museum work today is the reverential attention paid to products of craftsmanship which are (1) old, (2) rare, (3) high in price, (4) a little different from all others, and (5) illustrate a change in method of work or in the fashion of their time. Still more depressing is this reverence when it is accompanied, as it often is, with indifference, or scorn, or fear of commercial taint, toward products of craftsmanship which are (1) modern, (2) common, (3) not high in price, (4) a copy of the old, rare, and priceless.

What could be more ludicrous than the sight of those who, openly devoted to the worship of beauty, treat with scorn modern reproductions of old things which they have pronounced beautiful, even if they copy the old so well that only labels and microscopes can distinguish one from the other, or even if, not professing to be exact reproductions, they show originality and high skill in design, are technically quite perfect, and either disclose the taste of the time or are factors in the betterment of that taste.

Surely a function of a public art museum is the making of life more interesting, joyful, and wholesome; and surely a museum cannot very well exercise that function unless it relates itself quite closely to the life it should be influencing; and surely it cannot thus relate itself unless it comes in close contact with the material adornment of that life—its applied arts.

The necklace found on an Egyptian mummy is unique, old, and costly. But even if presented to a museum by someone of wealth and influence, it still may be hideous and it may have no suggestion whatever for the modern designer. If it has certain suggestive value in this line, it thereby becomes just as well worthy of its place in the museum as is a necklace made yesterday in a neighboring city. Being unique, it should be kept. Its origin gives it an archaeological value. But if it is admitted to a museum of art, it need not stand in the way of the display in the same museum of modern necklaces which may interest many and may give suggestion and stimulus to modern designers.

Of course, it is not the Egyptian mummy's necklace which stands in the way of the display of modern necklaces, but the spirit of curators, experts, directors, and trustees. They become enamored of rarity, of history, and, in this specific instance, of necklaces as indicative of steps in civilization. They become lost in their specialties and forget their museum. They become lost in their idea of a museum and forget its purpose. They become lost in working out their idea of a museum and forget their public. And soon, not being brought constantly in touch with the life of their community through handling and displaying that community's output in one or scores of lines, they become entirely separated from it and go on making beautifully complete and very expensive collections, but never construct a living, active, and effective institution.

Is the Department Store a Museum?

A great city department store of the first class is perhaps more like a good museum of art than are any of the museums we have yet established. It is centrally located; it is easily reached; it is open to all at all the hours when patrons wish to visit it; it receives all courteously and gives information freely; it displays its most attractive and interesting objects and shows countless others on request; its collections are classified according to the knowledge and needs of its patrons; it is well lighted; it has convenient and inexpensive rest rooms; it supplies guides free of charge; it advertises itself widely and continuously; and it changes its exhibits to meet daily changes in subjects of interest, changes of taste in art, and the progress of invention and discovery.

A department store is not a good museum, but so far are museums from being the active and influential agencies they might be that they may be compared with department stores and not altogether to their advantage.

The Museum as the Teacher and Advertiser

To make itself alive, a museum must do two things: It must teach and it must advertise. As soon as it begins to teach, it will of necessity begin to form an alliance with present teaching agencies, the public schools, the colleges and universities, and the art institutions of all kinds. It is only by bearing in mind the history of its development and the part that imitation has played in that development that one can understand how American communities have been able to establish, build up, and maintain great collections of works of art, beautifully and expensively housed and administered, which yet have almost no cooperative relations with all the other educational and social-betterment institutions of the same communities. Teaching tends to become dogmatic. Dogmatism in art is injurious, but museum teaching need not be dogmatic. Indeed, museums might well be less dogmatic than they now are. They buy high-priced paintings and spend vast sums for rare brocades, pottery, ancient wood carvings, and whatnot, and then set these (with an ample air of assurance of wisdom which may very well be called dogmatic) before their constituents, saying,

"Look, trust the expert, and admire." Far less dogmatic would it be to set side by side in a case ancient and rare modern and commercial pottery, and say, "Here are what some call the fine products of the potter's art when it was at its best in Italy long ago, and here are products of the potters of America today. You will find a comparative study of the two very interesting."

Would there be anything debasing in such an apposition? Would it be less dogmatic than is nearly all museum presentation of itself today?

By no right in reason whatever is a museum a mere collection of things, save by right of precedent. Yet precedent has so ruled in this field that our carefully organized museums have little more power to influence their communities than has a painting which hangs on the wall of some sanctuary, a sanctuary which few visit and they only to wonder as they gaze and to depart with the proud consciousness that they have seen. Some of the best of our museums, spending many thousands per year on administration and many other thousands on acquisitions, are now pluming themselves on the fact that they employ one—only one—person to make their collections more interesting to the thousands who visit them; that they have a hall in which during a winter a few lectures are given; and that they publish a bulletin recording their progress in piling up treasures, and catalogues which are as devoid of human interest as a perfect catalogue can be.

Museums of the future will not only teach at home, they will travel abroad through their photographs, their textbooks, and their periodicals. Books, leaflets, and journals—which will assist and supplement the work of teachers and will accompany, explain, and amplify the exhibits which art museums will send out—will all help to make museum expenditures seem worthwhile.

Why Not Branch Museums?

Museums will soon make themselves more effective through loan exhibits and through branches.

The museum is in most cases so remote from the city's center that even if it were to rival in attractiveness the theater, the cinema, and the department store, the time and money it takes to reach it would bar most from ever paying it a visit. It should establish branches, large and small, as many as funds permit, in which could be seen a few of the best things in one and another field that genius and skill have produced; in which could be seen the products of some of the city's industries, placed beside those of other cities, of other countries, and of other times; in which thousands of the citizens could each day see—at the cost of a few minutes only of their time—a few at least of the precious objects which their money has been used to collect.

Even though the main museum building is centrally situated, the need of branches—in a large city, at least—is quite obvious. The small branch would be more effective in the appeal it could make to many visitors than the main building could ever be. A half hour in the presence of one fine painting, a dozen Greek vases (with perhaps a few of other times and countries for comparison), one great piece of sculpture—each of these with ample descriptive notes and leaflets—would arouse more genuine feeling and a deeper interest than an aimless stroll through rooms full of the world's best art products.

These branches need not be in special buildings. Often, a single room conveniently located would serve as well as, or even better than, an elaborate and forbidding structure. How the idea would be worked out in detail no one can say. Apparently it has never been tried. But there seems to be no reason other than that found in precedent why the art treasures of a city—its own property, bought by itself to illuminate and broaden and make more enjoyable the life of its citizens—should rest always in the splendid isolation of that remote temple or palace erected for them.

Museum Objects May Be Lent

Art museums frequently borrow collections of objects and show them temporarily. Why do they not more often reverse the process?

More than 20 years ago, a self-constituted committee of women established in Massachusetts what was in effect a library art league. With the aid of the libraries which joined the league, they brought together a large number of interesting collections, chiefly of pictures of many kinds and dealing with many subjects, which traveled about and were shown at one library after another. For many years the University of the State of New York has been sending out from Albany collections of pictures to be exhibited in the libraries of the state and in other proper institutions.

Groups of museums, notably the group now operating under the direction of the Federation of Arts, have long been borrowing and successively showing collections of paintings, engravings, pottery, bronzes, and other objects. The Newark Library has prepared or arranged several exhibits of art and handicraft which have been shown in a total of more than 100 American cities. The American Museum of Natural History lends annually thousands of specially prepared exhibits to the schools of New York and vicinity. The Commercial Museums of Philadelphia prepare collections for the schools of the whole state of Pennsylvania. In St. Louis, an educational museum—geographical, scientific, and industrial, maintained by the board of education—lends many thousands of objects and collections each year to the schools of the city. In Germany, there go forth each year from a central bureau in Hagen many carefully prepared exhibitions of objects of art and handicraft gathered from the best workshops in the empire; and the South Kensington museum has been lending objects to towns and cities in Great Britain for many years.

In spite of all these good examples of the possibilities for helpfulness which lie in loan collections shown for brief periods in each of a score of cities or in each of a hundred schools of the same city, the habit of lending subjects from and by museums of art is almost unknown in this country.

Even the youngest and most modest of museums—unless it is of the purely mortuary type, housed in a temple, complete in all its appointments, installed for all time according to the museum laws of its founders and hastening to its destined end of disuse—even such a museum has objects which would find a hitherto useless life crowned with good works were they lent freely to schools, libraries, art schools, civic centers, and whatnot in the town to which they belong.

Museums of science are sending their exhibits to their patrons, old and young. It is quite evident that art museums will soon follow their example.

The art museums are just now greatly concerned over the question of how they shall make themselves of value to the young people of their respective communities. It is plain enough that it is impossible in a large city for the young people to make the journey to the central museum times enough to gain more than the most fleeting of impressions. They have not the money for car fares, they must go in crowds and teachers must accompany the crowds, and school time for this is lacking, and if they were to go times enough to get any enduring lessons from their visits, they would crowd the central building to the doors.

Why not take the museum to the young people? Public branches can serve the adults; and collections, groups, single objects, and photographs and other pictures can easily be placed in school houses, and surely soon will be.

Do We Need Museums at All?

I have ventured to mention the great department stores in the same sentence with museums of art. No sooner is the comparison made than other suggestive comparisons come to mind. The dealer in paintings has his art gallery, always convenient, open to all without charge, with exhibitions constantly changing. Dealers in works of art in general seem to approach even nearer to the museum ideal. Then on the industrial side we find that every factory and workshop is a museum in action, and, if it produces beautiful objects, is a living exhibit of arts and crafts.

Stores are each year more attractive and more informing; each year factories are more humanely and rationally managed, are more inviting and more informing, and are more freely open to interested visitors under reasonable restrictions. Each year the printing press produces better and cheaper illustrations of artworks of every kind, with a descriptive letter press which grows each year not only more ample but also more direct and simple. And each year the cinema reproduces for us more faithfully the activities of men in all lines of work and in all countries and makes it easier for us all to understand what books and journals try to tell us through text and pictures.

This question then arises: Does a world which is supplied by mere trade and industry with convenient storehouses of the world's products old and new, the best as well as the poorest, with industrial exhibits in factories of every kind, and with pictures and texts of amazing beauty and suggestiveness—does a world having all these things need the art museum at all?

The Museum as the Public's Friend and Guide

The question just asked answers itself at once, of course. Save for the very young, the opportunities for self-education offered by the street, the store, the factory, the movie, and the all-pervasive page of print are quite ample. Any boy or girl who will can gain an excellent education without the ministration of the school. But, on the whole, in spite of its manifest deficiencies, it seems wise to maintain the school and promote education through it.

Just so with those refinements of human nature—those betterments of manner and feeling, which I have ventured to name as good things which art museums exist to promote—these refinements may be attained by any, save the very young, who will attend thereto and will diligently use, to that end, the materials always at hand in dress, architecture, shop window, nature, and the ever-present picture and printed page. But in spite of the infinity of ever-present opportunity for everyone's education in the refinement of life and the enrichment of the leisure hour, it has seemed wise to establish and maintain the museum of art.

I have tried to show that this museum has been so absorbed in one aspect of its work that it has left untouched its more important and pressing duties. It has built itself an elaborate and costly home, beautiful after the fashion of its time and the taste of its community. In this home it has gathered the rare, the curious, the beautiful, and always, when possible, the unique and costly. So doing it has paid its debt to history and archaeology, has gained for its city a certain passing and rather meretricious distinction, and has given a select few an opportunity to pursue their study of fashion in taste, in ornament, and in technique.

Now seems to come the demand that the museum serve its people in the task of helping them to appreciate the high importance of manner, to hold by the laws of simplicity and restraint, and to broaden their sympathies and multiply their interests.

What Is a Museum?

Theodore Low

THE MUSEUM AND THE PRESENT

Slightly over two years ago Francis H. Taylor very emphatically stated the position of the museum in his article, *Museums in a Changing World.*[1] In the short time that has elapsed since the appearance of that article, the world has increased its rate of change with alarming rapidity. Museums have not followed suit. To discuss the situation of world affairs is far from the purpose of this report, and yet, it is only in their relationship to the vast changes which are taking place that the museums can find their rightful role.

No one can deny that museums have powers which are of the utmost importance in any war of ideologies. They have the power to make people see the truth, the power to make people recognize the importance of the individual as a member of society, and, of equal importance in combating subversive inroads, the power to keep minds happy and healthy. They have, in short, propaganda powers which should be far more effective in their truth and eternal character than those of the Axis which are based on falsehoods and half-truths. Museums with their potentiality of reaching millions of our citizens must not fail to recognize their responsibility. Adam saw the ability of the museums to carry on this work when he said,

> The antidote to cunning misinformation by emotion-rousing posters and enslaving prejudices is honest science, popular symbolic art, and the growth of independent judgment. Museums are powerful visual instruments to bring these gifts to the public. Their control is no routine or honorary matter but a frontline job in the continuous struggle to preserve social freedom.[2]

Theodore Low (1915–1987) was a museum educator at the Metropolitan Museum of Art. "What Is a Museum?" written by Low in 1942, was commissioned by the American Association of Museums. It is reprinted from *The Museum as a Social Instrument*, published in 1942 by the Metropolitan Museum of Art for the American Association of Museums.

That museum leaders are conscious of their part in the war effort is self-evident in the resolution passed on December 21, 1941, by the Association of Art Museum Directors with the concurrence of the Officers and Council of the American Association of Museums. The four steps in that resolution are as follows:

First, that American museums are prepared to do their utmost in the service of the people of this country during the present conflict;

Secondly, that they will continue to keep open their doors to all who seek refreshment of spirit;

Thirdly, that they will, with the sustained financial help of their communities broaden the scope and variety of their work;

Fourthly, that they will be sources of inspiration illuminating the past and vivifying the present; that they will fortify the spirit on which Victory depends.

Nothing but praise can be given to this resolution as it pertains to the war effort. However, the value of the museum in wartime must necessarily be limited to the maintenance of morale. In addition it must be admitted that museums today reach but a minute proportion of the public. Had the museums of yesterday realized the role which they should have had in community life, they would be infinitely better prepared to meet the emergency at hand today. Be that as it may, it is clearly apparent that the present job of museums goes far beyond the normal wartime duties. It is the army and navy which will win the war. The museum's task lies in preparation for the peace to come. It is then, in a world which we hope will be more ready to understand the problems of others, from nations down to individuals, and which will be searching for ways to make "peace" a word having real and lasting meaning, that the museum can assume a leadership befitting its position.

WHAT ARE MUSEUMS TODAY?

The word "museum" has little if any meaning the way it is used today. Actually one cannot define it because it has acquired so many different connotations. When a specific museum is mentioned, the scholar thinks of the magnificent collections and perhaps of his favorite objects; the man on the street thinks of a huge pseudo-something-or-other building with pigeons flying above and peanuts on the sidewalk in front. One could find a definition for most museums if one started with "a dynamic force in the cultural life of the community" and went down the list to "a collection of buttons." Most would be nearer the buttons, but in any case such a procedure does not help us. The fact is that a definition must be made for the word out of the actions of the institutions which it denotes.

The answer, then, to our question, "What is a museum?", is not to be found in words but in the nature of the institutions themselves. Many museums, of course, can hardly be called active, and for them the original meaning of the word may still hold. Not, however, for long, let us hope. Naturally it is toward the others which may rightfully be designated as active that this report is directed. That activity takes different forms, and the fact that it does is an added difficulty in discovering what a museum actually is. These different phases of activity, or if preferred, these functions, have been summarized by Paul M. Rea as

> ... the acquisition and preservation of objects, the advancement of knowledge by the study of objects, and the diffusion of knowledge for the enrichment of the life of the people.[3]

There can be little quarrel with that analysis in simply defining the functions. The trouble is that on paper such a statement makes it appear that the three functions are equal and receive an equal emphasis. Nothing could be farther from the truth. Stress has been and still is laid heavily on the first. Nor does Mr. Rea's statement give any indication of the fact such a thing as harmony does not exist among the three. The first two have forced the last to maintain a subordinate position creating a sharp inner division.

Let us face the issue fairly and squarely. Most museums are erected on the departmental structure. This type of division was started long before museums became aware that public education had any part to play in the life of museums. However, because that division into departments was already in existence, when education finally arrived, it was placed in a similar category and the "Department of Education" was born. The absurdity of giving education a place only equal in power to a single curatorial department was not realized. Often it did not even attain this status since at the beginning and as it too often remains at the present day, it was considered merely as a means to increase attendance. Mr. Taylor neatly phrased it when he said,

> And it has become the hallowed practice among all institutions to permit the educational department to be the legitimate tail to wag the rest of the dog. Thus, having paid a certain half-hearted tribute to the public welfare, they could turn to the more exciting pleasures of collecting and exposition.[4]

What he forgot to add was that it is the custom today among certain breeds to clip the tail to such an extent that it can produce nothing more than a comic wiggle.

Furthermore, in many cases public education has been placed in a moral quarantine by the rest of the staff. They have not only forced its submission but they have set it off as a necessary but isolated evil. This was the result, as we saw earlier, of the emphasis on collecting, the imitating of European museum manners, and the control of administration by men who were scholars and specialists in some curatorial field. Thus it was only natural that the directors should favor the attitudes of the curators from whose ranks they were drawn rather than the newer ideas of the educators. Certainly it is indicative of the American spirit that education forced its way into the museums to the extent that it did. Europe never has had education in our sense in its museums, and it has always been the educational aspects of American museums which have distinguished them from the European ones which they have tried so hard to imitate.

This battle which education has fought in the past to gain entrance into the museum has not been an easy one. Indeed, the odds have been almost overwhelmingly aligned on the opposite side. The opposition to consistent advance in the use of collections has been formed of a block of conservative men which may be divided into three sections. The first and largest are the curators. Since the beginning they have been the custodians and the purchasing agents for museums and in these positions are largely responsible for carrying out the first function as mentioned by Rea. They have also, however, gradually assumed complete control over the second function as well. Thus it has become their responsibility so to arrange the objects in their care that the scholars, students, and only incidentally the general public may see them and study them on their own initiative. This duty has been fulfilled by permanent arrangements, by the erection of study collections, and, most important, by the temporary exhibition. Obviously, this latter is essentially an educational feature of museum work, but, instead of being under the control of the educators, it has become the function of the curator. Once the exhibition has been arranged without consulting the educational staff the curator says, "Here it is. Now you explain it to the public."

The second groups of conservatives have been the directors. Because of tradition they have been much more interested in the building up of collections and in the scholarly prestige of the institution than in making it useful. Unfortunately, this scholastic bias has had the tendency to make most directors shy off from any form of popularization in the fear that it would lower standards. Frankly, there is some justification in this attitude when one sees some of the forms of popularization which have been attempted. On the other hand there is no reason in the world to maintain that popularization cannot be accomplished without loss of standards, and it may, in fact, raise them. In short, and it might as well be admitted, the majority of directors have not been administrators and have approached their task with an outlook and attitude which have prevented them from seeing the museum as something much more than the sum of its collections. More often than not this attitude was not their fault, and many strove to fight against themselves, but that in general what has been said is true must be affirmed when one looks at the present state of museums.

Finally, the third group of this body of loyal opposition consists of the trustees. Of the three there is no question but that the trustees represent the group which alone has the legitimate right to be conservative. Indeed, it is their beholden duty since they serve the cause of moderation. This does not mean that trustees should be adamant and oppose change merely because what is proposed is novel nor does it necessarily mean that a prerequisite for the position of trustee must be gray hair. On the contrary, trustees should be willing to abet and further the progressive ideas which are presented for their consideration, if the ideas represent carefully thought out plans for the future and not mere passing fancies. As representative members of the lay public and of the community, the trustees should remember that part of their responsibility is to see that their community is served as well and as efficiently as possible by their institution. Adam stated this clearly when he said,

> One of the first steps necessary is to clear away the legal fiction that museum trustees are mere guardians of funds and endowments. They are, in fact, active governing bodies in a field of great social movement and should be openly recognized as such by every element in the community.[5]

Another fact which bears mentioning is that the charge of ultra-conservatism which the educators have so often levelled at the trustees, although frequently justified, is not necessarily true in every case. Often they are conservative through no fault of their own since the progressive ideas of the educators fail to reach their ears or, if they do, they are drowned out by the arguments of the curators and directors. From a purely practical point of view this worked out all right as long as the question of public support did not materially affect the financial status of the museum. Recently, however, with a rapid decline in income, museums have been faced with a very acute financial problem which cannot be solved by trustees alone. Thus from a purely mercenary viewpoint the question of increased public support has become extremely important for the future of museums. Candidly, unless it is obtained, museums may soon cease to exist. That this is the wrong way to approach the vital problem of the museum's place in the community cannot be denied. On the other hand the educators should rejoice that the pressing need for financial support has become their ally albeit unwittingly. Because of this need the conservative block is beginning to wonder whether there is not something in this popular education after all. The danger lies in whether, once they realize this, their attitude is going to be one of grudging acceptance or of whole-hearted support. It is up to the educators to show them the way. In fact, before the public will be able to receive what it wants and needs, there must be a determined effort to reorient the ideas and attitudes of the curators, directors and trustees.

If these three groups contain the men who have consistently prevented the museum from taking its rightful course, who are the men who make up the progressive element within museums? They are, of course, as has already been intimated, the various educational staffs. Later, I wish to go into more detail on this subject. For the present, then, it must suffice to say that they are small in number but strong in spirit. Recently they have been able to add to their ranks men from the traditionally conservative groups. This cross-cutting of the opposition is a healthy sign and points to concrete results in the near future. Conversely, however, some of the educational people have been under fire for so long that their initiative and foresight have burned down to the point of extinction and they, too, have become ultra-conservative. Some may well be aroused again, but others must gradually sink from sight. As a group, however, they have the public at heart and are willing to accept new ideas and to fight to make the museum a more valuable institution.

The ultimate result of this conflict between scholarship and popular education is only too evident in the utter confusion as to purpose and function which characterizes museums today. They are little more than masses of conflicting ideas centering around masses of often unrelated objects. Some have gone a long way on the road to securing harmony and to making the museum into a distinctly American institution. Others are still in the state which provoked Dana to write against them. None, however, have been able completely to solve the problem. Until that problem is satisfactorily solved, museums will continue to wander in the darkness, fighting among and within themselves.

The first and foremost task, then, which faces museums is a realization of their potential force for good and the resolution of their internal strife so that they may put that force into action. There can be no doubt that this must be done and done now. The last ten years and the ten years to come will probably prove to be the test period for museums. Barring world conditions over which they have no control, it is possible for museums to make for themselves a permanent, useful place in society. There is a possibility that the turning point is past and that museums are already on the right road. If that is so, it is all to the good; if not, there is still time, albeit precious little. Let us become more specific now and look at what can be done to make the word "museum" actually mean something.

WHAT CAN MUSEUMS BECOME?

The first problem as we have seen is to weld the museum into a unit. This can be divided into two aspects. First there is the establishment of a single goal toward which all of the museum's activities are striving. Secondly, there is the discovery of the role which each activity is to play in relation to the others.

Some people might say that acquisition and preservation, scholarly study, and popular education are incompatible. That is far, far from the truth as they are all bound up in the same process and are so interrelated as to make one inseparable from the others. The difficulty is that museums have separated them in an artificial manner and have created jealousies which have resulted in the discord about which we have already spoken. Perhaps the most devastating result of this conflict (and universities are to blame as well as museums) has been that scholars have come to look with disdain on popular education and popular education has, in turn, come to decry the narrow-minded, haughtiness of the scholars. The fact is that both pursuits are

just as lofty, just as rewarding, just as difficult and both have distinct functions to perform. Furthermore, in the case of museums both are dependent on the function of
acquisition and preservation which supplies them with the objects to be used for
their respective ends.

What, then, is this common goal for which all three functions should be striving
and in the fulfillment of which they should abet rather than oppose each other?
Naturally, it can only be expressed broadly and, that being the case, the simpler the
explanation the better. Briefly, the purpose and the only purpose of museums is education in all its varied aspects from the most scholarly research to the simple
arousing of curiosity. That education, however, must be active, not passive, and it
must always be intimately connected with the life of the people. Each of the three
functions must be thought of as existing for the public and not as processes isolated
and self-sufficient unto themselves. Finally, to fulfill this purpose, the museum must
find its own place in the total process of education, since then and then only can it
make its own distinctive contribution to life itself.

The second step if museums are going to become a dynamic force must be the
realization that the functions are not static either in their relationship to one another or in their importance. Both aspects change even as do the times. Thus, if the
term "museum" is going to mean something in the future, museums of today must
be willing to alter and to modify their internal structure and their ideas to fit the
changing world conditions and the advances in social thought. Museums have failed
to do this and have shown a most extraordinary reluctance to accept new social theories and new social ideas.

If we go back into the recent past, it is possible to illustrate what is meant, function by function. In the early stages of their existence museums found it necessary
to place emphasis on the first function, acquisition and preservation. That was logical as we have pointed out. They were building up the collections of basic material
for the future. Today in our large museums those collections are formed, and acquisition has become a kind of scholar's jigsaw puzzle where he fits a piece in here
and fills a gap in there. Obviously museums will and should continue to make acquisitions but the importance of the role which that process has played must be diminished. The use which is made of objects bought in the past is of much greater
significance today than the occasional purchase of additional material. The other
aspect of this first function, preservation and all that it implies, need not be elaborated on.

The second or scholarly function grew up along with the first, and its development is best illustrated in the case of the art museum. The art historian is a relatively
recent addition to professional ranks, and it is quite safe to say that the American
version had his birth in the museum. For a long period the art museum was the natural place to teach art history for the simple reason that courses could not be found
elsewhere, and there was a definite need to be filled. This was all very well and nec-

essary at the time, but it had the unfortunate result of increasing the emphasis on the museum as an institute of higher learning reserved for the few and, at the same time, of overshadowing the fact that museums were founded for the benefit of the total population.

Today that emphasis still holds, and museums are still primarily interested in teaching art history when actually that function has been taken over by the colleges and universities. The art historian of today is not born in the museum, but in those colleges and universities, and the courses which he attends and will attend are not those given at the museum. Nor need it be emphasized that aside from the actual objects, the college and university can surpass the average museum in physical teaching equipment. The same holds true for the scholar as well. He will come to the museum to study the objects, but, if he does any teaching, it will be in a college or university. He may agree to give a lecture at a museum which may serve to sustain the museum's intellectual face, but which is usually far above the heads of the audience. If it is not, one may be fairly certain that the audience is composed of university people, and very likely a large portion are the lecturer's own students if he teaches in the same city. It would seem, then, that in trying to carry on in the old tradition museums are needlessly overlapping the functions of other educational organizations. Furthermore, it is likely that the future will bring more extension work on the part of the universities which will increase the duplication. At present the demand for the scholarly type of art lecture is certainly not exorbitant and can be easily handled by the universities, colleges and other organizations.

The point is brought to attention here because it is only too evident that the conception of the museum's duty to scholarship and thus to the performance of the second function must be thrown into a new light. The answer would seem to be to abolish all efforts at scholarly teaching and to substitute that kind of instruction which the museum can offer better than any other institution or organization. The museum will always have a duty toward scholarship as long as it has collections, but there is nothing that demands that that duty remain static.

The situation is, of course, complicated by the fact that as time goes on the overlap of function between the curator and the college or university professor becomes increasingly marked. Needless to say, both are scholars and specialists in the same fields and both write and publish works on the same subjects. Their existence side by side has never really been challenged but the time is not far away when that challenge must inevitably come. Actually the professorial ranks are on the increase both in numbers and proficiency while the curatorial position appears to be undergoing drastic modifications. At present the distinction between the two types of scholar lies in the fact that in putting his knowledge into action the professor teaches while the curator purchases works, cares for them, and arranges them in exhibitions. Were this division of duties to remain static, there would be no cause for confusion, but that is not the case.

One hesitates to make prophecies related to this problem because of the difficulties in determining which way current trends are leading. The common complaint of museum men that the college professor knows more about photographs than he does about objects is hardly tenable when one reviews the roster of the faculties of our large eastern universities. They are still the main sources of future art historians. On the other hand it is unfortunately true that whereas the faculties may have had wide experience with objects the students do get most of their knowledge second hand. Museums complain bitterly about this fact but few have done their share in counteracting the effect.

Actually the problem is far more complicated than it appears on the surface. With the present emphasis on degrees for degrees' sake and the rigidness of academic requirements few students have time to travel to the extent necessary. If by chance they do, they usually lack the money to do it. One suggestion which might help alleviate the difficulty would be for museums to have a type of in-school training which could be credited toward a degree. To draw students, however, the latter qualification is essential.

If, within the next twenty or thirty years, some system is worked out whereby everyone entering museum service will have had experience with objects, one begins to wonder whether or not the curatorial position will undergo some change. In this case the trend definitely points to an affirmative answer. Thus, in the first place, the curatorial function of arranging exhibitions should fall more and more under the aegis of the educational department. They and not the curators are closest to the public pulse. Secondly, the actual work of preservation and care of objects is coming more and more into the hands of scientists trained for the purpose. Particularly in our larger museums that will become a full time job. Finally one wonders whether or not the time now spent by curators in uncovering possible purchases will be decreased because of the simple fact that purchases themselves will be drastically curtailed.

Just how quickly this change in the curatorial position will come is impossible to tell. It is important, however, to face it now and to be considering what path will be followed. What is apparent is that the curator must be made to realize that he is a part of a working organism. At the present time most curators are amenable to limited demands made on their material by the educational departments. On the other hand it is extremely difficult to make many realize that the museum has a much more fundamental and worthwhile purpose than the mere preservation, acquisition, and exhibition of objects. Furthermore, it must be admitted that interdepartmental jealousy which is as needless as it is absurd is a very important factor in the failure of museums to do their duty. For their own sake and particularly in regard to the training of future museum men it is necessary for the curators to study their own situation with an open and critical mind. If they do not, they may well find themselves to be a group isolated from the main museum movement.

Whatever may eventually happen along that line, one thing is certain and that is that museums must shift the emphasis from scholarly work to the third function—popular education. Needless to say the latter may be increased without diminishing the former. On the other hand the curator's control over the use of his material must be modified to fit the interests of greatly extended and far more powerful education departments. In this connection it would be far more to the point to have one or two scholarly exhibitions a year devoted exclusively to the interests of the experts and have the rest of interest to the general public than to travel the present course which museums follow in presenting exhibitions which are neither one nor the other. There is no rule which says exhibitions must be intelligible to one and all. Such a procedure is not followed in other fields and there is no reason for it to be true in museums.

Still, however, with reference to the relation between scholarly work and popular education there is one factor which museums refuse to recognize. Museums are public institutions. Some it is true are semi-public and some private if the classification is made on the basis of finances. Despite that fact the swing of events points to the greater and greater need for public support and even those museums now classed as private may soon feel that need. Regardless of that, all types of museums are public institutions by virtue of the nature of their contents and as such have a distinct moral duty to the community in which they are situated. This being so, they must recognize that that duty automatically includes all types and all classes of people. I want later to discuss the question of the museum's public in greater detail, but it is necessary to bring this point up in this connection because it is a determining one in any discussion of museum purpose.

The fact is that museums have devoted a disproportionate amount of time and energy to the cultivation of the upper circles, both of intelligence and of society. More often than not they have been extremely fearful of getting "the wrong kind of people." It does not take any statistics to prove that the people who now frequent museums form a minute fraction of the total population of any one community. What becomes of the vast majority of the people? Are they not members of the public? Hasn't the museum a definite duty to fulfill toward them?

There is only one answer to the above questions. It is here, in the field of popular education, that the museum belongs today. It is here that the museum can make its own and its greatest contribution to the total cause of education. As we have said, the duty to scholarship remains, but in the light of the vital importance of this other work it must fade into a place in the background of the museum's consciousness. Museums are public institutions. That cannot be forgotten again. No doubt the scholars will verbally object to this altered conception of the museum's purpose and they are doing it already. They have enjoyed the feeling that the museums existed primarily for them, and they have enjoyed the ready-made retreats which were supplied to them. Some will and, it is true, some have already seen the importance of shifting the emphasis to the broader field. To the others it is well to issue one further warning. I know that in times like these it is the scholar's habit to say that only here in America can scholarship survive, and therefore it becomes the duty of every good scholar to bury himself deeper in his work, to maintain or, if possible, to raise standards, and to keep the flag of true scholarship waving in the breeze. The theory seems to be that, come what may, they will grit their teeth, close their eyes and forge ahead. It is a noble thought, but one which has a tendency to cloud the main issue. The fact is that scholarship will never die in a free land, but it is woefully dependent for its lifeblood on the latter condition. The intellectual sterility of the totalitarian countries is not a coincidence but a fundamental necessity for their continued existence. No one of intelligence, moreover, can deny the possibility of something similar happening here from without or, more likely, from within. Thus it would seem that the scholars, admittedly the best minds of the nation, should turn their efforts to the prevention of that possibility. That cannot be accomplished by further entrenchment in their own little corners of intellectual life. It makes little difference whether books on Byzantine ivories, Asiatic sarcophagi, or Borneo bushmen appear this year or next year as long as they eventually appear. The only way to assure that eventuality is to make certain that the social conditions under which they alone may survive are stable and ready to meet the threats which are so forcibly present today. Thus the scholars must be prepared to play their part in the struggle for maintaining that freedom without which scholarship dies, and the least that they can do is to throw their support whole-heartedly behind the movement for popular education.

What, then, is this popular education on which museums must concentrate their attention? To begin with it is not something narrow and clearly defined in the old sense of classes, courses, examinations, grades and degrees. Those words belong to the vocabulary of formal, academic education. Popular education is vastly more comprehensive, is part and parcel of the everyday experiences of life, and more often than not it cannot be recognized as education in the accepted sense of the word. On the one hand it embraces such things as books, the theatre, the movies, sports, radio, in fact, almost every branch of human activity to a greater or less degree depending on the relative power that each has to increase the knowledge, happiness, and experience of the individual. In these it is usually unconscious on the part of the individual. On the other hand it embraces the rapidly growing adult education movement. In this case it is more often a conscious effort on the part of the individual to improve himself in some way or other. Here it differs from formal education despite the organization of classes in that it is always a voluntary act of the individual. The success of the movement has long since proven that there is a demand for education of this sort and that the ability and desire of adults to learn is not a mere matter of wishful thinking on the part of those idealists who are set to remake the world.

To clarify the meaning of popular education still further I would like to quote two paragraphs from an article by C. A. Siepmann on *Can Radio Educate?* It is not a definition. I do not think that a definition is possible of a term which embraces so much. In it, however, one can find the type of spirit which is in back of the movement and which is far more important than any definition could possibly be. He asks why so little use of the radio has been made for purposes with educational significance and answers his own question in the following manner:

> The fault, I think, rests, as I have said, in part with the educators. We keep barking up the wrong tree. What we have failed to realize is that there exists today a new urgency for the wholesale dissemination of education. 'Money is like muck, not good but it be spread.' So with education. Radio disposes of our inability to spread education and offers us techniques peculiarly well suited to the kind of education that is wanted. We have been slow to appreciate the fact, slow to dispense with our own conceptions of what education is. We, as educators, suffer from the limitation of our own experience. Our background of education is that of a formal discipline extending over years, deriving from the teacher, or rather a succession of teachers, and from study, and directed toward the realization of a culture remote from that which can as yet be realized for the masses. We are the products of a selective process, aimed at the development of skills of an intellectual order and associated with cultural notions of taste and discrimination, the refinement and the good manners bred of the arts and of philosophy. We suffer, in fact, from a kind of intellectual inbreeding that tends to remove us both socially and in terms of experience from the hard facts and circumstances of suffering and strain of ordinary people. The fruits of such education stand unassailable in their own right. But having regard to the urgency of our time and the circumstance and background of the majority of our fellows, they are, for radio, largely irrelevant.
>
> It is for this reason among others that I believe we tend to shirk the adoption of techniques of interpretation which offend our taste and have for us little intellectual appeal. To have read the poets, to have studied art, to have a comprehensive understanding of history, to have shared the thoughts and speculations of the great philosophers is a great privilege, an unforgettable experience. But what highbrows tend to overlook is that in respect of fundamental values, in respect of fellowship, of honesty, the decencies of behavior, and the normal sympathies which make life worth living, there are other and cruder disciplines which approximate a similar achievement. If, without such a background of education, the good life is not possible, then indeed the condition of the world is parlous in the extreme. But that does not happen to be true. Poverty is not a bar to decency, nor is the lack of formal education a fatal obstacle to the appreciation of what citizenship and the practice of Christian virtues mean. Values derive from the heart and not the head. It is at the heart of the people and not at their heads that popular education should aim.[6]

The fact is that this type of education has been going on since time immemorial, but until recently the term education has had such a limited application that the educators never realized the wealth of teaching material which was lying by just waiting to be used. Belatedly leaders in the field have been attempting to bring order out of chaos, to study the ways and means of putting new mediums to good effect rather than to evil, and to reorient and reorganize the forces which can and should guide the movement. This is already being done to a very great extent by the various adult education organizations and in particular by the American Association for Adult Education. These are coordinating agencies and not sources of materials and teachers. They are the guiding lights, but they must be supported by other organizations and by other institutions.

It is here that the museum as an already established institution with vast resources of material of all kinds and description must take its place beside the library as a bulwark of the movement for popular education. These two institutions, one the exponent of the printed page and the other of the visual object, can provide a stability to the movement which it might otherwise lack and at the same time participate whole-heartedly in the drive which is necessary to keep the movement always going forward. Active public libraries and active public museums are an American creation and as such they can play an exceedingly important role in maintaining and strengthening that thing which we like to call "the American Way of Life."

It is, indeed, just this conception of a museum that was held by Choate and later by Dana. The difference between the times in which they spoke and today lies in the urgency of the situation. Two voices have spoken recently from the ranks of the adult educators. In an address delivered by Morse A. Cartwright before the American Association of Museums on the subject of *The Place of the Museum in Adult Education* he said,

> I think the museum, too, must realize its responsibility from top to toe as an agency for molding as well as for reflecting public taste and opinion. I think it must move out on its own initiative and that, in addition, it must be ready to serve as auxiliary to other agencies working for adult education in its multifarious forms within the community.[7]

T. R. Adam stated the case a little more fully when he said,

> Viewed in proper perspective, museums can be seen to be powerful instruments of popular education affecting the social history of our people. The need for rapid diffusion of new knowledge is not constant but varies in accordance with the rate of change in the social environment. When society can afford to pursue traditional paths, custom and habit are the best educators; when science or politics or industry suddenly breaks through into new fields, the community stands in danger of chaos until methods of spreading the essential facts of the new outlook have been discovered and perfected. There can be no social stability until a changed environment has been reduced in men's minds to accepted custom based on a common understanding of the forces at work.
>
> It is this element in museums—their use as modern weapons in the struggle for popular enlightenment—that has caused them to flourish so successfully in our times.

Separated from its social content a museum is meaningless to anyone but its curators. We are fortunate in possessing in this country a museum movement that is consciously seeking to base its fortunes on the performance of forward-looking tasks rather than on smug memories of the past. A time element exists that gives a dramatic quality to the present situation; cultural upheavals are taking place all around with a rapidity scarcely ever equaled in history. Museums, like all institutions, are slow and cautious in their adaptations. Whether the instruments we need to initiate men in the mysteries of our emergent civilization can be made ready in time, before ignorance and suffering destroy the physical basis of our culture, is a question few would be hardy enough to answer.[8]

Adam wrote those words in 1939 and in the intervening years events have shown that the cultural lag of which he spoke has increased rather than decreased. Museums have remained as part of that lag instead of taking their rightful position in the front rank of those struggling to close the gap. Moreover, that success in combating the evil forces now at work in the world can only come through popular enlightenment is clearly evident. Therefore it seems only logical that museums should turn from passive institutions used only by the scholars and the initiated into active institutions serving the total population of their respective communities.

NOTES

1. Taylor, F. H., *Museums in a Changing World*, The Atlantic Monthly, Vol. 164, No. 6, December 1939, pp. 785–792.

2. Adam, *op.cit.*, p. 28.

3. Rea, P. M., *What Are Museums For?*, Journal of Adult Education, Vol. II, June 1930, pp. 265–271.

4. Taylor, *op.cit.*

5. Adam, T. R., *op.cit.*, p. 29.

6. Siepmann, C. A., *Can Radio Educate?*, Journal of Educational Sociology, Vol. XIV, No. 6, Feb. 1941, pp. 352–353.

7. Cartwright, M. A., *The Place of the Museum in Adult Education*, Museum News, Oct. 15, 1939.

8. Adam, T. R., *op.cit.*

A Twelve Point Program
for Museum Renewal

Alma Wittlin

The finale is concerned mainly, and yet not exclusively, with museums in the United States, with which I am currently most familiar.

Some important directives into our museological future have gained in clarity in the course of the decades since the end of the Second World War—concern with the preservation of relics sheltered in museums; an increasing recognition of the need for the sharing of facilities by a number of institutions, first of all in the form of traveling exhibitions; the wish to get better insight into the motivations of people to view displays of objects—but in their sum, efforts have remained too scattered and halfhearted to hold out the promise of significant improvements in a situation that is widely recognized as unsatisfactory. Have we not been paying attention to detail mainly and to problems that are conducive to immediate action, with action being sometimes mistaken for a solution—another project, another committee, and maybe another wing to a building—without probing far enough into the ideological background in which all human actions and institutions are embedded? Without concentrating on strategies based on fundamentals and on priorities? Without evaluating the results of our actions, as if we were afraid of facing them?[1]

1. *The term museum.* International Council of Museums (ICOM) succinctly defined a museum as an establishment in which objects are the main means of communication. If we agree with this definition, an establishment in which objects are not used at all or are not used as main carriers of messages are not museums, whatever their qualities may be otherwise. A place in which people are exposed to changing lights or to a galaxy of light and sound unrelated to objects may offer a new kind of symphony or a carnival, according to its quality, but it

Alma Wittlin (1899–1990) was an international scholar who researched and wrote about visitor experience in museums and about museum history and practice. "A Twelve Point Program for Museum Renewal" appeared as a chapter in her book *Museums: In Search of a Usable Future*, published by MIT Press, Cambridge, Mass., in 1970.

is not a museum. If a few objects provided by a museum or by any source are used in a club or a recreation center among other items on the program, such as dancing or discussions of current problems and of vocational opportunities, the place still retains its identity. The term museum is neither better nor worse than the term club or center. We dim the outlook on our goals if we instill terms with connotations of borrowed status.

There is considerable scope for a combination of objects with other media, with brief motion pictures illustrating a single concept or with appropriately designed (and not overdesigned), suitably sized and placed graphics, but objects have to remain the stars of the cast.

2. *Museums are man-made institutions* in the service of men; they are not ends in themselves. While a recent letter from the White House requested an inquiry into the unmet needs of America's museums, I propose to vary the question, and to ask, "What can museums do with regard to unmet needs of people?" Within this very wide area every individual museum may decide on its share of intended accomplishment, and of resources required to reach its goals. Few individual institutions, if any, can be all things to all men. Even a very large museum will have to decide how much of its energies and financial resources is to serve the community of scholars or the general public, or specific sections of the public. Purposes have to be clearly defined in keeping with now existing needs. Proposals for the use of modern technology in making museum specimens available to scholars on video screens and in restricting the display of objects should be taken very seriously; they may be the key to the further existence of museums.[2] Dormant collections of innumerable small museums would in this manner become viable resources of thought. Scholars need not lose the unique experience that comes from the seeing and touching of actual specimens: all that has to be done is a distribution of the hoards of duplicates in the catacomb-like storage rooms of some very large and some not so large institutions to places in which they can serve human beings. Small, well-documented, collections could be kept in colleges which have no similar resources and in public libraries. Mr. Wilcomb Washburn reminded us that up to 1870 the Smithsonian Institution systematically distributed specimens.

A restriction in the number of materials displayed for the enjoyable education of the general public need by no means result in a lowering of their benefits; it may, indeed, lead to experiences of greater quality. There are signs that we are outgrowing the period of enchantment by statistics indicating growth in quantities and that we are on the way to the more mature appreciation of quality.[3] We need balanced mental diets in museums befitting the capacities of human minds seeking more than the satisfaction of a fleeting curiosity.

3. *Museums are not islands in space*; they have to be considered in the context of life outside their walls. The truism becomes a verity under present conditions

of accelerated change and at a time when every institution has to take measure of itself as a means to legitimate survival. Since public museums have developed from private collections, from recesses reflecting the moods and idiosyncrasies of select individuals and of bygone cultures, they are specially in need of considering their viability in terms of their capacity to enhance the overall potentialities of individuals and of society in years to come.

4. *The museum's uniqueness.* It is the three-dimensional reality and the authenticity of objects that matter, and the stimulation they offer to eye and hand. Most of man's traffic with his environment in the course of his perplexingly brief existence on earth has been directly through the senses: historically, written language is an invention of yesterday, and spoken language is comparatively new if we consider it as a means of communication in the context of the entire organic sector on earth. New evidence that emphasizes the effects of sensory deprivation on human beings confirms by implication the importance of visual and tactile stimulation.[4] So far museums have not availed themselves at all of findings made in psychological laboratories, although precisely these insights endow museums with genuine status: they begin to reveal one of the fundamental causes of the attraction exerted by museum materials on people. A wide field for experimentation opens up for a generation of museum workers interested in core problems rather than in fringe effects. What can a museum do that no other medium of communication can do, or cannot do at the same level of excellence?

Anybody is likely to welcome on occasion an encounter with the "First Signal Environment" of objects as a relief from overloads of symbolic communication, and such encounter is even more craved by people who are only functionally literate and who are one of the main current concerns of educators in a wide sense of this term.

A recognition of the importance of systematically developed environments of "things" inside museums leads far beyond their walls, into architecture and landscape design, into the appreciation of the physical appearance of objects of everyday use and into city planning. In all these cases we deal with a relationship between human beings and three-dimensional, concrete parts of the environment, complete with color and light.

The quality on which the museum's uniqueness rests implies a warning against the use of materials lacking object-concreteness. An exhibit which consists exclusively or largely of written sentences on screens is an alien body in a museum, however large the letters may be. Its existence may be due to a misunderstanding or to a self-betrayal of which those perpetrating it need not always be aware.

Another quality that endows museum materials with a high potential as a medium of communication is the opportunity they offer to present a number of facts simultaneously and in a context. Here again the museum worker has allies in psychological laboratories if he cares to turn to them. Information-in-a-context is easier and faster apprehended than unrelated items; it is easier recorded in human minds; and it is retrieved from memory with greater certainty. The assumption that the cumulative meaning of a number of appropriately selected items is superior to the sum of messages embodied in them is widely accepted in theory but is rarely put into practice in exhibits—sometimes because of a dearth of materials and more often because of their thought-scattering overabundance. When Kenneth E. Boulding wrote of the museum's function of providing developed images of the world, he may have considered the exhibit's aspect of simultaneity of impact of a number of items.[5]

Information-in-a-context is particularly important when knowledge is to be diffused among increasing numbers of people lacking background information and requiring aids to form mental associations.

5. *What is the museum's interpretation of "education"?* Is it our sole desire to feed information into people, or do we understand education to be a process of wider scope: a tuning of people to their best ability to think judiciously and to feel humanely? To realize new relationships between phenomena on earth, and between their own behaviors and what happens around them? And to develop a wider gamut of understandings and of appreciations, and—why not say it—of satisfaction with the fact of having been born and of being alive?

Obviously a museum exhibition can merely offer skeleton information and may light up interest with regard to a single point or to a few points, but if such impact is achieved with the help of the somewhat primordial forces of objects, a greater number of people may gain the necessary momentum to explore further by means of abstract media, first of all by verbal communication, oral or written. I venture to propose that the criterion of "good" education is its capacity to propel human beings along their evolutionary trajectory; in this case from the building of concrete models of the world to the use of more complex and abstract terms.

6. *What are the priorities among museum topics?* Smörgasbord-style exhibits drawn from accidentally available museum stores reveal a strange alienation of museum staffs from the human emergency situation of unprecedented rapid changes in ways of living. A parade of rocks, ancient timepieces, mounted birds, and exotic costumes had validity in a private cabinet of the seventeenth century where it represented a sampler of current knowledge. Each item was of relevance to the elite of scholars and amateurs who owned or viewed such things. Today's man, even the proverbial man of the street, has easy access to incomparably greater and more varied stores of information brought to his home by the mass media; the traditional museum offerings pale in comparison with the stimulation he receives otherwise—unless museum resources are presented to the layman in a context of either current issues or of perennial human affairs.

Modern man is not merely stimulated by his daily input of information, but he is overstimulated and fatigued by his exposure to a great deal of irrelevant input which is a fallout of our selling-buying culture. Most educational and recreational settings could cut down on their fatigue-without-return element, and a freewheeling institution like a museum is specially in need of self-imposed brakes. Museum people might do well to heed Kenneth Boulding's advice in his book *The Image* that we ought to seek a significant minimum curriculum rather than to try to expand our offerings.

Two basic questions may help in establishing priorities among topics in museums: how relevant is the subject matter or its presentation to man at this time of his history, and does the topic lend itself to a message based mainly on objects? Numerous topics of modern science may not lend themselves at all for presentation in exhibits, or in so grossly simplified models only as to defeat purposes implied in education—the conveyance of accurate information and the sharpening of the judgmatic capacity of people. An oversimplified model may encourage infantilization.

There are too many rather than too few topics that would pass the test of the two proposed basic questions—how often, if ever, do we ask them in museums?

Where are the exhibitions dealing with proposed model cities and other urban developments, together with illustrations of effects of environments on the socioeconomic life of human beings? Where are the exhibitions on facets of the population explosion on earth and of food production? UNESCO encouraged museums to deal with Hunger, but the situation calls for ongoing appeals to human awareness and for powerful communication; archaeological specimens of tools used in food production are important items, but they contain only fragmentary parts of the message.

Where are our museum exhibits which would contribute to the ongoing discussion of dissent and of aggression as parts of the congenital human endowment? We have among us scientists of a philosophical bent whose ideas await illustration in exhibits. They consider harmonious cooperation among groups as being favored by natural selection; to them aggression need not be of the essence of living but may turn into an obsolete and destructive feature of existence; they perceive the human being as fundamentally ethical owing to his capacity to foresee the consequences of his action.[6]

We see in museums the work of iconoclastic artists who replace paint and stone by changing lights, but their expression of dissent would gain in meaning if it were presented among other forms of dissent expressed by other groups of the population. Who expressed dissent in the past? And dissent from what? And why? And by what means? Relics and graphic interpretations of faded passions exist, and so do records of historical events that began with small actions of individual dissent from a majority. Is there any palpable thread of dissent running through human history, irrespective of any particular nation or country? How is religion or economics, political history, education, or any other aspect of civilization related to an individual's confrontation with the ruling mores of his day? Exhibits of this kind would help us to perceive better the continuities of human existence beyond the brief span of individual lives as well as changes in rationality and in humaneness, be they progressive or retrogressive.

What do people mean when they talk about the gulf between generations? How similar or dissimilar were two succeeding generations during various phases of the past? In appearance and in ways of life?

The current interest in ecology, including human ecology, can hardly be overestimated in its potential values: it is apt to multiply insights into peaceful group living, which biologists may sometimes achieve without the almost unavoidably inherited inhibitions which obstruct so much of the endeavor of humanists. Yet topics from biology alone do not exhaust the overall subject of human ecology.

"Futurism" has as yet not entered the halls of museums, but ample literature exists that can assist museum workers in lengthening their vistas toward the year 2000 and beyond.[7]

With leisure time becoming an increasingly prominent part of the lives of great numbers of people who in the past knew little leisure, exhibits on ways of using abundant time should receive attention; they may help us to understand what is meant by "leisure" as contrasted with "work." There is more to such exhibits than a case filled with baseball or golf equipment. We want to know what motivations came to the fore when people played certain games, and what satisfactions were sought, and perhaps found. Are volunteer workers engaged on a political campaign or on a community project, working or enjoying a leisure-time pursuit? What general human traits may be found in a comparison between the recreational activities of preindustrial natives of a South Sea Island, the ancient Greeks, and ourselves?

Since many of us at present live under conditions of hyperactivity and of stress, we would benefit from considerations of different forms of recreation as means of correcting ecological imbalances in our inner environment. Frequently museums offer opportunities for additional hyperactivity, which may attract some people, or many people on some occasions, but there are others who would appreciate or learn to appreciate a Silence Room. Even the Freer Gallery, my personal favorite, is too loud as long as one finds oneself engulfed by exhibits on all four walls of a room. Where is the museum where visual chamber concerts would be offered, with a few works of art stemming from different cultures being orchestrated with a beautiful crystal, a rare map, a photograph of excellence, or an exquisite flower arrangement? One such experience can hardly be equated to another, but noise and rush and small talk are alien to all of them.[8]

It is the unique privilege of man to act as a pilot in his evolutionary process, if he wishes to do so, and if he constrains himself to a distinction between advancing and retarding, or distorting, trends.[9] Are we as much concerned with the effects of noxious impressions on our minds as we are with air pollution? In the as yet to be created area of therapeutic man-made environments, museums could act as pioneers.

7. *Who is who in a museum?* You may be one of those who felt thoroughly disenchanted while visiting a museum whose director had fascinated you by his papers you heard at conferences or read in journals. You began to question whether you were in the right place: what you saw did not tally with what the director had said or written. He had advocated exhibits of musical instruments that would make entire cultural eras come to life—and you came face to face with a miscellany of musical instruments attached to long labels and crowded in a case, stamp–book style. You had listened to a rousing call to museum workers to interpret current racial problems in halls of ethnology—and what confronted you was yesteryear's habitat group of figures of Indians dropping to their knees before gun-toting white men taking control of a piece of the American continent. You expected to get an insight into events below the earth's crust which preceded a recent earthquake—and you walked along tedious cases of rows upon rows of igneous, sedimentary, and metamorphic rocks. Even if you kept your thoughts to yourself, the director is likely to have pointed to the villain of the story: the curator immured in his study and unavailable for comment, who had insisted on such presentation as you saw.

Subject-matter specialists have an inherited brief in many museums to judge what is to go into an exhibit case, even if some of them may prefer to be exempted from the task and to limit themselves to an advisory role. The diffusion of knowledge among laymen is as a rule outside their interests and competence, but their voices should be heard for the sake of offering to the public authenticated information. They should be members of a team composed of scholars of specific disciplines, of communicators with thorough knowledge of the psychology of human communication, and of designers; a consensus among the three is necessary. At present, communicators have as yet not entered the realm of museums, and a condition of imbalance exists due to the dominance of either the curator or the designer (compare Point number 9 in this section).

When a deadlock occurs between a curator and a member of the education department or a designer, one emphasizing the substance or the "what" of an exhibit, and the other the "how" of the presentation (educators and designers by no means representing the same museum staff species), the director is often called upon to act as a decision-maker, to solve a phantom problem that cannot be solved. Furthermore, the director's delicate relationship with the museum's governing board, trustees, committee chairmen, and big givers encourages compromise. Big gestures may be made in solving marginal problems, but the tensions and rifts that unavoidably exist in an organization lacking defined areas of authority have to be kept under wraps. How an individual director will survive under such circumstances, to what degree he himself will erode, depends on the predominant ingredient of this unenviable character of many parts—a manager with traits of a power-loving executive, a smooth public relations officer, a fund raiser, and maybe a scholar turning sour in the process of trading his former delight in intellectual pursuits for more palpable comforts. On occasion a member of the education department, a figure borrowed from the school classroom, climbs on the status and income ladder and reaches the chair behind the director's desk. This does not necessarily add to the nimbus of educators among their museum colleagues: everybody is ready to dabble in an area often thought of as being more nebulous than it is in fact. Although the planning of exhibits is even less trammeled by principles than what goes on in the name of education in museums, and is often a free-for-all, the exhibit designer has in recent years established a position for himself. In fact he often oversteps the bounds of his competence.[10]

We have to consider anew what categories of competence a specific museum requires as its human resources; some of the traditional figures may be unnecessary in an institution of certain goals and in a certain locality, while new talents may be called for. There is an urgent need for communication specialists using the museum environment, and mediating between the subject-matter expert, the museum curator or his equivalent in a university acting as adviser to a museum, and the designer. A practitioner of educational routines is no equivalent for a communication specialist grounded in theories pertinent to his task and gleaned from diverse fields of scholarship, from neurophysiology to a variety of psychological thought.

If museums wish to reach a level of professional competence and to become functioning public institutions to the limit of their potential, a task analysis of each staff member must become routine procedure, and his authority in decision-making must fit his competence and his task. A bad fit in this respect is a source of unending trouble. Furthermore: a single line of authority from the income-top down is obsolete in any kind of organization, and every organization has to create its own specific and most fruitful lines of interaction.[11]

8. *Exposure is not enough.* One of our blind spots, in all manners of educational environments, is the assumption that the exposure of people to experiences necessarily results in learning and stimulation. In public schools this pious belief is contradicted by an almost incredibly low achievement by large numbers of people, and by a variety of dropouts and malcontents.[12] In museums, I witnessed comparable results under experimental conditions. This is an area in which research has to go into high gear after a good deal of reflection in many

quarters. Unless we undertake this difficult, challenging, and often tedious task, we may just as well close much of our far-flung museum enterprise.

A museum, every single museum hall, every individual exhibit is a man-made environment; it is not a natural phenomenon resisting change; it can be changed. Before exposing large numbers of people to any such temporary, small-scale ecological niche, we have to test its effects on appropriate sample populations. The now generally accepted hit-and-miss procedure has a colossal and quite unnecessary margin of waste.

9. *Who are the testers?* To some people the answer is easily at hand: get a hard-nosed psychologist. But what if the mind behind that rocky nose is totally immersed in a single, perhaps momentarily fashionable, psychological dogma that does not take into account the needs of a museum environment? If a plant physiologist is needed to counsel people on the growing of plants in a semiarid soil, an oceanographer specializing in deep-sea fishes is not likely to be called. Psychology may be less diversified than biology, but it is diversified enough to lead to farcical situations unless, once again, competence in relation to specific tasks is considered very carefully.

Vision being the human sense acting as the main message receiver in a museum, a psychologist specializing in visual perception is needed; more than one may indeed be called for, since perception begins with the physiological capacity of the human eye and leads to the interpretation by the brain of what the eye perceives. Communication is in the early stages of becoming a special area of study, and the testing of the degree to which a message in any medium is communicable is of utmost importance. Motivation psychology has its uses, if those who practice it are familiar with the New Look school of motivation and do not completely disregard laws of visual perception. Since the viewing of exhibits is as a rule a voluntary occupation and is not linked to grades and other extraneous rewards, exhibits are an excellent opportunity for studying intrinsic motivations to man's congenital desire to seek information. A hundred-dollar bill cannot motivate a human being to read letters placed behind his back as a rabbit might do could he read, nor can anybody repeat and remember words spoken at great speed and out of context; the same applies to communication by visual means.

Another hazardous area for the selection of exhibit testers is the market survey. It may indeed be interesting to confront the motivations of museum visitors and of patrons of stores.

10. *Determine your visitor population.* It is one of the assets of museums to offer their facilities to everybody who wishes to come, be it for study or a few fleeting glances. Unforeseen interests may germinate under a variety of circumstances. Yet the probable margin of waste is the broader the more het-

erogeneous and anonymous the public is. All means of communication cater to somewhat defined consumers; most communities have several newspapers; public libraries provide popular books while specialized ones serve professional groups; there is a difference between a college library for undergraduates and a graduate library in a university. Why should museums not address themselves to specific segments of the population? Some might choose to do so at all times, or a few times in the year, apart from the offerings for everybody; and there would, of course, be no reason for excluding anybody while making a presentation with the view of the needs and interests of specific groups. I remember with pleasure an exhibition not intended for me and entitled "How to Look at Sculpture" in the Junior Museum of the Metropolitan Museum of Art.

A segment of the population which deserves special attention is our growing college population. Apart from collections illustrating the subject matter of their studies, there ought to be temporary interpretive survey exhibitions with stress laid on interdisciplinary relationships, and if possible with reference to current conditions of life. At this stage of life people make it their business to learn, or to receive information and to reflect on it; college youth is more interested in learning than others who give preference to empirical experience; and the demands of college courses and of examinations almost preclude wide, interdisciplinary reading.[13]

A special organization would be needed to plan, to prepare, and to circulate such campus exhibits, preferably on a regional basis, and serving a number of colleges. With an advisory committee drawn from the subscribing colleges, from both faculties and students; and wherever possible, with students being employed under professional guidance in the preparation of the exhibits, during school vacations if not otherwise.

11. *Problems of funds and of identity.* Museums are experiencing grave financial problems. Old endowments are being debilitated by diminishing purchasing power; large-scale donors are becoming scarce; and museums have as yet less access to public funds than other institutions. Admission fees lead to special problems in view of the fact that a nonprofit organization exempt from taxes may not be allowed to charge admission, yet it is the payment of the individual museum visitor for the service he receives which in my opinion holds out the greatest promise. The gist of the Belmont Report is an appeal for federal funds.[14] Since museum attendance in the United States has risen close to 300 million visits a year, or has passed this figure, and since museums have to turn down requests for services, it would seem logical to expect a financial contribution from individual visitors and from organizations based on memberships and associations. A federal contribution between $35 million and $60 million

for the first year could be doubled or tripled if each person paying for one of the 300 million museum visits would leave the token fee of 50 or 75 cents at the gate in the case of adults and less for children.

We live in a culture based on selling and buying, and a comparison with societies in which museums are state-supported has to include a reference to the loss of individual freedom that often is a part of the package. The time is not propitious for additional demands for federal support; there are other and awesome priorities. Further, would federal support in the sum of $35 million or even $60 million truly solve any of the fundamental problems of museums due to overextension or would it merely serve as a first-aid band?

There is no reason whatsoever to doubt the willingness of the public to pay for admission to museums; a visit would still be a bargain if compared with a ticket to a movie theater or to a concert. Visitors would, however, probably expect better evidence of the quality of a museum's offerings than they do now when few are aware of the indirect contribution they make to a tax-supported institution; a direct cash transaction tends to arouse alertness which in its turn may lead to a judiciously critical attitude which is now missing. And it is missing because of the absence of professional critics of museum exhibits whose interpretation would be made available in newspapers and magazines read by great numbers of people. Books, films, and sports are regularly reviewed; critics of drama and of music are established figures. They are important informal educators who quicken insight and refine sensitivity. Strangely enough some museum workers oppose the reviewing of exhibits. Their arguments are not persuasive and seem to be based on anxieties; they themselves may not be altogether convinced of the value of their displays or they may struggle to maintain the unquestioned authority of little feudal lords in their relationship with the anonymous public. Yet a stipulation of standards, which The Belmont Report rightly demands, can only be hoped for in a continuing process of rational analysis shared by many people. In the sciences, which have progressed in leaps, blunt and often abrasive criticism is considered to be a forward-moving force. René Dubos, of the Rockefeller University, wrote:

> All important human activities have given rise to a highly sophisticated profession concerned with the criticism of their values, achievements, trends and potentialities. The professional critics . . . play an essential and creative role even when they do not themselves contribute directly to the fields of activity they evaluate.[15]

Currently American museums sometimes run the hazard of losing their identity by courting donors of substantial funds and affluent people in search of status symbols. Occasionally an exhibit hall that is more stunning than informative is used as an advertisement that may attract the attention of a person of means and induce him to underwrite a research expedition; in the process of this enticement thousands of anonymous visitors are admitted free of charge to the exhibit hall and leave it without deriving any benefit from the experience.

In order to please buyers of expensive museum memberships, gala openings of new exhibitions are reserved for them; a great deal of effort is sometimes expended on not altogether needed temporary displays which offer opportunities for more frequent gala openings—a special form of cocktail party.

Some business corporations favor the soft sell by means of museum exhibits, preferably related to their work. They are not merely prepared to pay for them but to show favor in some other form. For example, by giving to the research division of the museum a contract which they may have otherwise placed in another laboratory, even though the research staff of the museum may be as competent as others. A loss of identity may also occur when a museum decides to enter a close partnership with a school system for the prime reason of obtaining access to public funds earmarked for education.

The risks of cheapening museums by accepting token fees at the museum door seem less than indirect bargains. Admission fees should not discourage low-income people from visiting museums; there are ways of attracting visitors from economically or culturally underprivileged backgrounds. One might, for example, offer a certain number of free admissions to various organizations at certain times of the year and in this manner arouse interest even among people who previously paid no attention to museums. Those whose earning capacity is severely curtailed by the style of our economy, students and senior citizens, should be given special privileges.

Individual admission fees to museums should, of course, not prevent public authorities from supporting specific projects, especially concerning research and clearly identified problems under the heading of education.

Our resistance to admission fees in museums stems from a general dislike or fear of changes of custom, or from a widely spread adjustment to times gone by. The numbers of dis-timed people are far greater than of the better known displaced ones.

12. *What do we mean by training in museology?* By its extensiveness "museology" is a vacuous term. What relationship is there between taxidermy and learning processes, or between security measures in museums, the preservation of tempera paintings, and the capacities of the human eye to view things? To acquire meaning the term has to be subdivided into a number of fields.

Most of the existing courses are held in museums of art, of anthropology, or of natural history, with stress laid on identification and on skills of preservation.[16] The National Endowment for the Humanities supports museum internships and fellowships, and the Smithsonian Institution appears to be aware of the many facets of training for museum personnel. My personal experience in conducting sessions with graduate students added to my conviction that young people are ready to pursue the study of communication by exhibits.[17] A few other museums are beginning to consider the need for an inclusion of the psychology of perception and of communication in the training of museum personnel. If plans are put into practice, it will be essential to offer workshops in addition to classes. A person has to go through the experience of selecting a theme, of writing an outline of an exhibition, of having the joys and frustrations of collecting materials, and of using them for a display.

Any such training ought to include prospective critics of museum activities who are not active members of the profession:

13. *The life and death of organizations.* John Gardner is credited with having stated that "most ailing organizations have developed a functional blindness to their own defects. They are not suffering because they can't *solve* their problems, but because they won't *see* their problems." Pauline Tompkins, president of Cedar Crest College, referred to Gardner's statement and added herself:

> . . . there are climactic times when developments within society stretch the capacity of existing institutions to cope with them. Such times require a qualitative reassessment, a breakthrough to new concepts, what Harrington describes as the "audacious use of the social imagination" to engineer radical change in institutions and to articulate new goals.[18]

In my estimation the main problem museums have to perceive is the need for a *change from an emphasis on hardware to an emphasis on software:* let us call a moratorium on the expansion of buildings and on the acquisition of additional gadgetry until we know more about the benefits people derive from what is going on in museums, or what could and should go on.

Let us delete all statistics which boast that a new museum is founded every 3.3 days. Do we always know what kind of misfits are created in addition to institutions of excellence? What meaning have rising attendance figures as long as they are not compared with increasing populations? With changing levels of general education? Or with increases in the demand for other media of education and information?

We have to recognize that a museum is not an all-purpose nostrum and that an instant museum is not likely to be a museum of quality.[19] It should be a fascinating goal to search for the specific, intrinsic contributions these institutions can make to human well-being. We may then at last be in a position to give an answer to the question "Would we invent museums if we did not have them?"

NOTES

The numbering of notes here is slightly different than in the original, which had two number ones followed by notes 2 through 18.

1. Dr. Grace Morley, the first director of UNESCO's Division of Museums, at the time of the agency's founding, wrote about the need for a more philosophical consideration of the aims and tendencies in museums. "Museums Today and Tomorrow," *Museum*, X, 3 (1957), p. 240.

2. "Museums Today," account of a symposium at the annual meeting of the American Association for the Advancement of Science, December 1967, *Science, 161* (August 9, 1968). See especially "The computer comes to the aid of museums," by Donald F. Squires, pp. 550–551.

   Wilcomb E. Washburn, "Are Museums Necessary?" *Museum News, 47* (1968), in the column "Opinion."

3. The visitor explosion in the National Parks equals if not surpasses that in museums. 300 million visits are expected by 1977. The administrators of the National Parks are beginning to change their policy and lay less emphasis on the travel statistics than on the quality of the experience—on bringing man and his environment into harmony. See *Science, 162* (October 18, 1968), p. 307. Letter from Douglas W. Scott, Department of Forestry, University of Michigan, Ann Arbor.

4. Fundamentally there appear to be two problem areas that await further exploration by neurophysiologists and psychologists specializing in visual perception and in processes of human learning:

   (a) One problem area is related to the stimulation of the brain of a person exposed to objects, irrespective of their appearance and meaning, and as distinguished from disembodied, symbolic communication, mainly in the form of language. To become visible, objects have to be struck by light, and the electromagnetic energy of light waves projected on the retina of the eye appears to have a stimulation effect on the brain.

   (b) The other problem area concerns the effects of a message expressed by a number of objects. In this context the physical properties of the objects represent only a part of the stimulus; the interpretation of the message by the brain provides additional stimulation. Are these two sources of stimulation related to one another? How are they related? Are there great differences on the reactions of different individuals? Are some people more "object-prone" than others?

   Museums have no exclusive claim to exposing people to objects of a variety of physical properties as well as of relevance to the beholders. Our daily environments of domestic and professional character include objects and the bodies of organisms; there are nature areas and cityscapes, good, bad, or indifferent. Yet museums could make it their business to act as optimal visual stimulators. It is easier to rebuild an exhibit hall than a city block. In this manner museums could provide people with a gratifying experience comparable with that of music; they would offer relief in the visually monotonous or depressing environment in which so many of us live.

Compare:

Conrad G. Mueller, *Sensory Psychology* (Englewood Cliffs, N.J.: Prentice-Hall, 1965).

Duane P. Schultz, *Sensory Restriction, Effects on Behavior* (New York-London: Academic Press, 1965).

Progress in Physiological Psychology, eds. Eliot Stellar and James M. Sprague (New York-London: Academic Press 1966), vol. 1.

None of these books provides answers to the raised questions, but all of them stimulate thinking.

5. Kenneth E. Boulding, "The Role of the Museum in the Propagation of Developed Images," *Technology and Culture*, 7, 1 (1966), pp. 64–66.

6. G. G. Simpson, *The Meaning of Evolution* (New York: Mentor Books, 1949). G. G. Simpson, "Naturalistic Ethics and the Social Sciences," *American Psychologist, 21* (1966), pp. 26–36.

Bentley Glass, *Science and Ethical Values* (Chapel Hill: University of North Carolina Press, 1965).

7. See, for example, Herman Kahn and Anthony J. Wiener, *The Year 2000* (New York: Macmillan, 1967).

8. For many years André Malreaux conducted a crusade against Western man's ways of exhibiting works of art, without coherence of either content or style, and crowded together on walls with people walking by them. He contrasted our ways with those of the Orient, where a single work of art is shown in isolation from conflicting experiences. *The Voices of Silence,* translated by Stuart Gilbert (New York: Doubleday, 1953).

Compare a modern sociologist's views about the homelessness of the visual arts in our society, where they are neither a mass entertainment nor an enhancement of class or group pride. He wrote of the "uncreative curiosity" of many visitors of art museums. Rudolph E. Morris, "The Art Museum as a Community Center," *Museum News*, 43, 5 (January 1965), esp. pp. 28, 30.

9. LaBarre Weston, *The Human Animal* (Chicago: Chicago University Press, 1954). Man has been facilitating his lot on earth by inventing devices magnifying his powers, contrary to other creatures, which very gradually undergo bodily changes. A microscope is a very advanced amplifier of the eye; an automobile tremendously amplifies the speed of human limbs. Other amplifiers are related to mental work.

10. The role of the curator in maintaining standards of knowledge, which some administrators and educators tend to downgrade, was stressed by Wilcomb E. Washburn in his article "Grandmotherology and Museology," *Curator*, X, 1 (1967). On page 45 he wrote: "The emergence of a powerful new administrative element has led to a further confusion of aim and purpose in the museum world."

The multiplicity of tasks and roles of a curator, and the lack of criteria in selecting personnel, were discussed by Donald F. Squires, "Schizophrenia: The Plight of the Natural History Curator," *Museum News*, 48, 7 (1969), pp. 18–21.

Organization men having to contend with problems on several fronts may draw comfort from the statement made by Joseph Henry, the first Secretary of the Smithsonian Institution, that votes ought to be weighed, not counted. Henry spoke up boldly against control of science by amateurs and politicians. Wilcomb E. Washburn, "The Influence of the Smithsonian Institution on Intellectual Life in the Mid-Nineteenth Century Washington," *Records of the Columbia Historical Society* (1966); see especially pp. 119 and 121.

11. Warren G. Dennis, *Changing Organizations* (New York: McGraw-Hill, 1966).

12. The low achievement standards of graduates of public schools in the United States became once again evident from results of The Armed Forces Qualifying Test. The estimated percent of illiteracy in the population over fourteen years old in 1960 was 2.9 for New York and stood at 5.3 in Louisiana. Average draftee failures in notoriously easy army tests amounted in 1965 to 10.1 percent in the national levels. According to an estimate of the U.S. Office of Education, published in the *New York Times*, October 11, 1969, p. H35, twenty-four million Americans aged eighteen and older are functionally illiterate. One million people are participating in courses in basic skills.

13. Dr. Hugo Rodeck, director of the University of Colorado Museum, wrote in a bulletin issued by the museum: "The presence of comprehensive and interpretive exhibits on an all-day, every-day basis on the campus offers the university student body the opportunity to gain some understanding of the aspects of our world which might otherwise remain eternally opaque."

14. *America's Museums: The Belmont Report*, ed. Michael W. Robbins (Washington, D.C.: The American Association of Museums, 1969), p. viii.

15. The statement made by René Dubos was published as a "Letter to the Editor," *Science, 154* (November 4, 1966), p. 595.
    Pleas for a professional critique of exhibits were made repeatedly. See Thomas W. Leavitt, "Toward a Standard of Excellence: The Nature and the Purpose of Exhibit Reviews," *Technology and Culture*, 9, 1 (1968). The conflicting views of museum workers with regard to the reviewing of exhibits are illustrated by "Letters" to *Museum News* (December 8 and April 10, 1968).

16. Training facilities are listed by William A. Burns, *Your Future in Museums* (New York: Rosen Press, 1967).

17. Among my most gratifying experiences were sessions at The Henry Francis Winterthur Museum, The University of Delaware, arranged by Mr. Craig Gilborn, of the Education Division of the museum.

18. ". . . Unless the Builder also Grows . . . ," *AAUW Journal* (Washington, D.C., January 1968), p. 52. Before assuming her position as the president of Cedar Crest College, Allentown, Pennsylvania, Dr. Pauline Tompkins was general director of the Association of American University Women.

19. THIS IS

    . . . a recreation center

    . . . a place to learn

    . . . a collector's paradise

    . . . a research laboratory

    . . . a craftsman's mecca

    . . . a "World's Fair" of art

THIS is YOUR family's PERSONAL Museum of Fine Arts

Walter Muir Whitehill, *Independent Historic Societies: An enquiry into their research and the public functions, and their financial future* (Boston: The Boston Athenaeum; distributed by Harvard University Press, 1962), p. 539, quoting a publication of the Boston Museum of Fine Arts.

4

The Museum, a Temple or the Forum[1]

Duncan F. Cameron

Our museums are in desperate need of psychotherapy. There is abundant evidence of an identity crisis in some of the major institutions, while others are in an advanced state of schizophrenia. These, of course, are relatively new museum ailments, and we still have to live with the more traditional complaints—delusions of grandeur on the one hand and psychotic withdrawal on the other—but the crisis at the moment, put in the simplest possible terms, is that our museums and art galleries seem not to know who or what they are. Our institutions are unable to resolve their problems of role definition.

Having made a statement as damning as that, one is obliged to provide some evidence. Here, in a more or less random way, are a few anecdotes and examples offered in the hope that the gestalt of these will justify the psychiatric diagnosis.

In Toronto the provincial government spent somewhere between thirty-five and fifty million dollars building and putting into operation the Ontario Science Centre. In its earliest days—from 1964 to 1966—this immense new institution was planned as a museum and was staffed by museum professionals with a variety of backgrounds. By the end of 1966, the government and some members of the board had decided that museums were somehow a bad thing. The word *museum* was unacceptable. A museum with collections and a research program, with a conservation laboratory and a research library—this kind of museum was of no real interest, in their view, to the modern public.

In the course of a few months, all but one of the staff members with any museum background had left. The planning and development of the institution switched to the design group, public service officials, and a staff borrowed from the provincial

Duncan F. Cameron is a Canadian museologist, onetime director of The Brooklyn Museum, and director emeritus of the Glenbow-Alberta Institute. His article "The Museum, a Temple or the Forum" appeared in *Curator: The Museum Journal* in 1971 and in UNESCO's *Journal of World History* in 1972. It is reprinted here by permission of UNESCO.

Department of Education. There was an absence of museum expertise and the Centre, as a matter of policy, was not to be a museum.

When the Science Centre opened to the public, with much fanfare, the brochure that was distributed carried this statement on the front cover:

> Make a list of everything you've been taught about public places, especially museums. Things like
>
> don't touch anything
> don't get excited
> don't take pictures
> don't laugh out loud
>
> Got your list? Good.
> Now tear it up in little pieces and throw it away.

The Ontario Science Centre is certainly not a museum, although it was originally planned as one. Today it contains a veritable chaos of science exhibits mixed with industrial and technological exhibits sponsored by corporations. There is an infinite number of buttons to push and cranks to turn. Interspersed among all of these are hot-dog stands and purveyors of soft ice cream in a claustrophobic maze of cacophonous noncommunication.

It is an "activity center," as the government promised, but how did a plan for a great museum of science and technology turn into the most expensive funfare in the world?

The Art Gallery of Ontario (AGO), also in Toronto, never had any doubt about its role as a museum of art history and a place for exhibitions of modern art. It was an art gallery, plain and simple. In the last twenty years, the gallery had to make difficult decisions about the exhibitions of local artists' societies. Perhaps the quality of the annual society shows was in question, but there was, quite rightfully, a concern with the maintenance of standards of excellence at the AGO. Then, during the 1960s, the problem of accommodating new contemporary forms, including happenings, electronic environments, and so forth, was faced by this gallery as it was by dozens of others. They did the best they could. Now, in the 1970s, there are plans for a greatly expanded art gallery building, and, at least in one stage of the planning, it was the intention to include large exhibition spaces, or environmental chambers, designed with maximum flexibility, wherein it was said that anything could be tried or made to happen.

The gallery had decided that it was no longer simply a place where proved works of excellence should be exhibited and interpreted to the public. Rather, it was also to be a place where the unknown and the experimental should be given a chance to happen, to become whatever it became, good or bad.

In Washington, D.C., in Anacostia (one of the great black ghettos of that city), there is a museum that has attracted international attention. The Anacostia Neighborhood Museum is sponsored by the Smithsonian Institution. It has an important program, which is defensible in every way. (Some readers may have seen the film about the rats exhibition. The purpose of that project was to examine the rat as an urban problem and especially a slum problem; to come to some understanding of the nature of the beast itself. Museum techniques were used, museum professionals were involved, but, most important of all, there was a remarkable degree of participation by members of the Anacostia community.) Here one must ask whether or not the name *museum* is appropriate to the operation of Anacostia. Is it not a community center serving an important and very necessary function in interpreting the immediate environment and the cultural heritage of that community by means of exhibition techniques but without permanent collections and curatorial functions? Is it not therefore a community exhibition center as distinct from a museum?

And what can be said of the new centers for contemporary art, of Sue Thurman's pioneering efforts in Boston or of Jan Vandermark's work in Chicago? In those instances, surely, the word *center* is more appropriate than the word *museum*. And if that is so, what of the Museum of Modern Art in New York? It is a center that became a great museum.

One can find many examples of the new science centers that hold no collections and do no original research but present a continuing program of science demonstration exhibits. There are many art history museums pushing back yesterday's heritage to make way for today's experiments. And then there are the growing numbers of cultural centers that strive to be all things to all men. Many of these include, somewhere in their complex and often frenetic programs, something called a museum.

Is a museum something that can be housed, with any degree of compatibility, side by side with ballet classes for three-year-olds, amateur arts programs of every variety, and the occasional bingo game benefit for a local charity?

There are institutions such as the Roberson Center for the Arts and Sciences in Binghamton, New York, that would say "yes" in answer to that question. The recent brochure from the Roberson says on the cover, "Roberson—the happening place—it is the center." And, on the back of the same handsomely designed piece, it says, "It is an art museum, a science museum, an historical museum, an arts council, an activity center for art, music, dance, drama—an educational center for all." There is little doubt that the Roberson is relevant, that it is serving its community well, and that the director and his staff are to be commended. But consider the question that is more significant than mere semantics: "Is there really a museum at the Roberson?"

Of course, none of these questions can be answered until it is decided what a museum is. Attempts to define a museum have been made for almost as long as there have been museums, yet there is no definition to my knowledge that meets with everyone's satisfaction. Another attempt is made here to provide a definition of a sort that may at least help to clarify the issue central to this discussion.

In order to approach the problem of definition, it is necessary to repeat some things that I have said elsewhere but which may not be familiar to the reader. The starting point is the idea of collecting as a universal behavior. It is argued that men, in all times and all places, have collected things and gathered objects around themselves and arranged them and rearranged them in an attempt to come to terms with the reality they perceived. It might be added that men also collect ideas and arrange them and rearrange them, collect words and sounds, have collections of stories and songs, and use these in a similar way. But, at the moment, the concern is with the collecting of objects.

The best evidence I can provide for this universal collecting behavior is not just the fact that collections and the arranging of collections of objects are recorded throughout history and are evidenced by archeological findings, but, more important, that this same behavior continues today on an intimate and individual basis. Here are examples that may strike chords in your own memories or recall earlier observations in a new light.

Consider what happens to a little boy or girl taken from the city into the country on a vacation for the first time. Does the child not bring into the house or the cottage or the hotel an unusual variety of objects that he has gathered from the new environment? Does he not bring in the dead toad and the mushroom and the colored leaves, as well as the pebbles, bits of driftwood, a dead fish, shells, and the jetsam of the seashore, depending upon where he may be? And, characteristically, will he not take these now prized possessions to a corner that he regards as his own (perhaps a window ledge or a table close by his bed)? And does he not arrange them and rearrange them as he examines and studies his new finds?

The child has been busy sampling a new environment, and with his sample he is attempting to structure a model that will help him to understand it. The importance of structuring a model is demonstrated by the child's reaction when a parent or brother or sister disturbs the child's arrangement of his collection. Mother, perhaps, while tidying up takes the childish array and reorganizes it in a neat row along the window ledge. The child is distressed not because his objects, his prizes, have been damaged but because the meaningful relationships he was establishing among them have been destroyed.

Over a period of time, if a child were to remain in that environment and it became familiar to him, he would collect in a somewhat different way. He would then be selecting objects from the environment that were significant or important in that environment—as he had come to understand it. Eventually, at a level of greater sophistication, he would select from the environment and enshrine in his collection those objects that best symbolized the operating values he employed in the environment or, alternately, the accepted values of the society in which he participated.

Isn't this a behavior common to us all in one way or another? Next time you have the opportunity, take a thoughtful look at the objects that are arranged in your own house or in your private room. Take a good look at an executive's desk with its collection of mementos and souvenirs and the so-called office equipment (much of which is not nearly as utilitarian as it first appears). These structured collections will tell you something about the way in which the collector perceives reality.

For a very dramatic demonstration of all of this, watch what happens in the private rooms of young people in their teens and even their early twenties. Their rooms very often appear to be in a state of constant chaos, upheaval, and unreasoned change from the viewpoint of the parent or the adult. In fact, what is happening there is that the young person, trying very hard to find his place in the scheme of things, is collecting, rejecting collections, building new collections, reorganizing them, establishing new relationships, and seeking a nonverbal reality model that will express his dreams and aspirations—the answer to his search for identity.

Another, and last, example of this untested hypothesis about the individual and collecting is that of the houses or rooms inhabited by the aged. In our time, especially, it is very difficult for those who have now lived the better part of their lives to accept the virtually revolutionary changes that continue to take place in society. Thus, in their rooms, we find extensive collections of memorabilia and souvenirs, photographs and keepsakes; they have structured them in their attempt to maintain belief in a reality they once perceived but which is, in fact, long passed. It becomes clear, then, that the collection as a reality model serves the collector first and may aid or deter not only the objective perceptions of the collector but also the perceptions of the visitor.

Until a century ago, or at most two centuries ago, collections were private collections, and public museums did not exist in any contemporary sense. These collections were autistic in that they reflected, in virtually all cases, some individual's private perception of reality and self-image. The collections may have said, "Look how curious I am and how meticulous and how thorough. Here is my scientific collection, which reaffirms my belief in the order of the universe and the laws of nature." The collection may have said, "See how rich I am," or, "Look at this. Look at how I surround myself with beautiful things. See what good taste I have, how civilized and cultivated I am." It may have said, "Oh! I am a man of the world who has traveled much. Look at all the places I have been. Look at all the mysterious things I have brought back from my adventures. Yes! I am an adventurer." And if you or I were invited to view one of these collections, it presented no serious problem. We weren't being told that this was *our* collection nor that *we* had to accept the collector's view of the world or of himself. We simply saw his collection and through it, perhaps, saw him more clearly.

Noting the exceptions, it can be said that it was but a century or a little more ago that we began, in western society, to create public museums. In large part, these public museums were private collections opened to the public, and, as long as that was made quite clear, there was, as mentioned earlier, no real problem. The trouble began with the introduction of a new idea: the democratic museum.

The idea was simple enough. It was to assemble collections of many different kinds and interpret them to the general public for the furtherance of its education, for its enlightenment, and for its recreation. In declaring these collections to be public in the sense of being publicly owned, however, it was no longer being said that this was someone else's collection that you, the visitor, could look at. Rather, it was being said that this was *your* collection and therefore it should be meaningful to *you*, the visitor.

The public museum was now an institutionalization of the individual collecting behavior. Thus the public had a right to expect that the collections presented and interpreted would in some way be consistent with the values of its society and with its collective perceptions of the environment or, if you wish, of reality. Unfortunately, there were two principal problems in creating such public collections and, it is suggested, these are problems that have not yet been solved in the majority of museums and art galleries.

The first of these was that the collectors and those responsible for organizing and structuring the collections were now the members of an academic, curatorial elite; they were most familiar and most comfortable with the models that were specific to their academic disciplines. Thus the public collections were structured as models that could only be meaningful to those with an education in which they had been introduced to scientific systems of classification, to prevailing theories of history, or to the academic approach to art and art history. One might almost say that the private collectors had been replaced by an exclusive, private club of curators. The public was still being offered private collections but with a new name over the door.

The second and related problem was that the value systems that determined not only the selection of material but also the priorities for its presentation tended to be the value systems of the middle class if not an upper-middle-class elite. This was, of course, most particularly true of museums of art.

We created great science museums that might be described as no more than three-dimensional textbooks. We created great art museums that reflected the heritage of bourgeois and aristocratic culture to the exclusion of popular or folk culture.

But, even given these faults or limitations, those segments of society with the power to do so at least created museums that were the temples within which they enshrined those things they held to be significant and valuable. The public generally accepted the idea that if it was in the museum, it was not only real but represented a standard of excellence. If the museum said that this and that was so, then that was a statement of truth. The museum, at least for a time, was the place where you could go to compare your own private perceptions of reality with the soi-disant objective view of reality that was accepted and approved in your society.

I suspect that it is for this reason that I have said from time to time that the museum, sociologically, is much closer in function to the church than it is to the school.

The museum provides opportunity for reaffirmation of the faith; it is a place for private and intimate experience, although it is shared with many others; it is, in concept, the temple of the muses where today's personal experience of life can be viewed in the context of "The Works of God Through All the Ages; the Arts of Man Through All the Years."[2]

It might be inferred from this attempt at a definition that this paper is to be a conservative and reactionary defense of the traditional museum; it may be useful, at this point, to deny the implication. It *is* argued that the museum as a temple is valid and furthermore that such museums are essential in the life of any society that pretends to civilization. But there will also be an argument for museum reform. That will lead to the question not of reform but forums, which are something else again.

Reference here to the reform of museums does not mean plans to convert them into social clubs or funfairs but reform to make them better and more effective museums in the sense of the museum as a temple. The initial step will be to reestablish the museum's role or, if you wish, its social function. The museum must be steadfast in its insistence on proved excellence, on the highest possible degree of objectivity in selection, organization, and interpretation. There must be a willingness to admit to the things that are not known, are not understood, as well as to argue with confidence for those things that are held to be true and for those things that are the considered judgments of time, if there is to be credibility.

The academic systems of classification, which constitute an undecipherable code for the majority of museum visitors, must either be replaced, or better, be supplemented by interpretation of the collections that is based on the probable experience and awareness of the museum audience. Those collections that are essentially representative of bourgeois and aristocratic cultures of the past must be put into the context of popular culture, folk art, and the life style of the peasant or working classes in the culture from which the collections are derived. Social history and the insights of the anthropologist must be used to develop techniques of interpretation that will put the collections, and especially the museum "treasures," in a more realistic perspective.

A very special task in reform for those museums concerned with alien, exotic, or historic cultures is to relate those collections to contemporary life and society. Most museum directors would be shocked if they knew how their visitors interpret oriental collections or collections from the classical world when they are presented in the traditional fashion. By failing to provide meaningful interpretation of the collections, museums are, by that omission, guilty of misrepresentation, distortion of fact, and the encouragement of attitudes toward cultures other than our own that are dangerous and destructive in what McLuhan has called today's "global village."

In effect, these museum reforms are part of social responsibility in cultural programming. They are necessary to the democratization of culture, or, to use an expression I prefer, to the creation of an *equality of cultural opportunity*.

These reforms, of which much more could be said, are in no way new suggestions, and they are certainly not original here. Such reforms of museums have been proposed for decades, and a great deal has been said and written about them since the end of World War II. Unfortunately, the majority of the great museums have yet to do very much about it. The time has come, however, when museums must institute these reforms or perish.

Some readers may have heard of the disruption of the meetings of the American Association of Museums in New York City in the spring of 1971. A protest group, composed principally of disenchanted artists in New York City, demanded admission to the meeting. When a representative group was admitted, they disrupted meetings, presented a manifesto, struggled for microphones on the platform, and refused to be silent. The majority of the American museum professionals present were not only shocked but greatly surprised by these developments. They did not expect to find protest against museums and art galleries. Having been in Paris and Brussels at museum meetings only a few months earlier, I was less surprised. The alliance of artists with the intellectuals and with the radical student movements of protest in Europe is a matter of record, and there I had heard much discussion of the antimuseum protest movement.

The argument that there can be no progress in the arts, or in the democratization of the arts, until the Louvre is burned is a cliché in the West European radical art movement. There is protest against the maintenance of great public museums that do nothing more than enshrine the evidence of bourgeois and aristocratic domination of society, and there is protest against arts education in which bourgeois values, exemplified by the Louvre, are imposed on the masses. One may or may not wish to use the vocabulary of radical protest, and I doubt that many in the museum world wish to set fire to the Louvre, but I do feel that it must be conceded that the protest against the museums and art galleries does have a basis in reality and that museum reform is long overdue.

A far more important inference that can be drawn from current protest is that there is something missing in the world of museums and art galleries. What is missing cannot be found through the reform of the museum as a temple. In my view, it is clear that there is a real and urgent need for the reestablishment of the forum as an institution in society. While our bona fide museums seek to become relevant, maintaining their role as temples, there must be concurrent creation of forums for confrontation, experimentation, and debate, where the forums are related but discrete institutions.

In an address to the Canadian Conference of the Arts in September 1970, Dr. Mavor Moore of York University summed up his proposals for democratization and the creation of equality in cultural opportunity, saying that the essence of the problem was, "Will the establishment finance the revolution?" I agree with Dr. Moore that the establishment (and by that is meant the corporations, governments, and private individuals) must, in effect, finance the revolution by creating opportunities for the artists and the critics of society to produce, to be heard, to be seen, and to confront established values and institutions. What they have to say must be subjected to public judgment and to the test of time! These are the functions of the forum.

In practical and specific terms, I am proposing not only exhibition halls and meeting places that are open to all, but also programs and funds for them that accept without reservation the most radical innovations in art forms, the most controversial interpretations of history, of our own society, of the nature of man, or, for that matter, of the nature of our world. It intrigues me and at the same time distresses me that the need for a forum applies primarily to experimentation and new thought in the arts and humanities but not in the sciences. The scientist who wishes to undertake research, even though his results may upset established scientific theory, is provided with laboratories, his work is published, we give him grants. And if he does upset the apple cart, we award him great honors even if the new theories he produces have disturbing effects upon our society and our way of life.

We are quite prepared to debate the virtues or evils of new birthcontrol methods, the fluoridation of water, test-tube babies, or the exploration of space, but it never occurs to us to put in jail the research scientists who created the very thing that we are prepared to argue about and which we oppose. In the arts and humanities this is not the case. The artist or scholar who criticizes our society and offends our sensitivities or our values is, in effect, regarded as an enemy of society even before we have allowed time for his work or his statements to be judged and considered.

At the outset it was suggested that there was schizophrenia and an identity crisis in the world of museums. Perhaps now that can be made more clear. Many institutions cannot decide whether they wish to be a museum, as a temple, or wish to become the public forum. Some have tried to bring the forum inside the temple. That is true of many of the institutions that call themselves museums but now claim to be "the place where it's at, an activity center, an institution swinging with a hip philosophy of social relevance." Unfortunately, the idea of bringing the forum—the place for confrontation and experimentation—inside the temple is to inhibit and, in effect, to castrate the performance in the forum.

Admission to the museum (even a swinging museum) is acceptance by the Establishment. So often the introduction of controversial, experimental, or radical activities into the museum is little more than paternalism. Some museums, I suspect, have decided to incorporate manifestations of the antiestablishment movement within their establishment institutions because they feared protest or perhaps violence and sought to neutralize the enemy. Others, I suspect, have gone this route because they simply wanted to be where the action was. (Surely it must be frustrating to follow the excitement and vitality of the contemporary art scene if you happen to be a curator of modern art, stuck in a museum, and you're not really a part of it.) But, regardless of the motivation, it is argued here that those museums that attempt to integrate these two discrete sociological functions of forum and temple are in error.

The error, as said, is in part that they rob the forum of its vitality and autonomy. There is an even more serious aspect to this error—the acceptance into the museum of the untried and experimental tends to devaluate those things that are properly in the museum. Museum collections, as suggested earlier, are based on the careful sampling of reality where both time and expert judgment determine what shall come in and what shall stay out. It has to be understood that the very nature of an object changes when it becomes a museum object. A work of art, an archeological specimen, or an antique is just that and nothing more when it is in the shop or in the street or perhaps in the forum. The moment that it is purchased or accepted by the museum it takes on a new quality. You and I will judge it differently. When the object was not in the museum, we were completely free to decide whether we approved or disapproved, liked it or disliked it. Once it is in the museum, we make our judgment in the knowledge, if not awe, of the fact that the experts have already said, "This is good," or "This is important," or "This is real." The object has been enshrined.

If the museum has opened its doors to all manner of innovation and experimentation, can we go on believing in the value of the museum's other judgments? Or, looking at another possibility, will we begin to accept with little reservation the importance of all innovations and experiments just because they happen to be in the museum?

To underline the point and to summarize for the moment, the forum is where the battles are fought, the temple is where the victors rest. The former is process, the latter is product.

Something must also be said about social responsibilities in museum programming that are somewhat apart from the issue of the museum as a temple or as a forum. It was suggested that protest, confrontation, the experiment, and the innovation were all appropriate to the forum and not to the temple. Some might infer an argument for the museum as a temple being apolitical, sitting on the fence, unconcerned with social issues, and so forth. That is not at all the case.

Years ago I worked in a museum where the natural scientists talked frequently at coffee breaks about problems of the pollution of our lakes and rivers. In the mid-1950s those scientists were deeply concerned with pollution and some of them sat on international commissions that were studying the growing problem. The galleries and special exhibition programs for which those scientists were responsible as curators did not reflect these concerns, however. It is only now, when pollution is a rather popular subject for discussion, that the museum in question is thinking of turning its resources toward the interpretation of the pollution of our environment.

That is a story of social irresponsibility in museum programming. Where museums, be they of art, history, or science, have the knowledge and the resources to interpret matters of public importance, no matter how controversial, they are obliged to do so.

Propaganda has, at no time, any place in the museum. Public education, the interpretation of science and of art, and attempts to explain what little we do know of the nature of man and of human society—these things have a place at all times, assuming objectivity and willingness to tell all sides of the story.

To return to forums and temples, certain organizational and functional relationships are important. It is desirable that each should have its own administration and governing body. Where there is a common administration, it seems far too likely that the forum would become a kind of purgatory and the museum a paradise, with the museum director playing the role of St. Peter at the pearly gates.

A most difficult question, because of the financial crisis in the world of museums and the increase in cost of construction, is whether or not the forum and the museum can be housed within the same structure. Ideally it would be most desirable to establish those manifestations of the forum that require a physical structure apart from the museum, but with a relationship such that they could not only share some common services but also could share the audience. Where both functions must coexist within one structure, then it is necessary to create a visual separation and a psychological distinction of the two by the use of color signs, and interior architectural modifications.

The important thing, and it need hardly be repeated again, is that they be recognized as distinct, one from the other; that each make its own function and its own role clear in the minds of the visitor. The distinction must be equally clear in the minds of the curators, the directors, the trustees, and the funding agencies.

Thought must also be given to the question of potential audience and communication effectiveness, whether we are concerned with the forum or a museum. Although there have been dramatic increases in museum audiences in the last two decades, it can safely be said that the majority of the population are not museum or art gallery goers. There should be great concern about the audience that museums do *not* have rather than excitement because the members of the present audience come more frequently and pump up the attendance statistics that are so gleefully printed in annual reports.

One of the studies of the use of leisure conducted in metropolitan Toronto[3] convinced me that museum visiting and attendance at spectator sports were very much alike in that they were functions of the characteristic use of leisure time rather than functions of special interests in either museums or baseball. It appears that there are some people who are not mobile in the use of leisure and who tend to rely heavily on television, radio, newspapers, magazines, books, records, and tapes. There are others who are highly mobile and seem to go everywhere to see everything and do everything.

There is evidence of a correlation between high educational achievement levels and the use of art museums and the more traditional performing arts. This does not appear to apply, however, to general museums, museums of history, archeology, or natural science. It can also be hypothesized from the study in question that individuals who have sophisticated or, if you wish, educated tastes in music, literature, and the visual arts may not be museum goers simply because they are not mobile, while others who would appear to be most unsophisticated show a high frequency of visitation.

All of this leads to the conclusion that, whether the concern is for the temple or the forum, the mass media must be used if the total audience which is prepared to listen is to be reached. Museum exhibitions should be designed from the very beginning so that they become the basis for television programs, films, feature articles in magazines, and well-designed, highly readable museum publications. There must also be extension or "outreach" programs that take museum materials into the community, into the inner-city areas of large urban concentrations, and especially into the schools. Similarly, the relatively unprogrammed and often unexpected events in the forum must be transmitted through the mass media. The public forum must be integrated into the circuits of electronic communication networks if it is to be significant in society. It must not be confused with the "forums" created by these networks.

More than half of the potential audience will not come to either the forum or museum. They will have to go to their audience. And even the roughest cost-benefit analysis will show that a telecast, a radio program, or a weekly newspaper column will get more information and experience to more people for fewer dollars than publicity campaigns designed to drive the unwilling in through the front doors.

Museums and art galleries, like the majority of other established cultural institutions, must institute reform and create an equality of cultural opportunity. Society will no longer tolerate institutions that either in fact or in appearance serve a minority audience of the elite. As public funds in support of these institutions increase, the public will demand its right to more than it has now. The public will make its demands known.

It is a difficult and precarious time for museums and art galleries, and those in the museum profession are charged with greater responsibilities than ever before.

Museums must concern themselves with the reform and development of museums *as museums*. They must meet society's need for that unique institution which fulfills a timeless and universal function—the use of the structured sample of reality, not just as a reference but as an objective model against which to compare individual perceptions. At the same time, and with a sense of urgency, the forums must be created, unfettered by convention and established values. The objective here is neither to neutralize nor to contain that which questions the established order. It is to ensure that the new and challenging perceptions of reality—the new values and their expressions—can be seen and heard by all. To ignore or suppress the innovation or the proposal for change is as mindless as to accept that which is new because it is novel.

In the absence of the forum, the museum as a temple stands alone as an obstacle to change. The temple is destroyed and the weapons of its destruction are venerated in the temple of tomorrow—but yesterday is lost. In the presence of the forum the museum serves as a temple, accepting and incorporating the manifestations of change. From the chaos and conflict of today's forum the museum must build the collections that will tell us tomorrow who we are and how we got there. After all, that's what museums are all about.

NOTES

1. This article is derived from the 1971 University of Colorado Museum Lecture. It is prepared for *The Journal of World History* special number, "Museums, Society, Knowledge" (1972), reprinted with the permission of Unesco.

2. Inscription at the entrance to the Royal Ontario Museum, Toronto, Canada.

3. An unpublished study of leisure and the use of cultural resources conducted for the Royal Ontario Museum by Dr. David S. Abbey and the author, 1961.

5

Rethinking the Museum:
An Emerging New Paradigm

Stephen E. Weil

It was nearly twenty years ago, in the April 1970 issue of *Museum News*, that Joseph Veach Noble—later to serve as a distinguished president of the American Association of Museums—published his "Museum Manifesto." In it, Noble briefly described what he took to be the five basic responsibilities of every museum: to *collect*, to *conserve*, to *study*, to *interpret*, and to *exhibit*. Stressed as well was the interrelationship among these responsibilities. "[T]hey form," he said, "an entity. They are like the five fingers of a hand, each independent but united for common purpose. If a museum omits or slights any of these five responsibilities, it has handicapped itself immeasurably."

During the two decades since, Noble's five-part analysis of museum functions has proven enormously useful. As an evaluative tool, it has supplied a series of perspectives from which a museum's performance might be systematically judged. Employed as an armature, it has provided a sturdy framework around which to build such diverse structures as museum organizational charts, collections management policies, and the curricula of various museum studies programs.

Despite its utility, however, a superseding paradigm now appears to be emerging. By no means entirely new, it amends rather than replaces Noble's 1970 formulation. In so doing, it is both prescriptive with respect to the future operation of museums and, to some degree, correspondingly questioning (if not actually critical) of certain of their recent past practices.

A version of this new paradigm was first introduced to me by Peter van Mensch, the Dutch museologist who teaches at the Reinwardt Academy in Leiden. As analyzed by van Mensch, the essential functions of museums are reduced to three: to *preserve*

Stephen E. Weil is senior scholar emeritus at the Center for Museum Studies, Smithsonian Institution. "Rethinking the Museum: An Emerging New Paradigm" was originally published in *Museum News* in 1990 and later featured in a collection of Weil's writings entitled *Rethinking the Museum and Other Meditations*, published by the Smithsonian Institution Press. It is reprinted here, with permission, from *Museum News*, March/April 1990.

(to collect being viewed as simply an early step in that process), to *study* (a function that remains unchanged) and to *communicate* (this third function being a combination of Noble's final two, i.e., to interpret and to exhibit). Noteworthy is the degree to which van Mensch's analysis parallels that of John Henry Merryman of the Stanford University Law School in his recent studies of public policy with respect to cultural property. The basic framework of any such policy, Merryman has concluded, must be based upon "the ordered triad of preservation, truth and access."

In seeking to establish a more direct link between the museum's activities as a collecting institution and its ability to preserve what it actually collects, this amended approach closely accords with the positions most recently taken by the major professional organizations representing the field. Thus, paragraph 3.1 of the *Code of Professional Ethics* adopted by the International Council of Museums at its 1986 triennial meeting in Buenos Aires provides: "Museums should not, except in very exceptional circumstances, acquire material that the museum is unlikely to be able to catalogue, conserve, store or exhibit, as appropriate, in a proper manner."

In a similar vein is the position taken by the AAM in its 1984 report *Museums for a New Century*. In the first recommendation of that report, museums were urged to collect "carefully and purposefully." Specifically suggested was that every museum must "exercise care by collecting within its capacity to house and preserve the objects, artifacts and specimens in its stewardship." Earlier pronouncements did not link these activities so strongly. Indeed, the AAM's 1925 ethics code—its first—did not address the matter of preservation at all.

To say that a museum ought not collect artifacts and specimens for which it cannot properly care—whether because of their inherent fragility or because the institution lacks the resources necessary to do so—has more than an ethical dimension. It has practical implications that extend to the acquisition process itself, potentially strengthening the role of the conservation specialist vis à vis that of the curator. The rarity, importance, or desirability of an object may no longer be a wholly sufficient (albeit still necessary) justification for its acquisition. Equally basic might be the question of its future care.

Such a fusion of the question of desirability with the question of preservability might, moreover, better undergird the increasingly made demand that the proffer to a museum of a collection object be accompanied by the proffer of the resources required for its long-term care. Museums are, for the most part, neither archives nor depositories of last resort. They can no longer (if they ever could) afford to look after boundless agglomerations of objects acquired for no better reason than that they became available. The careful shaping of a collection intended for a mission-driven use requires a more considered balance between the collection that is assembled and the museum's ability to provide that collection with a proper level of care.

Nonetheless, this perception of a tighter link between collecting and preserving—this sense that they should not, as Noble had originally conceived of them, be considered as interrelated functions but, rather, as different aspects of the same function—ought not cause any too great an alteration of current museum practices. Its implications are not nearly so far-reaching as those of the second change that this new paradigm contemplates—the fusion of the museum's interpretive and exhibition functions. In place today is a widely utilized scheme of museum organization that reflects the notion that interpretation is an activity distinct from (and most frequently posterior to) the display of museum objects in an exhibition format. This is most evident in the existence of separate departments of museum education.

Critical to understand is that this perceived fusion of interpretation and exhibition does not arise from any sense that these functions *should* be combined. It comes, rather, from the realization that these functions are so intertwined with one another as to be inseparable. What has become compellingly clear is the extent to which—like speech, like writing, like every other form of human discourse—an exhibition is shaped from its very outset by the values, attitudes, and assumptions of those who choose and arrange the objects that it contains. Whatever the power of the explanatory materials created to surround these objects—didactic labels, gallery handouts, catalogues, recorded tours, docent talks, lectures, films, and symposia—it is the exhibition itself, and not this educational nimbus, that radiates the strongest interpretive emanations. As the late René d'Harnoncourt, then director of New York's Museum of Modern Art, observed some thirty years ago: "There is no such thing as a neutral installation."

This phenomenon has recently drawn increasing attention. Writing in the summer 1987 issue of the Canadian magazine *Muse*, Deidre Sklar, a researcher working with Native American artifacts, discussed the paradox of displaying such materials under normal museum conditions. "Time and space in a museum," she wrote, "are defined in terms of the confines of the collection, not of the context from which [the collection is] drawn. Visiting hours from ten to five and glass exhibit cases define Euro-American, not native American time and space."

In that same issue, the Canadian anthropologist Chris Miller-Marti speculated as to whether museum exhibits, regardless of the time and place with which they ostensibly deal, must not inescapably reflect the values and beliefs of contemporary society. Central to these, she suggested, were the "concepts of progress, technology, rationality and domination over nature." What museum exhibits appear to be telling us, she concluded, is "more about ourselves than our ancestors, more about our own values and concepts than those of the culture they profess to portray."

The Smithsonian Institution addressed this same issue in the fall of 1988 when it played host to an international conference—*The Poetics and Politics of Representation*—that addressed the question of whether and how one culture could appropriately present another in a museum setting. In a preliminary description of the program, the organizers described it thus:

[We] will consider the fundamental relationship between ideas and objects, conception and presentation in the context of exhibitions. We will organize . . . around two general approaches: the poetics and politics of representation. Poetics, in this case, may be understood as identifying the underlying narrative/aesthetic patterns within exhibitions. The politics of representation refers to the social circumstances in which exhibitions are organized, presented, and understood. Clearly, these are intersecting domains which draw on a common pool of historical memory and shared (often unconscious) assumption.

As in anthropology, so in art. A workshop presented at the February 1989 conference of the College Art Association dealt with nineteenth-century American landscape painting and challenged the adequacy of how such works were generally exhibited. Specifically raised was the question of how museums "might find modes of installation and exhibition which illuminate more effectively the multivalent significance of images and the complexity of their ideological function as forms of cultural expressiveness."

This increasing recognition of the inseparability of the museum's interpretive and exhibition functions raises a host of important questions. Should museum education appropriately remain the responsibility of a separate department? If so, should that department—as distinct from a curatorial department—also be principally responsible for the organization of exhibitions? In either event, to what extent are museum workers able to articulate for themselves the values, attitudes, and assumptions that underlie the exhibitions they now organize? To what degree can or ought those values, attitudes, and assumptions be articulated to the visiting public as well? Must those values, attitudes, and assumptions always be considered as "givens," or might they sometimes (and, if so, when and by whose initiative) require some modification?

A further question—possibly even more important—concerns the scope of the interactions and experiences that we might envision this combined interpretive–exhibition function as embracing. Do we currently have available a single term that does full justice to the full range of these? So far as it goes, "communication"—the description proposed by van Mensch—has several distinct advantages. For one thing, it would be consonant with many of the most fundamental goals that museums have characterized themselves as pursuing, especially with respect to the education of their visitors. These goals—in a mix that varies widely from museum to museum—would certainly include: to provide access, to disseminate information, to instruct, to illuminate and clarify historic or contemporary situations and relationships, to set standards, to introduce and strengthen cultural values, to elevate taste, to pose issues, to develop skills, to offer a sense of empowerment, to establish and promote social identity and—in the most extreme instances—to inculcate and to persuade.

A second advantage of van Mensch's description is the ease with which it would permit some simple model of linear communication to be used as a tool to measure a museum's effectiveness. If we conceive of the museum fundamentally as a formulator and broadcaster of messages, then it ought be a relatively simple task to evaluate the success of its operations. Exactly what messages is the museum seeking to transmit? Is it able to formulate and transmit those messages in a manner that is consistently free of static, distortion, and interference? Are those messages being clearly received by their intended audience? Few competing models of the museum offer comparably useful tools.

Nonetheless, as a description, van Mensch's "communication" does not appear to go far enough. By equating the visitor's experience of museum-going with the successful receipt of a message, this notion of the "museum as transmitter" both overestimates the role of the museum's intentions and underestimates the wealth and emotional range of visitor responses. Moreover, its suggestion that museum-going ought be an experience in which, ideally, control lies wholly on the side of the museum seems unacceptable. Also unacceptable (and lacking, as well, in humility) is its implicit suggestion that the museum is a place of one-way communication in which the facts, values, and skills possessed by those responsible for its operation are consistently superior to the facts, values, and skills possessed by its visitors.

Our own common experience of attending museums—an experience that invariably preceded our experience of working in them—ought tell us that this is too restrictive. We all know that museums are *more* than just places of transmission. We know that they are also places of stimulation, not merely of their visitors alone but sometimes of their surrounding communities as well. We know that, sometimes, they can be far more even than that. If we are to have an amended paradigm through which to reorganize the way that we think about museums, then that paradigm must be inclusive enough fully to reflect such a "more." It requires room for the largest vision that those of us who work in museums have of what the museum experience can be.

Such an expanded vision must, moreover, acknowledge that museum visitors may and frequently do have agendas that are not *our* agendas (or, indeed, that the public may have museum-related experiences that are not part of any agenda at all). Museum-goers may legitimately be seeking frivolous diversion, consolation, social status, an opportunity for reverence, companionship, solitude, or innumerable other group or individual goals. Museum-going is neither a tidy nor a predictable activity. Parents and children, visiting a museum for wholly familial reasons, may find themselves unexpectedly awed or even enthralled.

The communication that takes place in a museum may as usefully occur between one visitor and another as between the museum and the visitor.

These experiences ought not be devalued simply because they were not part of our plan. At its finest, least calculable, and most magical moments, the museum can be more than merely a communicator or a stimulant. Museum-going can be a deeply affective experience. In the words with which the AAM's current president Joel N. Bloom closed his 1988 inaugural address, the museum can be and must remain "a place of wonder."

How can we capture this? Might some other term reflect this richness of possibility more adequately than "communicate"? "Make accessible," "make available," and "present" suggest themselves as terms descriptive of what museums do with respect to their collections, but they each appear too passive. Somewhat better might be "provide," i.e., museums not only provide their visiting and nonvisiting publics with access, information, standards, etc., but, as well, provide the setting for important experiences that may be wholly beyond the museum's control or intention. "Provide," though, also seems too passive. The failure thus far to find such a term ought not, however, be thought to undermine this model. Aside from its neatness in constructing a paradigm, the reduction of this broad range of museum experiences to a single term is not really necessary. More important would be to retain its breadth.

Still, if this emerging three-function paradigm appears to be of value, the effort to more fully articulate the range and consequences of its third term ought be pursued. It no longer seems adequate simply to say that this interpretative/exhibition function—essentially a museum's public program—is important because it contributes to (in Robert Hughes's wryly turned phrase) "human betterment." We need to be able to define the purposes for which a museum deals with its public in far finer and more precise ways than we thus far have. Acknowledging how greatly the answers might differ from one museum to another, or even at different times within the history of any single museum, we must be able to say just what a museum would like the outcome of its public program to be. Should this outcome impact a visitor's life in some significant way? If so, in what dimensions, when, how greatly, and how often? Do we believe that this outcome can come about wholly from our own exertions, or do we conceive of the visitor as a collaborator in this effort? Is the impact of the museum limited to its visitors or does its role—as an authority, as an arbiter—extend into the community generally? If so, in what ways, how far, and toward what ends?

Seeking to answer these questions more sharply might help us better to define what it is, ideally, that we envision the museum as doing in its third function. It might also provide us with a more solid justification than we have sometimes heretofore had in seeking the resources that we need to undertake and maintain our other, interconnected and equally vital functions—the preservation and study of our collections. If we can craft a new paradigm even nearly as sturdy as the one that Noble contributed to the museum field in 1970, we will indeed have performed an important service.

6

Museums in the Age of Deconstruction

Michael M. Ames

THE 'ETHNIC QUESTION' IN THE AGE OF DECONSTRUCTION

Problems relating to ethnicity appear to be occupying an increasing part of public discourse.[1] The 9 April 1990 issue of *Time*, for example, refers to the 'Browning of America,' suggesting that if present trends continue the average U.S. resident will be non-European by the middle of the twenty-first century (Henry III 1990). White pupils are already a minority in California schools. Independence, 'ethno-nationalist' or 'ethno-cultural' movements among indigenous and minority communities around the world receive regular media attention and scholarly debate. Under the circumstances it is hardly surprising that anthropologists also direct attention to ethnic phenomena, asking how ritual and aesthetic expressions, cultural performances, and political activities contribute to group identity formation, economic adaptation without cultural assimilation, and political separatism. As Williams (1989:401) notes in his review of ethnic studies: 'The concept of ethnicity has become a lightning rod for anthropologists trying to redefine their theoretical and methodological approaches and for lay persons trying to redefine the bases on which they might construct a sense of social and moral worth.'

My interests are not in ethnicity per se, but in the social anthropology of cultural institutions, such as museums and art galleries, and in the anthropology of public culture. Obviously, these institutions are involved in ethnicity, whether by default or by intent. Instead of looking at how such public forums help manifest ethnicity, I want to turn the question around: what is the impact of ethnicity on those institutions and on the public expressions of anthropology? Might we expect to see a gradual 'browning of anthropology'? At the very least visible and other 'minorities' or underrepresented populations are demanding more space or 'voice' in the mainstream institutions.

Michael M. Ames is the former director of the Museum of Anthropology and professor in the Department of Anthropology at the University of British Columbia. This excerpt is reprinted with permission of the Publisher from *Cannibal Tours and Glass Boxes: The Anthropology of Museums* by Michael M. Ames. © University of British Columbia Press 1992, pp. 139–50. All rights reserved by the Publisher.

The public concern with ethnicity seems like a natural outgrowth of our current disputatious times, which might be described as an 'Age of Deconstruction.' I do not know whether French philosopher Jacques Derrida invented or borrowed that term, nor do I know what he meant by it (he was not inclined to define it, and the term itself may soon go out of fashion after a brief run through literary circles). It nevertheless sounds like an apt term to summarize the past decade or so in the world of cultural affairs. Traditional standards of literacy were attacked for ethnocentric bias; traditional modes of scholarship in the social sciences and humanities were placed under siege by radical and feminist critiques from both the left and the right; the authority of cultural and educational institutions was questioned; and the traditional canon was criticized for its Eurocentric and male-oriented biases.

Not only did the Berlin Wall and the Soviet Union start to crumble in the early 1990s but so did the barriers between disciplines and around public institutions. The past few years have seemed like an age of deconstruction, reconstruction, and self-construction, where everything is questioned and almost anything goes, at least for awhile. Someone coined the term 'postmodern' to refer to such adventures, though the terms 'deconstructing' and 'reconstructing' come closer to describing what actually has been happening.

How have these issues of voice and self-representation impinged upon public museums and art galleries? Cultural institutions frequently serve as playing fields upon which the major social, political, and moral issues of the day are contested. Not only are the definitions of truth and beauty subject to debate, as one might expect, but so are other thorny issues, such as what constitutes public taste and who has the right to determine it, what kind of knowledge is deemed to be useful—indeed, even what constitutes proper knowledge, and who has the right to control its production and dissemination. Lying behind the rhetoric of these debates and controversies are larger questions about what kind of society we want to live in, how much social and cultural diversity we can tolerate, and how we wish to represent ourselves and others.

Thus, the activities and institutions dealing with 'art and culture'—subjects often considered secondary to the important things in life, such as earning a living—are, to the contrary, deeply implicated in the major issues confronting contemporary society. Museums also strongly affect the public understanding of anthropology, another reason to pay attention to what they are doing and what is being done to them. Public response to museums helps to redefine those disciplines they represent.

I will briefly review some of the controversies surrounding displays in public places to see what wider lessons can be learned. (Collecting controversies is a hobby of mine.) Cultural institutions certainly play paradoxical roles, sometimes reflecting popular opinion and at other times guiding it, sometimes reaffirming dominant ideas and at other times opposing them. In the cases to be considered here, and in all others I know about, one constant or recurring factor is the embeddedness of cultural affairs in political relationships, that is, relationships involving status and power. Art, artefacts, and their institutions have politics, including the politics of representation (the 'ethnic question' again). Other common threads may emerge as we proceed through the review.

PUBLIC ART: 'THE FIRST GREAT CANADIAN'

Stationed on a hillock overlooking the Ottawa River that runs between Ottawa, Ontario, and Hull, Quebec, and commanding a majestic view of five important Canadian landmarks—the Canadian Museum of Civilization, the National Gallery of Canada, the Parliament Buildings, the National Archives of Canada and the classic Chateau Laurier Hotel—stands an equally majestic bronze statue of Samuel de Champlain, described on the accompanying bronze plaque as 'The first great Canadian.'

Who is publicly proclaimed to be 'The first great Canadian' says much about who is considered a part of history and who is not. Crouching below the feet of de Champlain, who holds aloft an astrolabe as if to signal his territorial ambitions, is a scantily clad Indian, one-third the size of de Champlain, and presumably a representative of the peoples whose land de Champlain has claimed.

Ironically the Indian looks towards the new Canadian Museum of Civilization and has turned his back on the equally new National Gallery. This is an unintentional, but dramatic statement about the relations between indigenous peoples and white society and about how museums and art galleries deal with indigenous peoples' culture—by dividing and separating it into art and artefact, the separate and jealously guarded realms of art historians and anthropologists, each armed with their own particular 'astrolabes' of theory, method, and language. This division is contested by many indigenous peoples. From an academic point of view it is simply a matter of how to order the works of others through classification. From an indigenous perspective, it is a problem of how cultural patterns, which they view holistically, are being divided and segregated according to alien systems of conceptual domination.

Indigenous artists ask why their art is not collected and displayed in the National Gallery and other art museums and is always subjected to artificial contextualization by anthropologists. 'Free us from our ethnological fate,' they say.

What is to be done with the contemporary arts of indigenous peoples has become increasingly problematic (Duffek 1989; R. Phillips 1988). Anthropologists query whether it is really authentically indigenous, since it does not always look like earlier material, and art historians wonder whether it is authentically art since it does not always correspond to what white artists do, either. Probably most art curators and art historians still practise what Canadian art critic John Bentley Mays advocates: define what is art in terms of post-Renaissance Western experience. As

Mays (1990b) suggested in his review of an exhibition of Inuit carvings at Toronto's Art Gallery of Ontario:

> If it is to be useful, the word *sculpture* will surely be kept as an historical term applied restrictively to products of a certain practice, namely, the Western inquiry into plasticity, volume and visual meaning that has descended from the Greeks, through Rodin, to Duchamp and Carl Andre and beyond. Applied like a kind of honorary title to whatever we happen to like or think beautiful, the word *sculpture* is merely a grunt of approval, not a description of a class of related objects.

In contrast, the indigenous peoples view their creative works, contemporary and earlier alike, as neither art nor artefact but both or, even more likely, more than both. Deciding what is 'art' is not only a matter of academic tradition, semantics, or personal preference, it is also a political act. The label determines what is to be admitted into that inner sanctum of the cultural establishment, the prestigious gallery of art. To deny serious consideration of the art of indigenous peoples, that is, to exclude it from mainstream institutions, a reader (Millard 1990) wrote in response to Mays's newspaper review of the Inuit exhibition, is 'to collaborate in the suppression of their identity and in their continuing exclusion from the full life of this country.' There is always an 'on the other hand' to these issues, of course. As Susan Sontag remarked during the 1986 International PEN conference (Ozick 1989:125), 'Genius is not an equal-opportunity employer.' That is to say, there may be standards that transcend ethnicity, in which case works would be included or excluded according to merit rather than ethnic origin. But how then is genius defined?

Some major art galleries and museums in North America, Australia, and New Zealand have begun to recognize contemporary indigenous arts. They are following the lead of smaller institutions and commercial galleries, however, and the great divide between art and artefact continues to be a part of mainstream thinking and institutional practice in universities as well as in museums.

To make it more complicated, consider women's works. They are usually assigned to the lower status categories of 'craft' and 'decorative arts.' One example is Haida artist Dorothy Grant's 'Feastwear,' designer clothes for special occasions. If it is fashion, can it be art? And if it is not traditional, how can it be Haida? However, Haida art has always been usable and adaptable. Adapting Robert Davidson's Haida graphics to her elegant clothing allows Grant another way to express her creativity while also taking her culture into a broader arena (Fried 1990:10).

Beyond the question of where does one put it is the problem of how to interpret it. Do non-Natives any longer have the right to interpret Native creativity? And even if they do have a right, will they get it right? Will they have sufficient inside knowledge of, or intimacy with, the culture in question?

There is an 'irony,' noted First Nations writer Kerrie Charnley (1990:16), 'about people who claim to want to get to know who we are through the stereotypes they themselves have created about us rather than being receptive to who we are in the way that we express ourselves today.' Once scholars begin to debate their own social constructions of other peoples' lives, as they are prone to do, the people themselves are gradually dropped from sight. They become the 'disappeared' of the scholarly world.

The debate goes beyond cultural institutions and the question of ethnographic authority, of course, for it affects all systems of representation. This was illustrated by the controversy over W.P. Kinsella's 'humourous' stories about fictional residents of the real community of Hobbema, home of four Cree bands seventy kilometres south of Edmonton, Alberta (Lacey 1989). Some Hobbema residents objected to Kinsella's use of their community's name. Authors have the right to appropriate stories from another culture, Kinsella replied (Canadian Press 1989a): 'If minorities were doing an adequate job [of telling their stories], they wouldn't need to complain.'

Ojibway writer and storyteller Lenore Keeshig-Tobias also criticized Kinsella's appropriation. 'When someone else is telling your stories,' she said (Greer 1989:14), 'in effect what they're doing is defining to the world who you are, what you are, and what they think you are and what they think you should be.'

Do artists, scholars, or curators any longer have the right to claim free access to the world of knowledge, or should there be some limits to cultural trespassing? Shirley Thomson, director of the National Gallery of Canada, has said (Bennett 1990:12): 'Ideas don't recognize geographical boundaries. Why should the professionals who work in the institutions that house them?' York University (Toronto) professor of literature Terry Goldie offers the other view. We have hit an evolutionary moment, he says (Drainie 1989), at which it is no longer good enough for white writers to claim a spiritual kinship with Natives: 'Their culture is one of the only valuable commodities natives own in this country, and for white writers to keep telling their stories is inevitably appropriation.' People like Kinsella, writing stories about fictional Indians in a non-fictional Hobbema, are committing 'cultural theft, the theft of voice,' according to Keeshig-Tobias (Greer, ibid.). Stories are not just entertainment, 'stories are power.' They reflect and transmit cultural values. When non-Natives appropriate Native symbolism and monopolize the media, she continues, the Native voice is marginalized, or it has to be redefined to fit the format established by others: 'They are trivializing our gods' (Vincent 1990).

THE NATIONAL GALLERY: 'FIRE THE CURATORS'

The National Gallery of Canada faces other challenges to its curatorial prerogatives besides those presented by indigenous artists, and though they may not involve ethnic or minority issues, they still involve contests over the rights of representation. For example, the gallery's 1989 purchase of Barnett Newman's abstract *Voice of Fire* for $1.8 million (Canadian Museums Association 1990:1–2) was denounced. A National

Gallery spokesperson (Hunter 1990) described the painting as an 'electrifying . . . 18-foot punch.' Director Shirley Thomson said, 'We need something to take us away from the devastating cares of everyday life,' reminding us, as Toronto art critic John Bentley Mays noted (1990a), that art museums 'exist to serve the life of the mind.'

Those explanations were not enough to persuade everyone. 'Well, I'm not exactly impressed,' was the response from Manitoba Member of Parliament the Honourable Felix Holtmann (Canadian Press 1990a), who also chaired the House of Commons culture committee and was promising a committee inquiry into the purchase. 'It looks like two cans of paint and two rollers and about ten minutes would do the trick.' Others complained that public funds were being used to purchase a work from a deceased foreign (U.S.) artist rather than to support living Canadian artists. They should fire 'the irresponsible curators,' Canadian poet and editor John Robert Colombo (1990) wrote to a Toronto newspaper, for paying such a hefty amount for the work of a foreign artist who is 'a spent force.'

Perhaps what the National Gallery needed was to explain its purchase of an abstract painting in language ordinary citizens could understand and appreciate—but that is not what cultural experts are well trained to do.

INTO THE HEART OF AFRICA?

The theft of cultural or ethnic copyright or cultural trespassing is also what Afro-Canadians in Toronto accused the Royal Ontario Museum of committing in its 1989 exhibition, 'Into the Heart of Africa' (Da Breo 1989–90; Drainie 1990). This exhibition, curated by anthropologist Jeanne Cannizzo (1989), is an example of good intentions gone wrong or being misconstrued.

Cannizzo's mission was to show the origins of the ROM's African collection within the context of white Canadian imperialist history. It was first an exhibition of nineteenth-century Canadians *in* Africa and Canadian attitudes *towards* Africans. What may have been for some a passing comment on the questionable adventures of an earlier generation became for others a painful reminder of a history of oppression. Some Afro-Canadians picketed the ROM in protest, claiming that it was extolling colonialism when it should have recorded the great achievements of Africa. But how can an imperialist society talk about its own history without using imperialist emblems?

The protestors may have misread the intent of the exhibition, and/or it was too subtly stated. In any case, they found parts of it a painful, therefore offensive, reminder of colonial subjugation. Those picketing the ROM asked that the exhibition text be changed or the exhibition be closed. The ROM did neither, referring to the judgements of critics and the response of museum visitors who thought the exhibition provided a useful insight into Canada's imperialist past (Blizzard 1990; Freedman 1989). One is left to ponder how offensive it is permissible to be in the exercise of free speech and scholarly interest; if it matters who is offended; how offensive may the offended be in their protest; and whether a curator's good intentions count for anything any more. (The exhibition ran its course at the ROM, but its projected North American tour was cancelled when those museums scheduled to receive the exhibition bowed to protests by Afro-Canadians. Museums do not want to be offensive.)

THE QUESTION OF AUTHENTICITY: THE CANADIAN MUSEUM OF CIVILIZATION

When the new Canadian Museum of Civilization opened in June 1989 it was immediately and widely criticized for costing too much and for showing too little too poorly. The CMC was obliged by government decree to open before construction was completed. It did cost more than originally estimated (so far, about C$256 million), with a cost overrun of about C$9 to $12 million. Less than half the exhibition space was finished (at a cost of C$35 million), and it has been estimated that many millions more will be needed to complete the museum as planned (Jennings 1990). It probably will become, if it is not already, the most expensive public building in Canada and the largest museum in the world. But is it any good?

The CMC was accused of substituting Disneyland–style pyrotechnics for educational substance and for presenting, not artefacts, but contemporary reconstructions smelling like a lumberyard—'Disneyland on the Ottawa, with the emphasis on illusion rather than on the real artifact' (Canadian Press 1990b). Even the design by Alberta architect Douglas J. Cardinal did not escape criticism, being described by another architect as 'prairie gopher baroque.'

The illuminated Parliament Buildings in the background of the cover photo of MacDonald and Alsford's (1989), *A Museum for the Global Village: The Canadian Museum of Civilization*, fills in quite nicely for Fantasyland Castle. It was also appropriate, even if unintentional, that during the same week in 1987 when the then U.S. vice-president, George Bush, visited Prime Minister Brian Mulroney, someone dressed as Mickey Mouse visited Speaker of the House John Fraser and made him an honorary citizen of Walt Disney World (Canadian Press 1987:A5).

In the debate about cost overruns and the Disneyland–Global Village references by CMC director George MacDonald, what has tended to get lost are his and his staff's attempts to restructure the very nature of the museum enterprise. For example, they systematically integrate theatre and art gallery functions and associated disciplines with anthropology and history displays; consult with indigenous peoples and others on how they are to be represented; increase access to information about collections through electronic technology; develop marketing plans based on the concept of cultural tourism; borrow management and display techniques from theme parks; and substitute the authenticity of the visitor experience for the authenticity of the 'real' object.

The way the CMC is redefining the traditional concept of authenticity is particularly significant. Museums pride themselves on being the last refuge for the 'real thing,' the 'authentic object,' MacDonald has said, but they fail to portray the real cultures from which those real objects derive. North American curators, MacDonald notes (1988:29),

> are 98 per cent white Euro-Americans whose knowledge of North or South American Indian, African, Japanese or Chinese culture is definitely second-hand. Most curators, even in anthropology, spend at most a few years in the cultural milieu of their 'specialty.' In fact, they have the cultural credibility and often linguistic competence of a four-year-old child from that culture . . . They have never been cultural participants and will never have the credibility of 'the real thing.'

Collections become an expensive burden to museums because of the mandate to preserve and exhibit them even though so little is known about them that it is difficult to present them authentically:

> Most museum directors now feel like directors of geriatric hospitals whose budgets are devastated by patients whose survival for another day depends on expensive, high technology support systems. Conservators in museums are like a host of relatives who guard the wall plug of the life-support machines. Sixty per cent of most museum budgets are spent on life-support systems for the 'reserve' collections, and conservators constantly battle to increase that amount. There is no apparent solution to this dilemma. The museum is the final repository of 'the real thing.' (MacDonald 1987:213–14)

According to MacDonald museums should give more attention to presenting real experiences with the assistance of people from those cultures being represented, and redistributing reserve collections to regional museums. The authenticity of the experience, rather than the authenticity of the object, becomes the objective, and the use of replicas, simulations, performances, and electronic media intertwined with real objects—techniques in which theme parks excel—help recreate, reconstruct, or rerepresent near-authentic experiences (MacDonald 1988). The 'real thing' is the experience of the visitor, not the object or its interpretation by a curator.

One reason why proposals like MacDonald's are controversial within the museum community (Ames 1988b) is their implied shift of power and status away from curator, registrar, and conservator towards those more directly involved in public programming, performance, promotion, marketing, other public services, and revenue generation. These changes respond to growing pressures on museums to generate more of their own operating costs. The curatorial professions are, in a sense, coming under siege, their prerogatives increasingly encroached upon, even though they have been actively professionalizing or upgrading their own standards of work over the past decade. Unfortunately, this professionalization has been mostly oriented to behind-the-scenes collections management and has become costly. Registration, cataloguing, condition reporting, insurance reports, conserving and caring for the object, and so on, are all labour-intensive activities. Further professionalization, as presently envisaged, typically calls for even more labour. Museums are heading for a crunch. Curatorial staff want more support for backstage object-centred work while their programming colleagues try to expand frontstage activities to enlist more public support. Traditional museological notions about object care are being increasingly confronted by the seemingly more 'commercial' values of public service and cost-effectiveness. The bottom line is coming to the top of the agenda, making many uncomfortable.

If museums do not become more commercial and popular they may not survive in any useful form. Yet people continue to criticize museums like the CMC for sacrificing integrity and authenticity on the alter of populism (see Gray 1988; Thorsell 1989). But how is integrity to be judged? The answer from MacDonald and the Canadian government is straightforward: if about 80 per cent of the population rarely visit museums, new approaches must be tried to attract them; entertainment seems to be the way to do it. The fact that half a million people visited the CMC during the first few months, the then secretary-general of the National Museums, John Edwards (1989), said, demonstrates that they must be doing something right, despite what the critics are saying. The Canadian Museum of Civilization turned one year old Friday and its director says it's on its way to becoming the popular people's museum it was meant to be,' reported the Canadian Press (1990b) on the CMC's first anniversary. Integrity, from this point of view, means serving the public first, not the objects (or the curatorial professions).

THE POLITICS OF ART: 'THE SPIRIT SINGS' AND THE LUBICON BOYCOTT
The Glenbow Museum's 1988 exhibition 'The Spirit Sings: Artistic Traditions of Canada's First Peoples,' like 'Into the Heart of Africa,' also caused protest over messages stated, implied, and presumed—another example of good intentions leading to mixed results (Harrison 1988; Harrison et al., 1987; Harrison, Trigger, and Ames 1988; Trigger 1989; Ames 1989).

The Glenbow's six curators wanted to demonstrate the richness, diversity, and adaptability of indigenous peoples during the first years of contact with Europeans, but their exhibition got caught in the crossfire of a political campaign to support a land claim by the Lubicon Lake Cree in northern Alberta. The Lubicon called for a boycott of the 1988 Calgary Winter Olympics to draw attention to their fifty-year dispute with the Canadian government over land claims. Attention gradually shifted from the Olympics (and to some extent from the land dispute) to the Glenbow and its right to mount an exhibition of Native arts during the Olympics over the objections of a Native group not represented in the exhibition. Probably many would have agreed with Alberta Native artist Joane Cardinal-Schubert (Patterson 1988:8) who found the Glenbow exhibition 'so offensive': 'It shows 300-year-old stuff, which only serves to reinforce the lack of attention paid to the contemporary problems of tribes such as the Lubicon. Not only that, but the work itself, all taken from the Indian, is removed from its life involvement.'

The museological defence that some works displayed were gifted or sold by indigenous peoples rather than 'taken'; that museums have always been expected to preserve and represent the past (otherwise who would?); and that most of the 300-year-old materials probably only survived because they were removed from 'life involvement' sounds self-serving when placed against the poverty of these peoples whose lands have been expropriated and lifestyles almost destroyed. Whether they like it or not, museums have become a part of the discourse about endangered peoples. The question is whether they will have anything useful to say or do about the matter. Can museological principles be bent towards worldly concerns?

The strategy of those who proposed a boycott of the Glenbow was to disseminate criticisms of it and the proposed exhibition, effectively turning a debate about land claims into a moral critique of museological prerogatives. As Robert Paine (1985:190) noted about other indigenous protests: 'Much of Fourth World politics is about turning physical powerlessness into moral power and then putting that to good political account.' The 'politics of morality' become 'a politics of embarrassment' (ibid.:214) directed against the authorities and their sometimes hapless wards. The campaign against 'The Spirit Sings' received widespread attention and sympathy, including the support of many Canadian anthropologists (though it did not resolve the land claims dispute). We see again how the authority of cultural experts and cultural institutions is contested. The Glenbow Museum was challenged on a number of points that have wider implications, including its right to:

1. borrow or exhibit Native artefacts without their permission, even though those artefacts are legally owned by other museums;
2. use money from corporations involved in public disputes (the exhibit was sponsored by Shell Oil, which was drilling on land claimed by the Lubicon);
3. ignore contemporary political issues, such as land claims, even when presenting an exhibition of the history of indigenous peoples;
4. employ non-Natives to curate an exhibition about Native culture; and
5. claim neutrality in public disputes.

The broader issues underlying these challenges affect more than just the privileges of anthropology. Who should decide what constitutes knowledge about a people's history—scholars or the living descendants of those studied? When should moral and political claims outrank legal obligations (such as the Glenbow's agreements with donors and lenders)? And what should be the costs of public association with those accused? Some Lubicon supporters wanted 'The Spirit Sings' closed down because Glenbow curators did not change the exhibition text and because it was

sponsored by Shell Oil and the federal government. (Interestingly, there was no attempt to boycott Shell products or government agencies. Perhaps the Glenbow offered a better opportunity to define the issues in moral terms and was thought to be
more easily embarrassed.) The 'fire the curators' syndrome, adding punishment to
criticism, appears again. Lubicon supporters made a claim for the higher ground by
redefining an academic museum exhibition as a morality play between good and
evil. Once evil is identified, it has to be exorcised if goodness is to triumph.

THE POLITICS OF PUBLIC TASTE: PORNOGRAPHY AND BLASPHEMY

Possibly the biggest single debate in the arts community in North America in 1989
and extending into the 1990s, was over the question of who has the right to decide
public taste. What sparked the debate were two controversial exhibitions, one of the
works of photographer Robert Mapplethorpe, some of whose photos were said to
be pornographic and homophobic; and the other by photographer Andres Serrano,
whose photos, especially his *Piss Christ*, were called blasphemous trash.

'Fine Art or Foul?' read the headline to a *Newsweek* cover article (Mathews
1990:46). United States Congress representatives and senators threatened to cut the
budget allocation to the National Endowment for the Arts for financing such
'shocking' and 'abhorrent' materials in the name of 'art' and to deny future funding
to those galleries that displayed 'obscene' works (Alaton 1990; American Association
for State and Local History 1990:1). Senator Jesse Helms told the U.S. Senate (Vance
1989:39): 'I do not know Mr. Andres Serrano, and I hope I never meet him, because
he is not an artist, he is a jerk. Let him be a jerk on his own time and with his own
resources. Do not dishonor our Lord.' The Mapplethorpe exhibit continued to circulate through U.S. art galleries and got into trouble again in March 1990 in Cincinnati, Ohio, where the director of the Centre for the Contemporary Arts was charged
with obscenity for showing the exhibit.

Earlier in 1990 the Mendel Gallery in Saskatoon, Saskatchewan, was also temporarily besieged by the Saskatoon City Council and others for housing the National Photography Gallery's travelling exhibition 'Evergon,' which also included
sexually explicit imagery (Lacey and Vincent 1990; Milrod 1990). 'We have laws to
clean up pollution in our rivers,' one city councillor was quoted as saying, 'so we
should have laws to ban filth like this.' He was perhaps repeating *Washington Times*
columnist Patrick Buchanan's metaphor (cited in Vance 1989:41): 'As with our rivers
and lakes, we need to clean up our culture: for it is a well from which we must all
drink. Just as a poisoned land will yield up poisonous fruits, so a polluted culture,
left to fester and stink, can destroy a nation's soul.'

People called for Mendel director Linda Milrod to be fired and the gallery's
budget to be cut. (After weeks of debate, in council and through the local media, city
council voted to continue normal funding for the gallery. Milrod subsequently re-
signed but for reasons unrelated to this controversy.) When Andres Serrano at-

tended the 'Art and Outrage' conference on art and censorship at the Winnipeg Art Gallery on 31 March 1990, a Winnipeg councillor described him as 'a lunatic who should be in an asylum, not in the Winnipeg Art Gallery.' Anthropologist Carol Vance suggested at the same Winnipeg conference that the good people of Saskatoon and Winnipeg were experiencing a 'sex panic,' projecting upon people like Serrano, Evergon, and Mapplethorpe their anxieties about changes in family and gender relations, abortion, child abuse, and so on. (The Winnipeg conference was reported by Enright 1990. See also Vance 1989, 1990; Wallis 1990.)

Whatever the reasons, it is interesting to note that arguments which first seemed to centre around pornography, blasphemy, artistic freedom, and censorship, gradually began to encompass broader issues (see Robertson 1990) such as what is art, who is it for, who pays for it, and who calls the tune? We have returned to the politics of representation and the question of voice:

(a) What is art? Counterbalanced are two views about the purpose of art (and of exhibits, and even of anthropology, one might add): to be inspirational and supportive of mainstream values or to be critical, oppositional, or even sometimes offensive.

(b) Who is it for, the élites or everyone?

(c) Who pays for it? The debate here is over how much governments should support art or exhibitions that do not support the state or are not supported by the public 'in the marketplace.'

(d) Who calls the tune? Who should decide how taxpayers' dollars are used—legislators, panels of experts, peer review, or special-interest groups through public protest?

Without the freedom to offend, British author Salman Rushdie once said (Findley 1990), there is no freedom of expression: 'Without the freedom to challenge, even to satirize all orthodoxies, including religious orthodoxies, it ceases to exist. Language and the imagination cannot be imprisoned, or art dies, and with it, a little of what makes us human' (Rushdie 1990:6).

'It is perhaps in the nature of modern art to be offensive,' American writer John Updike (1989:12) wrote in response to the Mapplethorpe controversy. 'It wishes to astonish us and invites a revision of our prejudices.' What is more (1989:13): 'if we are not willing to risk giving offense, we have no claim to the title of artists, and if we are not willing to face the possibility of being ourselves revised, offended, and changed by a work of art, we should leave the book unopened, the picture unviewed, and the symphony unheard.' (Might one make the same claim for anthropologists that he makes for artists?)

On the other side—and there is always that other side in these matters (and usually more than one)—is the question of setting limits out of respect for community standards or the sensitivities of others. At some point it is necessary to stop and think about the people who might be offended. U.S. Senator Jesse Helms has frequently spoken out against the use of tax dollars for art he considered offensive. Let people be offensive at their own expense, he says. 'Should public standards of decency and civility be observed in determining which works of art or art events are to be selected for the government's support?' asked *The New York Observer* art critic Hilton Kramer (1989:1). Or, stating the issue another way, he continues, 'is everything and anything to be permitted in the name of art? Or, to state the issue in still another way, is art now to be considered such an absolute value that no other standard—no standard of taste, no social or moral standard—is to be allowed to play any role in determining what sort of art it is appropriate for the government to support?'

Canada's revenue minister, Otto Jelinek, referring to a Canada Council grant to a theatre that produced a play about homosexuals, remarked (Dafoe 1989) that 'some of these ridiculous grants are enough to make me bring up' and that his government should review the arms-length status of the Council.

We have returned to the marketplace as an arbiter of public taste. Public appeal is the test of virtue. As Senator Helms said in reference to the Mapplethorpe/Serrano controversies (Parachini 1989:3): 'I have fundamental questions about why the federal government is involved in supporting artists the taxpayers have refused to support in the marketplace.' Thus, the debate about the purpose of art becomes a language for examining broader questions about what constitutes a proper society, including the contest between the moral visions of the conservatives and liberals (Alaton 1990; Vance 1990). 'The fundamentalist attack on images and the art world,' Vance (1989:43) argues, 'must be recognized not as an improbable and silly outburst of Yahoo-ism, but as a systematic part of a right-wing political program to restore traditional social arrangements and reduce diversity.'

CONCLUSION: SOME COMMON THREADS

If we examined each case in detail we would find many differences and some similarities. I want to focus on the similarities here, especially those that lie behind the differences.

One pattern extends beyond these cases: the widespread inclination to question the authority of cultural agencies, such as museums and universities, and their professional representatives, to make decisions that go against those moral standards that are claimed by some to represent either the public's interest or the concerns of under-represented populations.

This is not new. Sociologist Alvin Gouldner, in his 1970 *The Coming Crisis of Western Sociology* (1970:115–16, passim), noted a long, continuous series of 'revolts' against the idea of applying empiricist methodologies to the study of society and its expressions. In his classic 1947 paper, 'The Expansion of the Scope of Science,' Leslie White suggested that the scientific or naturalistic perspective would appear latest, mature slowest, and receive the most opposition in the psychological, social, and cultural areas of our experience 'where the most intimate and powerful determinants of our behavior are found.' There have been renewed assaults on the notion of a scientific study of society during the past several decades, from within the disciplines as well as from outside, identifying the limitations, fallacies, and male-centric orientation of the naturalistic approaches. Some, perhaps buoyed along by a postmodernist enthusiasm, reject the possibility of any objective knowledge about society, opting for the equality of insider perspectives. Everyone is his or her own authority, just as the customer is always right. Consumerism and postmodernism, it would seem, share similar ideological foundations. The possibility of positive knowledge cannot be totally extinguished, however, no matter how often attacked by those claiming higher moral grounds.

Resistance and rebellion against naturalistic or empirical interpretations might be seen as recurring features of intellectual history, though their labels change from one age to the next—'postmodernism' being one of the more recent—and though intellectual discourse never totally succumbs to those onslaughts. Other features in our cases seem to be more emergent than repetitive.

One emergent feature concerns the type of morality that appears to be gaining ascendency—or, to use another trendy word, gaining 'hegemony'—in contemporary society. It is that populist/postmodernist/consumer ideological orientation referred to earlier and includes, in one form or another, the radical democratic idea that in the marketplace of ideas, customs, and morals, as in the marketplace of products, the customer is always right. As the Member of Parliament the Honourable Felix Holtmann noted in an interview (Godfrey 1990): 'I basically believe the people are always right. The customer is king.'

Another illustration of this view is Canadian economist Steven Globerman's (1983:37) argument that claims for government subsidy by the cultural sector based on the assumption that some tastes are better than others 'is an unacceptable basis for government action in a democratic society.' Good taste is popular taste. Or consider British Columbia's former premier Bill Vander Zalm's response (Moore 1987) to those concerned about the impact of free trade with United States on Canadian culture: 'What is culture? I'm not sure Canadians are all that concerned by what is traded away in culture . . . I don't think there's much wrong with the marketplace determining what people want in culture.'

There are other examples one could cite, but these will do for now. In the broader philosophy (Marchak 1988), of which these are individual expressions, there is a tendency to view citizens as consumers, to redefine cultures as commodities, to measure value by public opinion polls, referenda, head counts, and sales receipts, and to believe that justice is probably best determined by the play of so-called free market forces. In fact, the marketplace is typically represented as an ideal paradigm for organizing social as well as economic relations.

The second emerging feature, ambiguously related to the first, is the increasing public recognition of social and cultural pluralism. Contemporary society is not composed of an anonymous mass of consumers but rather—to borrow from the language of consumerism—of various 'market segments,' each with its special tastes and vested interests. What is significant about this pluralization or taste segmentation of society is not its existence, which is not new, but its growing visibility and acceptance, even if that growth is slow, frequently petulant, agonizing, and uneven. The implication for cultural institutions, such as museums and universities, is that they are increasingly being expected to meet the multiple demands of ethnically and socially diverse publics. In this new world order the minorities expect the same rights and privileges as the majority. For anthropologists that especially means giving consideration to the interests of Third World peoples and visible minorities. The introduction of third and fourth voices (worlds)—the traditional subjects of anthropological research—has been unnerving for anthropologists, who find themselves being publicly criticized and rejected by the very people they have tried to represent!

Fueling the assertion of minority rights is the idea of equality, which must be one of the most revolutionary ideas in all history. It is difficult to think of any other single principle that has had such an impact on social arrangements and personality formation, that throughout history has been as oppositional, confrontational, or destructive of traditional relations, and as transforming, emancipating, or liberating for individuals and groups. The belief that one has a natural right to be the equal of others is surely one of the most powerful of beliefs. Perhaps its most radical version is the assertion of collective (ethnic) rights over those of the individual and, thus, the right to be different as equal to the right of everyone to be the same.

The growth of cultural and ethnic pluralism and ideas about the equality of groups as well as of individuals in a consumer-oriented, postmodernist, deconstructing society raises several questions about the status of the anthropological perspective. First is the question of voice. In a plurality of tongues what happens to scholarly speech? Naturalistic interpretation, rooted in empiricism, has traditionally claimed cognitive superiority over those based on moral, communal, or popular considerations. But who can claim superiority in an equalitarian society? Is anthropology only to be regarded as one more voice among many, perhaps even inferior to the self-interpretations of underrepresented peoples? Has anthropology become just another story, yet another mythic 'discourse,' now that its colonial and sexist origins have been fully exposed? It is not just museum exhibits that are being criticized here, by the way—it is the very idea of studying others, never mind representing them, that is challenged. The contest is over the essence of anthropology. How, then, is anthropology to be reconstituted during this age of populist deconstruction?

The second question is about action. How will anthropologists and other cultural workers help people come to terms with the growing multicultural and multivocal realities—discordant realities, one might even say—of contemporary society? Will anthropologists in museums and elsewhere have the authority and public respect, not to mention the courage, to speak out? Or will they be lost in the cacophony of voices, reduced by public criticism, populist sentiments, funding restrictions, and the forces of the marketplace to bland pronouncements and tangled rhetoric?

NOTE

Note below is from the article as it appeared in Cannibal Tours and Glass Boxes: The Anthropology of Museums.

1. Earlier versions of this chapter were presented to the Plenary Session "Recent Developments in Canadian Anthropology" at the seventeenth annual meeting of the Canadian Anthropology Society, Calgary, Alberta, 2 May 1990, and to the University of Washington "Seminar on Ethnicity, Nationality, and the Arts," co-ordinated by Professor Simon Ottenberg, 8 May 1990. I am thankful for those opportunities. I am also indebted to Dr. Jeanne Cannizzo, research consultant of the Royal Ontario Museum, Lina Jabra, then director of the Burnaby Art Gallery, and Dr. Judith Mastai, director of Public Programmes at the Vancouver Art Gallery, for supplying information on a number of the case studies discussed here. This chapter is also to be published in a series edited by Professor Ottenberg. Materials from this chapter were included in a report to the Taonga Maori Conference, New Zealand, 20 November 1990, entitled 'Biculturalism in Exhibits' to be published by the government of New Zealand, also published in *Museum Anthropology* 15(1991)2.

REFERENCES

Alaton, Salem. "Liberals and conservatives in row over U.S. arts body." *Globe and Mail* (9 June 1990): D3.

American Association for State and Local History. "Reauthorization critical for NEH." *History News Dispatch* 5, no. 6 (1990): 1.

Ames, Michael M. "Daring to be different: an alternative." *Muse,* Journal of the Canadian Museums Association 6, no. 1 (1988b): 38–47.

———. "The liberation of anthropology: A rejoinder to professor trigger's 'a present of their past?'" *Culture,* Journal of the Canadian Anthropology Society 8, no. 1 (1989): 81–5.

Bennett, Julia. "High flyers: national gallery's Shirley Thomson masters the modern art world." *Privilege* 2, no. 1 (1990): 11–12.

Blizzard, Christina. "Exhibit mirrors history." *Toronto Sun* (8 May 1990): 29.

Canadian Museums Association. "MP's try to intervene on gallery's purchase." *Museogramme,* Newsletter of the Canadian Museums Association 18, no. 3 (1990): 1–2.

Canadian Press. "Goodwill ambassador [photograph]." *Globe and Mail* (22 January 1987): A5.

——. "Kinsella 'ripping off' Indians." *Globe and Mail* (8 December 1989a): C10.

——. "Gallery purchase raises questions." *Globe and Mail* (10 March 1990a): C6.

——. Civilization museum seeks popularity: a million visitors logged in first year." *Vancouver Sun* (2 July 1990b): B3.

Cannizzo, Jeanne. *Into the heart of Africa.* Royal Ontario Museum, 1989.

Charnley, Kerrie. "Neo-nativists: days without singing. *Front,* Newsletter of the Western Front Society, Vancouver (January 1990): 15–17.

Colombo, John Robert. "Fire the curators." Letter to *Globe and Mail* (17 March 1990): D7.

Da Breo, Hazel A. "Royal spoils: the museum confronts its colonial past." *Fuse* (Winter 1989–90): 28–37.

Dafoe, Chris. "Jelinek angers arts groups with remarks on grants." *Globe and Mail* (21 December 1989): C2.

Drainie, Bronwyn. "Minorities go toe to toe with majority." *Globe and Mail* (30 September · 1989): C1–2.

——. "Black groups protest African show at 'racist Ontario Museum.'" *Globe and Mail* (24 March 1990): C1.

Duffek, Karen. "Exhibitions of contemporary native art." *Muse,* Journal of the Canadian Museums Association 7, no. 3 (1989): 26–8.

Edwards John. "Novel approaches." Letter to *Globe and Mail* (21 October 1989): D7.

Enright, Robert. "Notes on 'the arts tonight.'" Canadian Broadcasting Corporation FM program, 2 and 5 April 1990.

Findley, Timothy. "The man who kissed books and bread out of respect." *Globe and Mail* (16 June 1990): C1.

Freedman, Adele. "A revealing journey through time and space." *Globe and Mail* (17 November 1989): C11.

Fried, Nicky. "Fashion by Dorothy Grant." *Design Vancouver* (1990): 9–10.

Globerman, Steven. *Cultural regulation in Canada.* Montreal: Institute of Public Policy, 1983.

Godfrey, Stephen. "Foe of elitism has had his say on arts." *Globe and Mail* (9 April 1990): A17.

Gouldner, Alvin A. *The coming crisis of western sociology.* New York: Avon Books, 1970.

Gray, Charlotte. "Museum pieces." *Saturday Night* 103, no. 9. (1988): 11–17.

Greer, Sandy. "Ojibway storyteller speaks out against film." *Kainai News* (9 November 1989): 14–15.

Harrison, Julia D. "'The spirit sings' and the future of anthropology." *Anthropology Today* 4, no. 6. (1988): 6–9.

Harrison, Julia D., et al. *The spirit sings: artistic traditions of Canada's first peoples.* Toronto: McClelland & Steward and Glenbow Museum, 1987.

Harrison, Julia D., Bruce Trigger, and Michael M. Ames. "Point/counterpoint: 'the spirit sings' and the Lubicon Boycott." *Muse,* Journal of the Canadian Museums Association 6, no. 3. (1988): 12–25.

Henry III, William A. "Cover stories: beyond the melting pot." *Time* 135, no. 15. (1990): 38–41.

Hunter, Don. "The $1.8-million stripe." *Province* (18 March 1990): 37.

Jennings, Sarah. "Museum's costs questioned." *Globe and Mail* (16 May 1990): A14.

Kramer, Hilton. "Is art above the laws of decency?" *New York Times* (2 July 1989): Section 2, 1, 7.

Lacey, Liam. "Colleague's attack only serves to motivate iconoclastic author." *Globe and Mail* (21 December 1989): A14.

Lacey, Liam and Isabel Vincent. "Saskatoon Gallery under fire for 'offensive' exhibition.'" *Globe and Mail* (23 March 1990): A13.

MacDonald, George F. "The future of museums in the global village." *Museum* 39, no. 3 (1987): 209–16.

———. "Epcot Center in museological perspective." *Muse,* Journal of the Canadian Museums Association 6, no. 1 (1988): 27–37.

MacDonald, George F. and Stephen Alsford. *A museum for the global village: the Canadian Museum of Civilization.* Hull, Quebec: Canadian Museum of Civilization, 1989.

Marchak, Patricia M. *Ideological perspectives on Canada.* 3rd ed. Toronto: McGraw-Hill Ryerson, 1988.

Mathews, Tom. "Fine art or foul?" *Newsweek* 116, no. 1 (1990): 46–52.

Mays, John Bentley. "National gallery should tune out static over painting." *Globe and Mail* (14 March 1990a): A11.

———. "Carving or sculpture?" *Globe and Mail* (16 June 1990b): C4.

Millard, Peter. "Art of the Inuit." Letter to *Globe and Mail* (26 June 1990): A18.

Milrod, Linda. "Message from the director" *Folio,* Newsletter of the Mendel Art Gallery (February/March 1990): 4.

Moore, Mavor. "Canada's cultural road takes a disturbing turn." *Globe and Mail* (27 June 1987): C2.

Ozick, Cynthia. "A critic at large (T.S. Eliot)." *New Yorker* 65, no. 4 (1989): 119–54.

Paine, Robert. "Ethnodrama and the 'fourth world': the Saami Action Group in Norway, 1979–1981. In Noel Dyck, ed., *Indigenous peoples and the nation-state: 'fourth world' politics in Canada, Australia and Norway.* Social and Economic Papers No. 14. St. John's Newfoundland: Institute of Social and Economic Research, Memorial University of Newfoundland, 1985.

Parachini, Allan. "The national endowment for the arts: arts agency—living up to its billing?" *Western Museums Conference Newsletter* (fall 1989): 1, 3–5.

Patterson, Pam. "Doreen Jensen and Joane Cardinal-Schubert: two native women artists tackle issues through their art." *Gallerie: Women's Art* 1, no. 2 (1988): 4–8.

Phillips, Ruth. "Indian art: where do you put it?" *Muse,* Journal of the Canadian Museums Association 6, no. 3 (1988): 64–71.

Robertson, Art. "Art gets much-needed publicity." *Saskatoon Sun* (31 March 1990).

Rushdie, Salman. *In good faith.* London: Granta, 1990.

Thorsell, William. "A spectacular disregard for cultural integrity" *Globe and Mail* (21 October 1989): D6.

Trigger, Bruce. "A present of their past? anthropologists, native people, and their heritage." *Culture,* Journal of the Canadian Anthropology Society 8, no. 1 (1989): 71–9.

Updike, John. "Modern art: always offensive to orthodoxy." *Western Museums Conference Newsletter* (fall 1989): 12–13.

Vance, Carol. "The war on culture." *Art in American* (September 1989): 39–43.

———. "Misunderstanding obscenity." *Art in America* (May 1990): 49–55.

Vincent, Isabel. "Minority artists assail the mainstream: delegates to conference accuse arts councils of racism." *Globe and Mail* (25 June 1990): A9.

Wallis, Brian. "Vice cops bust Mapplethorpe show for obscenity." *Art in America* (May 1990): 41–2.

Williams, B. "A class act: Enthropology and the race to nation across ethnic terrain." In Bernard J. Siegel, ed, *Annual Review of Anthropology* 18 (1989): 401–44.

7

The Real Multiculturalism:
A Struggle for Authority and Power

Amalia Mesa-Bains

For the last six or so years a number of us have been involved in conferences in the United States and abroad, talking about everything from the politics of culture to the center and margin, and I'm almost exhausted with the term *multicultural*. So I'm going to try to part the veil a little bit.

I grew up in the sixties, first in the black-power movement with my husband, then in the Chicano movement, and later, as an educator in that golden era of multicultural education in the public schools; so I've heard a lot of jargon come and go. *Multiculturalism* seems to be a term that we are comfortable with at present, possibly because of its euphemistic nature. It allows us to acknowledge our own ethnicity, but not the categorical differences in race, class, and gender that are below the surface and need to be addressed in order to deal in an appropriate and responsive way with the diversity we're talking about.

What we're really talking about is a kind of postcolonial diaspora. Much of art history and our ideas about art, the museum, and collecting have come out of the colonial ages. We are now dealing with the generations descendant from those colonial experiences and occupations, but they have come home to the colonies. In the case of indigenous Mesoamericans, these communities represent an experience of internal colonization. You are now meeting their grandchildren, dealing with those of us and our children who come from that experience of the postcolonial age.

Consequently, all of the institutional and theoretical developments from which your institutions spring conflict with what we, as people of color, represent. The contemporary expressions of individuals and communities who live between tradition and innovation simply don't fit Western categories. Multiculturalism has

Amalia Mesa-Bains is a MacArthur Foundation Fellow, professor at California State University, Monterey Bay, and activist in the Chicano artist movement. "The Real Multiculturalism: A Struggle for Authority and Power" was written for *Different Voices: A Social, Cultural, and Historical Framework for Change in the American Art Museum* published in 1992 by the Association of Art Museum Directors (AAMD). It is reprinted here by permission of the AAMD.

allowed the mainstream arts community to grow somewhat complacent. It has drawn a little closer perhaps, but on some levels still maintains a distance—a distance from the issues of racism and linguistics.

In this postcolonial, post-civil rights era we are faced, in many ways for the first time, not simply with issues of quantification, affirmative action, quotas, parity, access, and representation, but with the qualitative aspects of the diverse experiences of uniqueness, the polysemic voice that we speak of so often. These are the issues that I believe on some level have penetrated your institutions and with which you are struggling. Concepts like patrimony. Whose is it? Stewards of a commonwealth. Whose wealth? How was it gained?

We often speak of style, cultural style. I saw a photograph in which a young blond white boy was wearing dreadlocks; I also saw a full-page ad in *Glamour* showing a light-skinned black woman wearing blue lenses. Style has always been style, but the issues of real cross-cultural or transcultural exchange and, more important, the culturally specific values that people bring to those transcultural encounters are what we have had the most difficulty facing.

CULTURAL PATRIMONY

I come from a family that immigrated from Mexico, and I grew up in a community with other undocumented families. I'm the first in my family to receive a higher education and, to some degree, the first to encounter a larger institutional life; consequently, my family values have been put into question time and time again. This goes beyond code switching—learning what kind of clothes to wear or what voice to speak in—to fundamental questions of relationship.

It is in the areas of patrimony, cultural values, and something that Carlos More calls "interethnic intimacy" that we are presently struggling. By interethnic, or interracial, intimacy, we are not talking about that fearful thing called sex, which seemingly is one of the driving forces in racism. We're speaking of something much more intimate than that; that is respect, understanding, and exchange.

In many respects, patrimonial values and interethnic intimacy constitute the battleground in which we will work out the twenty-first century; and in this large-scale redefinition of aesthetic and cultural identity, there is on the most profound level a call to the institutions that broker learning, thinking, culture, and expressiveness. The Association of Art Museum Directors can play a major role here.

In order to push aside the veil of multiculturalism in its euphemistic sense and conquer the mystifications that come with it, we—as a transitional generation with an inherited view of patrimony, values, and interethnic intimacy—are called upon to assume another kind of moral leadership in what may be a very difficult time. It means we have to deal with some of the very issues that we brought up earlier: issues of power, authority, and privilege.

I define power as the ability to create self-definitions upon which one can act. Action is clearly the issue at hand. Dialogue has been going on for quite a long time. From your point of view, the questions may now be: How should we do this, and what will happen if we do? How far do we have to go with it? Must I give up the type of stewardship my institution represents? What happens when people from multiracial and multicultural communities come into the museum—when we begin to change our curatorial focus and to develop other kinds of exhibition and acquisition policies?

The ability to self-define—a complex task in a postcolonial age—is at the heart of the struggle. I am a Chicana, which means that my parents were born in Mexico. I was born in the United States, and I came to my own sense of power—self-definition followed by action—during the civil rights movement. The Chicano movement was pivotal to me and my self-definition. Chicana, after all these years, is an identity based on the ability to act upon a sense of who I am and what I come from. Even within my own community I have been guided by that sense of identity. But we're talking about something probably even more complex than that because it involves many identities and many struggles.

I would like to share with you a quote from Trinh T. Minh-Ha, whom many of you may know as an artist, critic, and filmmaker. She says: "You who understand the dehumanization of forced removal-relocation-reeducation-redefinition, the humiliation of having to falsify your reality, your voice—you know. And often you cannot say it. You try to keep on to unsay it, but please—we must say it. You try and keep on trying to unsay it, for if you don't, they will not fail to fill in the blanks on your behalf, and you will be said."[1] I believe Trinh is speaking of the very issue we are concerned with today, which is, How do we reflect previous history? It may seem that the art historical situation is set apart from such other contexts, but no art is beyond its social, political, and historical context. How do these issues of power, cultural democracy, and self-definition pertain to exhibitions, audiences, and resources?

Our institutions are ensconced in concepts of history based, as I stated earlier, in a colonial age. Anthropology, psychology, and archaeology originated in those times. The first typologies, which measured the distance between people's eyes to determine their intellectual capacities, included terms like *phlegmatic, choleric,* and *melancholic.* Those were the beginnings of psychology. Such colonial-age tools have set the stage for the historical understanding with which the paradigms of art history have been placed.

I was overjoyed to hear Irene Winter refer to James Clifford, because Clifford's work is very significant in helping us to understand why we find ourselves in confusion and disorder over the arts and culture of people of color. I can't refer to them as a minority, because numerically they're not. I could more accurately call them a distinct majority, or multiracial communities. We are talking primarily about issues of race. To some degree, race is also a euphemism of the colonial age, one that was designed to divide resources from linguistic groups. Nonetheless, we deal with these notions of race, and it is Clifford and others like him who compel us to question these original paradigms.

When Clifford talks about the way in which collecting has grown out of colonial-age acquisitions, he emphasizes how this chaotic collecting resulted in an order based on a kind of Western subjectivity. From this early date the cultural expressions of the non-Western world were reordered and misapprehended.

What Clifford points out is that we have devised a dual system in which Western art, construed within the parameters of the museum as masterpieces created by individual artists, is posed against ethnography, that is, the hall of man, the artifact, the culture in which it was created, the anonymous artisan.

Our dilemma is that after years of such a dichotomy, there have emerged in works by artists of color representations that blur and erase such categories as folk art and fine art. In many respects, this blurring allows us to see the contradiction between the dual standards of a Western subjectivity and those standards assigned to otherness. Only now are museums attempting to deal with the misunderstandings and misrepresentations of the post-colonial age.

RESOURCES, AUDIENCES, AND EXHIBITIONS

During the course of the day we have talked about the notion that art should be transcendent, apart from the body politic and certainly apart from economic relations (power and race relations). But, we also know that we're in a marketplace dilemma with regard to those very same pieces of art and that the artifact has joined the masterpiece in that marketplace. So, to some degree, the confusion over categories is an economic circumstance as well.

If the European masters are priced out, if Christie's and Sotheby's find that the Latin American market is financially more accessible with those masters of Latin America, such as Rivera, Kahlo, Matta, and Lam, having these familiar cousins in America (Arnaldo Roche, Carlos Almaraz, and Luis Cruz Azaceta to name but a few), then we must begin to deal with their work as well. Hence, the confusion, ambiguity, and disorder over resources, audience, and exhibitions.

To talk about the work, one must talk about the experience; so I'm going to talk first about resources. It is precisely because we often focus first on exhibitions, rather than resources, that we have had confounding experiences. We try to determine the art without understanding the cultural expressiveness of particular groups.

I don't have to say much about the exhibition *Hispanic Art in the United States: Thirty Contemporary Painters and Sculptors*, as I'm sure many of you are familiar with the controversy surrounding it. That was an instance where to some degree the curatorial perspectives started with traditional approaches to exhibitions, rather than an understanding of the resources of the Latino community. When I talk about resources, I am referring to those aspects that are within the worldview of the diverse cultures we are beginning to serve and respond to—their patrimony, values, and sense of an interethnic or interracial intimacy. As a psychologist I have to think first of the resource of cultural memory, because it is memory that allows us to assert our sense of continuity against all odds. Cultural memory allows spiritual and familial practices to be maintained, often through oral traditions. Many of the working-class people of color have not always had access to a formal education; yet learning is passed from generation to generation in other ways. It is from that cultural memory that much of the work of contemporary artists of color springs.

RESOURCES: HISTORICAL RESPONSIBILITY

The historical responsibility that is an element in those resources is a responsibility for both the past and the present, one that must be shared by cultural leaders. Historical responsibility involves the kind of history that critic Walter Benjamin speaks of: "Only that historian will have the gift of fanning the spark of hope in the past who is firmly convinced that even the dead will not be safe from the enemy if he wins."[2] This quote has to do with the concept of origin and the redemption of the past.

What we see in the African American, Latino, and certainly Asian American and Native American communities is a moving back toward the memory of origin. The African scholarship of people like Dr. Ben Yusef and Dr. Asa Hilliard, who question the relationship of Kehmt, or black Egypt, to the Greco-Roman world, of books such as Martin Bernal's *Black Athena*, and even such works as Cornel West's *Prophetic Fragments*—all are beginning to question the Eurocentric myth of origin.

It was with an awareness of historical responsibility that books like George James's *Stolen Legacy* (1954) and Chancellor Williams's *The Destruction of the Black Civilization* (1974) were written, years before they were accessible except in the most clandestine ways. The decentering of the humanities relies, to some degree, not just on cultural memory passed through communities, but on the historical responsibility of scholars, critics, artists, and institutional leaders who see themselves in this transitional generation as ready and able to move into another system of knowledge and thought.

RESOURCES: COMMUNITY PRACTICES

Community practices are also part of the resources of the community. Such practices have greatly influenced the development of aesthetic forms. For instance, the preponderance of the ceremonial and the spiritual in particular communities is an aspect of the collective history of religion, spirituality, and spectacle. Other practices reflect the dynamic and interactive processes of exchange and learning, the relationship between tradition and innovation, and the layering of experience that creates new measures of meaning.

At the core of many of the aesthetic representations that are a part of the contemporary school is ancestral legacy. In *The Decade Show: Frameworks of Identity in the 1980s*, concepts of historical responsibility and ancestral legacy are reflected in many of the artworks. Ancestral legacy allows us to consider more than one view of the upcoming quincentennial. For many of us, the ancestral legacy surrounding the quincentennial is not a five-hundred-year phenomenon, not a tabula rasa, or a fertile ground where culture was dropped. The ancestral legacy of which we speak—a splendor of thirty centuries even in Mesoamerica, which is only one part of this continent—is a very, very long one. It certainly outmarks a half a century.

If we are to understand ancestral legacy, we have to look at the forms in which we find it in our own institutions. The quincentenary celebration, which emphasizes historical and cultural Euro-Spanish developments, has to be questioned not only by those within the native communities, but also by the larger institutions that will determine the exhibitions, the outreach, and the activities related to that very market. For our native brothers and sisters, the quincentennial is a marking of genocide, hardly something that should be called a celebration. Nonetheless, it is one aspect of ancestral legacy.

AUDIENCES: AESTHETIC SENSIBILITY

An extension of ancestral legacy is reflected in family values and a worldview, even in the cultural styles of the audience. These issues are rarely addressed in major institutions. I've participated in several outreach panels in California and in a number of other places; so I've seen the proposals submitted by major institutions that are trying to outreach, or reach out.

One reason that outreach has not been more successful is the lack of recognition of community resources. Even the composition of the audiences themselves is an issue. I don't have to cite the demographic information. Most of you know that the major cities in America are increasingly made up of people of color. In California, for instance, by the year 2010 people of color will make up 50 percent of the state. These people are distinct, they are unique, and they have historical differences; but they also share certain aspects of a cultural worldview, and these have to be addressed in the audiences that we develop. So, composition reflects diversity in aesthetic perception and valuing. The programming of our institutions has to consider this diversity of aesthetic perceptions and valuing in deeper educational approaches.

A number of you are familiar with the Getty model, the discipline-based approach to education. Those of us in educational institutions, particularly public education in the primary grades, have really begun to question these models and examine how we can expand their limited vocabulary. Simply putting Marianne Anderson on the cover of your booklet and listing a number of artists of color as examples of those categories is not enough. Unless you actually deal with aesthetic perception and values as being as diverse as the experiences from which they spring, you will find yourself going in circles.

The Latino or Chicano sensibility is a perfect example of diversity, with its combination of the colonial baroque age and the dominance of the indigenous. The mixture of the Mexican healing worldview, *rasquachismo* (the aesthetics of the downtrodden), and popular barrio styles is characteristic of this bicultural sensibility. Ceremonial practices that have been anchored and maintained in home altars and healing rituals constitute an aesthetic domain in which we perceive and value those things around us. Beauty and power are concepts that are embedded in cultural experiences. They cannot be reduced to a single set of formal elements across all groups.

Aesthetic value and perception have a great deal to do with socioeconomic class. I lived in a rural valley and did not enter a museum until I was twenty years old. My parents didn't have access to those experiences. I was an artist, and they supported me in the forms that were endemic to my community. My uncles were carvers and welders and made things with their hands. I was privileged from the first day I showed my aptitude because I was marked with a spirit that was valued by everyone in my community and my neighborhood. From the age of six or seven I was referred to as "the artist" and given a kind of passport to experience.

Within the reality of what my family could provide for me, my artistry was singularly important to them and valued, yet access to the institutions of Western artistry was not available. Consequently, my only experiences of masterwork in the Western tradition were within the Catholic church. The tremendous influence of bricolage, display, and abundance is clearly marked in the work of many Latino artists and comes, to some degree, from the Catholic experience and liturgical spectacle.

When we talk about an aesthetic perception or value, we are not talking about superficial categories. We are talking about experience layered through time and aesthetic categories that are deep in their meaning and rooted in regional, topographical, and material realities. For example, what about the Japanese American sensibility, which springs from the insular island culture of Japan. What do such origins imply about the way one looks at things? What do they imply about the preference for a dominance of units, significance of nature, and spirituality in design? The Kimono Mind is a term that refers to the many Japanese American Women who still walk as though their bodies were wrapped in that garment. An aesthetic mentality is certainly part of one's culture. The many histories of a cultural aesthetic are the inheritances that we bring to a national patrimony. The capacity to respond to a diverse national patrimony is both an opportunity and a responsibility for our major institutions.

AUDIENCES: COMMUNICATION STYLE AND LEARNING STYLE

When we talk about audiences, we have to talk about communication styles and language. Surely we know multilingualism is an issue in signage, tours, docents, volunteers, catalogues, and brochures. To deal with this, we have to cultivate the resources of multilingual communities.

Communication style is another area that must be considered in audience development. The communication styles of Latin Americans, African Americans, and Asian Americans, just to name three, are very distinct. Cornel West calls the African American style "kinetic orality," or the movement of the body with language in a very specific way. Innovation in language reflects an African ancestry within African American speech.

The linguistic traditions of African American speech have survived the tremendous influences of mass media and education. African based, the language is one with its own rules for plurals, possessives, tenses, word endings, and colloquialisms. That does not mean that "standard" English should not be learned, but we have to recognize that our children come to us language-rich. If we are not capable of interacting with them, understanding them, and communicating with them, it is our problem, not theirs.

We should bring to the issue of audience, then, a greater understanding of communication style and cultural style. One aspect of cultural style that we have begun to look at is the way in which people interact even in something as simple as closure, the act of ending something. I often give the following example. Shortly after I married my husband, who by the way is African American, we were going to my mother's house for dinner. I said to him, "Now look, when we leave, pull the car out slowly and keep the windows down." He said, "Is something going to happen?" And I answered, "No, they just like to say goodbye for a while!" My husband soon learned that closure in a community that values relationships is not always desirable. All the nuances and manifestations of the highly prized communication is around extending the relationship, not around the end product. In such a value system, closure may often be in conflict with the American preference for closure. Attitudes towards closure must be taken into account when greeting and closing with an audience.

We have much to learn about the ways in which communication and cultural style affect cognition, apprehension, and learning, all of which are intertwined. Culture is a window on the world, and our processes of receiving, distributing, and processing information must pass through that window. The degree to which we Westerners don't understand this relates directly to the degree to which we have not been successful in our mainstream institutions, even those that deal specifically with education.

Differences in time and space, physicality, language, and communication affect the way people enter our institutions, the way they are received in our institutions, and the way in which they learn in our institutions. How we receive diverse communities and how we learn from them are elements we have largely ignored because we have come to think of audience as a problem, not as a resource.

EXHIBITIONS

My experience with exhibitions is both as an artist and a curator. I organized a show called *Ceremony of Memory*, which has been touring the United States. I did that show to put the ceremonial work of Chicano/Latino and Caribbean people in the same place at the same time so we could consider aspects of memory, spirituality, temporality, and spatiality. I wanted to look at what these elements mean and how they are similar or distinct as used by contemporary artists.

It's important to remember that we are the first generation to have had ethnic-studies departments on university campuses. We are therefore both artists and activists. We developed in many ways rather rapidly, not unlike the kind of fast-forward photography in which you see a little plant grow very quickly. Beginning with the seed, the bean goes up, the little leaves come out, and then there's a flower. In many ways, that's what happened to us. Many of us were raised in rural communities or newly urban communities; we had home practices of alternative spirituality and traditions of healing; we had folk tales and *corridos*, or ballads; we had ways of knowing the world that were from another generation, another time, and another culture.

We moved rapidly through the canon and through the academy, and that produced in us a very dense layering: For example, I was raised with Walt Disney and *norteno* music, with the concept of the Mayan ruins and black rhythm and blues. This is typical of the interpenetrations and fusions that characterize the not-so-easy-to-categorize work of artists of my generation, particularly those of color. It is the inability to distinguish folk from fine art, the canon from the other, that has confounded the development of particular exhibition practices among mainstream institutions.

In many ways, we are still struggling with the notion of quality or standards. As I've said before, quality is a euphemism for the familiar. It is a family of artists and ideas to which many have grown quite accustomed; but we are a new extended family. We are new artists, with new ideas that you have not had as much experience with.

The question is not simply one of criteria or standards: these can be amended or expanded. We have only to look at the history of scientific research in this country to understand that anything can be adjusted to encompass those things that we choose to prize. As curators in this transitional time our work is partly to make ourselves familiar with the new American canon.

In many ways, what we've come to understand about exhibitions is that it isn't enough for us to get into the museums; many of us have been in. Access is not the only issue. Interpretation is the new forefront. Sometimes very simple things like the translations of the signage can affect the understanding of the art. One example has to do with the exhibition *Hispanic Art in the United States: Thirty Contemporary*

Painters and Sculptors. Included was Cesar Martinez's painting of a very large man with a tattoo of the Virgin de Guadalupe and tattoos of a good woman and a bad woman on his shoulders. The painting is called *El hombre que gusta mujeres* (The Man Who Likes Women). The title was translated as *The Womanizer,* but that is not what it means! This is a man who *loves* women, a man to whom women are so central that he marks his body with them. The profound meaning of this work is reduced, limited, mystified, and misappropriated when a simple thing like a translation cannot be done with understanding, knowledge, and respect.

We've also been into museums where the sheer placement of our work—near lobbies or bathrooms, in rotundas or small rooms—has indicated the inferior value the institution attaches to the work. So access is not the only issue.

Exhibitions have to be formulated with expertise, and that has to be shared. Power—the ability to self-define in a way upon which we can act—must entail shared decision-making, leadership, empowerment, scholarship, and curatorial expertise between the diverse communities and mainstream institutions.

The expanded sense of an American aesthetic is an important part of what we are all struggling with. In many ways the dialogue is best understood when we look at the artists of this generation and the kinds of work they do: emblematic mythology in the hands of people like Lilianna Porter, Roberto Gil de Montes, Carlos Almaraz, Cecilia Vecuna; the indictment of social issues by artists such as Rupert Garcia, Ester Hernandez, Juan Sanchez, David Avalos, Ismael Frigerio, Daniel Martinez, Catalina Parra, and Judite Dos Santos. If we think of the ceremonial, the ways in which sacred space, memory, spirit, and time are located in a contemporary form, we think of Juan Boza, Pepon Osorio, Angel Suarez, George Crespo, and Peter Rodriguez. When we think about the issues pertinent to the environment—nature and spirit, the rain forest—we think about people like Regina Vater, Jonas Dos Santos, and Rimer Cardillo.

If we look at diversity while acknowledging the difficulties of racism and the limits of our own institutional knowledge, we can move toward those audiences with a recognition of their ways of knowing and being. If we use that cultural information to create programming, exhibitions, and educational outreach, we can share leadership and curatorial expertise and develop alliances and partnerships that are based on interethnic intimacy—not appropriation, nor co-optation, nor a good funding proposal, or even a way to get guilt off your back. If we do, then this transitional age is not so hopeless after all.

We must remember that the dialogue about the center/margin politics of culture finally and definitively demands action because to repeatedly speak to audiences (and this is a very personal statement from me) about things that matter so much, that are tied so much to the politics and economics of this country, as well as to your own institution, with no response, makes me feel as though the discourse is mere entertainment.

The definitive question becomes What changes should be instituted in acquisitions, programs, educational models, curatorial expertise, staffing, publications, and criticism within the mainstream institutions in order to respond more effectively to diverse cultures? Change has already begun in many of our institutions, but there is much much more to do. I like to refer to Rex Nettleford, who reminds us that there is such a thing as a "kingdom of the mind,"[3] a passionate creativity, and an emancipatory art that will set us free to understand the world relations of which we are a part.

NOTES

1. Trinh T. Minh-Ha, *Woman, Native, Other: Writing Postcoloniality and Feminism* (Bloomington and Indianapolis: Indiana University Press, 1989), 80.

2. Walter Benjamin, "Theses on the Philosophy of History," in *Illuminations*, edited with an introduction by Hannah Arendt (New York: Schocken Books, 1989), 255.

3. Rex Nettleford, unpublished remarks at "Cultural Diversity Through Cultural Grounding," conference sponsored by Caribbean Cultural Center, New York City, 1989.

8

"Hey! That's Mine": Thoughts on Pluralism and American Museums

Edmund Barry Gaither

In reflecting on the American experience, the authors of *Museums for a New Century* note that a "major force of change we believe to have implications for museums is our society's evolving sense of its own pluralism."[1] This view grows from two important observations: the recognition that many cultural groupings that previously have been rendered invisible in our population no longer accept that status, and the fact that recent immigration from other parts of the Western Hemisphere as well as more distant areas has altered the makeup of many communities—large and small, urban and semirural. African American people, whose numbers exceed thirty million, have become a meaningful political force able to wield considerable muscle and influence in many urban areas. Atlanta and other large cities easily demonstrate this truth. In all probability, African Americans and Hispanics will constitute one-fifth of the whole population of the United States by the year 2000. By that point, the Asian population will have risen from four million to eight million. To put it differently, minorities will be a much greater percentage of the population. Currently a full one-quarter of the annual growth of the U.S. population is the result of immigration, and the vast majority of these immigrants are both nonwhite and non-European.[2] The traditional dominance within the United States by whites of European ancestry will inevitably give way as a more pluralistic view of who is American takes firmer root.

There are clear consequences deriving from these demographic changes. As more formerly invisible social groups exercise political expression, public support by virtue of our tax laws will have to become more accountable to and reflective of a broader segment of the public. The story these institutions tell of the history of our

Edmund Barry Gaither is the Executive Director of the Museum of the National Center of Afro-American Artists in Boston and cofounder of the African American Museums Association. "Hey! That's Mine: Thoughts on Pluralism and America" was written for the © 1992 publication *Museums and Communities: The Politics of Public Culture*, edited by Ivan Karp, Christine Mullen Kreamer, and Steven D. Lavine, which includes the papers presented at a 1990 conference of the same name held at the Smithsonian Institution. It is reprinted here by permission of the Smithsonian Institution Press.

nation and its arts and sciences will have to be richer and more inclusive, which also means that it will have the potential to be both truer and more provocative.

Among the institutions that will be most affected are schools. All of us have come to think of schools, along with homes and religious institutions, as constituting the bedrock of society. Yet by almost all accounts, many urban schools are more mire than rock, more quicksand than stone. As you would expect from the demographics cited earlier, the majority of students at many public schools are now "minority," and other school populations are significantly more mixed than at any other point in our history. Overwhelmed by the scope of society's extra educational expectations, the schools need the cultural and educational benefits that museums offer. They need the profound and intimate understanding of different cultures that is fundamental to museum programming. They need the alternative approaches to education that museums—with their authentic objects—present. And they need the highly specialized types of encounters between people and their physical and cultural environment that museums provide. These encounters foster appreciation of the myriad accrued meanings of things, meanings which constitute the fabric that holds a community together. Without such a knitting together of our social fabric, we will become a still more fractured, fragmented, and violent society.

I believe that we must embrace a fresh understanding of the American experience. We must reject models of American experience that express—directly or indirectly—a concept of *either/or*. We must not tolerate thinking in which folk are *either* African American *or* American. Lurking behind such concepts are constructs such as *separatist/integrationist, we/they,* and *ours/theirs.* Instead, we must honor the comprehensive character of American experience. We must assert its inclusiveness and embrace the reality that folk can be simultaneously African American and American. We belong inseparably both to ourselves and to the whole. We are our own community while also being part of the larger community.

What does all of this mean for museums? Two implications stand out with immediate and perfect clarity. First, museums must serve an ever-broader public in ever-bolder ways. And second, museums must honor America's diversity without paternalism and condescension. To the extent that museums effectively address these broad objectives, they will move closer toward fully satisfying their mandate as institutions that receive public support. It must be noted here that I believe there exists an implied contract between museums, as tax-exempt entities, and the public, which directly or indirectly supports them. Museums have obligations as both educational and social institutions to participate in and contribute toward the restoration of wholeness in the communities of our country. They ought to increase understanding within and between cultural groups in the matrix of lives in which we exist. They ought to help give substance, correction, and reality to the often incomplete and distorted stories we hear about art and social history. They should not dodge the controversy that often arises from the reappraisal of our common and overlapping pasts. If our museums cannot muster the courage to tackle these considerations in ways appropriate to their various missions and scales, then concern must be raised for how they justify the receipt of support from the public. The United States' social health is too important to go unaddressed by any significant sector of its institutions.

How can museums have an impact on such concerns? Of course, there is a straightforward answer to this question. And as is almost always the case, that simple answer belies the complexity and the bedeviling multiplicity of dimensions of this problem. The straightforward answer is that museums can more accurately and more sensitively balance the programs they offer so that those programs not only would delight and educate but also would enhance understanding of humanistic and pluralistic values. Again I quote from *Museums for a New Century*: "When it comes to preserving cultural pluralism, museums have an important role to play. They represent cultural diversity in their collections and their exhibitions. The museum community—within its own institutional makeup—exemplifies our cultural pluralism. . . . But museums are in an uncomfortably contradictory situation in that their celebration of pluralism does not always extend to their internal hierarchies. Their staffs and boards generally do not represent the full diversity of our society."[3] This comment helps us see more clearly both what resources we already have and what areas badly need change.

After their reference to cultural pluralism within the institutional makeup of the museum community in the quotation immediately above, the authors of *Museums for a New Century* make the following observation: "Institutions dedicated to fostering and preserving particular ethnic heritages will be increasingly important in helping Americans understand their historical experience from different perspectives."[4] This is a key thought because it points to the role museums can play in reshaping their communities.

The American cultural arena is a vital and competitive place. In it, cultural expressions from all corners bump into and influence one another. Out of the resulting cacophony, new forms and ideas are born. Criticisms, interpretations, reassessments of values, claims, and counterclaims abound, and out of the muck come impressions of who we are as a people. Museums are important contributors to this dynamic process because they are institutional sponsors of discussions relevant to their disciplines and cultures. Museums that commit themselves to the criticism and fostering of specific cultural heritages—African American, Hispanic, Native American, Asian—have a unique role to play in such settings since they are at the center of the discussion of their own traditions. Unlike general museums, these institutions treat their cultural heritage neither as a short-term focus nor as an aspect of a larger story. Their heritage is their primary subject matter. The presentation of their own cultural traditions is the foundation on which their identity rests.

The existence of museums dedicated to specific cultural heritages does not diminish the need for other museums to share in the work of increasing knowledge and understanding. Instead, all museums become partners in the larger enterprise of education. Certainly, the complexity of a large American city is better reflected in a complementary network of many museums, each with its own primary and secondary foci, and all of which, in the aggregate, represent a fuller picture of the community's historical, cultural, and scientific life. Within this museum network, many and varied educational and exhibition opportunities exist for all partners. Large, medium-sized, and small museums can all enjoy reciprocal relationships with one another, underpinned by mutual respect.

I now wish to turn my attention toward the unique role in American society that can be played by culturally specific museums (also known as minority museums), couching my discussion in terms of African American museums, with which I have had two decades of experience. I believe that the general principles to be derived from the following discussion are by and large valid for Hispanics and other cultural groups in the United States that have been largely ignored or devalued in the telling of our national story.

Museums committed to specific heritages become the institutional buttresses of those traditions because they have unique features. Most often, they enjoy an intimate relationship with real communities of people, which are themselves extensions of those cultures. Because most African American museums were established after 1960, they are still at the outset of their development and are therefore freer to evolve new or different institutional forms. Free from historical association with discrimination and prejudice, these museums are able to provide a forum for the discussion of cultural issues and for the development of criticism without becoming bogged down in racism, which often attends European American museums' engagement of controversial issues.

The close relationship between African American museums and their communities permits the museums to validate the communities' experiences. For this reason, the museums' programs often have a familiarity and a truthfulness that cause the communities to feel a strong bond of kinship with the institutions. Using both conventional and new program formats, these museums provide exciting models for forging community–museum marriages.

For example, when John Kinard became the director of the Anacostia Museum—then the Anacostia Neighborhood Museum—he brought with him a deep love for African American people, a profound understanding of African American communities, and a sense that an African American museum ought to be the product of a dialogue with its immediate neighbors. Drawing on a background in social organization and valuation formation via theology, he did not look first to the museum field for guidance and sanction of his subject matter. Instead, he talked to people and discovered their concerns and issues. He framed an informed and constructive response to their reality and thereby helped teach them to see and understand their own situation more clearly. His now-famous 1969–70 exhibition *The Rat: Man's Invited Affliction* was a pioneering and audacious act that brought new meaning and relevance to exhibition: by exploring the impact of these rodents on poor city dwellers, what is a tragedy in urban neighborhoods was made a subject for examination in the museum. Kinard's boldness and the quality of the dialogue that he and his staff were able to sustain with the Anacostia community made the Anacostia Neighborhood Museum a worldwide model and a prototype for something new— a neighborhood museum. The museum was an experience that enfranchised a community of people and enabled them to talk about their lives and to take greater responsibility for the reconstruction of themselves and their children. The experience also provided an opportunity for the museum to teach conventional history, whether about Anacostia or about other places, more effectively.

Museums are collecting institutions. In amassing the objects and artifacts that will be the basis of their interpretations, museums also signal which materials they regard as important. In the process, they convey to their publics a sense of direction regarding cultural, scientific, and historical interests. The Rhode Island Black Heritage Society and the Afro-American Historical and Cultural Museum in Philadelphia, both of which (at different times) have been under the direction of Rowena Stewart, have set a high standard and offer excellent examples of how to weave a closer relationship between a museum and its community through the activity of collection. Their model demands closer attention. For example, Stewart and her associates have developed and published a five-step approach for collecting African American documents and artifacts.[5] The model is usable by any museum and is instructive for all. Their approach is rooted in a "people orientation" rather than an object search. The artifact holders, or "keepers of the tradition," are central: they provide not only the objects but also the initial interpretation of those objects. These keepers are for the most part ordinary people who may not have thought that the treasures they own were of the slightest interest for anyone beyond their immediate family and friends. They may even be folks who have not themselves placed much value on the evidence of their own personal and familial heritage.

Here are the five steps that are used by Stewart's museum in collecting African American materials. For openers, she or an appropriate member of her staff goes to visit a person who has been identified as an informal historian of the family or group whose material is of interest. Much time is spent, over many visits, becoming acquainted with the keeper and allowing the keeper to become knowledgeable about the museum. This portion of the process is concluded at the point when the keeper has fully accepted the credibility of the museum and feels that it is playing a vital and correct role vis-à-vis the keeper's understanding of his or her own heritage.

In the next stage, the keeper's help is enlisted in interpreting the objects, photographs, or documents to others who are close to and interested in the material. This may be done by arranging a small gathering of the keeper and his or her friends and family, and the event may take place in the museum. At this point, the keeper is the primary interpreter of artifacts that are personal extensions of that person's life and times. Following this event, the museum introduces a professional historian into the mix, who launches the work of more fully explaining and interpreting the larger matrix into which the objects fit. The historian also commences an assessment of the implications of the materials for a general discussion of African American experience and their place in that discussion. Next, attention turns to the preparation of what will become the exhibition or presentation of the materials. This aspect of the work is called giving the materials back to the community. It provides the occasion for the keepers and their peers and associates to share the materials with the community at large and to share their own experiences with other keepers. The final dimension of the process is the education plan and the publications that record the materials and their complete interpretation. This phase of the work may involve the use of the original keeper as a docent speaking to the public about his or her materials as well as those of others. Almost always it will also involve the release of a catalogue, which pulls together the contributions of all parties who were active agents in the collection, interpretation, and ultimate display of the new acquisitions. Significantly, this approach underscores the trust that can be built between a museum and its community. It brings to the museum an advocate whose relationship is predicted on the ennoblement of a shared heritage. Both the advocate and the museum are empowered by their teamwork and its product.

The issues that concern African American museums are not unrelated to larger, more general themes that draw attention in the international world of ideas, such as modernism, deconstructionism, and other thrusts in the arena of contemporary criticism. Because this is so, the critical, social-historical, and art-historical contributions of African American museums are urgently needed in mainstream discussions of such themes. Toward this end, the exhibition *Contemporary African Artists: Changing Traditions*, which debuted at the Studio Museum in Harlem in 1990, is noteworthy. Africa and its peoples have a strong historical and cultural relationship to black Americans. African cultures in all of their manifestations everywhere are perceived as part of the symbolic and actual legacy of black people in America. Thus it is especially appropriate that an African American museum should take the step of bringing critical definition to issues raised by contemporary African artists, who are redefining their historical relationship to their own cultures and influencing the international vocabulary of contemporary art. Participation in this kind of discussion is part of a continuing and full-time commitment of the African American museum toward understanding the growth and development of the visual arts and traditions of black people worldwide.

Knowing one's community means knowing its strengths and its weaknesses. Serving one's community means designing programs that are tailored to its needs and that anticipate its future requirements and demands. For small to moderate-sized museums, there exists a clear opportunity to develop programs and educational activities that respond very directly to community concerns and issues. For example, in the case of my own institution, the Museum of the National Center of Afro-American Artists, we have created several programs that were immediately inspired by observed needs in our primary public. A popular program called *Father and Son Sharing* was designed as a means of helping heal the sometimes strained male relationships that exist in separated families. Our program was focused around a newly commissioned public statue of an African American man reading to his son. John Wilson, the sculptor, is a Boston African American artist with a long history of working with father–son themes. Over the course of the ten-session program, the fathers and sons who participated visited the studio of the artist, created a portfolio of drawings and poems, and visited the foundry to observe how sculptures are cast in bronze. The program concluded with a public exhibition and reception for the participants' families and friends.

We are presently conducting an educational program based on the decorative appliqué traditions of the old African kingdom of Dahomey (the present-day Republic of Benin). In this program, teenage mothers draw on Dahomean textile traditions to create quilted blankets for their infants. Beyond the lessons in cultural history and the direct encounter with the art of Dahomey, these young women also gain social and family skills that will help them reconstruct their lives in more fruitful ways.

Being situated in a region with a large Caribbean population, we became concerned with helping the students we serve to better understand the cultural and social forces that created the Caribbean and that still inform its visual and performing arts. A quick examination of the materials available in the region's schools and from other cultural institutions in the Boston area revealed that no one had effectively addressed the cultural and social history of this region, which is so close to us and from which we have received such a large number of immigrants. With support from the Massachusetts Council for the Arts and Humanities we spent two years developing a series of three presentations that focus on the Caribbean and are accompanied by a substantial publication in four parts. Our Caribbean program, which began in 1969, is divided into parts based on language groups: French/Creole, English, and Spanish. Each subprogram is anchored by a widely recognized art-producing activity or festival from which we have acquired appropriate artworks. Through this series, we are able to provide an in-depth study of cultural traditions that are immediately influential in the lives of our primary community. We believe that such activities are important vehicles for fostering the marriage of a community and its museum(s).

The several examples I have mentioned above show the excitement that "minority" museums bring to the museum field. Without disregarding the professional standards demanded by the stewardship of collections, these institutions are increasingly able to introduce fresh ideas and suggest how museums may become more socially responsible and responsive. Through their programs, African American and Hispanic museums, among others, are developing new and growing audiences. Audiences who previously felt intimidated or alienated by museums now increasingly enjoy the remarkable educational and entertainment opportunities museums offer. Such new visitors are destined to become shared audiences as other museums also broaden their exhibition and educational offerings in response to the demands of American pluralism. When museums in the United States tell a more accurate and integrated story, more Americans from all cultural groups will feel ownership in them, and will say, "Hey! That's mine."

NOTES

1. American Association of Museums, Commission on Museums for a New Century, *Museums for a New Century* (Washington, D.C.: American Association of Museums, 1984), 24.

2. Ibid.

3. Ibid., 25.

4. Ibid.

5. Rowena Stewart, "Bringing Private Black Histories to the Public," in Janet W. Solinger, ed., *Museums and Universities: New Paths for Continuing Education* (New York: Macmillan, 1990).

9

An Agenda for Museums in the Twenty-first Century

Harold Skramstad

We live in a contradictory time. While Americans are increasingly impatient with any limitation on their individual rights, and loyalty to institutions such as the church, school, and community has been deeply eroded, they continue to seek out groups and institutions that can offer order, authority, and criteria that go beyond the imperatives of individualism. Those institutions that are able to recognize this contradiction and can help us find the required balance between our need for freedom and our need for authority are those that will be most successful in the next century.

One institution that is actively seeking that new balance is the American museum. Museums have helped shape the American experience in the past, and they have the potential to play an even more aggressive role in shaping American life in the future. They offer a powerful educational model that can help redesign and reform American education, and they can be important centers of community development and renewal. However, to accomplish these two things, museums must engage the world with a spirit of activism and openness far beyond what they are used to. They will have to reexamine and rethink some of the most fundamental assumptions they hold about what they do and how they do it. They will also have to reclaim the sense of bold entrepreneurship and experimentation that characterized the earliest days of the museum movement in America.

Museums came early to America, and the story of America's first museums is one of lively entrepreneurship combined with a strong sense of educational purpose. In a nation characterized by Daniel J. Boorstin as creating and recreating new, transient, "upstart" communities, most museums were formed as voluntary associations that brought together civic boosters in an eclectic mix of collecting, education, and

Harold Skramstad is president emeritus of the Henry Ford Museum and Greenfield Village in Dearborn, Michigan and former commissioner for the American Association of Museums Accreditation Commission. "An Agenda for Museums in the Twenty-first Century" appeared in a special issue of *Daedalus* devoted to museums and contemporary issues. It is reprinted here by permission of *Daedalus*, Journal of the American Academy of Arts and Sciences, from the issue entitled "America's Museums," Summer 1999, Vol. 128, No. 3.

entertainment activities. Museums, like other community institutions such as colleges and universities, theaters and opera houses, were often built and in business before roads were named or paved. They functioned to anchor and stretch the communities for which they were created. Characteristic of these museum enterprises was a practical bias toward community values and a governance structure that reflected a blurring of private and public spheres.

If there was a distinguishing feature of American museums from the outset, it was their diversity. They might focus on one particular area such as art, history, science, or archaeology, or they might take a mixture of subjects, each represented by a mass of collection materials. One of the earliest museums in America was the Peale Museum in Philadelphia, established by Charles Willson Peale in 1786. Peale saw his museum as a commercial as well as an educational undertaking; he understood the need to connect his content to his audience's interests in a lively manner if he expected them to pay the admission fees that his museum required for its operation. Peale's museum was characteristic of a genre that saw its collections as representing the entire world. Its collections grew to over one hundred thousand specimens, collected and exhibited with two purposes in mind—to entertain and to educate. It is important to remember that early museums such as Peale's developed long before universal public schooling became common; they, along with the church and the library, were important institutions concerned with public education.

If we look at the history of nineteenth-century American museums, we find again and again bold and diverse patterns of museum development carried out against a backdrop of a society hungry for information and knowledge but wanting to get it in a digestible form. One of the most successful early museum pioneers was P. T. Barnum, whose American Museum was founded in New York City in 1841. Barnum's museum provides us with a vivid example of educational entrepreneurship. Materials from around the world were presented in displays designed to blend education and entertainment. Barnum's intent was to create a personal experience of exoticism and wonder. Visitors to his museum were stimulated by the displays to learn and to enjoy themselves in the process. They were comfortable in knowing they were in a place where discovery, dialogue, and conversation were encouraged. They took pleasure in uncovering and trying to discover for themselves whether the material on display was real or not, as Barnum was well known for his staging of elaborate hoaxes to boost attendance. In capitalizing on Americans' almost insatiable desire for knowledge, Barnum understood instinctively that learning and entertainment could exist comfortably in a museum setting. In this he was a genuine museum pioneer.

Later in the century, as cities such as New York, Chicago, Cleveland, and Detroit became dominant centers of commerce, one of the strategies for displaying their economic and cultural power was the creation of large art museums. Because of their size, scale, and social prominence, these art museums came to dominate the cultural assumptions about museums for the next century and to establish a new, more conservative model for museum creation. Most were founded with governance and operating structures that made them less dependent on earned admissions from the visiting public than the earlier museums, such as those of Peale and Barnum, had been. They depended instead on private subsidies by wealthy patrons for much of their financial support. Their founding missions combined the inspirational and the practical: to educate and uplift the public and to improve the skills and taste of those who worked with their hands. The founding patrons of such museums recognized that museums, like libraries, universities, and symphony orchestras, were prudent investments in both social control and civic pride, essential ingredients in the growth and success of America's emerging industrial cities.

Building the collections of these museums fell to a new group of America's business and civic leaders. Their rapidly growing wealth, created by the vast economic expansion of the American economy, meant they were able to accumulate masterpieces of the artistic and cultural patrimony of Europe and the Orient, and these treasures began to find a permanent home in America's museums. As a result, museums began to focus less on the care of audiences and more on the care of their valuable and quickly expanding collections. The result was a gradual yet profound culture change as museums shifted the direction of their energies from public education and inspiration toward self-generated, internal, professional, and academic goals. Museums began to see their primary intellectual and cultural authority coming from their collections rather than their educational and community purpose. The great art museums of New York, Chicago, Cleveland, and Detroit set the dominant tone of this inward movement of museum culture. They were the recipients of many of the artistic masterpieces collected by wealthy Americans. The visibility of their museum collections and exhibitions was symbolic of America's need to prove that American museums could and would reach a quality and scale equal to any in the world.

Because of their visibility as symbols of civic pride, art museums defined the popular perception of a "museum." Once seen as a place of curiosity, wonder, and delight, the "museum" became associated with quiet galleries where artistic treasures were displayed for contemplation. This perception remains today. When journalists and others outside the museum field speak of "museums," they are generally referring to art museums. It was art museums that first saw themselves as preservers of rare and beautiful objects of intrinsic value, and their view of collecting has subsequently shaped the collections of many non-art museums. Until relatively recently, history museums have tended to collect examples of rare and beautiful objects from the past rather than those most characteristic or emblematic of the historical period or locale that was their focus. The word "museum quality" is taken from the culture of art museums and assumes aesthetic quality rather than appropriateness of historical or scientific context.

The great success of the American public-education system in the nineteenth century also worked to strengthen the trend among museums to focus inwardly on the study and display of their collections. As schools began to take on the role of the monopoly providers of public education, the public-education role of museums received less attention. By the first decade of the twentieth century what had too often disappeared from museum culture was a concern about education and respect for the public audience. The expansion of knowledge through museum collecting was now considered by museums to be the primary focus of their work. The more knowledge that was accumulated through museum collections, the more useful that knowledge would be. It was no longer necessary for the museum to be a missionary force on behalf of popular education; rather, it would be a preserver and protector of the rare, the unique, the beautiful, and the special in the arts, the humanities, and the sciences.

There were many in the museum field who expressed concern about this inward-moving perspective. Among many there remained a belief that museums and museum exhibitions had the power to create memorable experiences that could stimulate and inspire people, especially the young. One of the most articulate proponents of this point of view was the aviation pioneer Samuel P. Langley, who was Secretary of the Smithsonian Institution at the turn of the century. Soon after assuming his position, he became concerned that the Smithsonian was doing little to address the educational needs of children who did not understand the arcane labels of the natural history displays designed by scholars. To solve the problem he appointed himself as Honorary Curator of a new "Children's Room" with instructions "to see that a room was reserved and properly prepared for such things as little people most want to know." In a letter to himself accepting the position, Langley wrote:

The Secretary of the Smithsonian Institution has been pleased to confer upon me the honorable but arduous duties of the care of the Children's Room. He has at his service so many men learned in natural history that I do not know why he has chosen me, who knows so little about it, unless perhaps it's because these gentlemen may possibly not be also learned in the ways of children, for whom this little room is meant.

It has been my purpose to deserve his confidence, and to carry out what I believe to be his intention, by identifying myself with the interests of my young clients. Speaking, therefore, in their behalf, and as one of them, I should say that we never have a fair chance in museums. We cannot see the things on the top shelves, which only grown-up people are tall enough to look into, and most of the things we can see and would like to know about have Latin words on them, which we cannot understand: some things we do not care for at all, and other things which look entertaining have nothing on them to tell us what they are about. . . .

We think there is nothing in the world more entertaining than birds, animals, and live things; and next to these is our interest in the same things, even though they are not alive; and next to this is to read about them. All of us care about them and some of us hope to care for them all our lives long. We are not very much interested in the Latin names, and however much they may mean to grown-up people, we do not want to have our entertainment spoiled by its being made a lesson.[1]

In this letter Langley reveals an instinctive understanding of the educational power of museums and the degree to which that power is dependent on museum leaders' understanding of both their subject and their audience.

An important critique of the inward-moving trend in American museums appeared in a study done by Laurence Vail Coleman, commissioned by the American Association of Museums and published by the Association in 1939 as *The Museum in America: A Critical Study*. In his three-volume study, Coleman reminded museum workers that in America, "the museum, like the library, is a *community* enterprise in its very nature." He went on to criticize American museums as a "group of air-tight compartments" in which the "Instructors . . . are buffers between the public and the curatorial group that wants to be left alone. In large museums the instructors are gathered to a 'department of education' (named as though other departments might be dedicated to unenlightenment), and headed by a 'curator of education' (titled as though he had to take care of the stuff lest some of it get away)." Coleman's report remains an extremely insightful but too-little-read or -utilized artifact of American museum history.

The founders of America's first industrial museums, Julius Rosenwald and Henry Ford, provided another important counterforce to this inward focus among museums. Developed in the 1930s, Rosenwald's Museum of Science and Industry in Chicago and Ford's Edison Institute in Dearborn, Michigan, were driven by a strong sense of social purpose. The goal of their museums was to bring people into contact with new, educational, and potentially inspiring experiences. In describing his vision for the Museum of Science and Industry, Rosenwald argued:

> In an industrial center like Chicago there ought to be a permanent exhibit for the entertainment and instruction of the people; a place where workers in technical trades, students, engineers, and scientists might have an opportunity to enlarge their vision; to gain a better understanding of their own problems by contact with actual machinery, and by quiet examination in leisure hours of working models of apparatus; or, perhaps to make new contributions to the world's welfare through helpful inventions. The stimulating influence of such an exhibit upon the growing youth of the city needs only to be mentioned.[2]

This new type of museum was to be primarily a place of education, entertainment, and influence rather than research and scholarship. A formal, hands-on school was attached to Ford's museum; the experiences and artifacts in Rosenwald's Museum of Science and Industry would be chosen for their value in both entertaining and instructing its publics. For both men, the artifacts that formed their museum collections were of a different sort. Instead of focusing on the rare and the antiquarian, they focused on the vernacular and the everyday. Instead of focusing on artifacts that represented continuity, they focused on those that embodied and represented change. If original artifacts were not available, reproductions or models were commissioned. They created large and dramatic spaces and distinctive architecture to give a sense of theater and drama to the museum-going experience. Ford installed a dramatic eight-acre forest of technology behind a reproduction of the facade of Philadelphia's Independence Hall. Rosenwald focused on the creation of a number of vivid and theatrical exhibitions.

While the public responded positively to these new kinds of museums, other museums generally did not. The dominant focus of museum culture for most of the twentieth century remained the accumulation and management of museum collections and the professionalization of museum workers and museum work. The positive results of this focus are undeniable, indeed amazing. Extraordinary advances have been made in the building of new museum collections, the efficient management of existing collections, and the systematic study of those collections. Workers in the museum field have ceased to be seen as dilettantes or amateurs and are now for the most part well-educated and trained professionals. Yet this professionalism has too often widened the gap between museums and the publics who use and support them. Underlying much of contemporary museum culture is a fundamental belief that the collecting, research, and interpretation efforts of museums are intrinsic social goods and that members of the public who choose not to attend museum exhibitions and participate in museum programs do so because they are not quite up to the intellectual or aesthetic challenge. Museums have also increasingly adopted the conventions and privileges of academic culture, claiming the rights of academic freedom in both research and the production of museum exhibitions. In fact, in many museums the public is seen as a distraction from the study of the collection, the "real work" of the museum. The most cynical example of this is the way many museum professionals view "blockbuster" exhibitions. Blockbusters are often seen as little more than necessary pandering to the public rather than as opportunities to try to engage a broad audience in subjects and collections that in the long run benefit both the museum and the public.

Despite the inward focus that has dominated much of the museum culture during the twentieth century, there is no question that museums are almost universally acknowledged as an important part of the cultural landscape. The architecture of new museums has become an important source of civic pride and tourist dollars. Their collections have potency and their exhibitions are highly visible and can be important statements. For this reason, museums have begun to hear more clearly and bluntly from audiences that feel they have been either neglected or badly treated. These audiences are far more diverse and vocal than ever before in their expectations of museums. And because of their political power, they cannot be ignored. For example, when a broad coalition of American Indian groups objected that American museums were housing and studying the remains of their ancestors in a way that conflicted with their own beliefs, they forced federal legislation that gave hegemony to Indian values over museum collecting and research values.

Other groups have begun to look to museums to legitimize and validate their special claims or grievances and have found to their dismay and anger that their accomplishments and struggles are undocumented in museum collections and remain neglected in museum exhibitions and scholarship. Their response has often been to start their own museums so that their interests will not be diluted in the interests or purposes of larger museums. The continuing plethora of new museums (it is estimated that over one-half of the museums in America have been started since 1960) reminds us all that museum founding continues to be an important activity in the building of American communities. The extraordinary proliferation of these special-purpose museums, many of them focused around the history and story of a particular subject, community, or special interest group, is a vital sign of strength in the American museum movement.

THE MUSEUM AS A NEW EDUCATIONAL MODEL

Imagine the prototypical elementary school of the twenty-first century. It is an educational environment in which young children come together to learn about real subject-matter content and to develop critical thinking skills. They work with the real things and ideas of science, art, and the humanities. They work in a setting of participatory learning, led and mentored by adults who are themselves skilled practitioners of the particular craft or discipline the children are learning. The work is rigorous, involving projects that require team-based inquiry and demanding a variety of complementary learning skills. The rewards come in the form of recognition of the individual intellectual and emotional strengths of the learners as well as recognition of the strength of the working teams. All of the activities undertaken require basic skills in thoughtful and critical reading, analytical thinking, problem solving, clear writing, and computer understanding. The measurement of learning comes in a variety of forms, including standardized tests, teacher assessment, and student self-assessment.

Although this schooling model is rare today, it describes very closely the kind of learning that goes on presently in many American museums, especially children's museums and science and technology centers. These new types of museums developed out of community concerns that more traditional, collection-focused museums were not meeting the learning needs of their audiences. Most of these museums do not have large collections of objects, or if they do, the objects function as stimuli for the exploration and discovery of larger ideas or concepts, not as icons in themselves. During the past several decades, these two classes of museums have been great pioneers in improving the process of learning by the young. Their lead is now being followed by museums whose collections are rich in content and who have gained a renewed understanding of the potential of those collections as educational tools.

The museum educational model pioneered by children's museums and science and technology centers focuses on experiential and content-based problem-solving activities working with the real objects of art, history, and science; on participatory, "hands-on" learning; on apprenticeship under the tutelage of people engaged in real-world intellectual activity; and on learning experiences designed to engage all the senses. Its emphasis on educational experiences that address the diverse learning styles of students could, with a relatively small investment, take place in every museum of reasonable size. This model recognizes that education in tomorrow's world needs to be truly different from what it is today. Even the most disadvantaged child now has access to an extraordinary range of experiences in a variety of media. To respond with an educational model designed for a motivated and compliant middle-class student for whom the traditional rigor and rote learning of the classroom is an accepted form of education just will not work.

Yet too often museums are dismissed as institutions of "informal" education, which is taken to mean a less important and less powerful form of education than traditional schooling. The formal educational potential of the museum has been undervalued and greatly underestimated. Some important experiments are already underway in this area. A number of museums have close partnerships with schools so that work and study projects in the museum and at school are seen as a seamless educational experience. At Henry Ford Museum & Greenfield Village in Dearborn, Michigan, a new public high school based on the theme of innovation and focused on the development of critical thinking and problem-solving skills is actually located in the museum. A very diverse student body, chosen by lot, uses all of the facilities of the museum as a giant learning classroom and laboratory. Standardized tests of these students have shown very positive results. In a very different setting, the American Museum of Natural History has developed an extraordinarily ambitious, $25 million national program to educate children and adults about science. It will do this by making the research and discovery process of the museum "transparent" through sophisticated electronic technology available both on-line and through a variety of hardware and software packages. As these and other museum educational models become more fully developed in a variety of settings, it will be important to test and compare outcomes with those of more traditional models of schooling.

But the museum model of education should not be limited to the younger years. Museums can and should provide educational experiences for adult learning that are just as powerful. In museums adults can learn at their own speed and in their own way in a setting that is multisensory and engages the emotions as well as the intellect. With no mandated curriculum, learners can organize themselves by almost any criteria of interests. The mixing of education, age, gender, and race can become a strong asset in a shared learning process. The museum can provide a place that encourages and enables intergenerational learning. The closely controlled environment of the school, open during very limited hours and not available to all members of a family or community-based group, cannot match the environment of the museum for encouraging groups of all kinds to learn together.

THE MUSEUM AS A MODEL COMMUNITY INSTITUTION

Museums in America have been and remain the creations of diverse and distinctive communities. The pattern of civic enterprise that has brought and continues to bring museums into being needs continual nurturing and development. The dominant governance model of museums, the independent nonprofit organization led by lay citizens in service of broad community objectives, can provide an important center of leadership in a community. Changes in a community may well mean the need to reexamine a museum's mission, goals, and strategies. It may also involve the need for changes in the bylaws and other forms of self-regulation by the organization. Museums offer in their organizational model ample room for either minor course correction or major change. If the governing authority of the museum is not able or willing to make the necessary changes in the museum's mission, direction, or strategies to meet community needs, there is a good possibility that another leadership group will organize to form a new museum with a new mission and direction that more directly meet those community needs. While this is often seen by established museums as a wasteful dilution of community resources and leadership, it remains a critical element in the process of museum and community renewal.

But just as important as the organizational model of the museum is its focus on real content. Many community-based organizations such as service clubs, community centers, and fraternal organizations focus on very practical issues—i.e., how to solve a specific community problem. Other community-focused organizations, primarily social-service agencies, focus on how to deal with human problems at either the individual or the group level. These organizations must inevitably neglect what is even more important for any community—its need to create and sustain successful human beings who are capable of integrating their own lives into larger traditions of civic responsibility. To do this requires institutions that go beyond the immediate and practical concerns of people's lives and communities. In a museum, content, made real by contact with objects, stories, ideas, and lives from the realms of science, art, and the humanities, can offer a gathering point for exploration of an inexhaustible store of topics. The museum is a place for tactile, emotional, and intellectual contact with people, ideas, or objects that have the potential to inspire. It is a place where people can meet and make friendships with others who share similar interests or where they can be a part of something larger and more important than their own individual lives. In order to develop the community potential of museums,

museums have much work to do in developing new metaphors for their work that will emphasize their "caregiving" as well as their "collection-getting" focus.

THE MUSEUM AS A DESIGNER AND DELIVERER OF EXPERIENCES

Effective development of a much expanded educational and community role for museums in the next century will require museums to develop a much deeper competence in designing powerful and engaging educational experiences and delivering them to broad public audiences. More and more Americans expect that their social, economic, and cultural activities, though shaped by a variety of sources, will engage them in a way that is vivid, distinctive, and out of the ordinary. This is even more the case for children who are being brought up in a world of interactive media, which sets up new expectations of active participation. They expect to be treated as individuals who have a significant capacity to influence as well as be influenced by any experience in their lives. This means that in the world of the next century, these experiences will have to be developed with close interaction between their producers and their consumers. This interaction and the resulting relationship of trust is what increasingly will give authority to any experience. Organizations of all kinds, from theme parks to retail stores to restaurants, are beginning to structure their products and services in this way. The goals are always to make a connection with an audience, to establish a relationship of trust, and to cause some specific outcome, whether it be knowledge, fun, insight, or the purchase of a product or service. Museums need to recognize that they are in the experience business and that it is the distinctive theme, context, and value of the experiences they bring to a particular audience that will increasingly define their success.

There exists for museums great potential to orchestrate new and distinctive experiences that can give value to their audiences in a way that meets their individual needs. The key is that whatever is presented must offer an opportunity to go beyond passive learning to active involvement in the experience itself. This experiential dimension was a constant among the visionary and forward-thinking museums of the past. The displays in Barnum's American Museum were attempts to create an environment of the extraordinary, the wondrous, or the exotic. Langley's Children's Room at the Smithsonian was designed to inspire delight and discovery rather than convey specific information. The American museum experiences that are among the most memorable and influential tend to be those that are experientially rich, that have a sense of engagement, that have more similarity to a theatrical performance than a lesson plan. The pioneering dioramas of the American Museum of Natural History and other natural history museums, the planetarium as a new form of museum experience, the coal-mine exhibit at the Museum of Science and Industry, and the affecting exhibitions of the United States Holocaust Memorial Museum are examples of museum experiences that remain underutilized as models for future museum development. The producers of these museum experiences instinctively recognized that a museum's content or collections were not self-revealing guides to knowledge but were ingredients for the creation of special settings for undertaking exploration and discovery that acknowledged and respected the audiences' lives and experiences.

The refocused educational and community agenda for museums that I am advocating would make experience design and delivery central to the museum mission and would view artifacts and content as means rather than ends. It assumes that the content and collections are not the mission of the museum's work but powerful tools that enable it. It recognizes something that we all know through both common sense and research in museum learning: museums are not effective or efficient communicators of large amounts of information. People do not read very well standing up, and every study of the outcomes of museum experiences tells us that people remember very little of a museum's content. However, that same research reminds us that they do vividly remember museum experiences that somehow have a connection to their own lives. I am not suggesting here that museums create content to fit the needs of their audience, but rather that they create mission-related experiences to fit those needs.

Many museums recoil from this idea. The usual argument is that to focus on experience rather than on content is to pander to the audience and to attenuate the subtlety and nuance of what is being communicated. What is really being said in this argument is that the museum only wants to communicate to those people for whom nuance and subtlety will be an essential part of the experience. This is fine for internal discourse among professionals and connoisseurs but hardly acceptable for public museums. Experience design is a new and special skill, and it will be in great demand in the future. Museums need to better understand and develop this skill now, in collaboration with filmmakers, game creators, artists, poets, storytellers, and others who can bring necessary skills and talents to the process. In developing experiences, museums have an advantage over their competitors, whether they be electronic media, theme parks, or other entertainment venues. The real and authentic objects, stories, ideas, and lives that are the subject matter of museum experiences have a resonance that is more powerful than all but the most compelling imaginary experiences.

A focus on experience design and delivery will also allow museums to be more effective participants in the rapidly evolving field of cultural tourism. Travel and tourism are among the world's largest, most important, and fastest-growing industries. As tourism continues to rise, there will be an increased interest in what is unique and special about each tourist destination. Museums will be extremely important organizations in defining the specialness of a place, the "there" of a specific locale. Their ability to design and package powerful, content-rich tourist experiences will increasingly be critical not only to their educational success but to their economic success as well as the economic success of their communities.

A MODEL FOR SUCCESS

But more than conceptual and imaginative skills are required for museums to reach a central place in the American agenda. To become a forceful model for American education and a vital center for American communities, museums must develop three characteristics in their institutional culture in order to fully succeed. These characteristics are authority, connectedness, and trustworthiness.

Authority

Traditionally, museums have defined their authority primarily through the uniqueness of their collections and the special skills of their content specialists. Yet today all manner of resorts, hotels, casinos, restaurants, banks, and retail establishments have acquired collections of art and artifacts and engage in exhibitions and other collection and content-related activities that at one time would have been seen as the exclusive domain of museums. For example, the Hard Rock Cafe chain of restaurants has an important collection of artifacts related to its "core" content consisting of Elvis Presley, the Beatles, the Rolling Stones, U2, and Madonna. Its staff travels around the world soliciting donations and making purchases related to its "permanent" collection. Every artifact to be added to the Hard Rock Cafe's collection must be authenticated by a staff with special knowledge and training. And no artifact acquired for the core collection is ever sold. The recently opened Bellagio casino and resort in Las Vegas is developing heavily publicized art exhibitions from its own collections. The Rain Forest Cafe chain of restaurants has appropriated many of the elements of the interpretive programs of zoos. In each case, these commercial businesses have adopted the conventions of museum practice to lend a sense of deepened authenticity to their commercial experiences.

In addition to coming from the collections themselves, the authority of museums has come in large part from the larger and more transcendent ideas and values embodied in those collections and understood by traditional patrons, staffs, and audiences as intrinsically good and worthy of transmission to everyone without fear of controversy. More recently, museum exhibitions and other programs have become subject to increasingly sharp criticism from a variety of sources for a variety of reasons. This is not surprising. As museums engage the interest of more diverse and pluralistic audiences, they have become battlegrounds for larger cultural and historical debates. The contentiousness of the debate surrounding exhibitions mounted by institutions as varied as the Smithsonian Institution, the Library of Congress, and the Museum of the City of New York are recent examples. The most well-publicized example in recent times was the debate surrounding a Smithsonian exhibition that focused on the decision of the U.S. government to drop the atomic bomb on Japan during World War II. The curators of the exhibition did not fully understand the emotional issues that were at the root of the concern over their exhibition script, which questioned the need for dropping the bomb. The resulting controversy pitted the Smithsonian against a variety of outraged groups, some of which were both savvy and politically ruthless adversaries. The outcome, the canceling of the originally planned exhibition and the substitution of a much-simplified display, reflected badly on all parties to the debate. The lesson of this failed exhibition is that the development of the authority of museum exhibitions and experiences in the future will require continuous conversation and negotiation between museum staff with their specialized skills and knowledge and audiences now used to playing a more active role in the planning and development of the experiences in which they have an important stake. This is not to say that the skills of the specialist and the expert are no longer important in establishing the authority of a museum program or exhibition, but that a museum is not a university and that to expect audiences to yield to an absolute respect for and deference to the museum's cultural authority is no longer a reasonable expectation.

Connectedness

The controversy surrounding the Smithsonian exhibition on strategic bombing during World War II also evolved out of a lack of connectedness. Connectedness is nothing more than the process of a close, continuous, long-term connection between an organization and its audience. It is only through being connected to audiences in a close and continuous way that the museum will be trusted. In order to achieve connectedness in an ever more pluralistic society, both the governance and the staff makeup of American museums are going to have to become a lot more diverse. It will be impossible for museums to retain any sense of authority with the more pluralistic America outside museum walls unless there is diversity inside those walls. Connectedness also means that museums will have to master the skill of listening as well as the skill of talking—that is, how to listen and what questions to ask. And, most importantly, they will need to know what to do in response to the listening. The process of systematically listening to consumers and potential consumers goes against the grain of traditional museum practice, which assumes that the museum is teacher and the audience is learner and that the museum cannot allow its audiences to play a role in defining its programs. But if the museum has defined its mission clearly and if this mission is connected to the value the museum can give to its audiences, this is a false concern. Increasingly, museum mission statements are going to have to contain not only a concise statement of what the museum does but also a description of the outcome of what it does and of the value of that outcome to the community it serves. If there is nothing special about its work, nothing that connects what it does to people's lives, then what is the point of its existing and who should care? If we look at the museums that are most successful in their ability to carry out their public missions, we see those that work hardest at carrying on a continuous conversation of mutual respect with their audiences.

Trustworthiness

Museums could learn much about trustworthiness from the business world. There is among the best companies an almost fanatical concern about "brand" and "brand management." The result of good brand development and management over a long period of time is that the consumer can reasonably expect that any product or service carrying that brand will live up to or exceed expectations. The product or service will be seen as trustworthy, even before it is experienced. It also means that from time to time a mistake or a poor product or service will be forgiven in the marketplace. However, a string of poor-quality or unresponsive products or services results in an erosion of trust. Once eroded, this trust is very difficult, if not impossible, to rebuild. Whether in the more traditional world of organizations or in the new world of electronic connectivity and e-commerce, people always seek information, knowledge, and insight from people and organizations they trust. This is why businesses invest so much time and money in establishing a "relationship" with consumers and potential consumers, and work so hard at making a commercial transaction an "experience" that is positive and memorable. Establishing a relationship of trust requires both a great deal of time and an attitude of mutual respect between the producer and consumer of a product or service. This is nothing new. Anthropologists remind us that in traditional societies, language was used less for communicating content than for establishing bonds of trust and understanding. It is only in modern societies that language is primarily used to communicate content, but at the risk of reducing the bonds of communication and trust. It is no different for museums. Trustworthiness and authority in a museum grow directly out of skill and expertise well exercised as well as out of continual connection to the audiences served. In the new world of the new century, the authority that a museum claims will be built not primarily through its collections nor on its specialized expertise, but through those resources engaged in conversation and dialogue with those audiences the museum serves. Relentless focus on establishing continuous and direct connection to the audience will, over a long period of time, result in the museum being seen as worthy of authority, affiliation, support, and trust.

CONCLUSION

As the distinctions between nonprofit and profit, education and entertainment, form and content, and product and service become less clear, our view of institutions will inevitably change. The ability of any institution to give meaning and value to people's personal and collective lives will take on even greater importance than it has today. This is why American museums have so much to offer American life. The great age of collection building in museums is over. Now is the time for the next great agenda of museum development in America. This agenda needs to take as its mission nothing less than to engage actively in the design and delivery of experiences that have the power to inspire and change the way people see both the world and the possibility of their own lives. We have many practical institutions to help us work through our day-to-day problems. We have enough educational institutions that focus on training us to master the skills we need to graduate from school and get a job. Yet we have too few institutions that have as their goal to inspire and change us. American museums need to take this up as their new challenge. Up to now much of their time has been devoted to building their collections and sharing them through "outreach" to the larger world. Now they must help us create the new world of "inreach," in which people, young and old alike, can "reach in" to museums though experiences that will help give value and meaning to their own lives and at the same time stretch and enlarge their perceptions of the world. This will not be an easy task. It will require major changes in focus, organization, staffing, and funding for museums. But the potential benefit to America is tremendous. Working in partnership with each other and with their communities, America's museums remain one of America's best hopes for realizing the possibilities of the American future.

NOTES

1. Albert Bigelow Paine, "The Children's Room in the Smithsonian Institution," *Smithsonian Institution Annual Report 1901* (Washington, D.C.: Smithsonian Institution, 1901), 553–554.

2. Letter from Julius Rosenwald to Samuel Insull as quoted in Victor J. Danilov, "Science and Technology Museums Come of Age," *Curator* 16 (3) (1973): 30–46.

Additional Recommended Reading

American Association of Museums. *Excellence and Equity: Education and the Public Dimension of Museums.* Washington, DC: Author, 1992.

Association of Art Museum Directors. *Different Voices: A Social, Cultural, and Historical Framework for Change in the American Art Museum.* New York: Author, 1992.

Commission on Museums for a New Century. *Museums for a New Century.* Washington, DC: American Association of Museums, 1984.

Daedalus: America's Museums. Cambridge, MA: American Academy of Arts and Sciences, 1999.

Karp, Ivan, Christine Mullen Kreamer, and Steven D. Lavine. *Museums and Communities: The Politics of Public Culture.* Washington, DC: Smithsonian Institution Press, 1992.

Peniston, William A., ed. *The New Museum: Selected Writings by John Cotton Dana.* Washington, DC: American Association of Museums, 1999.

Ripley, Dillon. *The Sacred Grove.* Washington, DC: Smithsonian Institution Press, 1969.

Spiess, Philip D., II. "Toward a New Professionalism: American Museums in the 1920s and 1930s." *Museum News* (March/April 1996): 38–47.

Washburn, Wilcomb E. "Education and the New Elite: American Museums in the 1980s and 1990s." *Museum News* (March/April 1996): 60–65.

Weil, Stephen. *Rethinking the Museum and Other Meditations.* Washington, DC: Smithsonian Institution Press, 1990.

Zeller, Kerry. "From National Service to Social Protest: American Museums in the 1940s, '50s, '60s, and '70s." *Museum News* (March/April 1996): 48–59.

II

THE ROLE OF THE PUBLIC: THE NEED TO UNDERSTAND THE VISITOR'S PERSPECTIVE

The ever-expanding role of the museum visitor as critic, customer, consumer, and guest has slowly taken center stage in influencing many decisions and directions adopted by museums in recent years. Not that the public wasn't present before—it was always there—but the prevailing assumption was that the public *automatically* valued and benefited from the exhibitions and programs offered by museums. Ironically, while museums diligently counted the number of people passing through their doors as a measure of their success, most museums failed to examine what sort of experience those visitors were having or to consider why many people didn't visit museums at all.

The shift in museum leaders' awareness of the pivotal role of the public is striking. Many museums consider the perspective of the public when determining institutional directions and priorities, and others include community members and representatives in the development of the exhibitions and programs they mount. With increasing levels of competition from other leisure and educational options, museum leaders are turning to tactics long familiar in the business world, such as marketing and evaluation to inform decision making. Today a museum cannot afford to assume it has intrinsic value for the public. It must continually ask, "Is what we are doing relevant to our public?"

The soul-searching of the past two decades has been grueling at times and, as Dana would point out, long overdue—if he were here to comment. The impact has been a shift in management practices—in the way exhibitions are developed, in board recruitment strategies, in hiring practices, and in what they collect. It is a dramatic shift from the days of internally focused decisions made with little regard for public desire or interest. Today's museum leaders know that they cannot survive without ongoing feedback from and involvement with their constituents.

In their 1992 book *The Museum Experience*, John Falk and Lynn Dierking, directors of the Institute for Learning Innovation in Annapolis, Maryland, proposed a model for understanding why visitors go to museums that included social reasons—a motivation often considered by museum professionals as secondary to the central purpose of a museum visit—the educational experience of viewing an exhibition. Their work helped broaden the museum profession's view of the visitor experience and perspective. In "The Contextual Model of Learning" excerpted from their 2000 book *Learning from Museums*, they take their original work to a deeper level in discussing visitors and the complexities of learning in a museum setting.

Claudine Brown, a former deputy assistant secretary for museums at the Smithsonian Institution and current program officer for the Cummings Foundation, joined the then-ongoing dialogue on audience diversity with a slightly different perspective. In her 1992 article, "The Museum's Role in a Multicultural Society," she addresses inclusion and equity in museums by reminding museum leaders that fundamental affinities such as the universal categories of society—family, church, school—where and how people congregate and live, were more effective ways of thinking rather than the prevalent leaning toward groupings based on race or cultural background.

Marilyn Hood's article, "Staying Away: Why People Choose Not to Visit Museums," published in *Museum News* in 1983, is probably the best-known article to date about the public and why people choose to visit or not visit museums. Hood, a museum consultant specializing in audience development, evaluation, and market analysis, awakened many museum professionals from a complacent slumber—a state of confidence that what museums did was inherently valuable to the public and would naturally attract audiences. Hood's work brought visibility to the role of evaluation as a viable and necessary tool for enabling museums to better serve their audiences.

In a recent issue of *Curator: The Museum Journal*, Judy Rand, a consultant specializing in exhibit label writing and editing, outlines the cardinal concerns for museum professionals when considering the visitor perspective in their work. Her "Visitors' Bill of Rights" should be tacked to office doors, carried in briefcases, and posted over desks as a reminder not ever to let the visitor's comfort or perspective stray from the minds of museum workers. As the old adage says: Treat others as we would wish to be treated ourselves.

In "United States: A Science in the Making," published in 1993, C. G. Screven, a recognized pioneer and expert on museum evaluation, discusses the emergence of evaluation as a respected and necessary aspect of museum operations. He argues that the most important reason for using evaluation is to understand the visitor's perspective in relation to the work that museums undertake, especially in exhibition and program development. The real value of evaluation is experienced when the gathered results are used to influence decisions that improve the visitor experience.

Closing out Part II is "Can Museums Be All Things to All People?" by Neil Kotler, a program specialist at the Smithsonian Institution, and Philip Kotler, a professor of international marketing at Northwestern University's Kellogg Graduate School of Management, who discuss marketing and its impact on museums. Here they impart some of the basic tenets of their philosophy and provide a clear dissection of marketing, discuss market research and its implications, and offer suggestions for incorporating marketing strategies into museum decision making.

10

The Contextual Model of Learning

John H. Falk and Lynn D. Dierking

It is human nature to want simple explanations for complex reality. For example, in a book we recently read, a physician described how during his days in medical school he was constantly overwhelmed with the quantity of information.[1] He said some teachers could package the information very simply: "Here, this is what you need to know." Medical students loved those teachers, he said. But there were other teachers who always offered two or more (often contradictory) perspectives on things. This the students hated. "It involved more work on our part," said the doctor. "Who wants to be told that some people think this, and some people think that? It was so much easier just to be told what is what." But, he said, as the years went by and he became more and more experienced as a doctor, he realized that the concise, neatly packaged views were wrong. The teachers had chopped off all the rough edges that didn't fit into the system. In the end, the simplest solutions were not always the best.

For better or for worse, we believe, learning is a phenomenon of such complexity that a truly simple model or definition will not result in a sufficiently realistic and generalizable model. The complexities of learning can only be simplified so much before they become less than useful. Consequently, what we are proposing is not really a definition of learning but a model for thinking about learning that allows for the systematic understanding and organization of complexity. The Contextual Model of Learning is an effort to simultaneously provide a holistic picture of learning and accommodate the myriad specifics and details that give richness and authenticity to the learning process.

We have focused on the learning that occurs from museums, since this focus has permitted us to make concrete and tangible that which is inherently abstract and intangible. As we have repeatedly stressed, the where and why of learning does make a difference. Although it is probably true that at some fundamental, neurological level, learning is learning, the best available evidence indicates that at the level of individuals within the real world, learning does functionally differ depending upon the conditions under which it occurs. Hence, learning in museums is different from learning in any other setting by virtue of the unique nature of the museum context. Although the overall framework we provide should work equally well across a wide range of learning situations, compulsory as well as free choice, the specifics apply only to museums. In the final analysis, to truly understand how, why, and what people learn, specificity is essential. There is no simple, stripped-down, acontextual framework for understanding learning. Learning is situated.

Learning is a dialogue between the individual and his or her environment through time. Learning can be conceptualized as a contextually driven effort to make meaning in order to survive and prosper within the world. We have chosen to portray this contextually driven dialogue as the process/product of the interactions between an individual's personal, sociocultural, and physical contexts. As we have stated repeatedly, none of these three contexts is ever stable; all are changing.

EIGHT KEY FACTORS THAT INFLUENCE LEARNING

The Contextual Model of Learning provides the large-scale framework within which to organize information on learning; inside the framework hang myriad details. The factors that directly and indirectly influence learning from museums probably number in the hundreds, if not thousands. Some of these factors are apparent and have been described in this book. Many other factors are either not apparent or are currently perceived by us to be less important and have not been described. However, after considering the findings from the hundreds of research studies reviewed, we found that eight key factors, or more accurately suites of factors, emerged as particularly fundamental to museum learning experiences:

Personal Context
   1. Motivation and expectations
   2. Prior knowledge, interests, and beliefs
   3. Choice and control
Sociocultural Context
   4. Within-group sociocultural mediation
   5. Facilitated mediation by others
Physical Context
   6. Advance organizers and orientation
   7. Design
   8. Reinforcing events and experiences outside the museum

Individually and collectively, these eight factors significantly contribute to the quality of a museum experience. When any of these eight is absent, meaning-making is more difficult. Each of these factors, examined in detail in the preceding chapters, is summarized here.

Motivation and Expectations

People go to museums for many reasons and have predetermined expectations for their visit. These motivations and expectations directly affect what people do and learn. Usually the public's agendas are closely matched to the realities of the museum experience, but not always. When expectations are fulfilled, learning is facilitated. When expectations are unmet, learning suffers. Intrinsically motivated learners tend to be more successful learners than those who learn because they feel they have to. Museums succeed best when they attract and reinforce intrinsically motivated individuals.

Prior Knowledge, Interests, and Beliefs

Prior knowledge, interests, and beliefs play a tremendous role in all learning; this is particularly the case in museums. By virtue of prior knowledge, interests, and beliefs, learners actively self-select whether to go to a museum or not, which type of institution to visit, what exhibitions to view or programs to participate in, and which aspects of these experiences to attend to. The meaning that is made of museum experiences is framed within, and constrained by, prior knowledge, interests, and beliefs. At a very fundamental level, in the absence of appropriate prior knowledge, interests, and beliefs, no one would ever go to museums and no one would ever learn anything there even if they did. Because of the constructed nature of learning and the heterogeneous nature of museum-visiting populations, the prior knowledge, interests, and beliefs of museum visitors vary widely across, and even within, museums. For all these reasons, learning in museums is always highly personal.

Choice and Control

Learning is at its peak when individuals can exercise choice over what and when they learn and feel that they control their own learning. Because museums are quintessential free-choice learning settings, they more often than not afford visitors abundant opportunity for both choice and control. When museums try too hard to mimic compulsory education or force specific learning agendas on the public, they undermine their own success and value as learning institutions.

Within-Group Sociocultural Mediation

The vast majority of visitors go to museums as part of social groups—groups with histories, groups that separately and collectively form communities of learners. Parents help children understand and make meaning from their experiences. Children provide a way for parents to see the world with "new" eyes. Peers build social bonds through shared experiences and knowledge. All social groups in museums utilize each other as vehicles for deciphering information, for reinforcing shared beliefs, for making meaning. Museums create unique milieus for such collaborative learning.

Facilitated Mediation by Others

Socially mediated learning in museums does not only occur within an individual's own social group; powerful socially mediated learning can occur with strangers perceived to be knowledgeable. Such learning has long evolutionary and cultural antecedents, and few other museum experiences afford as much potential for significantly affecting visitor learning. Many such interactions occur with museum explainers, docents, guides, and performers, and they can either enhance or inhibit visitor learning experiences. When skillful, the staff of a museum can significantly facilitate visitor learning.

Orientation and Advance Organizers

Study after study has shown that people learn better when they feel secure in their surroundings and know what is expected of them. Museums tend to be large, visually and aurally novel settings. When people feel disoriented, it directly affects their ability to focus on anything else; when they feel oriented in museum spaces, the novelty enhances learning. Similarly, providing conceptual advance organizers significantly improves people's ability to construct meaning from experiences.

Design

Whether the medium is exhibitions, programs, or web sites, learning is influenced by design. Exhibitions, in particular, are design-rich educational experiences. People go to museums to see and experience real objects, placed within appropriate environments. Two-dimensional media they can see elsewhere, computer terminals they can find elsewhere, text they can read elsewhere. Not so authentic, real "stuff" in meaningful settings. Appropriately designed exhibitions are compelling learning tools, arguably one of the best educational mediums ever devised for facilitating concrete understanding of the world.

Reinforcing Events and Experiences outside the Museum

Learning does not respect institutional boundaries. People learn by accumulating understanding over time, from many sources in many different ways. Learning from museums is no exception. The public comes to museums with understanding, leaves (hopefully) with more, and then makes sense of this understanding as events in the world facilitate and demand. In a very real sense, the knowledge and experience gained from museums is incomplete; it requires enabling contexts to become whole. More often than not, these enabling contexts occur outside the museum walls weeks, months, and often years later. These subsequent reinforcing events and experiences outside the museum are as critical to learning from museums as are the events inside the museum.

NOTE

1. Hagen, S. *Buddhism Plain and Simple.* (Boston: Charles E. Tuttle, 1997), 1–2.

11

The Museum's Role
in a Multicultural Society

Claudine K. Brown

Culture in a societal context is the integrated pattern of human knowledge, belief, and behavior that depends upon a person's capacity for learning and transmitting knowledge to succeeding generations. Museums in American society are primary repositories devoted to the procurement, care, study, and display of cultural artifacts and objects of lasting interest and value.

As we approach the 21st century, museums around the globe are beginning to examine whose culture is being preserved and whose is not, from whose point of view the story is being told and whose point of view is being suppressed or distorted, whose culture is being respected and whose culture is being demeaned. In this country we are confronting these issues head-on as we watch the face of the nation change. We are living with the knowledge that by the year 2000 the word "minority" will have a completely different meaning, and we are espousing the notion of a cultural plurality.

The primary issues for museums of all types are cultural equity and equal access. In confronting these issues, the many cultural institutions that purport to interpret American life and the artistic endeavors of American people are beginning to reexamine the entity we call "the community."

WHO ARE OUR COMMUNITIES?

I have been concerned for some time at the easy codification of "the community." By definition, a "community" is an interacting population of various kinds of individuals in a common location. These individuals often share a common history or common societal, economic, or political interests. The community is not solely an

Claudine K. Brown is Program Director, Arts and Culture, for the Nathan Cummings Foundation and formerly was deputy assistant secretary for Arts and Humanities for the Smithsonian Institution. "The Museum's Role in a Multicultural Society" appeared in *Patterns in Practice: Selections from the Journal of Museum Education* © 1992 the Museum Education Roundtable. It is reprinted here with permission of Museum Education Roundtable, all rights reserved. For more information contact: Museum Education Roundtable, 621 Pennsylvania Ave., SE, Washington, DC, 20003; or www.mer-online.org or email info@mer-online.org.

ethnic group, a neighborhood, or the residents of a defined area. From the moment that we are born we find ourselves integrally involved with one community or another and with many different communities simultaneously.

In museums, the term "community" often refers to that audience whose needs we are not meeting: the poor, or in some instances specific ethnic groups. In truth, a community is any group of individuals who have the potential of being members of an institution's visiting public. As Barry Gaither and many others have recommended, if we were to draw concentric circles around our institutions, we would be able to identify potential visitors by their proximity.

Once we have identified groups with fairly easy access to our institutions who are not attendees, we must concern ourselves with whether our offerings are of interest to them and concurrently whether they have reason to believe they would be welcome at our institutions.

HOW DO WE PRESENTLY SERVE DIVERSE COMMUNITIES?

Over the past few years, many of us have tried a variety of methodologies to engage the interest of a wide range of ethnic groups and to encourage their visitation of our institutions. We have done special mailings and advertising for culturally specific exhibitions and programs to targeted communities; we have initiated collaborative programs with schools having a particular ethnic makeup. We have sponsored cultural festivals and special events; and we have offered outreach programs in underserved communities. We have convened focus groups, advisory boards, and in some instances brought non-European Americans onto our boards of trustees. We have hired more diverse staffs and recruited minority interns.

We have nonetheless often seen only minimal progress; and we have also witnessed some disturbing trends. Often these new audiences come to our institutions for programs and exhibitions that reflect their own cultures, but they do not return for other high-quality programs concerning other cultures. Some institutions have engaged in major membership recruitment efforts and targeted ethnic social organizations. The results have more often than not been most discouraging. Additionally, if the entire staff of an institution is not made aware that a particular underserved audience is being courted and should be made welcome, we have sometimes faced a situation in which the vision of management is not shared by the support staff and target audiences are the unwitting recipients of ill will on the part of guards, information desk staff, food service employees, and other service providers. Our efforts have frequently been hit or miss and seasonal, and the responses of our desired new audiences have been similar.

I suggest that we can attribute this lackluster response to our efforts to two distinct factors. The first is inconsistency. When an institution only programs for African Americans during Black History Month, it is no surprise that the largest turnout of black Americans is in February. I have also heard colleagues complain that when they do programs with signage for the deaf, deaf audiences rarely attend. There is a certain arrogance at work when a public program staff member does one program each month with signage, assuming that of all the institution's offerings this is the only program that appeals to deaf audiences. And as most programs with signage do not solicit response, we often assume that attendance is poor when in fact it may not be. If we begin not with black history or signage as a goal but with the notion of community within the context of social and human development, we will be able to define approaches to audience development that acknowledge ethnic and ability differences while taking into consideration similarities that grow out of the human experience.

The second issue that affects our inability to maintain "ethnic" audiences once we have gotten them through our doors involves our very limited way of viewing these groups. Our seduction of and newfound love for a new ethnic group each season gives rise to what one of my colleagues calls the flavor-of-the-month syndrome. This syndrome also suggests that there are easy ways of programming for these groups because their issues are simplistic. Often the scope of our programming involves booking a dance company, doing hands-on ethnic crafts workshops, having a great ethnic icon speak, and arranging for bilingual interpreters. While I don't seek to diminish these programs, I do fault the programmers for frequently failing to represent more than one point of view, for dealing with the issues of these cultures in isolation and not as they affect others, and for being reluctant to listen to youthful and radical voices.

ALTERNATIVE WAYS OF VIEWING COMMUNITIES

It is our inability to view non-European persons within the broader community context that most hinders our efforts in the area of effective audience development. With this in mind, I would like to consider four types of communities that are representative of the broader American experience. Though not bound by ethnicity, these groupings enable us to identify ethnic enclaves within a social, historical, and developmental context. Further, these groups give credence to the complexities of the human experience and enable us to look at Latino men as fathers, Asian women as managers, Caribbean men as educators, and African-American women as union organizers. This method for considering our communities allows us to look at ethnic groups by examining the many roles that they play in the many communities they find themselves in. The four communities I will focus on are the family, peer groups, educational communities, and the neighborhood and workplace.

FAMILY AS COMMUNITY

The community of family imparts the fundamental body of learning that shapes our formative years. Within the context of families we learn speech, how to stand upright, social interaction with others, and common courtesy. Our families can of course include the many individuals who contribute to our well-being, who are also known as our extended families.

While many museums have family programs, most don't look to these types of programs as endeavors geared toward increasing participation by more diverse audiences. Family programs are ideal for this purpose, but they must be reconsidered in terms of their structure if they are to become mechanisms for audience development. These programs must be responsive in terms of time, space, cost, and logistics so that they can accommodate family groups having different types of lifestyles and needs. Types of programs I recommend include:

- parent-child programs in which parents have briefings alone as well as time with their children so that they can take a competent leadership role in the shared experience
- foster grandparents co-parenting programs in which children interact with seniors and single adults who function as interpreters or facilitators in regularly scheduled programs
- special programs for noncustodial parents that facilitate their understanding of their children's needs in a nonthreatening interactive manner
- programs for volunteers and interns that provide child care.

All these programs look at ways of serving families that recognize parents and children in the role of teacher and/or learner. They are also programs that see museums as service providers as well as places where visitors can come to learn, be entertained, or just relax.

PEER GROUP COMMUNITIES

Peer groups can be educators who are off during the summer, adolescents doing a class assignment together, or friends just looking for something of interest to do together. They can be seniors from senior citizen centers, tourists, docents from other institutions, or Brownie troops engaging in activities that will help them get badges. Peer groups often share particular commonalities. They are often of similar age; they have shared interests, commitments, or purposes; and they sometimes have similar expectations based upon their common orientation to our institutions.

Within ethnic communities there are social clubs, civic organizations, service organizations, and block associations that attend to the articulated needs and concerns of their members. There are also many types of informal gatherings of neighbors and friends who form peer groups as a result of proximity, common purpose, and shared interest. The interests and concerns of these formal and informal groups need to be identified and considered as they relate to the mission, collections, and programmatic possibilities of an institution. They can then be translated into viable programs and exhibitions that can be culturally specific, cross-cultural, and cross-class.

EDUCATIONAL COMMUNITIES

While museums have enjoyed continued success with school groups, mostly with elementary school audiences, there are other age groups and educational constituencies we know are neglected or underserved. There are many successful programs for adolescents, and most museums offer internships for college students. I would nonetheless suggest that the term "educational institution" needs to be more broadly defined and the mechanisms for collaboration need to be reconsidered and expanded on.

Educational institutions serve a wide variety of audiences, many of which are overlooked when we engage in audience development initiatives. Special attention should be given to continuing education and certificate programs. Often large segments of underserved communities have not had opportunities for educational advancement, and they are frequently in programs that take place after work hours. Efforts need to be made to accommodate these groups.

There are other natural collaborations we should consider. American history museums are ideal venues for new immigrants who are studying to meet citizenship requirements. Teachers in these programs should be invited to use our institutions. College professors should be encouraged to teach sessions or entire courses in museum galleries, and they should be offered classroom space when it is available. Alliances should be made with community centers, especially where there is an underserved population that does not speak English. Museums should make an effort to have ongoing foreign language programs that address issues of importance to these groups in their new communities. Such programs can provide historical understanding of the environment new immigrants find themselves in and can offer them an opportunity to share their traditions with their neighbors.

NEIGHBORHOOD AND WORKPLACE

While we are making sense of our place in a school community, we have the concurrent responsibility for coming to terms with our neighborhood community. In our neighborhoods we begin to deal with definition of personality that is influenced by our race, class, and age; by our proximity to and interaction with other communities; and by our overall neighborhood personality. Neighborhoods are imbued with personality when we ascribe the following terms: urban or suburban, inner-city, middle-income, or gentrified. All of these factors help to shape one's sense of self and the role one plays in a neighborhood community. Our school and neighborhood communities represent those places where we spend the greatest amount of time and make bonds that last for a lifetime. Accordingly, every museum should see itself as a neighborhood museum. If an institution is not accessible to the individuals who must of necessity pass by its portals each day, then it is not a truly public institution.

Once we reach adulthood, there are a number of environments that can become communities and affect how we perceive ourselves. The primary entity that affects us in this manner is our work environment. But we might also be strongly influenced by other environments that we might find ourselves exposed to as a matter of personal choice or need, or necessity, or societal determinant. These might include hospitals, recreational facilities, correctional facilities, religious institutions, recreational facilities, and cultural institutions. In many of these places, we learn a language, a culture, rules, and sometimes a specific way of dressing. Our very survival is dependent upon our effective mastery of the tasks set before us and our grasp of the political situations that we find ourselves in.

OUR COMMUNITIES ARE NOT HOMOGENEOUS

In the world of work we find ourselves confronting issues daily that are often the premises for museum exhibitions, but these exhibitions are not pitched to us as workers. Exhibitions that deal with process, history, collecting, recording data, creation, and interpretation are all issues we face in the workplace. New materials in the construction and technology industries have found their way into art museums. Political issues being interpreted in history museums have antecedents in contemporary issues. Common objects we use today were preceded by similar objects made from different materials. Societies throughout the world have created mechanisms and systems for solving problems that have applications in the world today. Objects of beauty and wonder transcend ethnicity, race, and class.

What I am saying in a more concrete way is that:

- African-American children from Southeast Washington, D.C., would come to see "Dinosaurs Alive"
- workers of all ethnic backgrounds would find something of interest in a Jacob Lawrence or Lewis Hine show
- anyone with an interest in nature or the environment might see something worthwhile in a painting by Albert Bierstadt or Vincent Van Gogh.

There is no validity in programming for the homogeneous Latino community or a singular African-American community, because no such animals exist. Often when you target a people living in an area, you exclude persons of the same ethnic background from different classes and with different ideological and political points of view. Be wary of the community representative who purports to speak for all persons of that ethnic group, for while he or she may be an accepted leader in the community, no community is so simplistic that only one point of view prevails.

Pose thoughtful questions that speak to the human experience. What are the primary issues facing this community? (At one point in the Anacostia neighborhood of Washington, D.C., it was the rat, and that issue became the subject of one of the most innovative exhibitions of the past few decades.) How does this community view the museum? How can the museum meet the needs of the community? How do we provide means of access that allow human beings of every age to understand how the museum can serve them and how they, in turn, can serve the institution?

Museums are public institutions. They receive substantial support from public sources. It is our mission to preserve, exhibit, and interpret these collections for the public—not some of the public, but all of the public. Though we can't give all of the public what they want all of the time, we can provide more of the people with an honest representation of their achievements and contributions in this society. The time to begin is yesterday, and the place to begin is where you stand.

12

Staying Away: Why People Choose Not to Visit Museums

Marilyn G. Hood

Those of us who are museum professionals have frequently been puzzled by the elusive masses who never enter our museum doors—the nonparticipants. With all the treasures we offer, why don't we attract a broader spectrum of the public, a larger audience, a substantial clientele that comes regularly rather than just for blockbusters? Why do programs that are successful in one museum or with one group fail to garner equal response with other audiences?

Over the past half century we have tried numerous research techniques to gain answers to these questions. We have tracked visitors' traffic patterns, timed their stops at exhibits, observed them with time-lapse photography and interviewed them in the museum to find out what was satisfactory about their visit. It is not surprising that none of these *in*-museum studies has told us why the majority of the public does not visit museums.

From hundreds of such surveys in the United States and Canada, however, we have learned the demographic characteristics of those who do patronize museums: they are likely to be in the upper education, occupation and income groups, younger than the population in general and active in other community and leisure activities. Nevertheless, these demographic data have not indicated the *reasons* why some adults choose to frequent museums and why some do not, or why nonparticipants don't love museums.

It is apparent, then, that merely analyzing demographics will not reveal what these groups value in their leisure experiences. Instead we need to focus on how individuals make decisions about the use of their leisure time and energy, to concentrate on the *psychographic* characteristics of both current and potential visitors—their values, attitudes, perceptions, interests, expectations, satisfactions. Once these factors are identified, we can examine how nonparticipants differ from

---

Marilyn G. Hood is a museum consultant specializing in audience development, evaluation, and market analysis. "Staying Away: Why People Choose Not to Visit Museums" is reprinted here with permission from *Museum News*, April 1983. Copyright 1983, the American Association of Museums. All rights reserved.

participants in order to determine whether or not museums are offering or can offer the kinds of experiences that nonparticipants value and expect. Then we can develop ways, within the scope of our organizations and our abilities, to reach these elusive audiences.

In carrying out such a plan, the basic step is recognizing that people make *choices* about how they will use their leisure time and energy. We often assume that because we regard museums as unique and valuable, the public will similarly cherish them and want to share in them. Individuals do not just naturally gravitate to museums or to any other leisure place, however, no matter how worthwhile or unique it may be. Instead, before making selections, they consider which of several competing alternatives appears to offer them the most rewards, the greatest satisfactions—and they make their choice based on what will satisfy their criteria of a desirable leisure experience.

What are these criteria by which individuals judge leisure experiences, including museum visits? A review of 60 years of literature in museum studies, leisure science, sociology, psychology and consumer behavior identified six major attributes underlying adults' choices in their use of leisure time. They are, in alphabetical order,

- being with people, or social interaction
- doing something worthwhile
- feeling comfortable and at ease in one's surroundings
- having a challenge of new experiences
- having an opportunity to learn
- participating actively

Not every person values all of these attributes, and some are more pertinent to certain activities or places than to others. But all are fundamental criteria by which individuals make decisions about leisure.

To test how these criteria affect museum participation, a carefully designed and tightly controlled research project was undertaken in 1980–81 in cooperation with the Toledo Museum of Art, Toledo, Ohio. The purpose was to obtain quality information that would be useful for long-term decision making by the Toledo Museum and museums in general. To achieve valid and reliable results, several preparatory steps were taken: a 12-page questionnaire was developed, based on previous research and theory, and was tested and revised; the survey sponsor was identified as the Ohio State University, so respondents would not be biased in their answers to questions about museum going; a computer program generated telephone numbers for a probability sample of Toledo metropolitan area residents to be interviewed by telephone (in a probability sample, each person in the population has an equal chance of being selected, which assures that the sample is representative of the population); and 35 museum volunteers were trained to administer the 20-minute questionnaires.

The volunteers secured telephone interviews with 502 residents from across the Toledo metropolitan area (urban, suburban, exurban, rural) over a three-week period in spring 1980, and the data from the questionnaires were thoroughly analyzed by several sophisticated statistical tests, with the assistance of a statistician and a computer. A detailed report, including 67 tables, described the relationships between leisure attitudes and values and between museum going and demographic characteristics, and it outlined how these findings can be applied to museums generally and to other leisure-cultural organizations.[1]

The Toledo metropolitan area was a suitable locale for a major research project because its population was large enough to include representative socioeconomic, educational and age groups so that a probability sample of telephone respondents would accurately reflect the opinions and values of the community and the study results be applicable to other locations. In addition, it was assumed that the prestigious Toledo Museum of Art was well enough established to be identifiable by all groups within the community. This assumption was substantiated, since all respondents in the sample, regardless of socioeconomic status on length of residence, knew of the museum, even if they had never been there. Also, the types of problems that Toledo Museum faces are applicable to a greater or lesser extent to most museums, regardless of size, and the staff recognizes that it is in competition with other community activities for people's time, attention and energy.

Two major aims of the study were to determine how important the six leisure attributes were to the respondents and to ascertain their preferences for certain leisure activities and places. The study also assessed respondents' attitudes toward art museums and gauged their level of socialization toward 22 activities, including museum going. This article briefly discusses the results of the first two aims.

The results clearly show that our traditional assumptions about museum audiences are unfounded. Our long-held belief that there are just two audience segments—participants and nonparticipants—is incorrect.

There are *three* distinctly different audience segments in the current and potential museum clientele, based on their leisure values, interests and expectations: frequent participants, occasional participants and nonparticipants. Each group seeks different values and experiences through leisure activities, including museum going. Moreover, people decide to be or not to be involved in museums on the basis of how they evaluate the six leisure attributes and on how they were socialized—by family and other childhood influences—toward certain types of activities. Though other museum studies have identified levels of participation, they have not probed the *reasons* why audience segments develop and are maintained. Now, with these results, we are able to identify attendance patterns by leisure values and to show that leisure choices, although they may be correlated with demographics, are not determined by demographics.

This is strikingly clear when we examine the profiles of the three audience segments. The frequent visitors—those who go to museums at least three times a year (and some as often as 40 times a year) highly value all of the six leisure attributes and perceive all of them to be present in museums. The three that they value most are distinct for this group: having an opportunity to learn, having a challenge of new experiences and doing something worthwhile in leisure time.

Though the frequent visitors constitute a minority of the community (14 percent in the Toledo metropolitan area), they account for 45 to 50 percent of museum visitation (the Toledo Museum's annual visitation is 300,000–400,000). These are the people who are usually interviewed *in* the museum; hence, they fit the typical museum visitor demographic profile.

These loyalists go to museums wherever they are and whatever is showing, because some time ago they chose to place museums on their leisure agenda. Since their experience with museums has developed over time, they identify with museum values and understand the "museum code" of exhibits and objects. Museums are satisfying places for them because they find that the three leisure attributes they value most highly are regularly available in substantial quantities in museums.

For frequent attenders, the benefits offered by museum visits consistently outweigh the costs (time, money, travel, mental saturation, fatigue, inconvenience). Because they come so often, we museum professionals should make sure the museum is not a static place remaining always the same; these visitors want to find the challenge of new experiences on a continuing basis in their leisure activities.

At nearly the opposite pole from the frequent participants—in leisure values, preferences and expectations, as well as most demographic characteristics—are the nonparticipants (who represented the largest segment, 46 percent, of the Toledo metropolitan community). In their leisure experiences they most value the three leisure attributes that were less important to the frequent visitors: being with people (social interaction), participating actively and feeling comfortable and at ease in their surroundings. And, underscoring their differences, they rank low the three attributes the frequent visitors preferred.

Generally, nonparticipants as children were not socialized into museum going in fact, they are likely to have adopted more cultural activities as adults than they were acquainted with as children. We museum professionals and devotees need to be wary, however, of labeling these persons as apathetic or uninvolved simply because they do not participate in cultural activities. Their interests and commitments lie elsewhere, and they choose leisure experiences that compete with museum going because they find more of what is satisfying to them in activities that emphasize active participation, casual and familiar surroundings and interacting socially with other people.

Nonparticipants perceive that these three leisure attributes—the ones they value most highly—are not present at all in museums, or are present in such small amounts that investing themselves in a museum experience brings minimal bene-fits. They perceive museums to be formal, formidable places, inaccessible to them because they usually have had little preparation to read the "museum code"—places that invoke restrictions on group social behavior and on active participation. Sports, picnicking, visiting and browsing in shopping malls better meet their crite-ria of desirable leisure activities.

The most notable finding from this research involves the occasional participants—those who visit museums once or twice a year (40 percent of the Toledo metropolitan community). We have long assumed that museum visitors, regardless of frequency of attendance, share many common values, interests and characteristics. The research re-sults emphasize, however, that the occasional visitors are distinctly different from the frequent visitors in their socialization patterns and leisure values. In fact, they more closely resemble the nonparticipants.

The occasional visitors were socialized as children into activities that emphasized active participation, entertainment and social interaction. As adults, they maintain high levels of participation in these types of activities—outdoor experiences such as camping, hiking, swimming, skiing, ice skating, playing a musical instrument or en-gaging in arts and crafts; going to amusement parks and movies; sightseeing and at-tending sports events.

Family-centered activities are much more important to the occasional partici-pants and nonparticipants than they are to the frequent participants, who are more likely to visit the museum alone. Places like parks, zoos and picnic areas that are natural centers for family outings and for extended-family visiting attract the occa-sional participants because they offer all three of their most highly valued leisure at-tributes. Going to outdoor art and music festivals and participating as a family in a craft or discovery workshop also meet their criteria of desirable leisure experiences.

Occasional participants, who value comfortable surroundings in their leisure places, feel that museums offer little in the way of comfort—not simply physical comfort but a feeling of "this is where my friends and I belong, a place where I feel at ease and am able to cope with the message." For this group, leisure is equated with relaxation, which is more akin to interacting socially with a family or friendship group than it is to the intense involvement in a special interest that is evidenced by museum enthusiasts. Because these persons do not feel entirely at home in a mu-seum setting, the presence of a support group—family, club, co-workers, friends—provides social approval and validation on a visit.

Occasional participants perceive that some of the attributes they value in leisure experiences are available in museums, but not in sufficient quantity to warrant reg-ular visits—especially when compared with the benefits afforded by competing in-terests. Consequently, they come for the special occasions, the major events, the family days, which seem to promise them greater fulfillment of their expectations and wants. Since museum values and intentions more closely resemble those of the frequent visitors, museums generally offer or emphasize the very qualities that are least appealing to the occasional participants and nonparticipants, who are looking for significantly different leisure satisfactions.

The findings from this study provide a new perspective by which to assess current and potential museum audiences and the programs that museums can develop to appeal to and satisfy various sizable groups. If we are to reach those who are not coming frequently or at all, it is essential to program for more than one type of audience. Each attendance group is looking for different types of benefits in leisure experiences. Frequent visitors—the smallest group—are, for the most part, finding what they want in museums. But for the occasionals and the nonparticipants, who seek an opportunity to interact with people and to relax, the prospect of going to a museum for a learning experience, for a challenge, for doing something worthwhile in leisure time, is not enticing. Particularly if these people have had negative experiences with formal education, the idea of going to a museum for a learning activity connotes an exacting, ponderous undertaking rather than an enjoyable, casual experience.

If we museum professionals are concerned about reaching new audiences—the occasionals and the nonparticipants—we must appeal to them on the basis of what satisfies *their* criteria of a desirable leisure experience. Endeavoring to reach these elusive audiences by providing more of the same type of programs now offered, regardless of their quality, will not pay dividends for either audiences or museums; a different emphasis and presentation are necessary.

For instance, instead of portraying itself as an educational institution, where the family learns together, the museum seeking to reach occasional participants and nonparticipants might stress that it is a place for exploring and discovering, for enjoying a relaxed family outing and for having a good time with other people.

Discovery workshops that offer the family the opportunity to participate as a unit—to identify insects, fungi or fossils in a natural history museum, to work with clay or on a mural in an art museum, to try on or make facsimile costumes in a history museum—are examples of current museum programs that occasional visitors prize. These activities, though, should not be just ends in themselves but utilized as entrees, transitions, into the collections. If skillfully handled they can prepare the occasional visitors to cope with the "museum code" as well as enhance their positive perceptions of museums as places that meet their criteria of satisfying leisure locales. If they find their preferred attributes are present, they will *choose* to return. Other museums are providing tours and talks geared to the interests of specific groups—construction workers, sports fans, hobbyists of all hues—to demonstrate the relevance of museum collections to persons who do not perceive any connection between museums and their lives.

None of these approaches implies that the museum will abandon its current purposes or programs. They do require that museum staff and trustees view exhibits and programs from a different perspective, presenting them in as many appealing manners as possible.

Before we solicit the nonparticipants' attendance, therefore, we will have to consider what the uninitiated expect in the way of assistance with the "museum code." Are adequate helps provided so that those who make the initial venture onto untried turf will receive enough benefits to want to return? This does not mean diluting the message, but it does mean communicating the message in the nonparticipants' terms, on several levels of detail and comprehension, in order for them to perceive it as meaningful to their lives.

In addition, it is essential to remember that occasional participants weigh each museum visit against other leisure options. They may choose to attend on a particular occasion *instead* of watching television, browsing at a shopping mall, participating in a sport or working in the garden. A museum outing for them is likely to be a vehicle for having an enjoyable time with other people rather than for concentrating on the content of the exhibits. While participating, they hope to find comfortable surroundings in which they can feel at ease, both physically and psychologically.

Applying these findings and doing follow-up studies can benefit all museum professionals by helping to build a fund of reliable information about audiences. Although a major study of similar scope cannot be accomplished without expertise in audience development and scientific research techniques, each museum can utilize systematic procedures to obtain psychographic information on its audiences, on their perceptions of the museum and on ways to deal with practical situations such as communicating more effectively with a variety of publics. Gathering quality information for long-term decision making is worth effort, time and money, for the value received is in direct proportion to the care invested in designing and carrying out a carefully controlled study.

The Toledo Museum of Art has benefited itself and its audiences by incorporating the findings of this study into its planning and programming. Most important has been a heightened awareness by the staff of the diversity of visitors' expectations, leisure values and needs.

The primary influence of the research results on the museum's major structural renovation was in recognizing the need for public amenities. People need a sense of where they are in relation to the whole museum and to other areas in it. They need to feel comfortable. New graphics greatly improved visitor orientation, and comfortable seating was added to the new entrance lobby. An information office to welcome visitors was located just inside the entrance.

For the recent *El Greco* exhibit, the museum targeted the area's Hispanic and Greek communities for special attention. Both groups attended in greater numbers than might have been otherwise expected, especially the Greek residents, who constitute a small, closely knit community. Still under way are efforts to improve labeling and explanatory handouts to assist the less-prepared visitors in understanding why certain art works are grouped together.

Most of all, the study results prompted the staff to think beyond only internal concerns and "to consider the public we're doing this for," explains Gregory Allgire Smith, assistant director for administration. "We now realize we should plan more on their terms, not just on our own terms."

We, too, can solve many of our audience development problems if we recognize that occasional participants and nonparticipants are looking for experiences and rewards different from those they now find in museums. If we want them to love museums, we must offer them some of the values that are important to them, in programs that meet some of their needs, while we continue to provide what the frequent visitors already find satisfying and rewarding.

NOTE

1. Marilyn G. Hood, "Adult Attitudes toward Leisure Choices in Relation to Museum Participation" (Ph.D. diss., Ohio State University, 1981).

13

The Visitors' Bill of Rights

Judy Rand

- **Comfort—"Meet my basic needs."**
  Visitors need fast, easy, obvious access to clean, safe, barrier-free restrooms, fountains, food, baby-changing tables, and plenty of seating. They also need full access to exhibits.

- **Orientation—"Make it easy for me to find my way around."**
  Visitors need to make sense of their surroundings. Clear signs and well-planned spaces help them know what to expect, where to go, how to get there and what it's about.

- **Welcome/belonging—"Make me feel welcome."**
  Friendly, helpful staff ease visitors' anxieties. If they see themselves represented in exhibits and programs and on the staff, they'll feel more like they belong.

- **Enjoyment—"I want to have fun!"**
  Visitors want to have a good time. If they run into barriers (like broken exhibits, activities they can't relate to, intimidating labels) they can get frustrated, bored, confused.

- **Socializing—"I came to spend time with my family and friends."**
  Visitors come for a social outing with family or friends (or connect with society at large). They expect to talk, interact and share the experience; exhibits can set the stage for this.

- **Respect—"Accept me for who I am and what I know."**
  Visitors want to be accepted at their own level of knowledge and interest. They don't want exhibits, labels or staff to exclude them, patronize them or make them feel dumb.

Judy Rand is a consultant specializing in exhibit label writing and editing and a prior member of exhibit teams at both the Monterey Bay Aquarium and the Field Museum in Chicago. She is a member of the national group of consultants, The Museum Group. *The Visitors' Bill of Rights* is from "The 227-Mile Museum, or a Visitors' Bill of Rights," which appeared in *Curator: The Museum Journal* (Vol. 44, No. 1, January 2000, pp. 7–14). It is reprinted here by permission of AltaMira Press, a division of Rowman & Littlefield Publishers, Inc.

- **Communication**—"Help me understand, and let me talk, too."

  Visitors need accuracy, honesty and clear communication from labels, programs and docents. They want to ask questions, and hear and express differing points of view.

- **Learning**—"I want to learn something new."

  Visitors come (and bring the kids) "to learn something new," but they learn in different ways. It's important to know how visitors learn, and assess their knowledge and interests. Controlling distractions (like crowds, noise and information overload) helps them, too.

- **Choice and control**—"Let me choose; give me some control."

  Visitors need some autonomy: freedom to choose, and exert some control, touching and getting close to whatever they can. They need to use their bodies and move around freely.

- **Challenge and confidence**—"Give me a challenge I know I can handle."

  Visitors want to succeed. A task that's too easy bores them; too hard makes them anxious. Providing a wide variety of experiences will match their wide range of skills.

- **Revitalization**—"Help me leave refreshed, restored."

  When visitors are focused, fully engaged, and enjoying themselves, time stands still and they feel refreshed: a "flow" experience that exhibits can aim to create.

14

United States: A Science in the Making

C. G. Screven

The term 'visitor studies' has undergone important changes over the past twenty-five years. Its original association was with visitor surveys conducted to help administrators justify expenditure, predict attendance or improve efforts to cater to larger audiences. Today, visitor studies encompass not only demographics and attendance data, but such activities and topics as:

The 'psychology' and 'personality' of visitors, for example, learning styles, attitudes, knowledge about exhibit topics, language skills and time frames.

Observable behaviour patterns of visitors in museum environments, such as where they go, whom they come with, time spent, label reading, fatigue, family and social behaviour, return visits, use of services and preferences for hands-on and interactive devices or other exhibit formats.

The ability of visitors to understand exhibit messages and the impact of exhibit information on visitor attitudes, behaviour, misconceptions, interest, etc.

How the design and presentation format of signposting, labels, objects, layout, media, noise, information density, etc., affect reading behaviour, comprehension, way-finding, attention, the ability to follow directions, time spent, attitudes and other reactions.

The development and improvement of measurement and evaluation methods for assessing visitor learning, short- and long-term impact of exhibit experiences, involvement, effort, social-behaviour patterns, attendance and post-visit interests.

C. G. Screven is a veteran museum evaluator and promoter of evaluation as an essential decision-making tool for museums. "United States: A Science in the Making" originally appeared in *Museum International* (Vol. XLV, No. 2, 1993), a publication of UNESCO. It is reprinted here by permission of Blackwell Publishing Ltd.

Evaluation in visitor studies involves the systematic effort to obtain data about museum audiences that contribute to planning educational exhibits (visitor demographics, knowledge, pre-conceptions, interest, attitudes). Evaluation seeks information on whether an exhibition is successful or not, how early versions of exhibit ideas (mock-ups) appeal to visitors so that potential problems can be anticipated or improvements suggested. The use of evaluation in visitor studies is not the same as formal research. It simply provides concrete information to help improve decisions about exhibits such as the placing of labels or other practical matters. Today, evaluation in American museums mainly seeks cost-effective solutions to immediate questions that arise during the planning and design process.

Evaluation tools in use during different stages of exhibition development include:

Surveys, questionnaires, focus groups, observations providing basic information about targeted audiences, tasks and goals used during the planning stage of exhibit development (*front-end* evaluation).

Observations and testing visitor reactions to quickly made mock-ups of exhibit ideas during early stages of their design (*formative* evaluation).

Observations, testing and evaluation of the overall impact of the exhibit after it is installed and occupied (*summative* evaluation).

Using formative evaluation to improve installed exhibits (*remedial* evaluation).

The different kinds of information provided here form a basis for exhibit developers to make more informed decisions about exhibit goals, to avoid problems and, in general, to increase the chances for success both educationally and motivationally.

A LITTLE HISTORY

In 1916, Benjamin Gillman [sic], a museologist, wrote an article in *Scientific Monthly* on museum fatigue. He photographed visitors to test the idea that visitor fatigue resulted from the poor designs of exhibit cases. His photos showed the physical efforts visitors had to make (kneeling, twisting, stretching, etc.) to examine objects on display. He concluded that this encouraged superficial viewing and suggested that designers should take the physical and psychological aspects of visitors into account when designing display cases. He predicted that this would improve the quality of visitor attention. During this early period, there was lively criticism of museums in which they were characterized as 'places of gloom', 'cemeteries of bric-à-brac' which were generally insensitive to visitors' needs, boring and difficult to understand. Gilman's concerns and study anticipated the visitor-studies viewpoint of the 1980s.

In the 1920s, the first evidence of a visitor-oriented methodology was applied by Otto Neurath to an educational exhibition on social change in the Social and Economic Museum in Vienna. Each exhibit's 'message' was first analysed, graphics and other features were then developed and, finally, efforts to improve their quality were made through trial and error. Known as the Isotype method (International System of Typographic Picture Education), the process began with visitors' needs and communication goals and proceeded to designs that best served these goals—a 'bottom-up' model for exhibit development—anticipating what later would be regarded as a visitor-studies approach to exhibit planning and development.

Between 1928 and 1931, Edward S. Robinson and Arthur Melton, with help from the American Association of Museums and the Carnegie Foundation, conducted a series of classic empirical studies of visitors as they moved freely through galleries and at choice points, recording the number and location of stops, and their use of exits and other aspects of behaviour. Their data yielded reliable behaviour patterns, distribution of visitor attention within galleries and other information which revealed orderly behaviour patterns in response to architecture, fatigue, exhibit layout and interpretive labels.

In the 1940s, various studies gathered data on ways exhibit designs affected participatory behaviour, traffic flow, label usage, the role of story lines in enhancing visitor interest, the effects of live demonstrations, light and colour, and how the ratings of exhibits by museum experts compared with those by ordinary visitors. Although this shift towards the psychology of lay visitors developed slowly, several significant and sophisticated evaluations were conducted which paved the way to what was to come in the 1970s. Most notable among these were pioneering studies by Harris Shettel, which were the first to use mock-ups systematically to pre-test viewers' reactions and revise text and illustrations prior to final production. Shettel also employed an array of measurement strategies: unobtrusive observation, photography, closed-circuit TV, interviews, objective tests, as well as pre-testing experimental mock-ups.

By 1970, interest in experimentation and evaluation research in the United States had gathered momentum. An increasing body of knowledge on museums as learning environments took shape, and included pioneering work on visitor and family behaviour patterns, visitor movement, attitudes and learning, testing the attention capabilities of interactive response devices, criteria for evaluating exhibit effectiveness, applying naturalistic evaluation methods and comparing the effectiveness of visitor orientation strategies.

This emerging knowledge base supported the idea that information obtained from and about visitors should improve the ability to design exhibits and programmes that more effectively communicated to lay audiences. The burst of interest and activity in the 1970s was facilitated by a series of national forums initiated by the Smithsonian Institution on museums as educational environments that brought together and helped focus the field toward multi-disciplinary approaches to the educational aspects of museums.

In the 1980s, growing interest in informal education and visitor studies spread to more museums and zoological and botanic gardens. Private funding also increased. The Kellogg Foundation took an interest in and funded a national series of training programmes for museum directors, educators and curators aimed at increasing their awareness of the potential for visitor-centred exhibits. The American Association of Museums' publication *Museum News* ran a series of articles on visitor learning, evaluation and educational programming. In 1990, the AAM gave Standing Committee status to the Committee on Visitor Research and Evaluation and a new national organization, the Visitor Studies Association, was formed in 1991.

But, in spite of all this attention in the name of education, museum planners were still not employing visitor methods en masse. Most exhibit decisions remained 'top-down' and design features were determined mainly by artistic and subject-matter specialists with little or no information on how lay visitors might respond. By the beginning of the 1990s, exhibit planning and design were promoted in the name of education, but remained, in practice, more or less isolated from the public.

MUSEUMS AND EDUCATION

Traditionally, the educational role of museums has taken the form of school programmes, guided tours, outreach programmes, interpretive kits and publications aimed at helping different age-groups and kinds of visitors to make sense of exhibitions. Before the mid-1980s, education staff were seldom concerned with planning exhibitions that, later, they were expected to interpret to the public. In developing their own programmes and materials, their background and daily contact with real visitors have given them the advantage of knowing something about the general public and the educational process. These programmes have generally been more educationally productive than exhibitions for unguided visitors.

Like museums elsewhere, those in the United States began as places for the care and study of collections by scholars. Museum mission statements have long asserted that 'educating and informing the public at large' was a major mission. In practice, however, priorities usually have been on collections and scholarly research in which the focus is the exhibit's value for knowledgeable rather than lay audiences. Objects were said to 'speak for themselves' and it was the visitor's responsibility to derive meaning from them. Exhibits simply provided the opportunity for learning by those with the interests and background to benefit rather than the general public. Only recently have museums begun to give priority to exhibitions as an educational medium for general and non-traditional audiences. The great assets of museums—their expertise and collections—are being redirected to provide the needed support for the role of the exhibition as a teaching medium.

This new priority, however, has not resulted in a new influx of understandable exhibits. While exhibitions have become more entertaining, their educational substance, despite the best of intentions, is rarely getting through to most visitors. One reason for this is that their planners are designers, curators and copy-writers who have had no formal course-work in educational psychology, tests and measurement, or communication. Their view of the 'public' has been formed mostly by their experience with graduate students, peers and other knowledgeable people. This means that their well-intentioned efforts to design educationally effective exhibits are handicapped by their isolation from the public and their unrealistic views about the exhibit medium.

The scholarly focus of exhibits and 'top-down' decision-making processes have probably been the chief contributors to the poor track record of would-be educational exhibits. From a visitor-studies point of view, the problem is a systemic one that requires shifting responsibilities from curators/specialists and exhibit/graphics-designers to educators, instructional designers and evaluators. In other words, exhibit planning, design and installation would start by identifying the message, or messages, and work backwards to the objects, layout, presentation media and formats most likely to convey the message. Subject-matter specialists (curators) would have prime responsibility for identifying exhibit content and communications specialists would translate messages and shape presentation formats to attract visitors. Samples of target visitors would become a part of the 'editing' process at various planning stages through responses to questionnaires, interviews and focus groups. The critical stages for visitor involvement would be prior to and during stages of exhibit design, after installation to assess overall performance and after a period of public visits to correct or adjust interpretive signposting. An evaluator would be on the exhibition team with responsibility for maintaining linkage between exhibit messages (or purposes) and visitor reactions, attitudes and learning. The evaluator would (a) collect front-end data on visitor knowledge, attitudes and preconceptions and reactions to mock-ups of visuals, text and presentation formats; (b) co-ordinate summative and remedial evaluation; and (c) report results to the exhibition team with recommendations. Each team would be led by a 'team director', responsible for guiding the exhibit through planning and installation to post-installation adjustments, and maintaining communication between members. A 'summary protocol' covering all exhibit elements and evaluations would serve as the co-ordinating document to keep the team informed of progress.

There appears to be a growing consensus in the United States that preparing and co-ordinating such activities should not be the job of curators or other subject-matter specialists whose role should be confined to tasks for which they are uniquely qualified: that is, elaborating the messages to be delivered by an exhibit or programme. Planning for the delivery of these messages would be left to persons experienced in educational communication and evaluation processes.

SOME WORKING PRINCIPLES

A few of the working principles that have emerged from the accumulated experiences of the past thirty years would include the following.

Audience information should be available to planners before decisions are made concerning exhibit content and presentation. Such information would include data on the knowledge, attitudes, expectations and misconceptions that visitors have about prospective exhibit topics, objects and artists and on the kinds of questions they might pose, their special interests, personal experiences, beliefs and preferences. This could be obtained from the visitors themselves and from published literature. The most important educational goals of the exhibit—primary messages, what visitors are expected to do, feel and learn—need to be carefully identified beforehand using this information.

Just as much attention should be given to ways to motivate visitor involvement with the content of key exhibits. There must be a fun element in the experience or visitors will ignore the exhibit.

Rewarding features of exhibits must be designed to encourage visitors to give focused attention to exhibit content, visuals and text, which are keys to the learning that should take place (for example, asking visitors to make comparisons, discovering answers to leading questions, solving a problem) and to discourage random, unfocused attention. Lots of activity at popular exhibits does not necessarily mean that useful ideas are being conveyed.

Exhibitions that require visitors to follow a specific path should be avoided or minimized. Orientation panels can provide a 'menu' of approaches, sequences and structures that visitors can then adapt to their interests, personal learning styles and time-frames. These measures can reduce visitor fatigue and encourage more efficient use of the visit.

Visitors should be able to skip from one panel to another without becoming 'lost' or confused. Whenever possible, understanding a display should not depend on immediately understanding it or interacting with another display.

Most visitors notice objects, pictures, movement and manipulative/action elements more than they do text. Such elements can generate enough interest to encourage visitors to seek more information from text, graphics or other materials. However, they are likely to do so only if the text is *easily* and *quickly* found, as close to the object as possible, well illuminated, using large print and having high contrast. Avoid placing text too far away from the exhibit or on an opposite wall, numbering labels to be matched to exhibit objects, or see-through mountings on glass. Text should require minimal time for comprehension; however, it must not be too short. Visitors prefer more text when explanation is needed and they resent shortened text that does not answer a question. Length, positioning and other features should always be pre-tested with visitors.

Objects, illustrations, text, headings, questions and processes must use familiar, active language and visual formats whenever possible.

Time is crucial to most visitors. The less time required to decipher an exhibit's message the better. Pursuing the content of an otherwise interesting exhibit is influenced by the amount of time visitors believe will be needed to get an answer to a question or to find desired information.

Noise, crowds, sight-lines and unfamiliarity often distract attention from individual panels or confuse visitors. They can be corrected only with observations made after public occupancy. A portion of the exhibit budget (commonly 10 per cent) should be set aside to make adjustments to interpretive components after public occupancy (remedial evaluation). Signposting, headings, text and graphics are the components that most often require remedial adjustments.

The potential of museums as places for alternative educational enrichment will require some time before it can be fully achieved. However, it seems clear that museums today have reached a stage where their benefits as real educational institutions are beginning to be realized. There are good reasons for optimism that there will be rapid changes in the next few years. Many museum planners are convinced that visitor studies can play a useful role in making exhibits more effective educationally. Large and small museums of all kinds are already sending key staff to pre-conference workshops on visitor studies methods despite tight budgets and are re-assessing priorities so they can, at least, try to incorporate some aspects of visitor studies and evaluation into staff operations, schedules and budgets. Some are holding back portions of exhibit budgets to make adjustments to exhibits after installation and are reporting dramatic improvements in increased attention and self-directed learning of children and adults as a result. Eventually, these successes should lead others to follow the same path.

15

Can Museums Be All Things to All People? Missions, Goals, and Marketing's Role

Neil Kotler and Philip Kotler

INTRODUCTION

Museum managers struggle with the issues of maintaining their museum's integrity as a distinctive collecting, conserving, research, exhibiting and educational institution, and, at the same time, making their museum more popular and competitive. The traditional standard for collections based museums has been well articulated by a former Director of London's British Museum, Sir David M. Wilson: "Museums are about the material they contain. The first duty of the museum curator is to look after that material. . . . His second duty is to make that material available to whoever wants to see it."[1] Yet, as museum activist Kenneth Hudson has pointed out, the shift in museum focus to serving audiences has been developing over nearly a half-century. Hudson writes: ". . . [O]ne can assert with confidence that the most fundamental change that has affected museums . . . is the now almost universal conviction that they exist in order to serve the public. The old-style museum felt itself to be under no such obligation. . . . The museum's prime responsibility was to its collections, not to its visitors."[2]

Whatever the reason for the focus on audience (e.g., public subsidy and accountability, need to generate revenue, pressure to include under-served groups), museums are seeking ways to reach a broader public, forge community ties, and compete effectively with alternative providers of leisure and educational activities. Museums, decades ago, were content to reach a small, narrow and self-selected audience. Their narrow programmatic focus in the past (i.e., the focus on collections and scholarly and professional activities) reflected their small, relatively homogeneous constituency base. Today, museums are not only reaching out to larger audiences and building demand among new groups, they are designing proactively the

Neil Kotler is a program specialist at the Smithsonian Institution, and Philip Kotler is professor of international marketing at Northwestern University's Kellogg Graduate School of Management. Their article "Can Museums Be All Things to All People? Missions, Goals, and Marketing's Role" appeared in *Museum Management and Curatorship* (Vol. 18, No. 3, 2000, pp. 271–289). It is reprinted here with permission from Elsevier.

arrangements, services and offerings which will generate satisfaction and positive outcomes for their visitors. In the process, museum managers and staff are discovering assets and resources which museums possess and were in the past often overlooked.

Change is pervasive in today's museums, and the boundaries which once separated museums from other recreational and educational organizations are blurring or breaking down altogether. A growing number of museum leaders is concerned about competition from the entertainment and cultural districts in central cities, cyberspace, restaurants, sports arenas, and those shopping malls which also present collections and exhibitions, as well as from the growing number of new museums proper, and history and science centers. Sony built the $160 million, 350,000 square-foot Metreon in downtown San Francisco as the urban equivalent of a Disney theme park combined with a suburban shopping mall. Four floors contain shops, restaurants, a movie theater and a 3-D IMAX screen, along with a fantasy land inspired by the Maurice Sendak children's books, a video game arcade and an interactive computer gallery which explores how technology works. In Chicago, Disney opened Disney Quest, a theme park and play space fitted into a department store. Virtually every entertainment conglomerate is building its own variation. At other museums which occupy grand, imposing buildings and generate popular perceptions of inaccessibility and elitism, managers are seeking ways to make their facilities more congenial, comfortable, and even mundane. The Cleveland Museum of Art, with one of the loveliest classical buildings in the museum world, convenes each year a colored chalk competition on the sidewalks surrounding the Museum building. Children and families are encouraged to express their creativity by chalking up the sidewalks and, in the process, they feel more at home at the Museum. Other museums are focusing their energies on building bridges to their neighbors and making themselves increasingly a vital part of community life.

If the public today stands at the center of museum thinking, how do visitors view the museums they visit? Casual visitors, according to audience research, enjoy their visits, but want more information and orientation, a higher level of comforts and services, and more human contact in museums. Increasingly, museum constituencies are asserting their claims for programs and services. Claims on resources are multiplying, as are the constituencies which are demanding more services. The result is that museum managers are working double-time, to raise the comfort level for visitors, provide a range of programs, and, in addition, expand their overall audience. Not surprisingly, museum managers, laboring under tight budgets, are hiring marketers and business experts to help them identify tradeoffs, make choices and keep costs down. The challenge in running museums, then, is to determine, in the midst of competing claims for resources, a realistic set of goals and the strategies and tools which can accomplish the desired changes.

Museums engage in goal-setting and strategic planning and marketing to achieve greater visibility, enlarge their offerings, develop a broader audience, and raise income. At the core of the challenge is making the right choices of goals and strategies and allocating adequate resources. Museum managers are honing in on several questions to guide the choices. What goals fit with the museum's strengths and best promote its core mission? Who are the museum's main constituencies and what is the relative level of attention to pay to each constituency? What goals and strategies should be set for each constituency? What is the optimal program mix, including exhibits, interactive elements, and other interpretative methods, which can promote a diversified offering for visitors and satisfy their varying needs? What indicators can be used to measure goal achievement?

A related challenge to goal setting and strategy implementation is the challenge of defining the outcomes and results which managers seek to achieve from their programs and operations and their audiences. As Peter Drucker has observed about all organizations, whether for-profit or non-profit: "Marketing is so basic that it cannot be considered a separate function. It is the whole business seen from the point of view of its final result, that is, from the customer's point of view."[3] This article examines three museum strategies for building audience, support and income (common goals on today's museum agendas), explores the inter-relationships of missions, goals and strategies, brings to bear research on visitor and staff perspectives, and delineates the role of strategy and marketing in museums.

SETTING GOALS

Setting goals and monitoring progress in achieving them form a critical part of the strategic marketing process in which many museums are engaged. A museum, for example, may enjoy support from members and important constituencies, yet it has to expand and diversify its audience in order to achieve broader community support as well as increased income. In this case, the museum has to frame a goal of attracting under-served groups, among others. In other cases, a museum can enjoy a relatively stable visitorship, including a flow of tourists, but lack connections with and loyalty from important constituency groups. Or, a museum may find it necessary to position itself differently, forging a new image and identity, as a means to attract new segments such as young people, families with young children and young professionals.

Goal setting has to reflect a sense of mission and knowledge of a museum's strengths and weaknesses, as well as research regarding the visitors the museum seeks to serve and the competitive environment in which the museum exists. The latter is a significant factor. Museums which seek to expand their audience or bolster their community ties have, first, to identify the competition they face and then determine the distinctive niche they can occupy in relation to the segments of the public they want to serve and their audience needs. In other words, goals ultimately have to reflect the interests and needs of consumers (the museum audience, members and supporters). And the relation of a museum to its audience is an exchange relationship: visitors derive benefits from museums and at the same time incur certain costs (in time, convenience and expenses) in participating in museums; and museums derive benefits from the public such as revenue, donations and political support.

Goals are interrelated, forming part of a larger pattern of activity, and, therefore, have to be determined as part of a broader strategic framework. For example, a museum may seek to build a larger audience. Yet the goal of audience development can depend on another goal: raising public awareness and visibility. The latter goal, in turn, may depend on achieving yet a third goal: redefining the museum image and identity and, in particular, correcting negative information and image. Goals have to be viewed as instrumental in nature, contributing to or detracting from yet other goals and the enterprise as a whole. Goals in the museum world, in addition, can be differentiated, for analytical purposes, as audience goals—offering or product goals—and organizational and competitive goals, although each set is interrelated and interdependent. Once goals are set, a strategic plan can be established for ordering them as a set of priorities, sequencing them over time, and finally accomplishing the goals. Lastly, goals have to be specific, measurable, and achievable. Table 1 lists ten major museum goals in relation to three strategies. Goals are sorted into three groups. Audience growth, membership growth, donor growth (the latter, in particular, deal with business and organizational support), and community service, comprise the audience goals. Improving offerings and programs, and improvement of the museum's services, including exterior and interior design, constitute product or offering goals. Four goals comprise the organizational and competitive category: redefining a museum's image and raising public visibility; expanding earned income; building a more customer-centered organization (in which staff training forms a major element); and building collaborations and partnerships with other museums and organizations in the community, which can include co-marketing, cost-sharing, and other functions.

The three sets of goals are interrelated. For example, audience goals and product goals have to interpenetrate one another for either set to be successful. From a marketing perspective, successful organizations, including museums, have to reflect their audiences and, specifically, the needs of different groups and segments and the benefits they seek as consumers. Yet, as an analytical tool, it is useful to differentiate museum goals into three sets. Traditional-minded museums, while never static or oblivious of their audience, tend to focus on their collections and other resources and, typically, they generate organizational change from the inside outward. Art museums and natural history museums tend to focus more on their collections and internal resources than science centers and museums. The latter, typically, have

Table 1. Museum goals and strategies

Strategies	Audience Goals			Product Goals			Organization/Competitive Goals		
	Audience Growth	Membership Growth	Donor Growth	Community Service	Improving Offerings & Programs	Improving Design & Services	Image-Building	Building a Consumer-Centered Organization	Increasing Income	Generating Collaborations & Partnerships
Strategy #1 Improving museum-going experience										
Strategy #2 Community Service										
Strategy #3 Market repositioning toward entertainment										

smaller collections and are more focused on developing programs for particular audience segments, especially children and their families.

THREE STRATEGIES FOR BUILDING AUDIENCES
AND IMPROVING THE MUSEUM-GOING EXPERIENCE

Now let us turn to the three strategies outlined in Table 1. Strategies are gameplans which occur in a given period of time and reveal how an organization can reach its goals. The first strategy, improving the museum-going experience, will have a large impact on the museum's audience and offering goals. The second strategy, community service, will raise the museum's image and local impact. The third strategy, market repositioning toward entertainment, aims to increase the museum's attractiveness and competitiveness in relation to alternative leisure activities. These strategies are not mutually exclusive. Indeed, elements of each can be combined, depending on the end-goals involved. Each strategy, however, represents a different direction and emphasis, roughly corresponding to the distinction among 'audience goals'; 'product goals', and 'organizational/competitive goals', as outlined in Table 1. As models, these strategies represent different tradeoffs, divergent agendas, and they generate varying degrees of tension and conflict with core museum missions. For example, the first strategy of improving the overall museum-going experience of visitors corresponds closely to the emphasis implicit in achieving audience and offering goals. The third strategy, 'market repositioning', is most closely related to achieving organizational change and competitive goals. Each strategy, in addition, involves different choices in allocating a museum's resources.

STRATEGY # 1: IMPROVING THE MUSEUM-GOING EXPERIENCE

The first strategy aims to improve the museum-going experience for visitors by providing richer exhibits and programs, better services and design elements, and more accessible and comfortable facilities. Strong exhibitions and programming, as well as good design and services, are major ingredients, but form only part of the experience. Casual visitors to large museums, typically, spend an hour or so in a museum and divide their time between exhibits, the restaurant and the gift shop. Audience research reveals that, for the majority of visitors, social and recreational experiences are as important or more important than educational and intellectual ones. Exhibitions, with their limited texts, selective objects and compressed narratives, are often less efficient means of gathering information than books, magazines, newspapers and the Internet. Research on European museum audiences indicates further that diversion, curiosity and spontaneity are more characteristic of visitor intentions than structured learning.[4] For this reason, museum managers, aiming to improve visit quality, have to consider the range of visitor expectations and experiences, as well as the range of the museum's offerings and services, as integral parts of a total visitor experience.

Improving the museum-going experience involves going beyond the traditional emphasis on objects and collections and even the emphasis in recent years on information and education. Generating experiences involves activities in which visitors can directly participate, intensive sensory perception combining sight, sound, and motion, environments in which visitors can immerse themselves rather than behave merely as spectators, and out-of-the-ordinary stimuli and effects that make museum visits unique and memorable. Not all museum offerings have to be intense and immersion-like; what is needed is variety and balance in offerings along with scope and range. Research into visitors' expectations, needs and behaviors should guide the design of museum-going experiences. Museum managers, years ago, were content with counting visitors and, later on, sought to identify types and backgrounds of those visitors. In recent years, audience research has been providing data which illuminates visitor perceptions and attitudes, thus enabling managers to respond pro-actively to the visitor needs and design environments and experiences those visitors can enjoy.

To improve offerings and services, museum staff have to go beyond imagining what they think visitors want. They have to question visitors directly, and a good deal of relevant audience research already exists. For example, pioneering studies by Marilyn Hood in the 1980s described visitor attitudes and behaviors in all types of recreational arenas, including museums. Hood found that consumers sought six types of benefits and values in their recreational activity: 1) being with people and enjoying social interaction; 2) doing something worthwhile; 3) feeling comfortable with the surroundings; 4) enjoying the challenge of a new or unusual experience; 5) having a learning opportunity; and 6) participating actively. In the museum setting Hood found that active museum-goers looked for a set of benefits different from casual, occasional visitors. The former sought the benefit of learning, coupled with the challenge of novel experiences and doing something worthwhile, to a greater degree than the latter.[5]

Audience research further reveals that the majority of visitors are part of social groups (family or friends) and that their behavior is influenced by the interests and attitudes of the group. John Falk points out that museum visitors vary in their backgrounds and interests and that, while some are focused on ideas, information, and cognitive learning, others favor emotional, sensory, and kinesthetic modalities. Furthermore, visitors expect recreational and social experiences and perceive museum visits as an interconnected mosaic which begins with the outing and incorporates all aspects of the visit, including the departure. The availability of convenient parking, ease of physical access to the museum building, cleanliness of the facilities and friendliness of staff, all rank high in importance alongside quality exhibitions and programs.[6]

Museum visitors seek variety in the offerings. Many feel a reverence toward the objects and collections in museums. Visitors seek after celebrative experiences in which they connect with the past, encounter inspiring examples, express pride in their heritage, honor important events, and bask in great achievements in art and culture, science and governance. Regular visitors to art museums, in particular, embody a keenness for aesthetic experiences and things of beauty which can sweep them away in experiences of awe and enchantment. Visitors expect learning and cognitive experiences as well, and to encounter things in museums which contrast with the routines of work and everyday life.[7]

Zahava Doering, Director of the Institutional Studies Office at the Smithsonian Institution, has studied visitors' expectations, attitudes and behaviors over a number of years. Her studies shed light on predispositions and assumptions which visitors bring to their museum visits. Doering's studies indicate that visitors arrive in museums with "their own visit agendas and sense of time," frequent those exhibits and programs "with whose point of view they expect to agree," and they respond best to museum activities "that are personally relevant and with which they can easily connect." The great majority of visitors are involved in four types of museum-going experience: social experiences; cognitive (information-gathering, meaning-making) experiences; object experiences (viewing beautiful, rare or valuable things, such as the Hope Diamond at the Smithsonian's Natural History Museum); and introspective experiences, in which objects and settings trigger memories and associations, feelings of spiritual connection, and a sense of connectedness to a culture and community.[8]

In making improvements in exhibits and programs, managers have choices in terms of exhibit designs which offer different levels of information, reach different groups, and employ different formats such as interpretative text, storytelling, interactive elements, and simulation of an environment, mood or historical situation. Creating a variety of exhibits and programs has the advantage of appealing to several different audience segments. An example is the First Division Museum at the Cantigny Estate in Wheaton, Illinois, built by Col. Robert McCormick, publisher of *The Chicago Tribune* newspaper, to honor the fighting men of this army division and their wartime experiences. Vintage tanks and other military equipment from two World Wars stand in a park outside the museum, not unlike pieces of sculpture a visitor can find in a sculpture garden, while inside the Museum, war-related events and military achievements are richly interpreted in a series of galleries. In the newest section, visitors can walk through a World War I battlefield trench, listen to the sounds of war, and experience the travail and suffering. They also walk through a French village as it stood just after being shelled and can imagine the civilian calamity which has been inflicted.

Large museums organize 'blockbuster' exhibitions which offer visitors one-of-a kind experiences, and years afterwards visitors can recall these exhibitions vividly because of their intensity and scale. Smaller museums, lacking the resources to organize such large-scale exhibitions, have to find ways to change and renew their displays from time to time and exploit creatively their collections and presentational designs. More and more museums are utilizing media and interactive elements to expand the visitor's sense of immediacy and participation. One element in the museum-going experience usually can be improved: the extent of visitor contact with staff. The majority of visitors arrive with friends or family, yet they express a desire for added contact with staff. Exhibition programs and behind-the-scenes tours with docents and staff offer opportunities for visitors to ask questions, offer comments, and share their experiences. Museums are experimenting with programs which allow visitors at designated times to come together in a museum space, along with staff, to reflect together on their museum experiences. The latter activities enrich museum visits and humanize what can be intimidating objects and settings. Services form a significant part of museum offerings and include: convenient parking and access to mass transit; outdoor lighting and security; ample seating, dining and shopping facilities; trained staff who are responsive and friendly to visitors; way-finding and user-friendly gallery design that make it easier for visitors to move around the museum; and furnishing richer information and context regarding objects, collections, and exhibits, such as narratives, historical analysis, databases, biography, and a variety of interpretative tools.

Finding one's way around museums with large, complex buildings, for example, can be a stumbling block for first-time visitors. Large museums typically provide visitors with maps of galleries, exhibitions and other physical facilities within the museum. The National Gallery of Art in Washington, D.C. has taken this one step further in its electronic Micro-Gallery. Visitors to the Micro-Gallery, situated at one of the major entrances, can sample the Gallery's collection and temporary exhibitions on a computer screen; absorb all kinds of contextual information such as biographies, time-lines, historical information, and art criticism; locate the specific works and treasures they want to view; and design their own personal tours with instructions printed out for finding their way. The Hirshhorn Museum and Sculpture Garden, part of the Smithsonian Institution in Washington, D.C., moved its gift shop from an out-of-the-way basement area to the main entrance area and combined it with a visitor information desk operated by volunteers. Prior to the change, visitors entered the Museum with little opportunity to obtain information and orientation. Information desks and gift shops at entrances work well in acclimating visitors.

The Museum of Science in Boston has invested in recent years considerable resources in way-finding improvements. Today, visitors move about the Museum, using color-coded signage and directions as well as computer-generated and brochure maps. The Baltimore Museum of Art provides, on request, lightweight folding chairs for visitors who like to sit down in the galleries. It is a flexible arrangement which encourages visitors to spend more time viewing the art works. The Oregon Museum of Science and Industry has created a family room with board games and abundant seating so that large or extended families can move about at different paces, allowing, for example, grandparents to relax and play the board games while the grandchildren are running off in multiple directions. Museums contain a great deal of sensory stimuli and visitors can easily feel overwhelmed and exhausted by the experience. Improved services such as seating, activity rooms, gift shops and restaurants not only satisfy a visitor's need for comfort and diversion, but also encourage visitors to spend more time in museums.

Augmented services such as social events and continuing education are yet another form of service museums are increasingly offering. Museum visits usually are sociable experiences and managers are organizing a rich array of events which deepen a visitor's or member's relationship with the museum: e.g., opening night events for new exhibitions; holiday, seasonal, and commemorative events; special programs for targeted groups, such as art workshops for families with young children, and young professionals' socials.

Museum staff have choices regarding the extent to which they can influence and manage the museum-going experiences of their visitors. Years ago, museum audiences were smaller, more homogeneous, and more self-selective. Today, museum audiences are wide-ranging and more diverse and, therefore, are seeking after a variety of experiences, benefits and satisfactions. Museums are better-equipped today as a result of both visitor research and technological means to provide differing levels of information, narrative, and cognitive experience as part of their displays. The issue is the extent to which managers want to influence proactively or design the elements of visitors' experiences, as against the degree to which they want to leave their visitors alone. For art museums, particularly, the matter of designing the visitor experience is a complicated one. On the one hand, art museums seek to safeguard the visitor's direct encounter with works of art, minimizing distractions in the form of noise, congestion, and a deluge of media and printed material. On the other hand, art museums recognize that many visitors need information and interpretative tools in order to appreciate the artworks they are encountering.

There is no single formula which museums can employ for shaping visitors' museum experiences. Different types of museums will strike different balances. Yet from a consumer point of view, managers should look upon their museum, in varying degrees, as a designed environment and arrangement of activities, services, and experiences which will have value for their visitors. Managing services and orchestrating experiences is a direction managers are taking to transform museums from being simply places to visit on the occasion of a special event or 'blockbuster exhibition' to being places to visit regularly because they offer exceptional services, settings, and ambiences in every season.

Figure 1 outlines three dimensions of a designed museum-going experience. The horizontal axis indicates a range of visitor experiences, which includes visual, sensory, and aesthetic experience, recreational, sociable, and learning experiences, and

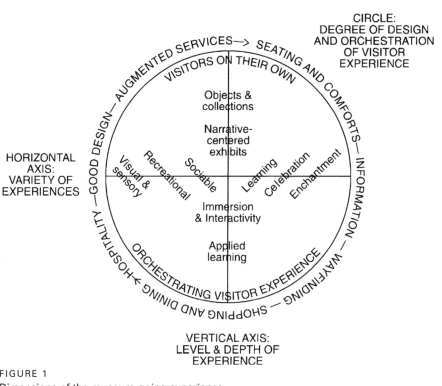

FIGURE 1
Dimensions of the museum-going experience.

the experiences of celebration and enchantment. The vertical axis identifies levels of intensity in museum-going experience, from relatively passive viewing of collections to active immersion experience and applied learning. The circle indicates the degree of services, including interior and architectural design, augmented services, information, hospitality, dining and shopping. In this first strategy, objects, exhibitions and interpretative programs continue to be the focal points of the museum-going experience, while improvements in facilities, services and programs serve to facilitate and reinforce the museum-going experience for a broader audience. An emphasis on improving services, to be sure, may divert resources from collections care and exhibition development, but overall, this strategy, of the three, is that most closely linked to the traditional core activities of museums.

STRATEGY # 2: COMMUNITY SERVICE

The second strategy places its emphasis on expanding community service. Many American museums developed out of a sense of place and community. Local historical societies organized museums in the 19th century to celebrate heritage and community history. Historic houses have commemorated great figures, families, and historic periods, while historic sites captured the drama of great events. Art museums presented regional art and natural history museums illustrated regional flora and fauna and their natural development. At a later time, 'halls of fame' arose, celebrating great achievements in sports, invention, industry and technology, while their sponsors, followers and enthusiasts represented extended communities of memory, spirit and ideas.

In the early decades of the 20th century, John Cotton Dana at the Newark Museum in New Jersey was a pioneer in developing the educational role of museums and links to schools, a major expression of community service. Dana conceived a museum "to be of immediate, practical aid to all of the community that supports it." Museum collections were seen as educational tools which could be useful to young people; collections of industrial tools, of design elements, and of art and crafts, were made available to help young people appreciate the practical arts and train some to become tradesmen, craftsmen and artists. Special collections were used in schools and students became apprentices in the museum.[9] Adult education was a goal of several prominent Chicago museums, such as the Field Museum of Natural History and the Museum of Science and Industry. Set in public parks and nature preserves, these museums were designed to inspire an appreciation of nature and educate adults who lacked formal education or who were recent immigrants. Today, museums are building partnerships with schools. The Smithsonian Institution, for example, provides technical training and support, along with instruction and curriculum materials, for museum-oriented model schools in Washington, D.C.

Community service in recent years has assumed a broader meaning than education. Some museums have made themselves a vital part of community life and instruments in fostering a community's sense of identity and solidarity. Local historical museums have played significant roles in deepening the sense of communal identity, celebrating heritage and interpreting community traditions and mores. Regional museums such as the Genesee Country Village and Museum: in upstate New York organize a variety of holiday, commemorative and seasonal events to strengthen community ties, reinforce the sense of belonging, and, additionally, augment their audiences. The Missouri Historical Society in St. Louis has evolved into a leading forum for discussion of neighborhood and community issues and of efforts to generate policy to solve those problems. The Johnson County Museum in Shawnee, Kansas, in the early 1990s, forged a new identity as a community-centered museum emphasizing the cultural practice and heritage of different ethnic and cultural groups in the region. The Museum invited residents to help the Museum build its collections by donating objects which illustrate local history and culture. It reoriented its displays to focus on different groups, generating a far higher level of participation among community members than had occurred in the past. Museums function as community meeting places, and children's and youth museums, especially, have developed important roles as educational centers, meeting places, and community development arms.

Museums in the late 20th century have evolved yet another community function, as economic development engines in the form of attractions and tourist destinations which can contribute to a community's growth in jobs and income. Downtown developers and city governments view museums, cultural and entertainment districts, as projects to stimulate economic revitalization. An example is the Davenport (Iowa) Art Museum which is situated in a hard-to-reach, outlying neighborhood. With support from the municipal government, as well as private donors, the museum board will build a new $15 million downtown museum which is expected to infuse new life in the downtown area and serve to attract other cultural and entertainment organizations. In the summer of 1999, a British architect was hired to design the new museum. Museum architecture as well as exhibitions and public programs are tourist attractions. An example is the Guggenheim Museum in Bilbao, Spain. Public authorities in Bilbao, in the depressed Basque region of Spain, invested $100 million to build the extraordinary Frank Gehry-designed museum in Bilbao, which has overnight become one of Europe's greatest tourist destinations.

Community service embraces services which are useful in fulfilling the common needs of a community as a whole, yet it also includes initiatives which reach specific groups, such as under-served ethnic groups, families with children, and young professionals, whose participation can be vital. The Memorial Art Gallery in Rochester, New York, in the late 1980s and early 1990s, became aware of its aging membership and declining support groups. As a means to attract younger visitors and members, the Gallery created a monthly event for young professionals known as 'First Friday', offering a variety of activities, including drinks, light meals, lectures, gallery tours and jazz performances which has become a leading social event for younger members of the community. The monthly events average more than 1,000 participants and a growing number are recruited as members and patrons. The Field Museum in Chicago has reached out to new segments, such as under-served ethnic and cultural groups, by organizing outdoor summer ethnic arts and cultural festivals. Community service also has manifested itself in recent years in the form of museum collaborations and partnerships to promote art and culture and raise the visibility of museum offerings and services. A group of museums in Providence, Rhode Island, for example, has joined together in leasing a downtown building to generate a cultural district of greater visibility, appeal and service. Groups of local museums have formed marketing partnerships to generate joint advertising, collaborate on admissions fees and offer common tickets, and to build purchasing co-operatives to reduce operating costs.

The second strategy, it can be argued, gives the most emphasis to identifying, segmenting, and targeting the public, the consumers and the members of a given community and region. Community participation and support, after all, is accomplished by the involvement of the various segments of the community and new museum offerings and programs have to be tailored to meet the needs of different segments. The community service strategy, thus, can be viewed as a change strategy which moves from the outside (the audience, the public) inward into the museum organization (the offerings and services). Embracing community service also is a means to build audience and support over the long run. Thus the community service direction has evolved from a focus on education based on collections and exhibitions to a focus on community needs in a broader sense. In the process, what were once known as 'ancillary' services have become major elements of museum operations alongside core functions. A focus on community service does not necessarily involve sacrificing the core mission of a museum, and in the best of worlds the former will bring in more visitors and active participants. However, greater interaction with and dependence on the community can lead museums to rethink their collections, displays and programs, and move in the direction of diversifying their collections and programs, and, perhaps, replacing some parts with others.

STRATEGY # 3: MARKET REPOSITIONING TOWARD ENTERTAINMENT

The third strategy can involve far-reaching change. It occurs when a museum redesigns its facilities and offerings in a sweeping rather than incremental manner in order to attract an entirely new audience to make itself competitive with other leisure activity organizations, or to become a place which is popular and entertaining with a broad and diverse audience. Market repositioning means, in some cases, a substantial move away from a museum's traditional audience and thus the need to build entirely new constituencies. Although this third strategy involves potentially the most drastic transformation of the core activities of collecting, conserving, exhibiting and educating, it is not always easy to judge when a museum's range of offerings, overall, reinforce its educational mission and when new offerings change the balance and tip the museum instead in the direction of an entertainment center. The very definition of 'entertainment' has changed during the past century and more. The American museum pioneer, Charles Willson Peale, opened a museum in Philadelphia in the 1780s and promoted it as a place of "rational entertainment", by which he meant a combination of designed settings and experiences for recreation along with educational offerings. Although a museum director, Peale was also a showman who understood that visitors had to perceive an attraction to exist before they would be available for learning. The contemporary concept, 'edutainment', sets out to capture the same idea: attractive and entertaining presentation and design can facilitate educational goals.

From early times, museums have presented themselves, in part, as akin to performances, happenings and theatrical experiences. These sometimes functioned as interpretative devices for collections and at other times as atmospherics and extra attractions. Dioramas built in natural history museums from the late 19th century, for example, sought to provide visitors with richer interpretative contexts for stuffed animals and birds. Historical museums and historic homes have featured displays of costumes, story-telling and quasi-theatrical performances as means of helping visitors to understand better different historical situations. Many museums are hybrids composed of collecting institutions with story-driven and interactive learning and entertainment centers. A growing number of them call themselves history and science centers precisely as a means to build an identity as broader-based learning centers rather than simply organizations devoted purely to objects and material culture. What basically differentiates museums from non-museums are the collections of authentic objects and materials, assembled and conserved in accordance with the core purposes of preservation, enlightenment, edification and education, which museum staff are expected to accomplish.

Museums seek to fulfill their educational missions in varied and innovative ways. Objects and collections alone may not be the most effective means to cover a particular topic or tell a particular story, and museums may offer displays with hands-on and interactive elements, immersive environments, multiple media and narratives. The Exploratorium in San Francisco, one of the most celebrated science centers in the world, has an overriding goal of teaching science and inspiring young people to engage in scientific experiments. To accomplish that mission, it offers visitors hundreds of scientific experiments and demonstrations as well as themed displays which tell the story of science. Yet very few of the Exploratorium's offerings contain original scientific instruments, artifacts or archival material. The Smithsonian Institution installed in the summer of 1999 an interactive display entitled, *Microbes: Invisible Invaders . . . Amazing Allies.* Designed primarily for children and their parents, this display generated large, enthusiastic audiences, although it was a departure from traditional Smithsonian exhibitions. *Microbes* offered an exuberant educational experience without including treasured objects of medical history, even though great treasures of the history of medicine reside in Smithsonian collections, such as the original vial of Salk polio vaccine. Many museums are experimenting with different combinations of collections, themed displays and interactive offerings. Indeed, the Minnesota History Center, in Minneapolis, has redesigned its offerings and galleries to engage visitors in the process of reliving history. A series of small theaters offer visitors emotional, even cathartic, experiences revolving around the sense of family and the sense of place. Visitors can manipulate cubes with layered information in the exhibit halls which offer different types of visitors varying levels of information and engagement.

Transformation can take other forms too. Changes at the Smithsonian's National Museum of Natural History in Washington, D.C. exemplify a movement toward greater entertainment-oriented experience, while the museum works to maintain a balance between museum purposes and marketing requirements. The museum opened its Discovery Center in 1998–1999, consisting of three facilities which set out to serve the needs of a large audience: a significantly enlarged and redesigned gift shop with better quality merchandise; an expanded restaurant with a greater variety of cuisines; and a new 3-D IMAX theater. Although the new center has generated increased visitors and revenue, some argue the museum should have invested the funds in refurbishing its 50-year old displays rather than investing in a new entertainment facility within the museum. Another example of repositioning is the Guggenheim's summer 1998 exhibition 'The Art of the Motorcycle.' The Guggenheim often has exhibitions dealing with design. The motorcycle exhibition aimed, in addition, to reach into popular culture and segments of the public that rarely if ever visited art museums. The exhibition was one of the most popular ever held at the museum.

Market repositioning can also involve examining a museum's community, finding out what needs are not being addressed, and repositioning the museum to serve the community better. The last example is the most transforming. The Strong Museum in Rochester, New York, was a traditional museum known for having one of the world's most distinguished doll collections, along with regional historical artifacts. Visitor numbers had declined precipitously by the early 1990s and museum leaders decided to strike out in new directions. They commissioned substantial market research and launched a strategic planning process, in which members of the community were asked to recommend alternative museum concepts. This resulted in transforming the Strong into a family- and children-centered museum, for which there was an unmet need in the community. Today collections co-exist with hands-on, interactive programs, narrative-driven displays, performances, and family activities, and this has generated significant additional community involvement and has expanded both audience and income. These examples illustrate the range of market repositioning strategies available: innovation in offerings; innovation in community service; and innovation in competing in recreational and tourist markets.

CRITICISM OF MARKET REPOSITIONING STRATEGY

What are the objections to the market repositioning strategy? The first objection is that the strategy can diminish scholarship, authenticity of the collections, and staff professionalism, which lie at the core of the museum mission. Museums are standard bearers in which the public should place its trust, while converting museums into mere entertainment centers renders them no different from ordinary entertainment media and robs them of their primary educational purpose. Once museums lose their distinctive core mission, they will have to compete in the marketplace with the entertainment industry, whose resources are far more substantial. Competing as entertainment arenas will not provide museums with a level playing field; on the contrary, museums will have to compete with real entertainment products and they are likely to be perceived as second-rate in comparison.

A second objection is that museums are distinctive institutions which focus on the role of objects and material culture in understanding history, science, art and culture. Few other institutions can play this role and any movement of museums toward non-collection-based displays and programs denies society of alternative approaches to knowledge. A third and related objection is that in giving emphasis to entertainment, museums remove from society the few remaining varieties of recreational activity. Popular tastes run to thrills, adventure, and emotional stimulation and these are readily available in existing mass media. What is needed are counterpoints—influences which will elevate public taste—for which museums are uniquely suited. Furthermore, audience research shows that museum visitors appreciate the extraordinary range of collections presented that allow them to step outside of the routines of work and everyday life. The ideal situation in a museum, as veteran managers have observed, is to nurture staff devotion to collections and their interpretation and at the same time motivate staff commitment to helping visitors fully enjoy what a museum has to offer. The passion which curatorial staff have toward collections and encouraging the public to be equally passionate about them lies at the heart of the museum mission. This is what generates care and quality. The manager's role is to encourage staff, mollify their fears, and demonstrate that opening up the museum to new and broader audiences will not jeopardize integrity and standards.

MARKETING'S ROLE IN MUSEUM GOAL SETTING AND STRATEGY

A growing number of museums are hiring marketing experts to help them accomplish their goals. Goals which relate to external factors, audiences, and the environment (e.g., building audiences, improving the museum-going experience, increasing sales, developing competitive programs) are particularly well suited to marketing. Table 2 identifies a series of marketing tools and techniques which can help museums achieve their goals, and these include the so-called marketing mix, the five basic factors which affect consumer behavior. The list is as follows: 1) research, including environmental and competitive analysis, organizational assessment, audience and market research; 2) techniques of segmenting different audiences, targeting the groups the museum seeks to attract, and positioning the museum as delivering the benefits sought by the target groups; 3) product development, including management of existing products as well as generating new ones; 4) distribution, ways a museum can distribute its offerings widely, beyond the museum walls; 5) promotion, consisting of tools of advertising, public relations, direct marketing, which communicate offerings to different target groups; 6) pricing, or the determination of what to charge for different museum offerings which will increase audience and income; 7) service and relationship marketing, that aims to create close bonds with target groups (in the case of museums, repeat visitors); and 8) strategic planning, the long-range activity by which the museum visualizes and plans its future and sets its priorities. These represent the tool box which museum managers can apply to their particular challenges and problem-solving. Basic to

Table 2.   Marketing tools and techniques for museums

Research and analysis	Researching the environment, including market opportunities and competitive threats, organizational assessment, including strengths and weaknesses, market and visitor analysis
STP: Segmentation	Identifying different segments of museum audiences, consumers of other recreational activities, and non-visitor groups, and their differing needs and expectations
Targeting	Selecting segments to target for the museum audience (e.g., families with young children, educated adults, senior citizens, young professionals, tourists)
Positioning	Defining an image identity that will differentiate a museum from other comparable organizations and satisfy needs of target segments
Marketing mix: Product	Managing and renewing exhibits, collections, programs creating new offerings and services
Place	Designing a comfortable museum facility as well as distributing museum offerings to schools, traveling exhibits and websites and other electronic media
Promotion	Advertising public relations, directing marketing, sales promotion, and integrated communications to audiences, collaborators and competitors
Price	Pricing admissions, memberships, gift shop merchandise, special events, donor acknowledgment, discounts, to attract visitors in all seasons, including off-season, and to attract under-served constituencies

each of the tools and techniques, and a basic assumption behind marketing, is that a transaction and a relationship with museum visitors, members and supporters has to reflect an exchange of benefits and costs, both for the public and for the museum.

Marketing's ability to assist museums flows both from the tools and techniques it offers and from the ability of marketing staff to influence constructively the museum organization in all its operations. Some museums have hired marketing staff but have relegated them to one corner of the museum operation, typically promotional activity. Marketing, however, is broader than simply promotion. Marketing is best able to facilitate a museum's goals and strategy when marketing staff can participate in and lend their expertise to all museum tasks, including programs and education, facility and interior design, as well as membership and development. Marketing professionals, under the best circumstances, will have relationships with all other museum staff and offices and a marketing director's advice will be sought in all roles, especially those affecting audiences, supporters, and other parts of the external environment.

MARKETING TOOLS AND TECHNIQUES
Can Museums Be All Things to All People?
The challenge for museum managers is to safeguard the museum mission while reaching out to a larger public and offering a richer museum-going experience for visitors. The risks in diluting the core activities of collections, scholarship, and edu-

cation cannot be minimized. Yet, without an audience and community support, even the greatest exhibition and collection will fail to generate response. While museums cannot respond to every demand put forward by a constituency group, they can make sound choices. Managers have alternatives in designing and orchestrating visitors' experiences. They can leave visitors alone, to fend for themselves, or else they can provide ample orientation and information, welcoming behavior by staff, and design satisfying experiences for their visitors.

Can a museum be all things to all people? Not easily or productively, simply because most museums are strapped for funds, especially the program funds needed to satisfy diverse constituency demands. Experience has shown that museums, like other organizations, are best able to play to their strengths and are foolish to offer things of indifferent quality at which other competitors excel. From a marketing point of view, museums have to address their audience needs while cultivating new groups of visitors and leading their audience to even greater experiences and benefits. If museums cannot serve everybody in a uniform way, they can set priorities for the target groups they can best serve and fit programs and staff to meet their needs. And museums can develop a fuller relationship with their constituencies, converting one-time transactions involving a single visit or occasional visits into relationships involving regular, active participation.

In setting goals and strategies, museums develop a clear view of their strengths and weaknesses and a vision of the kind of internal culture and structure which is most likely to generate desired outcomes. Having ambitious though realistic goals, relating these to the mission and the desired audience mix, knowing the audience and how to lead it, and finding the strategies and tools most effective in reaching the goals, is the best recipe to put forward for museums grappling with issues of change, innovation, and preserving integrity.

NOTES

1. David M. Wilson, 'What Do We Need Money For?' in T. Ambrose (ed.), *Money, Money, Money, and Museums*, Edinburgh (Scottish Museums Council) 1991, p. 11

2. Kenneth Hudson, 'The Museum Refuses to Stand Still', *Museum International*, No. 197, January–March, 1998, p. 43

3. Neil Kotler and Philip Kotler, *Museum Strategy and Marketing: Designing Missions, Building Audiences, Generating Revenue and Resources.* San Francisco (Jossey-Bass) 1998, p. 348

4. Zahava D. Doering, 'Strangers, Guests or Clients? Visitor Experiences in Museums', paper, presented at a Weimar, Germany, conference, *Managing the Arts*, 17–19 March 1999, Washington, D.C. (Institutional Studies Office, Smithsonian Institution) 1999, p. 4; see, also, Nobuko Kawashima, 'Knowing the Public: A Review of Museum Marketing Literature and Research', *Museum Management and Curatorship*, vol. 17, no.1, 1998, p. 32

5. Marilyn G. Hood, 'Staying Away: Why People Choose Not to Visit Museums', *Museum News*, April 1983, pp. 50–57

6. John H. Falk and Lynn D. Dierking, *The Museum Experience*, Washington, D.C. (Whalesback Books), 1992, pp. 25–37; 129–133

7. Kotler and Kotler, op. cit., pp. 34–36

8. Doering, op. cit., pp. 7–13

9. John Cotton Dana, *The New Museum*, Woodstock, VT (Elm Tree Press) 1917

Additional Recommended Reading

Diamond, Judy. *Practical Evaluation Guide: Tools for Museums and Other Informal Educational Settings.* Walnut Creek, CA: AltaMira, 1999.

Falk, John H., and Lynn D. Dierking. *Learning from Museums: Visitor Experiences and the Making of Meaning.* Walnut Creek, CA: AltaMira, 2000.

———. *The Museum Experience.* Washington, DC: Whalesback, 1992.

Gardner, Howard. *Frames of Mind: The Theory of Multiple Intelligences.* New York: Basic Books, 1983.

Hein, George E. *Learning in the Museum.* New York: Routledge, 1998.

Kotler, Neil, and Philip Kotler. *Museum Strategy and Marketing: Designing Missions, Building Audiences, Generating Revenue and Resources.* San Francisco: Jossey-Bass, 1998.

Museum Educators of the American Association of Museums. *The Visitor and the Museum.* Berkeley: University of California Press, 1977.

THE ROLE OF PUBLIC SERVICE:
THE EVOLUTION OF EXHIBITIONS
AND PROGRAMS

Today public programs and offerings span a wide range of choices, many made possible by the advent of diverse technologies in recent decades and a new ideology about service to the public. Traditional exhibitions—in-house and traveling—may coexist with computer stations where visitors can pull up images of objects in the collection, or visitors can experience science firsthand in an active science laboratory. Docent programs, tours, lectures, workshops, classes, organized trips, publications, websites, and behind-the-scene tours are some additional ways museums offer access to and interaction with their specific content. The transformation of public offerings over the past century has been dramatic; the nature and appearance of museum exhibitions and public services continue to evolve.

Exhibitions display the most transformation, and many are now a far cry from an object with an identity label. Today some exhibitions may feature one extraordinary object interpreted from the point of view of a scientist, an artist, a historian, and a member of the public; or an exhibition may present different experiences of one historical event; or the visitor may be immersed in a re-created scene designed to conjure up the emotions of a significant place or moment in time. As the public has become more sophisticated in its expectations, museums have been rethinking the why, what, when, where, and how of developing and mounting exhibitions, as well as who should be doing them. Old assumptions have been abandoned and replaced with questions that test ideas and approaches in an effort to reach the visitor with the greatest success.

The question of who should develop exhibitions and what should be said in them spurs some of the most impassioned debates. Roles and responsibilities have come under scrutiny. Curators or content specialists were traditionally considered the only individuals capable of researching and developing exhibitions based on a topic, a particular collection, or current research. The old exhibition development model was based on a chain reaction—the curator/researcher choosing and developing the exhibit concept, then passing it on to the exhibit designer, who designed and installed the exhibit, and then passed it on to the educator, who with no prior input was faced with the challenge of determining how and what to convey in public programs and how to make tours of the exhibition engaging and meaningful.

This singular model has been replaced by a range of exhibition development models. Some exhibition development approaches now involve community representatives throughout the process to help the museum shape the message and story line of the exhibit, locate objects from the community for display, and participate in the design of the exhibit space. Occasionally, some museums pass the baton to an artist, who is given creative license to interpret and shape an exhibition from a nontraditional, noncuratorial perspective. Natural history museums often work with environmentalists or scientists to convey the pressing issues of the natural world in their exhibitions. Perhaps most common is the team of diverse staff members who shape the exhibit development and design process. Members of these teams vary but may include educators, evaluators, content specialists/curators, exhibition developers, marketing specialists, audience advocates, conservators, exhibit designers, and graphic designers—all with the goal of merging diverse perspectives in order to achieve a more balanced exhibition message and a more effective visitor experience.

Educational programs are frequently cocreated in order to marry the resources of the museum with the needs and capabilities of another public organization. One of the most common partnerships is between schools and museums; however, museums are also partnering with social organizations, universities, police departments, hospitals, corporations, and others. Partnerships are driven in part by limited resources but also by the understanding that museums can expand their impact by collaborating with organizations that are able to provide more effective entry or insight into communities or subjects. Successful partnerships enable both organizations to broaden audiences, expand their collective impact, and empower the community at large.

The articles in this part document the evolution of thinking about exhibitions, educational programs, and public services. Kathleen McLean is perhaps best known for introducing exhibition critiques in the national conference program of AAM over ten years ago and for her book *Planning for People in Museum Exhibitions.* Here she chronicles the metamorphosis of thinking on exhibitions in "Museum Exhibitions and the Dynamics of Dialogue," which appeared in the 1999 summer issue of *Daedalus.* She cites specific exhibitions that changed the museum industry and traces the emergence of the many roles of exhibitions, including that of a vehicle for dialogue with visitors.

Lisa Roberts, a consummate museum educator, now at the City of Chicago Garfield Park Conservatory, in 1997 wrote the book *Knowledge to Narrative: Educators and the Changing Museum.* Here in "Changing Practices of Interpretation," an excerpt taken from that book, she traces the evolution of educational offerings in museums, illuminating the changing definition of interpretation to accommodate today's more holistic view of museums as educational institutions. Like McLean, she presents a historical perspective on this evolution while tracing the impact of contemporary issues as instigators of change in museum interpretation.

Lois Silverman, an educator and professor of museum studies, in her 1993 article "Making Meaning Together: Lessons from the Field of American History" discusses the concept of meaning making as a lens through which to consider the visitor experience in exhibitions. This topic remains critical in helping exhibit developers understand the range of personal meaning and insights that visitors can derive from experiencing exhibitions.

Mary Ellen Munley, a longtime educator, the former director of the Department of Education and Outreach at the Field Museum in Chicago, and now an independent practitioner, presents a frank discussion in "Is There Method in Our Madness? Improvisation in the Practice of Museum Education" about making sense of the wide range of public programs. She provides a fresh perspective on the nature of the educational offerings museums develop in order to reach various audiences.

Lisa Corrin's article, "Mining the Museum: An Installation Confronting History," documents one of the most revolutionary museum exhibit installations of the twentieth century, *Mining the Museum*, which was conceived and installed by the artist Fred Wilson. Given the opportunity to interpret the collections and mount an exhibit at the Maryland Historical Society in Baltimore, Wilson took ordinary objects and juxtaposed them with unlikely partners to make poignant visual statements about prejudices and racial inequities in the world and frequently present in museum displays.

Closing out Part III is "Evaluating the Ethics and Consciences of Museum" by Robert Sullivan, the associate director of public programs at the National Museum of Natural History at the Smithsonian Institution. In this article, published in 1994, Sullivan outlines a series of questions designed to stimulate and encourage museum practitioners to take stock in the power of words—the associated assumptions and value-laden meanings that accompany word choice and use. The implications of his questions reach far beyond museum interpretation and have applications in all aspects of museum operations. This diverse field of issues Sullivan highlights is also the bed of riches that museums will draw upon as they shape the stories to be told in tomorrow's exhibitions.

16

Museum Exhibitions
and the Dynamics of Dialogue

Kathleen McLean

Museums are not museums without exhibitions. The most prominent and public of all museum offerings, exhibitions are the soul of a museum experience for the millions of people who visit them, as well as for many of the people who create them. As unique three-dimensional compositions, exhibitions show things, whether a work of art or a working machine, a history timeline or a bit of bone. This showing or exhibition is the one feature common to all museums, from institutions engaged in scholarly research for a small professional audience to large multidisciplinary organizations providing services for the broadest spectrum of people.

The act of showing brings with it an inherent dialectic between the intentions of the presenter and the experiences of the spectator. Even in the earliest temples of the muses, someone set forth some object for others to experience, and who selected what for whom is the question at the heart of all conversation about exhibitions. The objects may be trophies of conquest, curious things from the natural world, masterpieces, or constructed environments, but embedded in their presentation is material evidence of the presenter's intentions and values. Teasing out and uncovering this evidence has been an increasingly attractive activity for some museum professionals, critics, and social theorists, particularly since the intentions of exhibit creators are often opaque or hidden from public view, and sometimes even unconscious.

The belief in a universal truth made apparent through the research and scholarship of curators has given way in some circles to the notion that display is no more than the act of promoting some truths at the expense of others. As museums give more credence to the diversity of ideas, cultures, and values in our society, museum

Kathleen McLean is Director of Public Programs and the Center for Public Exhibition at The Exploratorium in San Francisco and author of *Planning for People in Museum Exhibitions*. "Museum Exhibitions and the Dynamics of Dialogue" appeared in the special issue of *Daedalus* devoted to museums and contemporary issues. It is reprinted here by permission of *Daedalus*, Journal of the American Academy of Arts and Sciences, from the issue entitled "America's Museums," Summer 1999, Vol. 128, No. 3.

professionals are becoming increasingly conscious of the need to diversify the pool of curators, exhibit developers, and designers who have control of exhibition content and style of presentation. And those who traditionally have been doing the "talking" in exhibitions—with the often anonymous voices of curatorial authority—are increasingly expected to state their motivations and authorship up front.

On the other side of the equation are museum visitors—the people doing most of the "listening." Museums are getting to know them better, particularly since they have become more vocal in recent years, and possibly more discriminating. And museum professionals are coming to think of them less as passive spectators and more as active participants. Visitors now sit on exhibit-development committees, speak their minds in research and assessment programs, and even contribute to visitor-generated exhibits and labels in exhibition galleries.

As museums seek to attract and engage greater numbers of people, they are meeting, often for the first time, increasingly diverse audiences. People with different lifestyles and learning styles, cultural backgrounds and social perspectives are being enticed into museums. Whether they return will depend, to a great extent, on whether they can make personal connections and see something of themselves within. It will also depend on whether museums can keep up with the competition— the profusion of social, educational, and cultural activities vying for people's attention.

We have come a long way from the days when exhibitions were organized exclusively by and for collectors and curators. Nowhere will you find a museum closed on Saturdays, Sundays, and public holidays "to keep out the 'vulgar class,' such as 'sailors from the dockyards and the girls whom they might bring in with them.'"[1] Museums increasingly look to a general public audience for support, and competition for a market share of people's leisure time is a driving force that focuses the heat on exhibitions. In the rush to attract more visitors, exhibit professionals across the country are making profound changes in their exhibitions—expanding their range of exhibitable and often controversial themes and experimenting with new exhibition techniques and styles of development. Exhibitions are increasingly filled with interactive elements, multimedia and networked technologies, catchy and conversational labels, and objects out from under the glass.

The public nature of exhibitions makes them the obvious stage on which to play out the tensions of our times—tensions between access and exclusivity, common and expert knowledge, the prescribing and the challenging of meaning, and market and mission. The proposition that exhibition creators must pay attention to the interests and needs of their visitors still meets with resistance, particularly among those who hold to the notion of museums as temples and sites primarily of scholarship. They express concern about focusing on entertainment at the expense of learning and other high-minded museum experiences. Much farther along the continuum, a growing number of administrators are equating rigorous scholarship and depth of content with an outdated and elitist model of museum exhibitry, convinced that the public will not attend serious exhibitions. A majority of professionals stake their claim somewhere in between, characterizing museums and their exhibitions with metaphors like sanctuary, showcase, ritual, forum, and celebration.[2]

Profound social change has led museum professionals to an almost obsessive self-reflection: what value does the museum, as a civic institution, bring to the social mix? Where is our unique niche? When attempting to characterize and distinguish exhibitions, museum professionals naturally associate them with books and classrooms, comfortable with a resemblance to the academy. But they also, somewhat cautiously, compare exhibitions with television, motion pictures, and theme parks, acknowledging family ties to the world of entertainment. Like books and classrooms, exhibitions provide a framework for learning, and like good films, television, and books, exhibitions take us on revelatory journeys to destinations as close as neighborhood streets and as distant as the beginnings of life on Earth.

But books, films, and television are relatively uniform media that deliver an experience to physically passive individuals. Much more like the theme park, the multiformity of exhibitions ensures that museum visitors will interact in an almost endless variety of ways with the exhibits and with each other. In a contemporary exhibition of any discipline, it is not uncommon to find an introductory film; a collection of objects for viewing; elements to manipulate; labels and text panels to read (and sometimes even a reading area with books and comfortable chairs); photos, maps, and other graphics; a learning center with Internet stations and computers; embedded film and video loops; an "immersion environment"; and an adjacent gift shop. That same exhibition might house a quiet area for contemplation, a demonstration area for public programs, and even a conversation area for discussion with other visitors.

SCHOOL CHILDREN AND SCHOLARS, BABY-SITTERS AND PIPE FITTERS: WHO IS LISTENING?

Demographic and psychographic studies reveal that most museum visitors are well educated and value worthwhile leisure time experiences that focus on learning and discovery.[3] While this is not new information, it is astonishing how little it seems to affect staff perceptions that visitors are less informed and knowledgeable than they. A 1974 survey of museum professionals and their attitudes toward their primarily college-educated visitors revealed that visitors were considered to be "untutored" or the "laity," "as if some great and sacred gap separated museum worker and the educated middle class visitor."[4] To some extent, this attitude is still with us today, although it gets played out in different ways.

While exhibit creators insist that their exhibitions are designed for the general public, empty museum galleries are evidence of pedantic or esoteric intentions at work. More often than not, the creators of these exhibitions ignore public interests, assuming they are out of line with their own. With a bit of investigation, they could probably find common ground, providing more relevant experiences for visitors while retaining intellectual depth. Conversely, the characterization of the public as "Joe Six-pack," espoused by an increasing number of marketing advocates, results in cheerful exhibitions that attract visitors in the short run, but may erode the quality and depth of the experience that the visitors ultimately expect.

Research on how and why visitors use museums has played a major role in helping to turn exhibitions into more connected two-way conversations. Although formal visitor research in museums had its start in the 1930s, it did not really begin to take hold until the 1980s, prompted by a sincere desire on the part of some professionals to better understand the effects of their exhibitions on visitors and by expectations of funding agencies that museums be able to back up with real evidence their claims of audience impact. For those exhibitions claiming to make an educational difference, visitor research and evaluation provide the tools by which to measure at least some aspects of their educational and communicative success.

While the science of visitor research has become an increasingly sophisticated art in recent years, many art museums have been reluctant to embrace the practice, perhaps out of a fear that by talking to visitors, they will lose the high ground. As one arts administrator put it, "The public does not know. Their responses will be anecdotal, so why are we asking them? Why can't we use creative intelligence and take intellectual risk?" A curator explained, "If we pander to what the public wants, we'll lose the poetry and beauty."[5] Besides raising the question of just what "public" these professionals are envisioning, it is clear that their attitudes come from a confusion of visitor research and evaluation with a "give-'em-what-they-want" style of market research not unlike Russian artists' Komar and Melamid's nightmarish *People's Choice* paintings, which were based on the results of public-opinion polls about preferred elements in a work of art. (Visitor research, on the other hand, is a process of inquiry and discovery that can lead to new theories for practice, and evaluation helps us measure our own performance against our own goals.)[6]

Of course, with the increasing emphasis on articulating *easily achievable* research and evaluation goals, there is a danger in focusing goals too restrictively and reducing them to discrete subject nuggets that do not embody the potential depth of an experience or capture what is really important. In developing an exhibition for one of the nation's most significant natural history museums, for example, exhibit developers articulated the following goals: "Visitors will be able to name three different organisms on display in the hall, and a fact about each one," and "After attending this exhibition, visitors will be able to give one specific research scientist's name, research program name, or general area of research interest." Exhibitions resulting from such a process will suffer a dreary half-life. But good visitor research can lead to rich discoveries about visitor perceptions and the quality of their experiences and can encourage curators and designers to question their own assumptions about their intentions, their methods, and their audiences.

Exhibit creators focus a great deal of time on the ideas they are trying to convey and the forms their exhibitions will take, while visitor experiences are often inspired by more earthly constraints. Access to public transportation, ease of parking, and the availability of food services all have an influence on a person's decision to visit a museum. Once inside, a visitor may decide to attend a particular exhibition depending on its location within the museum, access to the restrooms, and other museum programs competing for attention. Exhibitions are places where people interact over time—an important factor in any exhibition experience—and people today never seem to have enough of it. On average, visitors usually spend less than 20 minutes in an exhibition, and a typical museum visit usually lasts from one-and-a-half to two-and-a-half hours.[7]

Visitors' experiences in an exhibition, over time and within a three-dimensional environment, will be as affected by the quality of air and the condition of their feet as the openness of their minds. And they are just as likely to have their most memorable encounter with another visitor as they are with an object or idea, no matter how intentional the presentation. Exhibitions provide a safe and interesting environment in which to bring people together, and the presence of people—whether they are visitors or staff—transforms a constructed exhibition setting into a dynamic public space. Staff explainers, docents, storytellers, artists, and actors enliven exhibitions, create context, and encourage people to interact with each other and with the exhibits. Even without staff, an exhibition designed to encourage face-to-face interaction and dialogue among visitors—often strangers—is arguably one of the most vital contributions museums can make to the social dynamics of our times.

THE CURATOR, THE EDUCATOR, THE DESIGNER, AND THE COMMITTEE: WHO IS TALKING?

Traditionally, most museum exhibitions have been a one-way conversation "designed around the cognitive order in the minds of curators."[8] Curators assembled the objects, established the conceptual framework, and wrote the exhibition "statement" and labels. Designers then packaged the curatorial material in a three-dimensional form, usually embodying the curator's vision. Afterwards, educators prepared interpretive materials that could help visitors make sense of the exhibition experience. While this process ensured that the depth of a curator's passion and knowledge made it out into the galleries, it was fraught with problems, particularly when the curator's true affections were aimed at other scholars, leaving a majority of visitors in the dark.

In the challenging times of the 1960s and 1970s, the curator as the voice of authority was, of course, one of the first to be challenged. In some circles, this was characterized as wresting content and interpretive control away from curators and putting it firmly in the hands of educators. In the encyclopedic tome *The Art Museum as Educator*, editor Barbara Newsom reflects on the tenor of the times:

> For both observers and administrators of art museums, the curatorial-educational encounter has become increasingly bothersome in the last decade. Joshua Taylor, director of the National Collection of Fine Arts, calls the relationship between the curatorial staff and "the activity of the increasingly aggressive education department" in art museums of the 1960s "a major problem," noting that it grew "with the orientation of museums more and more towards the public." Hilton Kramer, who covered the 1975 meetings of the American Association of Museums in Los Angeles for the *New York Times*, has found the division between curatorial and education departments that exists in most art museums "an endless source of conflict."[9]

Art museums were not the only arena for this debate. In 1963, Albert Parr, then senior scientist at the American Museum of Natural History, suggested:

> Whenever two entirely different types of skill and creative imagination have to be called upon to act together with equal authority, administrative problems arise, but it is, in my opinion, quite impossible to maintain high standards of exhibition quality by placing the functions of design under curatorial command. On the other hand, it seems quite possible to make the entire execution of the exhibition program an autonomous function within the museum's organization by including one or more educators or educational designers on the staff of the exhibition department itself.[10]

This proposition was a radical one for its time, with Parr offering the disclaimer that his idea was not meant as a general recommendation but only as a possible solution in cases when educational aims were given short shrift by curators.

In response to a need for more professional dialogue, museum educators formed the Museum Education Roundtable in 1969, and in 1971 the American Association of Museums created the President's Committee on Education to provide a more formal venue for the voice of the educator. Some museums actually reorganized their management structures to accommodate an increased emphasis on education in exhibit development. The New York State Museum, for example, formed a division of museum services in 1968 that was staffed with exhibit developers who came out of the school system, ultimately focusing exhibitions on educational goals.[11]

At the same time, Frank Oppenheimer at the Exploratorium in San Francisco was creating a new kind of museum altogether, born from the philosophies of self-directed learning, interactivity, and individual discovery that were growing out of a burgeoning educational reform movement. At the heart of the new Exploratorium—"A Museum of Science, Art, and Human Perception"—was a fundamental mission to empower the public and "bridge the gap between the experts and the laymen" with exhibits and experiments that visitors could activate on their own.[12] Michael Spock, at the Boston Children's Museum, was on a similar mission to create a highly dynamic, hands-on learning environment where visitors took center stage. While this populist attitude was essential in opening up museums to a whole new model of public embrace, it was often taken to the extreme, with sometimes unpleasant side effects. In the redesign of the Brooklyn Children's Museum (the oldest children's museum in the world), the museum's collection objects, at the heart of a rich and successful tradition of teaching about nature and culture, were, for the most part, warehoused in favor of "The Learning Environment," an interactive construction based on the laws of the physical world.

> We do not want to have precious items but we want to have respect for precious children. . . . In museums the experiential component of learning is usually not present. Elements which are denoted as being interesting by their inclusion in the museum are placed behind glass or in textual or pictorial display which deny active participation and discovery. . . . Without arbitrary elements in the learning environment, without textual guidelines to the experiences, without objects behind glass that tell children that the objects' survival is more important than their own, without static pictorial explanations, without static human information sources, without fixed expectations of informational absorption, we will try and provide a learning environment for the children who arrive at the BCM.[13]

Although the underlying goals of open exploration and self-directed learning were admirable, the wholesale break with the tradition of using collection objects—a previously successful strategy for the museum—led to a more homogenous, less diverse program that eventually slid into neglect. Spock and Oppenheimer, on the other hand, understood the complexity of the public exhibit experience and worked at blending a variety of media—objects, text, images, and interactive experiences—to create richly textured multiform environments.

While educators were unrelenting in their pressure to influence exhibition perspectives, museum audiences were also getting into the act. Democratization of museums, at the heart of the struggle, focused on access and representation. In 1969, the landmark exhibition *Harlem on My Mind* opened at the Metropolitan Museum of Art, igniting a series of conversations that has continued to this day. The exhibition attempted, through a new immersion-environment technique of super-graphics and multimedia, to tell the story of the history of blacks in Harlem, from the early days at the turn of the century through the civil-rights movement and the unrest of the 1960s. What was perhaps most troubling was that in the rush to create a new type of exhibition, the museum went too far. The exhibition was designed with techniques and curatorial methods unlike any other display at the Met, exoticizing an already disenfranchised African-American community. To make matters more contentious, this black history exhibition was organized by a white curator. In a *New York Times* article twenty-six years later, Michael Kimmelman reflects, "From the distance of a generation it seems clear what went wrong with 'Harlem on my Mind.' Coming as it did in the midst of racial crises, the show was a Molotov cocktail of then-radical exhibition techniques and reckless social politics."[14]

On the other side of the country, the Oakland Museum in California opened its doors in 1969 to pickets over the blatant lack of representation of many in the community whose taxes had paid for the new institution. The museum's response was to create a Special Exhibits and Education Department with its Guild for Cultural and Ethnic Affairs, which organized its own exhibitions developed by designers working cooperatively with representatives from the community. Exhibitions like *Black Pioneers: Scientists and Inventors, Mine Okubo: An American Experience*, and *Three Generations of Chinese: East and West* were added to the traditional mix of art, history, and natural science exhibitions. Because these designers and community participants worked primarily outside curatorial terrain, they were free to organize themselves and their exhibitions in unusual ways. Juxtaposing diverse and often controversial points of view within theatrical environments, these exhibitions were more celebratory and dialogic than most of the exhibitions of the time.

Taking their cues from the educators, exhibition designers began to speak out. Despite the experimental exhibition designs of artists like El Lissitzky (in the 1920s) and Herbert Bayer (in the 1930s–1950s), most museum exhibitions were formulaic in their design and installation. And most exhibition designers were expected to be stylists at best, and more likely tradesmen, simply necessary for the building of walls, the application of plaster, and the positioning of furniture. During the 1960s and 1970s, innovative designers like James Gardner in England and Charles and Ray Eames in the United States were creating some of the more interesting exhibitions in museums. In the Eamses' exhibitions, *Mathematica: A World of Numbers and Beyond* and *The World of Franklin and Jefferson*, the designers replaced the curator as auteur, creating conceptual frameworks for the exhibitions and developing the content as well as the design. The exhibitions contained objects, models, dense collages of graphics, some of the first history timelines, and, in the case of *Mathematica*, a collection of participatory exhibits.[15]

Although these holistic designers had a salutary effect on the way some exhibitions were developed in museums, for the most part designers were considered extraneous to the development of ideas in exhibitions. In 1981, designers and other exhibit-focused professionals organized the National Association for Museum Exhibition (NAME) in order to have a voice in the professional arena and promote more designer involvement in the conceptual development of exhibitions. A major impetus in organizing was to "promote excellence in the creation and installation of museum exhibitions; to provide a means of communicating among museum exhibition professionals; and to organize workshops and seminars on design and all other aspects of museum exhibition."[16]

As museums struggled to create more effective frameworks for exhibit development, models employed in other fields provided alternatives for coordinating all of the people involved. While the auteur approach of film directors (and art museum curators) worked for some, the collaborative spirit of ensemble theater better suited those museums that emphasized community involvement and democratic representation. Additionally, the sensibilities of cross-functional business and industrial design "teams" infused exhibition practice with a market-driven emphasis. In the 1980s, museums embraced the "team approach" to exhibition development as a way of improving exhibit quality and ultimately diversifying exhibition presentations. In the team model, an assortment of specialists (usually a content specialist or curator, a form specialist or designer, an audience specialist or educator, and sometimes a process specialist or project manager) work together to create exhibitions, with the assumption that an equal relationship among specialists would produce exhibitions more cohesive, accessible, and richly textured than the curator-driven model. While team proponents consistently pointed to mutual appreciation among team members as a significant outcome of the process, there was no discernible improvement in the quality of exhibitions developed by teams. And pseudo-teams often generated a committee-style process that dulled creative vision.

ACKNOWLEDGING THE DIALOGUE

By the late 1980s, exhibition creators had become much more sensitive to the subjective representations inherent in exhibition display. In 1988, the Smithsonian Institution and the Rockefeller Foundation organized "The Poetics and Politics of Representation," an international conference on interpretation in exhibitions, culminating in a book of essays from the museum administrators, curators, historians, anthropologists, and folklorists who attended.[17] One of the most interesting and clarifying essays was by Stephen Greenblatt, who identified "resonance" and "wonder" as two conceptual models in art exhibitions (although these models can also apply to natural history, history, and science exhibitions):

> By *resonance*, I mean the power of the displayed object to reach out beyond its formal boundaries to a larger world, to evoke in the viewer the complex, dynamic cultural forces from which it has emerged and for which it may be taken by a viewer to stand. By *wonder* I mean the power of the displayed object to stop the viewer in his or her tracks, to convey an arresting sense of uniqueness, to evoke an exalted attention.[18]

As an example, Greenblatt described the then newly installed collection of late-nineteenth-century French art at the Musée d'Orsay, which was designed to present a social history by juxtaposing furniture, decorative arts, photographs, and sculpture with masterpieces as well as with paintings by lesser-known artists:

> The museum remakes a remarkable group of highly individuated geniuses into engaged participants in a vital, immensely productive period in French cultural history. . . . But what has been sacrificed on the altar of cultural resonance is visual wonder centered on the aesthetic masterpiece. Attention is dispersed among a wide range of lesser objects . . . many of the greatest paintings have been demoted, as it were, to small spaces where it is difficult to view them adequately, as if the design of the museum were trying to assure the triumph of resonance over wonder. . . .[19]

Greenblatt articulates the polarization of conceptual intent taking place in the exhibition-development arena, and he goes on to make the case that the triumph of one over the other is unnecessary, that "almost every exhibition worth viewing has elements of both" and that the goal "should be to press beyond the limits of the models, cross boundaries, create strong hybrids. For both the poetics and politics of representation are most completely fulfilled in the experience of wonderful resonance and resonant wonder."[20]

Heeding a recurring call for more experimentation in exhibit design (something that NAME had been proposing for some time), the Smithsonian opened its Experimental Gallery in 1991. Its mission was to "present techniques [that] are pushing the edges of our museum experience and/or take chances in their choice of subject matter or viewpoint . . . to celebrate and encourage innovation in exhibition technique and . . . the exchange and development of management styles and peer relationships across cultural lines."[21] The mission of the gallery was commendable, and a few of its exhibitions truly "pushed the edges" of practice, although most were focused on cultural resonance and rarely strove for the hybridization of resonance and wonder that Greenblatt encouraged.

One of the more memorable exhibitions at the Experimental Gallery was *Etiquette of the Undercaste*, a mazelike interactive installation that attempted to replicate symbolically the experiences of loneliness and alienation. In this highly resonant "social simulation," developed by Antenna Theater, visitors would lie down on a mortuary slab and get pushed into the exhibition. Once inside, people were "reborn" and forced to follow a constricted path through a series of tight corridors and claustrophobic rooms constructed of flimsy cardboard, tape, string, and glue. The prerecorded audio provided a voices-in-the-head narrative that was designed to give visitors "a sense of helplessness when faced by a series of disasters, where every solution attempted only leads to more problems."[22] What was, perhaps, most significant about this exhibition was that it was not created by museum professionals at all, but by artistic directors of a theater company.

Indeed, some of the most interesting and thought-provoking exhibitions were being created by artists, who played a major role in creating a new genre of self-reflective exhibitions that challenged the traditional values and interpretations of exhibit planners and the conventional contexts of museum display. Ripe for deconstruction, the environmental settings employed by many history, science, and natural history museums and the cultural interpretations in art museums—particularly when people of one culture interpret cultural objects of another—led to landmark exhibitions like *Mining the Museum* by artist Fred Wilson at the Maryland Historical Society. Wilson juxtaposed startling combinations of collection objects that called into question notions of context, value, and point of view. In the case labeled *Metalwork 1793–1880*, for example, ornate silver vessels were displayed with a pair of slave shackles. Wilson reflects, "Quite possibly, both of these could have been made by the same hand. To my mind, how things are displayed in galleries and museums makes a huge difference in how one sees the world."[23] Wilson's more recent installation, *Speaking in Tongues: A Look at the Language of Display*, at the M. H. de Young Memorial Museum in San Francisco, contained a thought-provoking room, "Secret/Sacred," that was "closed to the public and accessible only to members of indigenous groups who have cultural affiliations with the objects included in the collection," highlighting some of the behind-the-scenes tensions of museum ownership and access to collections.

Artist David Wilson, on the other hand, went even further and created his own museum. After moving his provocative installations from space to space, he finally settled on Los Angeles as the permanent site for the Museum of Jurassic Technology in the late 1980s. Wilson employs the traditional display elements of a natural history museum: specimens stuffed by a taxidermist, curious objects in vitrines, scholarly text, environmental recreations, and even a visitor-activated orientation slide show and a small gift shop. What is unusual about this museum is that, while the voice of museum authority rings out, the elicitation of wonder comes from a dense environment of semi-real and hoax-like tableaux. Destabilized, visitors certainly come away from the experience questioning the fixed nature of "truth" and are perhaps more wary of the creator's intent.

Artists were not the only ones deconstructing exhibition curatorship and display. In the exhibition *ART/artifact*, organized by art historian Susan Vogel at the Center for African Art in New York City in 1988, four different display environments for African objects over the past century—a 1905 curiosity room, a natural history museum presentation complete with diorama, a reverential art museum presentation, and a contemporary art gallery installation—were elegantly inverted into a critique of exhibition practice. As Vogel described it, "The exhibition stressed that these different styles reflected differences in attitude and interpretation, and that the viewer was manipulated by all of them."[24]

The most recent and ambitious in this self-reflective genre is the Museum of Modern Art's exhibition *The Museum as Muse: Artists Reflect*, organized by curator Kynaston McShine. More than sixty artists explored the notion of "museum" in all of its manifestations, as arbiter of culture and solicitor of patronage, as storehouse and funhouse. From Charles Willson Peale's iconic painting *The Artist in His Museum* to Hiroshi Sugimoto's photographs of museum dioramas, from Lothar Baumgarten's *Unsettled Objects* to Claes Oldenburg's *Mouse Museum*, the exhibition eloquently captured all that is poignant and problematic about museums and the exhibition medium.[25]

While one might assume that these exhibitions would appeal primarily to exhibition practitioners, museum administrators, and critics, many have attracted larger-than-average public audiences. *Mining the Museum*, for example, was extended from its original run of six weeks to one year, and during that time, attendance at the Maryland Historical Society increased tremendously. At the same time, these exhibitions have contributed to changing attitudes within the profession, as the *Excellence and Equity* report from the American Association of Museums indicates:

> Concepts of the "meaning" of objects and the way museums communicate about them are changing. Objects are no longer viewed solely as things in themselves, but as things with complex contexts and associated value-laden significance. Each visitor supplies yet another context and another layer of meaning by bringing individual experiences and values to the encounter with objects in a museum setting. Changing interpretive approaches will have a strong impact on museum collections and the public's understanding of them.[26]

Of course, many of these changes have not gone uncontested. In a 1997 article in *The New Criterion* about changes at the Smithsonian Institution, for example, the author declared:

> The Institution has been transformed by a wholesale embrace of the worst elements of America's academic culture. The staples of cutting-edge academic "research"—smirking irony, cultural relativism, celebration of putative victims, facile attacks on science—are all thriving in America's premier museum and research complex, its showcase to itself and to the world. The changes at the Smithsonian are not unique to that institution. Museums across the country have rushed headlong into what may be called the "new museology," based on a mindless parroting of academic fads.[27]

While this kind of hostility tends to make reasonable people dismiss it as a rant, it should at least sound a note of caution and inspire a more critical look at the quality and depth of exhibition enterprises.

As museum professionals have attempted to assess and appraise the quality of exhibitions, there has been an increasing need for a forum for exhibition critique or review. Historically, exhibition reviews have focused on curator-based content concerns with little or no analysis of form and experience, or design-based aesthetic concerns with no consideration of content and experience. Rarely were museum exhibitions held to the holistic scrutiny necessary to create a theoretical base and actually improve the practice. Since 1990, critique sessions at the American Association of Museums' annual meetings have attracted standing-room-only audiences, suggesting that exhibition professionals are hungry for a more substantial dialogue about the quality of museum exhibitions.

Exhibitions featured in these critiques have ranged from newly installed African galleries at the Seattle Art Museum to the Sixth Floor Museum, a historical display on John F. Kennedy's assassination in Dallas, to the Rock and Roll Hall of Fame and Museum in Cleveland. Critiques have focused on organizational clarity of exhibit concepts and elements, the ability of the exhibition environment to welcome and accommodate visitors while reinforcing themes and goals, the appropriateness of different media, and the overall effectiveness of communication between the exhibition and visitors.

An increasing body of academic literature on museum practice has been published over the last five years, much of it highly theoretical and not well-grounded in practice. While some of the discourse provides exhibition creators with a postmodern sociopolitical view from outside the field, one wonders how much the work will actually inform exhibition practice. On the other hand, museum curators, designers, and evaluators from the Standing Professional Committees Council of the American Association of Museums have recently developed "The Standards for Museum Exhibitions and Indicators of Excellence," and while there is always a danger in interpreting standards in too literal or concrete a fashion, they at least provide a more holistic baseline for exhibition practice and a window onto the current values and aspirations of the field.

Most exhibit creators agree that organizing a good museum exhibition requires the passion, intuition, scholarship, and expertise of a wide range of people, and more professionals are becoming multilingual (or fluent) in the languages of environmental psychology, aesthetics, learning theory, conceptual and spatial design, and interpretation. They are essentially "expert generalists," able to synthesize the variety of disciplines that inform the exhibit-development process—to recognize the importance of accurate and meaningful content, to comprehend and be able to manipulate the dynamics at play in the three-dimensional environment, and to be sensitive to the expectations and interests of a diverse audience. They are first and foremost communicators, dedicated to sustaining the relationships and enriching the conversations between exhibition and visitor.[28]

OF DIFFERENT PERSUASIONS

All exhibitions are three-dimensional experiences, compositions of images, objects, and architecture. But they are as varied as the subjects they examine. Art, history, natural science, and technology exhibitions may require different planning, design, and pedagogical considerations. Exhibitions designed for a number of locations will form around different constraints from those of exhibitions planned for one space, and exhibits that demonstrate the effects of natural phenomena may have different goals and require different development and design processes from those of object-oriented or topical exhibitions. But while museum professionals often view their exhibitions from within their own disciplinary boundaries, the current trend in exhibition development to provide a variety of visitor experiences is shifting exhibitions into multidisciplinary territory. Creators of art, history, and science exhibitions—traditionally strangers—would be well served to communicate with and learn from each other, since their collaborations should result in richer exhibit experiences for visitors.

In the recent *Memory* exhibition at the Exploratorium, exhibit creators intentionally combined scientific specimens, psychological models, and installations by artists with historical artifacts and interactive science exhibits in an effort to capture the notion of memory in its broadest sense. While each of these elements required different conceptual and display approaches in its development, when experienced by visitors the individual disciplines simply became pieces in the larger puzzle. Additionally, some exhibits were designed so that visitors created their own exhibits by adding their memories to the mix.

Temporary exhibitions have been the traditional testing ground for new exhibition philosophies and techniques, since they are usually open for only weeks or months and require lower development, design, and installation budgets than the permanent installations, which are often designed to last five to ten years (or longer). Blockbusters in the service of the box office are the exception, often lavished with big budgets and intense attention. "Big" is the key word here, and many professionals argue that too big a percentage of museum resources is spent on blockbusters, to the neglect of other programs and permanent exhibitions. In art and science museums alike, administrators dream of blockbusters as "cash cows," drawing huge crowds and generating a frenzy of activity. And when these dreams turn into reality, visitors will often find themselves spending more time in lines than in the actual exhibition.

While temporary exhibitions can focus more immediately on a theme of current interest, like the lighting of the Statue of Liberty, commemorations of the quincentennial, or reflections on the millennium, for example, permanent exhibitions—the core museum experiences—must remain relevant during the entire time they are open to the public, able to weather trendy viewpoints and fickle fashions. Additionally, permanent exhibitions require enough material to attract repeat visitors and provide them with opportunities for new discoveries on each visit. This means that while experiments on risky new techniques, interpretation, and subject matter, if attempted at all, find their home in temporary exhibition halls, the permanent galleries tend to prefer more traditional inhabitants.

PAYING THE PIPER

Each year, more museums open their doors while the money available for them does not increase proportionately. Since exhibitions are among the most expensive of enterprises in any museum, their costs come under greater scrutiny as administrators attempt to stretch limited financial resources. There is competition for funding from corporations and foundations, and funders often expect high visibility and high attendance in exchange for financial support. While some corporations, through their philanthropic foundations, still support museum exhibitions without any strings attached, funding today more often comes from corporate marketing departments, and it may be accompanied by the expectation of special treatment, such as exclusive use of particular products, direct access to exhibit audiences in order to advertise or distribute products and services, and, in some instances, influence in editorial decision-making.

The fund-raising practice of naming exhibits, facilities, and even museums after donors—euphemistically called "naming opportunities"—has long provided museums with an avenue for generating revenue. While generally a benign and gracious method of recognizing philanthropists, it can create identity and credibility problems when used indiscriminately. Perhaps the most extreme recent example is the Taco Bell Discovery Science Center, presenting "science Southern California Style . . . where science becomes a full-body contact sport."[29]

Limited resources have compelled museum professionals to improve efficiency, collaborate on a wide range of projects, and share the effort and expense of costly exhibition development, particularly for traveling exhibitions, interactive multimedia, and educational programs. More exhibits are available off the shelf, when one museum undertakes the costly research and development and then sells the plans or copies of exhibit units to other institutions. The advantage of using cloned exhibits is that they have been market-tested with visitors and are known to be durable and popular, but museum administrators must weigh the economic appeal of prepackaged programs against the risk of losing the distinct institutional voice essential in maintaining a clear public identity.

Shrinking pools of donated funds bring an increased reliance on "the gate" (admissions revenues) and other sources of earned income, shifting institutional emphasis even more towards the market. But broad public access may be jeopardized in the process. While museum exhibitions are being designed to provide for audiences with a wide variety of interests, learning styles, physical capabilities, and cultural and social orientations, they are also expected to increase gate revenues. Attendance fees at some museums may run as high as fifteen dollars per person, and, increasingly, museums are charging additional fees for entrance to special temporary exhibitions. In some museums, exhibition budgets are balanced against projected attendance revenues, and if revenues fall below projections, budgets are cut accordingly. For those museums attempting to attract new audiences, this makes life even more complicated.

At the same time that exhibition budgets are coming under greater scrutiny, museum marketing budgets are growing, in some cases dramatically. While advertising clearly keeps information about museum exhibitions in the public eye, too often museum administrators confuse marketing with audience development. Audience attraction is not necessarily audience development, and, in some cases, attracting audiences in the short run may actually work against building a visitorship that returns over and over again. The "spikes" in attendance for temporary exhibitions often translate into the unbearable crowds most of us like to avoid. (It is ironic to note that while some museum professionals are convinced that "spikes" in attendance are essential to the health of the museum, they also often prefer after-hours and special tours of other museums to avoid the crowds.) Building a sustained audience means building participation in decision-making and meaning-making, activities that must take place in many ways over an extended period of time.

EMBRACING THE TENSIONS

Our times seem to be framed by an increasingly complex and layered dialectic of privilege, expert knowledge, and prescriptive meaning-making on the one hand, and access, popular culture, and the negotiation of meaning on the other. The public spectacle of exhibitions makes them a particularly dynamic stage for this unfolding dialogue.

The current trend to create "public-program" and "guest-services" divisions, in which exhibitions and educational programs are combined and the research and curatorial functions are often separated out, has educators replacing curators and science educators replacing scientists. While this reorganization has been essential in making exhibitions more relevant, accessible, and "user-friendly" for a wider range of visitors, educators, in shifting away from the pedantic style of curators, have come up with their own style problems. Didactic, highly filtered "teaching tools" fill exhibition halls, and cognitive learning goals articulated with the reductionism of a multiple-choice test have begun to drive the exhibition-development process. Where museums once displayed a multiplicity of objects in their galleries, exhibit developers now favor the technique of selective display, with objects carefully selected to drive home a particular educational message. The hearts of these "audience advocates" might well be in the right place, but their exhibitions often suffer from an unnecessarily simplistic tenor.

As exhibitions pull away from the curator's grip, the momentum may have swung us too far in the other direction. The effects of splitting off the researchers and content creators from the public presenters have, in some instances, forced museum exhibitions to lose their essential relationship to the pursuit of inquiry and the world of mind in favor of a superficial and simulated experience much more connected to the world of mindlessness. This is particularly the case in science museums, in which elements like simulator rides and giant robotic insects are becoming de rigueur. While some of these techniques, if used intelligently, could contribute to the culture of learning that museums have traditionally embraced, for the most part the demeaning phrase "lowest common denominator" applies. In the traveling exhibition *Ice Age Mammals*, for example, a robotic woolly rhino and saber-toothed tiger were displayed alongside non-Ice-Age hominids, tossing scientific accuracy right out the window. Surprisingly, staff scientists at host museums either were ignored or shrugged off the exhibition as superficial entertainment, since the exhibition made its rounds to many of the nation's natural history museums. Defining "entertainment" with the mind-set of a scholar or "education" with the mind-set of a theme-park operator does a great disservice to the complexity and sophistication of our audiences. As Marshall McLuhan was fond of observing, "Anyone who does not understand the relationship between entertainment and education doesn't know much about either."

Many people, when recalling childhood museum memories, describe strange things in jars, sculptures larger than life, and chicken eggs hatching every few minutes. These unusual and amazing things have the powerful capacity to surprise, fascinate, and inspire people—something that may be overlooked in the rush to prove the educational and marketing values of exhibitions (values that can translate into funding). Some would argue that in shifting our emphasis from temple (a place of contemplation or wonder) to forum (a place for negotiation and experimentation), we have lost the essential qualities that make museums unique.

But museums are both temple *and* forum. Just as Greenblatt urged us to strive towards a hybridization of resonance and wonder, we—like genetics researchers—will need to select this element for one characteristic and that for another. Focusing entirely on either market or mission engenders a static sameness that no longer suits our relative world. It may be difficult to create dynamic channels for dialogue between those with expert knowledge and the visiting public (those with common knowledge), but it is also more interesting. By embracing the tensions inherent in a dialogue, we will better understand how each form of knowledge informs the other, and, most importantly, we will become better able to articulate our issues *in common*.

Like other cultural and educational media, exhibitions are about people communicating with each other. How this conversation takes place, and who is responsible for conversing with whom, will depend on museum missions and the visions of exhibit creators, administrators, visitors, and their constituencies. No matter how the dialogue is approached—a dialogue as diverse as lectures and stories, pronouncements and prayers—it is inevitable that exhibitions will be judged by the societies of which they are a part. Museums have long been places of inspiration, conversation, investigation, and celebration—places that feed our natural curiosity about the world. Our most important work lies in more fully articulating the quality and tenor of the dialogues museum exhibitions could be having with visitors.

NOTES

1. Kenneth Hudson, *Museums of Influence* (Cambridge: Cambridge University Press, 1987), 23.

2. Although Duncan Cameron first juxtaposed the notions of temple and forum in the early 1970s, museum professionals still struggle with these dynamics today. See Duncan Cameron, "The Museum, A Temple or the Forum," *Curator* XIV (1) (1971): 11–24; for a description of one museum's metaphorical scope, see George MacDonald and Stephen Alsford, *A Museum for the Global Village* (Hull, Quebec: Canadian Museum of Civilization, 1989).

3. John Falk, "Visitors: Toward a Better Understanding of Why People Go to Museums," *Museum News* 77 (2) (1999): 38–40.

4. Barbara Y. Newsom and Adele Z. Silver, eds., *The Art Museum as Educator* (Berkeley: University of California Press, 1978), 77.

5. In conversation with the author.

6. Not all art museums are adverse to visitor research, and several, including the Cleveland Museum of Art, the Hirshhorn, the Denver Art Museum, and the Minneapolis Institute of Arts, have embraced it as an essential element of museum practice on some level.

7. For more information on time spent in museums and exhibitions, see Beverly Serrell, *Paying Attention: Visitors and Museum Exhibitions* (Washington, D.C.: American Association of Museums, 1998).

8. Sheldon Annis, "The Museum as Staging Ground for Symbolic Action," *Museum 151* 38 (3) (1986): 170.

9. Newsom and Silver, eds., *The Art Museum as Educator*, 37.

10. Albert E. Parr, "Curatorial Functions in Education," *Curator* VI (4) (1963): 290.

11. Robert Sullivan, in conversation with the author, March 1993.

12. Frank Oppenheimer, "A Rationale for a Science Museum," *Curator* XI (3) (1968): 206–209.

13. Edwin Schlossberg, *The Learning Environment for the Brooklyn Children's Museum* (Brooklyn, N.Y.: Brooklyn Institute of Arts and Sciences, 1975), 24.

14. Michael Kimmelman, "Culture and Race: Still on America's Mind," *New York Times,* 19 November 1995, p. 1, sec. 2.

15. John Neuhart, Marilyn Neuhart, and Ray Eames, *Eames Design: The Work of the Office of Charles and Ray Eames* (New York: Harry N. Abrams, Inc., 1989), 254–259. The exhibition is still on view today at the Boston Museum of Science.

16. "Exhibition Group Formed," *Exhibitionist*, October 1981.

17. Ivan Karp and Steven D. Lavine, eds., *Exhibiting Cultures: The Poetics and Politics of Museum Display* (Washington, D.C.: Smithsonian Institution Press, 1991).

18. Stephen Greenblatt, "Resonance and Wonder," in Karp and Lavine, *Exhibiting Cultures*, 42.

19. Ibid., 54.

20. Ibid.

21. From a Smithsonian Institution press release, December 1990.

22. From the exhibition catalog, February 1992.

23. Ivan Karp and Fred Wilson, "Constructing the Spectacle of Culture in Museums," in Reesa Greenberg, Bruce W. Ferguson, and Sandy Nairne, eds., *Thinking about Exhibitions* (London: Routledge, 1996), 256.

24. Susan Vogel, "Always True to the Object, in Our Fashion," in Karp and Lavine, *Exhibiting Cultures*, 198.

25. The exhibition was on display at the Museum of Modern Art in New York from March 14 through June 1, 1999. For more information, see the catalog: Kynaston McShine, *The Museum as Muse: Artists Reflect* (New York: The Museum of Modern Art, 1999).

26. American Association of Museums, *Excellence and Equity: Education and the Public Dimension of Museums* (Washington, D.C.: American Association of Museums, 1992), 11–12.

27. Heather MacDonald, "Revisionist Lust: The Smithsonian Today," *The New Criterion* 15 (9) (1997): 17–31.

28. Kathleen McLean, *Planning for People in Museum Exhibitions* (Washington, D.C.: Association of Science-Technology Centers, 1993), 37.

29. From an invitation to the president's opening reception, 9 December 1998.

17

Changing Practices of Interpretation

Lisa C. Roberts

The use of interpretation was inaugurated early in museum history by curators, particularly those devoted to the public welfare.[1] Employed sporadically throughout the nineteenth century, interpretive devices like labels, brochures, and lectures became a permanent fixture in museum halls by World War I. Initially, their content was largely information-based: dates, places, and facts were the norm. Some curators, however, began experimenting with new ways of presenting collections that, they hoped, would more effectively reach visitors. The most innovative of these figures was John Cotton Dana, director of the Newark Museum. Contemptuous of what he called "gazing museums," Dana hesitated to call the Newark a "museum," preferring instead "institute of visual instruction."[2] His many special exhibitions stretched the boundaries of conventional display by featuring, for example, applied and industrial arts, textile and clay products manufactured by local firms, immigrants' handicrafts, and "inexpensive articles of good design." Dana hoped that these exhibits would draw new visitors like housewives, workers, immigrants, and others who might have a natural interest in the objects on display.

More important to Dana than what was displayed, however, was how it was used. He established many now common practices to increase the museum's usefulness: for example, loaning objects to school classrooms, shops, and hospitals; creating a teacher-training course at local colleges; opening a "junior museum" for children only; establishing branch museums in local libraries.

Dana was not the only such innovator. Others came, interestingly enough, from the art-museum establishment, which then even as now had a strong conservative strain. Many art museum officials were moved by wider social failings that they hoped their institutions might help to redress. Others, concerned about

---

Lisa C. Roberts is Director of Conservatories for the Chicago Park District and is the former manager of public programming at the Chicago Public Gardens. "Changing Practices of Interpretation" is an excerpt from her 1997 book *From Knowledge to Narrative: Educators and the Changing Museum.* It is reprinted here by permission of the Smithsonian Institution Press.

America's weakness in design, felt that museums could have a hand in elevating patrons' taste, thereby educating not only the producers of fine and applied arts but also their consumers, thus creating a demand and model for quality work.

Not lost on museum officials was the more subtle character-building that exposure to good art could induce. Historian Terry Zeller has cited numerous examples of ways museums sought to refine citizens and to raise their standards of beauty and taste.[3] The Toledo Museum of Art, for example, was an early pioneer, engineering a number of civic improvement projects and preaching "the gospel of simplicity and truth." The museum exhibited model homes and landscaping scenes and mounted two period rooms, one "furnished inexpensively and in good taste," and "the other room exhibiting as many as possible of the most common offenses against the laws of truth and beauty."[4] Other museums involved in the beautification movement included the Art Institute of Chicago, through the Better Homes Institute of its Extension Department; the Boston Museum of Fine Arts; and the Milwaukee Art Institute.

Other innovators included the Rochester Museum of Arts and Sciences' Arthur Parker, who labored to make museums active service centers in their communities. Like Dana, Parker mounted exhibits with broad popular appeal and initiated services intended to break down museums' psychological and intellectual barriers. To him, the measure of museums was not their wealth and collections but the values they disseminated. Activities like loaning materials to schools, sponsoring programs for the unemployed, and offering programs to promote patriotism during World War II were just a few of the ways Parker sought to expand museums' community-service role.

In sum, many genuine efforts were made to make collections accessible to viewers before the arrival of professional educators.[5] Most of those efforts, however, whatever their express motives, sought to inculcate the public with specific aesthetic values. Naturally, they were the values of the propertied class who chose and controlled the culture enshrined in museums. Ideology, then, was as much a part of the mission as cultural uplift. As T. J. Jackson Lears has observed,

> Many middle- and upper-class Americans felt that if only the proper educational balance could be struck, immigrants could be assimilated, angry workers calmed, and an incipient leisure class returned to productive life.[6] Like the museum proprietors of the founding republic, then, many early twentieth-century curators saw in museums the possibility of achieving social and cultural uplift for their public. They, too, were guided by specific, usually middle- to upper-class, ideas of what was good and what was beautiful.

As innovative and successful as some of these early approaches to reaching visitors appeared to be, they were not the norm; most occurred in small pockets throughout the nation, usually in metropolitan museums. Many innovators still faced resistance from colleagues who had differing philosophies about museums' public role, and few were furthering their cause in a broader, professional sense. As Paul Rea noted in his study on the problems and needs of U.S. museums:

> [While] a great diversity of educational methods has been developed and a high order of results has been achieved . . . few methods of juvenile museum education have become universal. There seems to be more interest in devising new small-scale experiments than in the more prosaic work of extending to the whole field such methods as have been found most generally effective.[7]

Still, the foundation was clearly laid for museums' involvement in a variety of public activities. The next stage would be ushered in with the newly emerging museum educators.

As museum education evolved into an autonomous profession, what affect did educators have on the interpretation of collections? Insofar as educators have lobbied for visitors' interests in practically everything museums do, including—and especially—interpretation, their influence has been substantial. It has been most significant in three areas: first, in the mere presence of interpretation; second, in the language used to interpret; and third, in the content of the messages. Educators' impact in these three areas occurred roughly chronologically, although there was considerable overlap.

The first issue—advocating the presence of interpretation—has been an ongoing cause for educators. Providing interpretation was the single most important thing museums could do to engage visitors with their collections. Of course, by the time educators came onto the scene in the 1930s and 1940s, many museums had interpretive and educational programs in place. Many more, however, remained underdeveloped with respect to their public functions; and even those with established programs were subjected to the backlash of conflicting professional opinion.

Art museums, for example, may have been the seat of many innovative programs, but not everyone supported their innovations. Many curators opposed educational activities that appeared to interfere with the direct contemplation of the object. In their eyes, interpretation demeaned art by turning it from an aesthetic phenomenon into a social or historical construct. The following statement by John Walker of the National Gallery of Art exemplifies this position:

> A work of art is not a specimen, not primarily an historical document, but a source of pleasure, analogous to, say, a musical composition. The major purpose of the National Gallery is to allow each painting, piece of sculpture, or other object of art to communicate to the spectator, with as little interference as possible, the enjoyment it was designed to give.[8]

While critiques such as this did not oppose the educational value of art collections, they did oppose the provision of aids to that education. It was precisely this sort of attitude that educators sought to change. In his study about the educational values to be derived from museums, T. R. Adam observed:

> To someone outside the world of art criticism, there must seem an element of almost mystic faith in this belief in the power of great paintings to communicate abstract ideas of beauty to the uninformed spectator. . . . When background is lacking—where there is no knowledge of what the artist is attempting to say in terms of time, place, or social meaning—the resulting impression is confused and is likely to be painful as pleasurable.[9]

Despite such views, many art museum staff have persisted to advocate unadulterated contemplation as the proper means to understanding. Anything else alters, simplifies, and trivializes not only the art on view but also the experience of looking. Such sentiments were given eloquent voice by Walter Pach. In *The American Art Museum*, he argued that museums could not (and therefore should not) reach the public without lowering their standards:

> In the confusion of values amid which the world is struggling, the man in the street may be so misled by the blare of loud-speakers and the dazzle of fierce lights that his chances of achieving good judgment and good taste are progressively endangered. Much of what he gets over the radio, at the movie house, and from posters, magazine covers, and the like is making his "street" always more unhealthy. In that case, the museum cannot go halfway in meeting him.[10]

In other museums, the issue of scholarship continued to be raised periodically as the proper and primary focus of museum activities. In his 1932 study, Paul Rea admitted that "except in a few more favored or braver museums, scholarship has probably suffered from the public museum movement."[11] Additionally, Herbert J. Spinden in a 1940 *Museum News* article, "The Curators in the New Public Museum," observed:

> It seems that in some institutions curators have little to say about new specimens and little opportunity to develop their scholarship. The great American enigma is why men who have achieved a reputation in some special field are hired because of that reputation and then given no opportunity to do the kind of work for which they are best fitted.[12]

Despite such opposition, educators continued to press forward. Grace Fisher Ramsey's 1938 study of educational work in museums recorded dozens of examples of educational activity in museums nationwide: gallery talks, discussion groups, teacher training, school visits, museum clubs for children, extension work, and programs for disabled people.[13] In 1942 the AAM appointed a Committee on Education to review the social and educational problems facing museums; the result was *The Museum as a Social Instrument*.[14] While Ramsey's and the AAM's studies clearly supported museums' educational potential, they cautioned readers against jumping to conclusions about the effectiveness of museum education.[15] A 1952 study conducted at Chicago's Museum of Science and Industry echoed their concerns: just because visitors look does not mean that they learn.[16]

Still, educational activity in museums proceeded unabated. By 1960, 79 percent of museums were reportedly offering some kind of organized educational program (up from 15 percent in 1932);[17] and from 1952 to 1962 the gross attendance to museums more than doubled.[18] While impossible to establish a direct association between the expansion of educational offerings and the growth in attendance owing to the former, it is not a far stretch to suppose the two may be linked.

It would seem that museum education had finally taken root in the institution. Yet, despite the widespread allocation of staff and budgets to educational services, education remained a minor institutional mission. Throughout the 1960s and well into the 1970s, educators worked with minuscule budgets in substandard office space; they were rarely involved in exhibit development, and they had little or no voice in museum affairs. Curators still reigned supreme; they kept alive old concerns about the treatment of collections, while educators continued to advocate the inclusion of interpretation that was directed toward visitors, not scholars. In the early 1960s, for example, curator Wilcomb Washburn of the Smithsonian Institution lamented the changes wrought by

> professional educationists, who consider education a professional skill too abstruse to be left in the hands of the scholars, and who, typically, substituted functions and techniques for purpose and content.[19]

Echoing his concerns, Daniel Catton Rich, director of the Worcester Art Museum, exhorted:

> Though from time to time we will be advised to arrange our collections by the latest department store techniques, we must resist. The Kress stores and the Kress collections are quite separate things. Never must we be persuaded to become the supermarkets of culture.[20]

Keeping the debate alive during his tenure at Cleveland's Museum of Art, the irascible director Sherman Lee declared in 1971: "I part company with the concept of a museum as an instrument of mass education."[21] Meanwhile, director Thomas Leavitt of the Museum of American Textile History pushed for the placement of educators under curatorial supervision: "Left to its own devices, a museum education department is like a nervous system detached from the cerebrum, like the chicken's conduct after its head has been cut off."[22]

Fortunately for educators, the AAM did not share these views. In 1973 it approved the creation of a standing professional committee on education to serve as the profession's mouthpiece and advocate. By the end of the decade, educators finally began to achieve parity within the museum institution. Pressure was mounting on museums to address a variety of public issues, such as assisting ailing school systems, diversifying audiences, undertaking community outreach, and increasing attendance to generate revenue and to demonstrate public service. These factors, combined with the growing professionalization of museum-education practice, began to make educators more valuable to administrators. Consequently, many began participating on exhibit-development and marketing teams. A few managed to break the glass ceiling with appointments to senior administrative positions.

As educators became more involved in decision- and policy-making, different issues came to the fore. No longer was it the case that they had to push for the inclusion of interpretation. With the possible exception of art museums, where "unadulterated contemplation" remained in high favor, by the 1980s interpretation was an accepted institutional function. However, the nature of that interpretation became a contested issue. Hence, the second area in which educators affected interpretation was language.

If interpretation was to be effective, it had to be expressed in a manner that was both comprehensible and engaging. More often than not, it was neither. Interpretive writing was typically the purview of curators who had the expertise to know what to say but whose ability to say it often left something to be desired. As a result, labels and other interpretive materials often bore a voice that was technical, verbose, and eminently curatorial. "Rules" for effective labels had been put forth ever since Goode's time.[23] But it was the rare curator who practiced what the rules preached. Not surprisingly, few visitors had the wherewithal to absorb label text.

It was not until visitor-studies procedures became a more regular museum practice and interpretation was subject to evaluation that it became clear just how ineffective exhibit labels had often been. Some suffered the pitfalls of poor writing or design; others failed on the grounds of being simply uninteresting.[24] It is probably no coincidence that the bulk of these studies began to appear when the climate in museums was becoming more friendly toward educators and their interests. Museum officials were finally beginning to get the message: interpretation was about communication; and effective communication required bridging the world of the expert and the world of the layperson with language that was intelligible to the latter without being a misrepresentation of the former.

Achieving this balance between accuracy and intelligibility resulted in the development of new writing styles, many of which were reinventions of old rules. Many museums, for example, began to adopt a prose style that was short, simple, and direct. Others, notably the Monterey Bay Aquarium, began experimenting with the organization of information, producing a label hierarchy that distinguished between general and specialized messages. Label writer Judy Rand set a new standard and form of speech at the aquarium through the use of humor, colloquialism, questions, and second-person voice.[25] While many museum professionals balked at the sacrifice or oversimplification of information, evaluations of these new labels showed visitors engaging in such behaviors as reading aloud, pointing to objects, and sharing information. More importantly, visitors understood and were able to reiterate exhibit messages.[26]

Elsewhere, visitor researches studied various narrative strategies that contributed to label effectiveness. At the Brookfield Zoo, for example, Beverly Serrell found that labels which included explicit visual references to what was on display held attention longer than labels lacking such references.[27] Steve Bitgood, while working at the Anniston Museum of Natural History, found that dividing a single label's text into several discrete chunks of information increased reading time significantly.[28] Separate studies conducted by Bitgood and other researchers confirmed that the inclusion of questions and directives in labels helped to focus visitors' attention and to increase their time spent reading.[29]

Of course, communication extends beyond the words on the wall. Messages are equally borne by the visual presentation, from interpretive graphics to display elements. With the growing acceptance of educative ways of thinking, researchers were conducting more studies on how the design of interpretive devices could improve visitor learning. With the incorporation of interactive elements into labels, along with improvements in legibility and attractiveness, exhibit halls began to receive a long-needed facelift. Standards and guidelines were established regarding type size, placement, figure-to-background contrast, and other design issues. Consequently, interpretive graphics were employed more boldly—both to illustrate messages and to provide atmosphere. Artifacts increasingly shared the stage with elaborate set dressings designed to establish a broader interpretive context. Significantly, these activities marked the growing participation of education and design personnel in exhibit development decisions.

Not everyone welcomed these changes. Critics raised anew questions about the proper treatment and selection of artifacts. When the Field Museum appointed "exhibit developers" from outside the curatorial division to head its exhibit teams, anthropology curator John Terrell had this response:

> [B]ecause curators can't remember how little museum visitors know—and so expect much more from visitors than they reasonably should—from now on, museum educators are to be the "choosers," the lucky ones to decide what visitors may and may not see in museums.

What? The powers-that-be honestly believe exhibitions can be mounted without curators? Preposterous. But, sadly, we have no ruby slippers in our collections at Field Museum to tap together to return to better times.[30]

Terrell is not alone in his views. As educators have become more involved in exhibit and interpretive functions, once the domain of curators, more curators have begun to speak out against what some have called the "Disney-fication" of museum halls.[31]

Educators, however, were to leave their most radical mark in their third area of influence—the content of messages. No matter how engaging the interpretation of, for example, a Cambrian fossil, the question remained: Do visitors even care that another set of creatures once roamed the earth? Indeed, why should they care? The issue of language in museum-exhibit text has to do with not just presentation but also context, which has as much to do with the visitors as with the object. In other words, visitors' interest and attention is determined not by an object's inherent appeal but its relevance to their own framework of knowledge and experience. It was but a small step from visitor-centered language to visitor-centered content, and label writers experimented accordingly.

The Denver Art Museum, for example, proposed for labels a new "experience-driven paradigm" in contrast to the traditional information-driven paradigm. Based on their research about how novices view art, the new labels focused on what the visitors wanted to derive from the art instead of what the museum wanted to impart to visitors.[32] Making a human connection, for example, was found to be important to art novices. "Human-connection labels" focused on people—artists, patrons, users, and viewers—and employed such strategies as relaying first-person testimony and referring to the viewers' cultural context.[33]

Other museums also began employing front-end evaluation as a part of exhibit planning to determine visitors' interests in and knowledge about a particular topic. For example, when Minda Borun was education director at the Franklin Institute of Science, she conducted extensive interviews with visitors about their notions of gravity. Visitors' input helped exhibit developers to frame the subject in a way that was sensitive to visitors' preconceptions.[34]

As the climate in museums warmed to visitor input and feedback, exhibit developers also began to seek advice on exhibit content from outside advisory groups that represented various communities—for example, cultural groups, neighborhood residents, and teachers. This cooperative spirit marked an important step in making the production of knowledge and exhibits a shared process, open to everyone who might have a stake.

Finally, a handful of curators who were sensitive to the changing academic tide began to incorporate overlooked perspectives into museum exhibitions. Historians, for example, changed the face of Colonial Williamsburg by bringing to public view interpretations that deal with slavery and the African American experience that had previously been excluded. More exhibits began to consider long-neglected versions of history and culture, thereby giving voice to the perspectives of laborers,[35] women,[36] and other underrepresented groups.[37]

Exhibit content would receive its greatest makeover, however, with the entry of other noncuratorial, nonscientific meanings into the interpretive domain. As studies continued to reveal the vast range of interests, expectations, and experiences that visitors brought to museums, the question of relevance took on new dimensions: for example, who was to say that what was significant about an object to a visitor was any less valid or significant than what was significant to a curator? If a visitor was moved by a crystal decanter that reminded her of a family heirloom, did it matter that she did not learn something further about the Waterford line that had produced it?[38] Museum educator Patterson Williams explained:

> I would argue that the essence of a museum's public function is to enable the visitor to use museum objects to his own greatest advantage. To call for museum literacy, therefore, is to call for a theory of instruction focused on teaching visitors how to have personally significant experiences with objects. . . . The goal [of such a theory of instruction] must be an experience on the part of the visitor which *the visitor values*; therefore the significance, if any, of the encounter will be determined by the visitor's value system, not by our own.[39] [emphasis mine]

It became clear that the task of interpretation was first and foremost a task of connection: getting visitors to connect to what they see, on whatever terms that might be. At issue was the legitimization of personal experience as a source of meaning *different from but no less valid than* curatorial knowledge. Advocates of this view began experimenting with interpretation that encouraged visitors to look inside themselves.

Characteristic of this approach was a shift in focus from the object to the process of looking at it. For some, the goal was to impart not facts, but tools—skills of perception and interpretation. At the Brooklyn Children's Museum, for example, an exhibit entitled "The Mystery of Things" introduces children to the process by which identifications and meanings are assigned to objects. Based on Csikszentmihalyi's work on the meaning of things,[40] the exhibit presents dozens of unfamiliar objects from around the world; interpretation guides visitors to use their senses and make associations to identify the objects. Of special interest is the fact that the exhibit is self-reflective, so that its messages also apply to museums and how they look at and decipher objects.[41]

Other museums have experimented with ways of evoking and validating visitors' personal responses to museum pieces. The Denver Art Museum, for example, developed a two-columned label for some of their paintings that reads on one side, "If you like this painting, is it because . . . ", and on the other, "If you don't like this painting, is it because . . ." A series of statements on each side helped visitors sort out their reactions to the paintings.

Similarly, in one of the earliest of such examples, the "Game Room" at San Francisco Fine Arts Museums made important use of the idea of visitor-centered meanings. Designed as the art world's answer to the participatory-learning stations so popular at science museums, the room actually achieved a far more radical result. Its four "games" elicited visitors' personal judgments and opinions by challenging one of curators' most sacred cows: the idea of the masterpiece. In "Guess the Masterpiece," for example, visitors chose their favorite painting and played a computer program that helped them to characterize what they found appealing about it. "The Masterpiece Comparison Game" allowed visitors to compare their assessments of various masterpieces with that of curators.[42]

Another example of museums' experimenting with visitors' responses can be found at the Art Gallery of Ontario, where Doug Worts has been experimenting with different ways of stimulating visitors' personal responses to paintings. For example, "Share Your Reaction" cards, dispensed in some two dozen locations throughout the museum, have encouraged visitors to reflect upon their experiences with the art through writing or drawing. "Explore a Painting in Depth" uses audio to model different ways of engaging with an artwork. Most unusual is a reflective imaging exercise that has guided visitors into a reverie with a particular painting and has helped them to explore the personal reactions, feelings, and memories that it evokes. Both of these methods have elicited some rather dramatic and moving responses.[43]

Again, the significance of these approaches does not lie exclusively in their novelty, because no one denies the power of art to trigger an emotional response. But explanations of art's meaning and significance have always rested on external historical and aesthetic standards. The significance of these experimental approaches for eliciting visitors' response lies precisely in their insistence on internal, personal standards of meaning that are legitimate and that can stand on equal footing with traditional external standards.

Over the course of a few years, educators' interpretive role has thus shifted dramatically from representing the curatorial view to experimenting with new languages and methods for representing that view, and finally to authorizing alternative views altogether. Educators' immediate goal may have been to develop innovative ways of making collections intelligible and interesting; but in so doing they found themselves challenging not only traditional ways of speaking about objects but also the very basis and authority for speaking about them at all. At stake was nothing less than the conditions for knowledge by which museums have traditionally abided. Exactly what that means—for museums, for exhibitions, and for the nature of the interpretive task—is the subject of the next section.

IMPLICATIONS FOR MUSEUMS' INTERPRETIVE ROLE

By promoting interpretations that reflect visitors' worlds and experiences, museum educators have brought the debate about canon into the institution. Questions about what collections represent and who controls their representation parallel closely wider disputes over how knowledge should be defined. As advocates for visitors and their perspectives, museum educators have served as the catalysts of the wider shift to a more context-based definition of knowledge. If museums today are more attentive to displayed objects' contexts, and if they employ advisory groups and other mechanisms to solicit input from those with a special relationship to or knowledge about their collections, then it is largely because educative modes of thinking have pervaded the way exhibits are conceived and developed.

Although educators did not generate the new scholarship and interpretations that have allowed them to make exhibits more inclusive, they are to be credited with taking an activist role in insisting that such interpretations be considered. Their efforts, as a result, go beyond the educational task of imparting understanding, and have had far-reaching political and epistemological ramifications. Three of these ramifications are examined below.

First, the inclusion of alternative ways of interpreting museum collections is open acknowledgment that there is more than one way of knowing. What is so revolutionary, however, is not the fact itself but the legitimacy conferred on those new knowledges by their mere presence in the museum. Ironically, it is that very authority to legitimate that their presence stands to challenge. Museums have traditionally been tremendously authoritative institutions. The history of their development, the architecture of their presence, and the gravity of their responsibility as stewards over the nation's cultural heritage have all bestowed on the institution authority over matters of knowledge. Inherent to this authority is the long scholarly legacy out of which museums grew.

So to permit, even to encourage, the inclusion of alternative interpretations is to acknowledge other modes of knowledge besides that on which museums were built. While practices such as the use of popular linguistic forms and nonscholarly contexts of meaning were promoted as aids to understanding, in fact they achieved a far more radical result. As the literary critics have so ably demonstrated, meaning is intimately connected to both the context in which it arises and the language with which it is crafted. To refer to an object in a different manner is to present not just an alternative way of communicating about it but also an alternative way of conceiving its meaning. The difference may seem insignificant, but it can have tremendous impact. For example, compare these three ways of labeling a gorilla specimen, all of which—until a 1992 renovation—could be found in different exhibits at Chicago's Field Museum of Natural History: "Western Lowland Gorilla"; "Man-like Ape"; and "'Bushman' lived in Chicago most of his life." The first presents viewers with a biological specimen; the second, with an animal depicted in anthropocentric terms; and the third, with an individual who has not only a name but also a history.

Second, curators no longer wield the same authority over museums' interpretive function. Educators now have a hand in that function, although their role is still often confined to presentation: making interpretation available and intelligible. Presentation, however, has turned out be more than mere window dressing. As the above example shows, the manner of presentation affects not just the effectiveness of the communication but also the particular meaning it bears. Furthermore, as educators have become more knowledgeable about visitors' interests and needs, they have campaigned more strongly for interpretations whose content is more reflective of visitors' worlds.

Although curators might hold authority over interpretations stemming from their technical and scholarly knowledge, that does not necessarily qualify them to speak to meanings that are based on nonscholarly criteria of knowing. As visitors' representatives, educators are better versed in the diversity of languages and backgrounds that define visitors' ways of knowing. As a result, they are also more sensitive to the multifaceted nature of the interpretive enterprise. After all, there is no one "visitor-centered" way of interpreting something because museums do not have a single, homogenous audience. One of educators' biggest challenges has been to deal with the fact that even visitor-friendly interpretations only reach those visitors to whom those interpretations are indeed friendly. One solution to reaching a diverse population has been to hand the interpretive process itself over to visitors, so that they may discover for themselves the meanings that speak to them. By providing guides to questioning and looking, visitors are empowered to look for themselves from their own particular vantage point.[44]

Just as the work of white, Euro-American men may not be representative of other Americans' experience, so too may the specialized perspectives of curators never hold meaning for many visitors. By acknowledging such disjunctions and promoting alternative interpretations, educators have begun to shift the balance of power. On the surface, this shift might appear to be primarily territorial: educators now share some of the same interpretive functions that were once the domain of the curators. But it runs far deeper, touching basic assumptions about what museums are and do by authorizing other criteria of knowing and legitimizing other knowledge producers. Not just educators but also visitors themselves may now have a hand in the meaning-making process.

Third, the very nature of museums' exhibit function has been altered. Once a seemingly straightforward matter of displaying collections, exhibition can now be viewed as an eminently interpretive endeavor: not just that the information exhibits present is subject to multiple interpretations, but the very act of presentation is fundamentally interpretive.

As a practice, exhibits were first developed for the sole purpose of presenting collections to public view. Over time, they were embellished in ways that were thought to improve that view: draped fabrics, painted backdrops, illustrative props and graphics were incorporated into exhibits. Such elements served to frame an object, providing not only the intended ambience but also shaping the object's apparent meaning. Literary critics have shown how messages may be borne by nonverbal texts. The props surrounding an object may thus carry a message in their own right by creating a visual context that shapes the way an object is seen and thus comprehended.[45]

Exhibits then are not simply displays; exhibits are systems of signs in and of themselves. They express messages about objects and the worlds from which they came, as well as about the institutions from which those messages emanate. The interpretive act does not end with a decision about what an object shall say, because the arrival at that very decision entails a translation of particular objects and their contexts into language and hence meaning.

The very act of creating an exhibit is thus subject to the same conditions and limitations that apply to the production of knowledge. The function of exhibits is, therefore, no longer driven strictly by the collections they exist to showcase so much as by what is done with them. In other words, many exhibits are now driven by messages for which the collections, when they exist, serve as a vehicle, since an object's presented meaning is ultimately shaped by decisions about its interpretation and display. Once again, it is the literary critics who have demonstrated how signs shape that to which they point. Messages no longer emerge from an object's "inherent" meaning. Messages express meanings that people create.

The exhibition enterprise may be fundamentally interpretive; but museums have been slow to share that fact with the viewing public. Despite the gains that have been made in making collections more accessible, few museums share the decision-making process through which their interpretations are derived. Even though curators may acknowledge the interpretive basis of their work, they generally continue to present those interpretations authoritatively and anonymously. Visitors, as a result, remain uninformed about even the most basic assumptions and rationales behind the messages they are given.

From an educational standpoint, this is the worst kind of teaching: spoon-feeding information without the learner's involvement. More seriously, it preserves the institution's authority to dictate "truth" by denying visitors access to the assumptions and logic on which their messages stand. What is problematic is not that those messages are invalid, but that without an awareness of either the factors or the fact of knowledge production, visitors lack the tools to engage in even the most rudimentary critique of what they are being told. Museums may present various views and knowledges; but their role in doing so remains invisible and thus protected.

A few art exhibits, however, have tackled the issue of how display is an eminently interpretive act. For art curators, exhibition is a primary medium of scholarship. Since debates about quality and value (the art "canon," as it were) are quite lively in the art world, it is to be expected that one should find exhibitions created to address them.[46] Some of the most provocative of such exhibitions have been mounted at the Center for African Art (now the Museum for African Art) in New York. "Art/artifact," for example, displayed a series of African artifacts in four different settings: a nineteenth-century curiosity cabinet, a "typical" art museum, a natural history diorama, and a contemporary gallery. This extraordinary exhibit thus sought to demonstrate how objects' meanings are linked to what we do with them, and thus to how we choose to see them.[47] "Perspectives: Angles on African Art" interpreted African ritual objects through labels written by a variety of individuals both inside and outside of the museum profession. Each person wrote about the feelings and thoughts that some piece evoked in him or her. This manner of interpretation introduced visitors not only to the variety of meanings these objects might hold but also to the idea that the "knowledge" presented about them consisted of an interpretation.[48] Other art exhibits designed to reflect upon themselves have appeared at such esteemed institutions as the Whitney Museum of American Art, Downtown, and the Parrish Art Museum.[49]

Since exhibition is an integral part of the history and nature of Western art, it is not surprising that art itself has also been created to explore the nature of museums and exhibitions. Furthermore, artwork, unlike other museum objects, can and has expressed a relentless self-consciousness about what it is and how it is experienced. Much twentieth-century artwork, in particular, addresses its own institutionalization by dealers, historians, and curators. Some of this work deals specifically with what it means to be enclosed by a museum, by challenging either the museum's scripture (what artwork goes in), its audience (the elitist knowledge they require), or its edge (that there is an inner and an outer that are different).[50] A handful of artists have tackled the issue head-on by creating fictionalized museums and museum exhibits whose very fabrication points out the myriad ways that museums shape objects' meaning through the imposition of such elements as frame, story, and context.[51] Some artists have been so fortunate, and some museums so bold, as to curate an exhibition using an institution's permanent collection to critique conventional notions of interpretation and display.[52]

Outside the art world, however, there are few examples of exhibits that address the basis for their own messages.[53] Without good models of what such interpretations might even look like, it is not surprising that exhibit developers have been slow to incorporate messages that reflect upon themselves.

One of the few noteworthy non-art examples appeared in the late 1980s at Chicago's Field Museum of Natural History in response to protests about a particular interpretation. Tucked away in one of the Native American galleries, a diorama of the Pawnee Morning Star ceremony showed a young woman about to be sacrificed. Naked and bound, she was surrounded by men, one with arrow poised, ready to shoot. On a bulletin board next to the exhibit, a letter was posted from a visitor protesting the depiction of images of violence against women in a respectable, public institution. Also posted was a response from the Pawnee Tribal Council defending the museum's decision not to hide history from public view, however unpleasant it may be. Visitors were invited to comment, and they did—in profusion. The bulletin board was dotted with index cards on which people scribbled their thoughts about everything from women's rights to the historical enterprise to the nature of museums' responsibilities.[54]

Implicit in this approach was an effort to involve visitors in the decision-making process. As visitors learned basic information about how the Pawnee practiced this ceremony, they were also given the means to consider the wider context in which this information is represented and to judge it for themselves. For art museum educator Danielle Rice, this is not just good pedagogy; it is an ethical responsibility:

> [The educator's task is] to bridge the gaps between the value systems of the scholars who collect and exhibit art and those of the individual visitors who come to the museum to look at, and perhaps to learn about art. . . . It is the educator's ethical responsibility to represent, from within the institution, the position that art is only valuable because of ideas conceived by human beings about what constitutes value. . . . In showing that it is people who structure and control institutions, rather than the other way around, and in helping people to analyze the decisions by which aesthetic and other value judgments are made, we empower people to act with greater awareness.[55]

Likewise, it is the educator's ethical responsibility to ensure that history, anthropology, and even science are presented in a manner that reflects people's ideas about what constitutes history, anthropology, and science.

How do we really know what we know? The question is readily addressed by scholars. We would do well to apply it to museums, for museums present not just straight information, but information that is interpreted and communicated in a particular manner based on particular assumptions and decisions.

By omitting any mention about the decisions behind the determination of an object's meaning, museums exclude visitors not only from an awareness that knowledge is something that is produced but also from the possibility that they themselves may participate in its production. Inasmuch as museum educators represent visitors' perspectives, they have paved the way for interpretations that both address alternative contexts of meaning and reflect upon publicly—to visitors—the basis for and decisions behind selecting those contexts. Thus stated, the work of interpretation becomes an act of empowerment, because it provides visitors with both the knowledge and the consent to engage in critical dialogue about the messages museums present.

NOTES

The notes in this article vary from the original in that they have been renumbered sequentially beginning at one. In the original they begin at 13 and run through 67.

1. So short has been their existence that when museums educators looked back for evidence of museum education, they found that early efforts were carried out by the then dominant personnel: curators and directors. As a result, many of the profession's founding fathers such as Dana and Goode were, in fact, curators by profession.

2. John Cotton Dana, *The New Museum,* vol. I (Woodstock, Vt.: Elm Tree Press, 1917), 19.

3. Terry Zeller, "The Historical and Philosophical Foundations of Art Museum Education in American," *Museum Education: History, Theory, and Practice,* ed. Nancy Berry and Susan Mayer (Reston, Va.: National Art Education Association, 1989), 10–89.

4. "The City Beautiful Campaign," *Museum News* 22 (October 1914), quoted in Zeller, "Art Museum Education," 21.

5. For a more complete sense of the scope and nature of these efforts, see John Cotton Dana's list of fifty-one "Helpful Museums" (for reference by those who may be starting a museum), many of which include educational activities. Dana, *New Museum,* 42–47.

6. T. J. Jackson Lears, *No Place of Grace: Antimodernism and the Transformation of American Culture, 1880–1920* (New York: Pantheon Books, 1981), 78.

7. Paul Marshall Rea, *The Museum and the Community with a Chapter on the Library and the Community: A Study of Social Laws and Consequences* (Lancaster, Pa.: Science Press, 1932), 31.

8. John Walker, "The Genesis of the National Gallery of Art," *Art in America* 32, no. 4 (1944), 167.

9. T. R. Adam, *The Civic Value of Museums* (New York: American Association for Adult Education, 1937), 26.

10. Walter Pach, *The American Art Museum* (New York: Pantheon Books, 1948), 229–30.

11. Rea, *The Museum and the Community,* 29–30.

12. Herbert J. Spinden, "The Curators in the New Public Museum," *Museum News* 18, no. 6 (1940), 7.

13. Grace Fisher Ramsey, *Educational Work in Museums of the United States: Development, Methods, and Trends* (New York: H. W. Wilson Company, 1938).

14. Theodore Low, *The Museum as a Social Instrument: A Study Undertaken for the Committee on Education of the American Association of Museums* (New York: Metropolitan Museum of Art, 1942).

15. Ramsey, *Educational Work in Museums of the United States,* 43, 217, 252–54; Low, *The Museum as a Social Instrument,* 30.

16. Lucy Nielsen Nedzel, "The Motivation and Education of the General Public through Museum Experiences" (Ph.D. diss., University of Chicago, 1952).

17. Joseph Allen Patterson, "Points of View," *Museum News* 40, no. 1 (1961), 3.

18. American Association of Museums, *A Statistical Survey of Museums in the United States and Canada* (Washington, D.C.: American Association of Museums, 1965), 16.

19. Wilcomb Washburn, "Scholarship and the Museum," *Museum News* 40, no. 2 (1961), 17–18.

20. Daniel Catton Rich, "Museums at the Crossroads," *Museum News* 39, no. 6 (1961), 81.

21. Grace Glueck, "The Ivory Tower versus the Discotheque," *Art in America* 59 (1971), 81.

22. Thomas W. Leavitt and Dennis O'Toole, "Two Views on Museum Education," *Museum News* 64, no. 2 (1985), 27.

23. George Brown Goode, "Museum-History and Museums of History," *Papers of the American Historical Association* 3, ed. Herbert Baxter Adams (New York: G. P. Putnam's Sons, 1888), 262–64; Louise Connolly, *The Educational Value of Museums* (Newark, N.J.: Newark (Museum Association, 1914), 34–36; William L. Bryant, "Experiments with Museum Labels," *Museum Work* 6, no. 4 (1923), 114–20; Charles H. Blake, "Sizes of Type for Museum Labels," *Museum News* 22, no. 15 (1945), 8; George Weiner, "Why Johnny Can't Read Labels," *Curator* 6, no. 2 (1963), 143–56; Beverly Serrell, *Making Exhibit Labels: A Step-by-Step Guide* (Nashville: American Association for State and Local History, 1983); and Beverly Serrell, *Exhibit Labels: An Interpretative Approach* (Walnut Creek: Calif.: AltaMira Press, 1996).

24. See, for example, Chandler Screven, "The Effectiveness of Guidance Devices on Visitor Learning," *Curator* 18, no. 3 (1975), 219–43; Minda Borun and Maryanne Miller, *What's in a Name? A Study of the Effectiveness of Explanatory Labels in a Science Museum* (Philadelphia: Franklin Institute, 1980); and Beverly Serrell, "Zoo Label Study at Brookfield Zoo," *International Zoo Yearbook* 21 (1981), 54–61. For a summary of the results of some two dozen studies on the effects of label length, placement, type size, and graphics, see *Visitor Behavior* 4, no. 3 (1989), 8–13.

25. Examples of her approach and a statement of the philosophy behind it can be found in Judy Rand, "Fish Stories That Hook Readers: Interpretive Graphics at the Monterey Bay Aquarium," in *American Association of Zoological Parks and Aquaria 1985 Annual Conference Proceedings* (Columbus, Ohio: American Association of Zoological Parks and Aquaria, 1985), 404–13.

26. Judy Rand, personal communication, 6 October 1995.

27. Beverly Serrell, "Zoo Label Study."

28. Stephen Bitgood et al., *Effect of Label Characteristics on Visitor Behavior,* technical report no. 86–55 (Jacksonville, Ala.: Center for Social Design, 1986).

29. Steve Bitgood et al., *The Effects of Instructional Signs on Museum Visitors,* technical report no. 86-70 (Jacksonville, Ala.: Center for Social Design, 1986); K. D. Hirschi and Chandler Screven, "Effects of Questions on Visitor Reading Behavior," *ILVS Review* 1 (1988): 50–61; Robert Farrington et al., "Tyrannosaurus Label Study," *Current Trends in Audience Research and Evaluation* (Washington, D.C.: American Association of Museums Evaluation and Research Committee, 1989), 6–12.

30. John Terrell, "Disneyland and the Future of Museum Anthropology," *American Anthropologist* 93, no. 1 (1991), 149.

31. Peter Cannon-Brookes and Caroline Cannon-Brookes, eds., "Editorial: False Gods," *International Journal of Museum Management and Curatorship* 8, no. 1 (1989), 5–9; Lynda Murdin, "'Director's Gone Disney' Claims South Kensington Union," *Museums Journal* 90, no. 6 (1990): 8–9; and "Editorial: A Major Museum Goes 'Populist,'" *Nature* 345 (1990), 1–2.

32. Marlene Chambers, "Improving the Esthetic Experience for Art Novices: A New Paradigm for Interpretive Labels," *Program Sourcebook* (Washington, D.C.: American Association of Museums, 1988), 213–27.

33. Patterson B. Williams, "Making the Human Connection: A Label Experiment," *The Sourcebook* (Washington, D.C.: American Association of Museums, 1989), 177–91.

34. Minda Borun, "Naive Notions and the Design of Science Museum Exhibits," *Proceedings of the 1989 Visitor Studies Conference,* ed. Stephen Bitgood et al. (Jacksonville, Ala.: Center for Social Design, 1989), 158–62. Results of the complete "Naive Knowledge" study appear in Borun et al., "Naive Knowledge and the Design of Science Museum Exhibits," *Curator* 36, no. 3 (1993), 201–19.

35. "The Way We Worked: Baltimore's People, Port, and Industries," Baltimore Museum of Industry, Baltimore, 1980; "Worker's World," Hagley Museum, Wilmington, Del., 1981; "Homestead," Historical Society of Western Pennsylvania, Pittsburgh, 1989; "By Hammer and Hand," South Street Seaport Museum, New York, 1990.

36. "Dress for Greater Freedom," Oakland Museum, Oakland, Calif., 1972: "Eleanor Roosevelt: First Person Singular," Smithsonian Institution Traveling Exhibition Service, Washington, D.C., 1984; and "Men and Women: A History of Costume, Gender, and Power," National Museum of American History, Washington, D.C., 1989.

37. "Pawnee Earth Lodge," Field Museum of Natural History, Chicago, 1977; "Essence of Indian Art," Asian Art Museum of San Francisco, San Francisco, 1984; "The Way to Independence: Memories of a Hidatsa Indian Family, 1840–1920," Minnesota Historical

Society, St. Paul, 1987; "Field to Factory: Afro-American Migration, 1915–1940," National Museum of American History, Washington, D.C., 1989; and "Chiefly Feasts: The Enduring Kwakiutl Potlach," American Museum of National History, New York, 1991–1992.

38. In his study of visitors to the Steinhart Aquarium in San Francisco, Sam Taylor found that the exhibits were frequently used for discussion of past experiences and memories. In fact, reinforcement of previously held knowledge or experience was found to be a more frequent use of exhibits than the acquisition of new knowledge. Samuel M. Taylor, "Understanding Processes of Informal Education: A Naturalistic Study of Visitors to a Public Aquarium" (Ph.D. diss., University of California, Berkeley, 1986).

39. Patterson Williams, "Object Contemplation: Theory into Practice," *Journal of Museum Education* 9, no. 1 (1984), 10–14, 22.

40. Mihaly Csikszentmihalyi and Eugene Rochberg-Halton, *The Meaning of Things: Domestic Symbols and the Self* (Cambridge, England: Cambridge University Press, 1981).

41. "The Mystery of Things," Brooklyn Children's Museum, 1988. For more on fostering looking skills, see Danielle Rice, "Making Sense of Art," *Journal of the Washington Academy of Science* 76, no. 2 (1986), 106–14.

42. For a more complete description of the Game Room, see Kathleen Berrin, "Activating the Art Museum Experience," *Museums News* 56, no. 4 (1978), 42–45.

43. Douglas Worts, "Extending the Frame: Forging a New Partnership with the Public," *Art in Museums* 5, New Research in Museum Studies, An International Series, ed. Susan Pearce (London and Atlantic Highlands, N.J.: Athlone, 1995), 164–91.

44. Of course, even guides to questioning carry an implicit perspective by attempting to elicit another perspective—that of the visitor.

45. It is not just the inclusion of props that makes an exhibit "interpretive." Their exclusion itself constitutes a statement and a context that shapes the way an object is seen. When the Art Institute of Chicago places a kachina doll on a bare white pedestal under a Plexiglas cube, the viewer's eye is drawn to formal characteristics like color and shape. This is a different sight from that at the Field Museum of Natural History, where kachina dolls are placed in a diorama that depicts a Hopi apartment. Hanging on either side of a hearth in which a woman is baking cornbread, the kachinas prompt viewers to consider their purpose and use.

46. It is worth remembering that the revolutionary director John Cotton Dana himself raised these questions about seventy years ago. Dana proposed displaying an ordinary drinking glass half filled with water and labeled thus:

   Is it a work of art? The glass surely is; the water is a natural product, like a landscape; look carefully at line and mass, at the gleams and reflections on the glass, on the water within, on the water's surface, on the color gathered from the textile—and perhaps what you are looking at will cease, for a moment, to be merely water in a cheap tumbler, and will come to be an exquisitely beautiful thing. If you thus see it, is it then a work of art?

John Cotton Dana, "In a Changing World Should Museums Change?" *Papers and Reports Read at the Twenty-first Annual Meeting of the American Association of Museums* (Washington, D.C.: American Association of Museums, 1926), 21.

47. "Art/artifact," Center for African Art, New York, 1988.

48. "Perspectives: Angles on African Art," Center for African Art, New York, 1987.

49. "The Desire of the Museum," Whitney Museum of American Art, New York, 1989; "A Museum Looks at Itself: Mapping Past and Present at the Parrish Art Museum, 1897–1992," Parrish Art Museum, Southampton, N.Y., 1992.

50. Examples include Marcel Duchamp, Claes Oldenburg, George Segal, Robert Smithson, and Andy Warhol. Forms such as earthworks, graffiti, and performance art seek to challenge traditional definitions of art and proper modes of viewing it.

51. Marcel Duchamp, "Boîte-en-valise," portable museum, 1936; Robert Fillliou, "La Galerie Légitime," gallery in a hat, Paris, 1961; Marcel Broodthaers, "Musée d'Art Moderne," artist's home, Brussels, 1968; "Museum," Städtische Kunsthalle Düsseldorf, Düsseldorf, 1972; "Décors," several versions mounted in major European cities, 1974–75; Claes Oldenburg, "Mouse Museum," Neue Galerie, Kassel, 1972; Jean-François Lyotard, "Les Immatériaux," Beaubourg, Paris, 1985; David Wilson, "The Museum of Jurassic Technology," Los Angeles, 1988; various artists, "Theatergarden Bestiarium," Institute for Contemporary Art, P. S. 1 Museum, Long Island City, N.Y., 1989; Fred Wilson, "The Other Museum," White Columns, New York City, 1990; Danny Tisdale, "The Black Museum," INTAR Gallery, New York City, 1990; and Guillermo-Gómaz Peña and Coco Fusco, "The Year of the White Bear," Mexican Fine Arts Center Museum, Field Museum of Natural History, Chicago, 1993.

52. Simon Grennan and Christopher Sperandio, "At Home with the Collection," Lakeview Museum of Art, Peoria, Ill., 1992; Joseph Kosuth, "The Brooklyn Museum Collection: The Play of the Unmentionable," Brooklyn Museum, Brooklyn, 1990; Fred Wilson, "Mining the Museum: An Installation by Fred Wilson," The Contemporary and the Maryland Historical Society, Baltimore, 1992–1993; and Wilson, "The Museum: Mixed Metaphors," Seattle Art Museum, Seattle, 1993.

53. Again, for every generalization, there exist exceptions. For a more complete overview of self-reflective exhibitions and artworks, see Lisa G. Corrin, "Mining the Museum: Artists Look at Museums, Museums Look at Themselves," in *Mining the Museum: An Installation by Fred Wilson,* ed. Lisa G. Corrin (New York: New Press, Baltimore: Contemporary, 1994).

54. At the end of 1990, the Field Museum renovated the exhibit, correcting some of its inaccuracies (for example, making the sacrificial victim a thirteen-year-old girl instead of a mature woman) and adding more background information. The bulletin board was

removed and new labels that explained the controversy were installed. A few of the visitor comments have since been printed and are available at the museum's Native American Resource Center.

55. Danielle Rice, "On the Ethics of Museum Education," *Museum News* 65, no. 5 (1987), 17–19.

18

Making Meaning Together: Lessons from the Field of American History

Lois H. Silverman

Over the last few years; the field of American history has witnessed an explosion of interest in how contemporary individuals understand and use the past. In 1989, the leading scholarly publication in the field, the *Journal of American History*, devoted a special issue exclusively to the topic of history and memory;[1] prestigious universities have held conferences with titles like "History and Memory" and "How We Learn History: The Past, the Classroom, and Society"; and in 1990, a group consisting primarily of historians founded the Center on History-Making in America, an interdisciplinary initiative at Indiana University that promotes and conducts research on people and the past. While those who call themselves "public historians" have long been interested in citizens' encounters with history, much of the recent movement has gone beyond professionals theorizing about the experiences of others to include gathering and analyzing empirical data such as the attitudes and behaviors of contemporary Americans. These data have allowed scholars to document the range of ways in which people make meaning of the past and explore the workings of memory, narrative, and historical consciousness. Fueling this trend is some serious "reflective practice" in what has been one of the most authoritarian of academic disciplines. The results are a growing concern among some historians with the audiences of history and an increasing desire to see the discipline become more democratic, relevant, and meaningful to a wide range of citizens. What's this got to do with museum education?

Those who work in history museums, historic sites, and historic houses may already be familiar with this movement, given its potential impact on the interpretation

Lois H. Silverman is a museum consultant specializing in visitor experience and human needs. She was formerly associate professor and director of the Center on History-Making in America at Indiana University in Bloomington, Indiana. "Making Meaning Together: Lessons from the Field of American History" appeared in the *Journal of Museum Education* (Vol. 18, No. 3, Fall 1993, pp. 7–11). It is reprinted here with permission of Museum Education Roundtable, all rights reserved. For more information contact: Museum Education Roundtable, 621 Pennsylvania Ave., SE, Washington, DC, 20003; or www.mer-online.org or email info@mer-online.org.

of history. Since the concept of the past is an integral component of many other disciplines, including art, archeology, and science, the importance of this work is clearly
not limited to institutions with "history" in their titles. Indeed, a growing understanding of how people make sense of the past is likely to influence the interpretation
of art, archeology, and other fields. Yet the connection of this work to museum education is at once more subtle and more complex than the issue of subject matter. The
movement afoot in the theory and practice of history is a mirror of quite similar—
and fundamental—issues and challenges facing museology today: What is the nature
of interpretation? Who makes meaning? How? How might we move beyond the dichotomy that separates "professionals" from "laypersons" to more beneficial and inclusive ways if interacting? How can we revitalize the field and its institutions so that
they might serve as tools for all people? Given new understandings of interpretation
and of audiences, what new or revised skills might we need to accomplish these goals?
As a museum educator, audience researcher, and director of the Center on History-
Making in America, I have been amazed to see firsthand how similar are the challenges that face history and museology today—and many other fields of knowledge as
well. In the next few pages, I'd like to offer an overview of recent developments in
American history and illustrate how similar application of the meaning-making paradigm and related ideas to museum education can help us to create more inclusive
and democratic museums—model institutions for a functional and healthy multicultural society. In short, here are some lessons from history for museum education in
the present.

THE PARADIGM OF MEANING-MAKING:
RECALLING THE NATURE OF "INTERPRETATION"

As this issue of the *Journal of Museum Education* illustrates, the American academy is
clearly in the midst of a powerful paradigm shift to embrace the notion of "meaning-
making." This paradigm seems to have emerged as a response to and means for dealing with the country's changing cultural landscape and the fact that multiple and
often conflicting points of view indeed exist and clash in our society. In the field of
communications, many scholars now believe that communication does not occur in
a linear fashion, with one active party conveying information to a passive other, but
that communication is a process in which meaning is jointly and actively constructed
through interaction. Developed further in the work known as cultural studies, this
notion has surfaced in a variety of other fields as well. While differences do exist in approaches to the notion, most share the growing belief that people who are communicating negotiate power and authority in the making of meaning.

This paradigm has profound implications for history. Long considered by many
to involve the expert retrieval of objective truth, recovered through documentable
evidence by highly trained individuals, the meaning-making paradigm offers a
powerful reminder that history, when viewed as a process, is an *interpretation*—a

story or perspective that is crafted, albeit with expert documentation, by certain people for certain ends. And even though the historian might communicate his or her particular interpretation with authority, another person who encounters it may yet make very different meaning of it from that which the historian intended. Thus while historians may continue to be the most recognized and valued presenters of the past in our society, their products are interpretations, which can then be interpreted further by those who read them. It seems increasingly clear that professionals and citizens "share authority" for constructing meaning of the past.[2] It is no wonder that growing numbers of historians are working to understand the ways that audiences think and interact with history.

Much of the same may be said for museum educators, for, like historians, the act of "interpretation" is our raison d'être. And like our fellow "keepers of culture," we seem to have lost sight of the meaning of the term "interpretation" as a viewpoint or particular understanding and have defined it instead in our minds and in the minds of many visitors as immutable truth, operating as if the results of our work can and must be experienced in just one way. Like historians, museum educators do not need to abandon the role of purveyors of excellent interpretation. The paradigm of meaning-making simply opens the door for museology, as well as history, to consider some desperately needed expansion.

WHO DOES IT AND HOW? EVERYPERSON HIS OR HER OWN HISTORIAN

At the core of the recent movement in history is the revival and advancement of a concept expressed eloquently, accessibly, but unfortunately in gendered language by Carl Becker in 1932: "Everyman his own historian." Arguing that all history is essentially the same, whether it is about military figures or everyday life, Becker shows that all people regularly use knowledge of the past to various ends in the present and in the process exercise research skills that are similar to those of the "expert" historian.

> If the essence of history is the memory of things said and done, then it is obvious that every normal person, Mr. Everyman, knows some history. . . . Mr. Everyman, as well as you and I, remembers things said and done and must do so at every waking moment.

Becker also recognized the social nature of the meaning-making process. History is

> an imaginative creation, a personal possession which each one of us, Mr. Everyman, fashions out of his individual experience, adapts to his practical or emotional needs, and adorns as well as may be to suit his aesthetic tastes. In thus creating his own history, there are, nevertheless, limits which Mr. Everyman may not overstep without incurring penalties. The limits are set by his fellows. If Mr. Everyman lived quite alone in an unconditioned world he would be free to affirm and hold in memory any ideal series of events that struck his fancy, and thus create a world of semblance quite in

accord with the heart's desire. Unfortunately, Mr. Everyman has to live in a world of Browns and Smiths . . . which has taught him the expediency of recalling certain events with much exactness.[3]

Building on these ideas in recent work, David Thelen and others have coined and promoted the term "history-making" to refer to all the different ways humans interpret or make meaning of the past, from "reminiscence beside a fireplace or restoration of a piece of furniture"[4] to the writing of books and the production of exhibits and documentaries. The concept of "history-making" joins the notion of history as process with the meaning-making paradigm. Two important effects of this concept are to further Becker's effort to democratize history activity and to suggest that understanding the ways people make history is a critical step in understanding how meaning about the past is negotiated.

Indeed, recent empirical studies in a number of fields illuminate the pervasive and varied ways in which ordinary people relate to the past. Using ethnography, for example, Henry Glassie studied an Irish community called Ballymenone and described how people interpret the past by telling stories, arranging their household goods, and going about their everyday occupations. Drawing upon sociology and communications theory, Tamer Katriel and Thomas Farrell examined the making and using of scrapbooks for pleasure, reminiscence, communication, and the maintenance of relationships.[5] Other explorations of history-making activity can be found in the literature of psychology, anthropology, and communications.

As Thelen describes, understanding the range of ways that people make meaning of the past and using that broad spectrum as the basis for public history can open the door to new directions in exhibits, textbooks, activities, films, and other media that might indeed excite and involve Americans in history.[6] Research as well as reflective practice in public history has shown that many of the ways people relate to the past in their everyday lives are quite active and integral components of the ways they make sense of interpretations about the past presented to them by historians in museums, theaters, and classrooms. Such expansion, therefore, seems not only logical but necessary if historians wish to communicate meaningfully with the public.

While this philosophy can lead to exciting new projects and programs, it can also help to explain the success of certain techniques and practices. For example, many historians wondered why Ken Burns's television film The Civil War was so popular and successful in the eyes of the public. To explore how viewers made sense of the series, David Glassberg analyzed 444 letters received by Ken Burns in response to the film. The letters suggest that those writing viewed The Civil War most often in the context of their own family history but also in the content of their previous television watching experiences and their previous knowledge of the war. Glassberg concluded that Burns's series created "spaces for sharing information," which "viewers filled with stories," and that the letters and diaries "made viewers feel closer to the process of history-making, not passive and removed."[7] In sum, *The Civil War* encouraged and supported some of the personal ways people relate to the past far more effectively than have many documentaries before it.

WHO AND HOW? EVERYPERSON HIS OR HER OWN INTERPRETER

What about museum education? Once again, we may see our field mirrored in the history movement, but there's a lesson to be learned from Becker: namely, everyperson his or her own interpreter. Like history, making meaning of objects is something we do all the time, not just in museums and not just those of us who get paid for it. Whether art, history, science, anthropology, popular culture, or kitsch, we each exercise a variety of skills—including identification, description, and evaluation—that are similar to those of the museum professional in responding to objects in most contexts. Like history-making, those processes are social; the meanings we make are influenced and constrained by other people, including those with whom we participate in relationships and social groups.[8] And as is the case with history-making, there exists a range of ways in which we respond to and make sense of objects: we reminisce about them, imagine and fantasize with them, worship and revere them, treat them as symbols, react unconsciously to them, and use them to tell stories to others—often on topics having little to do with the museum's intended "messages." Many of these ways of relating to objects are typically deemed "naive" and inappropriate behavior in museums. Yet our own experiences and recent research attest to the fact that such behaviors can be integral parts of the museum experience, important and satisfying to many visitors. As in the case of history, it seems that understanding the range of ways that people make meaning of objects and using that broadened spectrum as the basis for museum programs and exhibits can open the door to more democratic practices in museums. Such practices can provide opportunities to model and communicate basic values such as pride, respect, and tolerance that grow increasingly crucial for the functioning of multicultural society.

Literature on objects in anthropology, sociology, psychology, communications, ethnic studies, and folklore can help to stimulate our thinking along these lines. Communications research, for example, certainly sheds light on the ways in which people relate to objects as symbolic of values and mnemonic of stories that express those values. In a case study of a rural Pennsylvania community, for example, Christopher Musello examined the use of family objects within the daily lives of community members. He found that families use their possessions to symbolize important people and events and to pass on family values embedded in stories.

> Furnishings are largely dependent for their interpretation on the rounds of talk they generate and support about the range of references they embody. In conjunction with

talk, they are employed to stimulate and facilitate the transmission of . . . accounts of people and events.[9]

We know that visitors engage in such storytelling in museums all the time. Should that activity and those meanings continue to take second place to the interpretations of museum staff? The popularity of comment books, self-made videos, and computer databases for visitor input in more and more museums suggests otherwise. Understanding the many ways we make meaning of objects in our culture may in fact help us see a wider range of behaviors that museums could be supporting and promoting. In so doing, museums could become cultural havens for, as well as models for, the respectful exploration and exchange of ideas.

BEYOND EXPERT AND NOVICE:
UNDERSTANDING SIMILARITIES AND DIFFERENCES

Recognizing the spectrum of history-making activity and the ways that people relate to objects offers hope that we might move beyond the often condescending and limiting dichotomy of professional-expert/layperson-novice that still exists in history and museology alike. Letting go of judging responses as "right" or "wrong" can provide room for something more. But what?

To move toward a practice of history that is more inclusive and democratic, Thelen argues for the need to understand the *similarities and differences* in the ways that people interpret and use the past as a means to create new dialogues among all history-makers.[10] Through the exchange of opinions, reactions, and perspectives, multiple viewpoints and meanings can be explored.

Struck in the expert/novice linear communication model, some historians do not think to encourage such dialogue or see its great potential for educating about diversity. Michael Frisch relates one such missed opportunity at the point at which history was being presented to the public: an experience of attending a labor history symposium with academics, trade unionists, and community people. The symposium featured the presentation of oral history interviews about steelworkers' strikes organized in the 1930s.

It was not clear until one overheard comments in the lobby, however, that people had seen it very differently: many of the academics heard in the tapes evidence of the pervasiveness of class conflict and a call to militance inspired by labor's heritage of struggle. But the trade-unionists seemed to come away with a very different message: recalling the "bad old days," they said, made them appreciate the distance between then and now, as measured by their current no-strike contracts, grievance procedures, and pension benefits. But the interviews had not focused on such messages in either sense, and the program offered no opportunity or framework for discussing, contrasting, and evaluating the connection of this particular past to the present. . . . The program ended where it should have begun.[11]

If different voices were to share "interpretive" authority from the start of the process of creating history, there is hope that common ground might also be forged and methods developed for supporting multiple points of view. A new, more inclusive vocabulary could become a shared goal, as well as less judgmental criteria for comparing perspectives. New frameworks and techniques for the practice of history, born of "shared authority," might then emerge. Thelen offers the idea of a history textbook in which

> teachers, government officials, community activists, history buffs, stamp collectors, farmers, and school children would discuss and negotiate its content. In the course of listening to each other, they might construct a new historical experience.[12]

It is not hard to fantasize the challenge and excitement of such a project or the ideas and educational approaches that could result from such dialogue and others like it.

MUSEUMS AND DIALOGUES

In creating museum exhibits and programs that interpret objects, it is similarly time for museum educators to take further steps beyond the expert/novice dichotomy to create more effective ways to share authority for the making of meaning in museums. As in history, such steps can be facilitated by affording more opportunities to explore and promote differences among perspective while also working toward the creation of expanded but common ground.

In the realm of products, such as exhibits and programs, we have laid some important groundwork already, through the growing use of feedback books, computer databases, and other mechanisms for incorporating diverse visitor responses. But in addition to such techniques that provide a relatively small space for visitor choices, imagine: a gallery with the explicit goal of fostering the sharing and exchange of various perspectives on objects; an exhibit that makes equal room for other "interpreters" by giving visitors space and materials to create and add labels and other devices for communicating their interpretations to others, including suggestions to others on how to relate to the object as they do; a museum program that begins, as Frisch suggested, with audience members' multiple interpretations of what they've seen and then challenges visitors and staff alike to truly understand each other's perspectives.

In the realm of process, or the ways in which we create exhibits and programs, we also have experience on which we can build in our efforts to create expanded dialogues. In many museums, tremendous gains have come from the difficult but rewarding work of using teams, community advisory groups, and focus groups in planning and design. It's time to explore further what such groups could look like, what purposes they could serve, and how they would operate. How about casting our nets wider than staff and community membership and involving individuals who make meaning of objects in many different ways? How about, as Thelen suggests for history, convening a group to discuss the vast "meaning of things," in which teachers, collectors, shamans, the elderly, anthropologists, shopkeepers, museum educators, children, and others would discuss and negotiate the content of an exhibit and, in the process, construct new experiences with objects?[13]

What might the outcome be? While it's hard to know in advance, negotiation specialists suggest that shared authority for a group goal is likely to produce common ground.[14] Could museum exhibits and programs find such common ground? The popularity of Fred Wilson's exhibits suggests so. While largely the vision of one individual, Wilson's unique installations suggest the great potential museums have to be places that can transcend differences as well as communicate about them. As Donald Garfield describes Wilson's philosophy, "The key element for Wilson is to let the *shared humanity* of the museum, its collections, and visitors come through." As Wilson explains:

> Even the most standard exhibition can be more human. Because you are human. The people who organize exhibitions are human. If they . . . tap into what led them to get excited about museums in the first place, and put THAT out there along with the scholarship, that is how to reach people.[15]

While individual artists or museum educators may well possess the sensitivity and skill to hypothesize what constitutes "shared humanity," imagine the challenge and potential rewards of seeking answers to that question through broad dialogues among diverse groups. And imagine developing exhibits and programs that reflect those answers as well as the processes involved in finding them!

ON THE ROLE OF THE MUSEUM EDUCATOR

What new or revised skills do we need to accomplish these goals? How might we rethink the role of the museum educator as a result? While the field of history has not yet imparted much advice in this realm, the paradigm itself broadens our notion of the museum educator's role to be one who is knowledgeable in the ways people make meaning of objects and skilled in facilitating dialogue and negotiation.

As we move from a model of the museum professional as exclusively a one-way expert communicator to one who participates and facilitates in shared processes of meaning-making, these needs become clear. While subject matter knowledge, excellent interpretive abilities, and the ability to communicate information clearly and effectively are and will always be necessary skills for museum educators, we will increasingly need to understand the diverse ways that people make meaning of objects if we hope to support these perspectives effectively. While the field of museum visitor studies offers great insights and new developments, we must also look toward research and observations on the role of objects in our lives from psychologists, folklorists, artists, religious leaders, anthropologists, poets, collectors, historians, novelists, and our friends, relatives, children, and selves. What more could museums do and be?

To truly support, encourage, and promote dialogues in museums, museum educators (and others) must also hone our skills as *facilitators*—learning and improving in the areas of listening, supporting, prodding, and negotiating—skills that grow increasingly vital to the functioning of a multicultural society. Many of these skills have long been the hallmark of a good educator in any context; yet focused on communicating the "museums' message," we may have lost sight of their importance. In this area, too, we may look to literature on conflict resolution, therapy, counseling, and management as well as to firsthand experience and experimentation, for guidance and inspiration.

To preserve differences, to facilitate mutual respect, and to forge the discovery of "shared humanity" are tremendous challenges that face the field of history—and nearly every other realm of our society today. What better place to uphold these goals and model paths to their accomplishment than museums, the places that house objects of so many different meanings?

NOTES

1. *Journal of American History* 75, no. 4 (1989): entire issue.

2. Michael Frisch, *A Shared Authority: Essays on the Craft and Meaning of Oral and Public History* (Albany: State University of New York Press, 1990).

3. Carl L. Becker, "Everyman His Own Historian," *American Historical Review* 37, no. (1932): 223, 228.

4. David Thelen, "History-Making in America," *Historian* 53, no. 4 (1991): 631.

5. Henry Glassie, *Passing the Time in Ballymenone: Culture and History of an Ulster Community* (Philadelphia: University of Pennsylvania Press, 1982); Tamar Katriel and Thomas Farrell, "Scrapbooks as Cultural Texts: An American Art of Memory," *Text and Performance Quarterly* 11, no. 1 (1991): 117.

6. Thelen, "History-Making in America."

7. David Glassberg, "'Dear Ken Burns': Letters to a Filmmaker," *Mosaic* 1, no. 3 (1991): 8.

8. Lois Silverman, "Of Us and Other 'Things': The Content and Functions of Talk by Adult Visitor Pairs in an Art and a History Museum" (Ph.D. diss., University of Pennsylvania, 1990).

9. Christopher Musello, "Family Houses and Personal Identity" (Ph.D. diss., Annenberg School for Communication, University of Pennsylvania, 1986), p. 388.

10. Thelen, "History-Making in America."

11. Frisch, *Shared Authority*, p. 190.

12. Thelen, "History-Making in America," p. 648.

13. Ibid. See also Mihali Csikszentmihalyi and Eugene Rochberg-Halton, *The Meaning of Things: Domestic Symbols and the Self* (Cambridge: Cambridge University Press, 1981).

14. Roger Fisher and William Ury, *Getting to Yes: Negotiating Agreement without Giving In* (New York: Penguin Books, 1981).

15. Donald Garfield, "Making the Museum Mine: An Interview with Fred Wilson," *Museum News* 72, no. 3 (May/June 1993): 49, including quotation from Fred Wilson.

Is There Method in Our Madness?
Improvisation in the Practice
of Museum Education

Mary Ellen Munley

What is the role of museum education? What kinds of programs and activities should be part of museum education departments? Is there a coherent vision behind the expansion of museum education beyond structuring and guiding field trips to promoting a variety of learning activities—after-school programs, literacy programs, festivals, speaker series, symposia, overnight events, summer camps, library collaborations, programs for parents, video productions, Web sites, interactive exhibits, museum schools, and electronic field trips? What are we to make of this seemingly endless variety of offerings? Have we gone mad?

One of the challenges museum educators face is to ensure that there is a guiding vision for program development so that museums are presenting something more than a hodge-podge collection of public activities. To understand the essential vision and value of museum education, it is instructive to reflect on the improvisational quality of many recent educational programs. For a successful educator is one who responds to changing times by improvising new programs while remaining focused on the underlying convictions that provide continuity and direction. Variation has allowed museums to evolve, but constancy has set our course.

In her remarkable book, *Composing a Life*, author Mary Catherine Bateson recommends using the forms and practice of improvisational jazz to understand growth, development, and change. Bateson's writings on women's lives have influenced my own thoughts on museum education. She offers a framework for understanding accomplishment when the path is not a traditional one: "Each of us has worked by improvisation, discovering the shape of our creation along the way,

Mary Ellen Munley is an independent consultant specializing in museum education and a member of the national group of consultants, The Museum Group. She is the former director of the Department of Education and Outreach at the Field Museum in Chicago. "Is There Method in Our Madness? Improvisation in the Practice of Museum Education" appeared in *Presence of Mind: Museums and the Spirit of Learning*, edited by Bonnie Pitman. Copyright 1999, the American Association of Museums. It is reprinted with permission from the American Association of Museums. All rights reserved.

rather than pursuing a vision already defined . . . solving problems for the first time . . . [finding it] no longer possible to follow the paths of previous generations."[1]

Indeed, museum educators work by experimentation. They must be responsive to the public, and they are often the first to identify the barriers that keep people away from museums and their collections. Museum educators identify problems, turn them into challenges, and improvise responses. Their improvisation has resulted in many "firsts" for museums, including outreach programs, neighborhood museums, discovery rooms, gallery games, interactive exhibits, community advisory groups, and museum schools. These programs may not have been anticipated, but they were carefully crafted nonetheless.

There is, I believe, a pattern underlying the variations. Together, these solo improvisations create an evolving definition of museums as educational institutions. As Bateson writes, "Practicing improvisation [is] clearly not a contradiction. Jazz exemplifies artistic activity that is at once individual and communal, performance that is both repetitive and innovative, each participant sometimes providing background support and sometimes flying free."[2]

This collective act of creativity is at the heart of museum education. Despite all the variation and improvisation, there are underlying convictions that provide continuity and direction to this work. As Bateson writes, "Improvisation can be either a last resort or an established way of evoking creativity."[3] I believe that the improvisational art of responding to new situations with focused innovations has allowed museum education to evolve and has strengthened the educational relevance of museums in modern times. This has happened—and will continue to happen—because there are some fundamental principles that guide the practice of museum education. If we remain true to these convictions, we will lose neither our minds nor our way as we delve into the limitless possibilities of program format and design.

THE FOUNDATIONS OF MUSEUM EDUCATION

Our work as museum educators is predicated on our beliefs about our audiences and our beliefs about human learning and capacity for understanding. It is these beliefs that set the foundation for our evolving vision for the museum experience.

What do we believe about our audiences? In many museums, there is a decided tension between audiences and professional staff, and that tension can be traced to very different ideas about what a museum is and why people visit. Most people do not go to museums with the intention of being students who will learn what the teacher (the museum) has decided they should know. Yet museum staff, who have planned each detail of an exhibit or program, frequently become frustrated, even angry, with visitors who "fail" to follow their lead, go in the "right" direction, or attend sufficiently to the intended message.

At issue here is something very fundamental: the ability to understand who our visitors are and what coming to the museum means to them. Traveling, rather than schooling, strikes me as a useful metaphor for understanding museum-going. With leisure travel, experience accumulates over time. Travel can be fun, not tedious. We are attentive to our own needs when we travel. When visiting a new place, we do not feel the obligation to focus only on history, geography, architecture, and "high" culture. We allow ourselves to explore the landscape in a holistic way. We concern ourselves with the comforts of accommodations. We soak in the ambiance. We can delight in the cuisine without being considered frivolous. The point is that we bring our entire person—mind, heart, body—when we travel. Rarely are we invited to bring so much of ourselves to a place of learning—to a museum. But if museums create an atmosphere in which their visitors can think, feel, and sense, they will begin to better understand their audiences, and rethink the design of their exhibits, programs, food services, rest areas, and more.

Coming to terms with visitors' needs and interests is at the heart of attempts to expand and diversify audiences—a hallmark of museum education activities for decades. Although demographic profiles of visitors to most museums do not support our claims, most museum professionals believe that museums are for everyone.

We need to understand the ramifications of our commitment to broaden and expand our audiences. To accomplish this goal, we will work with and serve people from diverse racial and ethnic backgrounds, people who have not been part of the museum world in the past. We will serve the very young and the very old, and we will serve people who draw a wide range of meanings from the museum experience. As we invite more people to visit museums and actively participate in many different ways, we may wonder if our programming is still educational. Obviously, the answer to this question depends on how we define education.

What do we believe about education and the capacity for human beings to learn? At its best, museum learning encourages independent thought. Museums have the capacity to stimulate meaningful learning for their visitors. Meaningful learning is about making connections, and it occurs when new information is linked with existing concepts in the visitor's system of understanding. Meaningful learning results in visitors creating a variety of messages and meanings.

Therefore, many museum educators do not expect, or even aim, for each visitor to learn the same thing. Each visitor will experience the museum differently because there are endless and unpredictable ways in which people acquire, retain, and use knowledge. In fact, it is this unpredictability—indeed, the creative imagination—that is at the heart of the educational matter in museums.

Research in the fields of human learning, cognition and human intelligence suggests radical shifts in how we design exhibits, programs, and learning experiences. Most widely touted, certainly in the museum world, is the work of Howard Gardner. Identifying musical, spatial, bodily kinesthetic, interpersonal and intrapersonal intelligences along with the verbal and logical mathematical intelligences, he places many people among the ranks of talented human beings for the first time. He thereby challenges educational institutions of all types to rethink their aims and their designs. For museums, this rethinking challenges us to expand the traditional role of the museum as educator.

THE FUTURE OF MUSEUM EDUCATION

These two beliefs structure the evolution of educational programming as museum educators strive to provoke independent thought and foster active participation in museum programs by a broader audience. Museums therefore offer a range of learning experiences. Some engage our visitors with the traditional program formats that will continue to be valuable in sharing what we know. However, the traditional way of thinking about museum education offerings (i.e., workshops, classes for schools, and family programs) is simply not robust enough to address the needs of an expanded audience and an expanded definition of human learning. Although lists of program ideas come easily, more of the same is not an advisable direction for most museum education departments. We must break with tradition and develop new approaches to program development and design that reflect our expanded audiences and an expanded understanding of learning. To do this, we must establish the museum as a center of learning in the community. The following presents one possible framework for understanding how museum education is evolving.

1. The museum as educator. Museum programs have the capacity to inform people of all ages. Content knowledge is important, and museums will continue to excel in introducing large public audiences to valuable information about art, science, history, and more. Education programs focused on sharing information are important first steps in educating our audiences.

In addition to information exchange, museums have the potential to address important societal issues. Through a mixture of entertaining, inspiring, enlightening, and challenging experiences, museum programs can inform people of all ages about science, technology, history, the environment, and cultural diversity. However, education is not just sharing what we know. It is also about encouraging conversation and participation. Museum educators should respond creatively to this challenge by developing programming innovations that will allow institutions to remain meaningful and purposeful by evolving into community centers, community forums, and community catalysts.

2. The museum as public forum. Museum programs can introduce participants to thoughtful presentations and discussions about complex and important global, national, and community issues. Working in partnership with community leaders and organizations, museums can give life to their mission and collections by organizing meetings, lectures, and debates on topics important to our collective quality of life. In their capacity as forums, museums also can invite people to meet on site and use collections and exhibits as stimuli for reflection and discussion.

3. *The museum as community center.* Museums create community spaces. They have the capacity to unite people who would not normally meet. If we create inviting spaces and more open-ended programs, over time people of all backgrounds will come together to share social learning experiences. Indeed, museums have a history of fashioning programs around drumming, storytelling, dancing, cooking, and festivals—forms and formats used through the ages by people with an interest in coming together. The new twist for museums and their audiences is that these programs can be ongoing and the participants can be performers, not observers. Museums can, for instance, establish storytelling and drumming circles, dance groups, artist colonies, and ecology groups.

4. *The museum as provocateur.* Why do humans fight change? How is technology changing our world? Why do we see hate crimes in our communities? How can we sustain the biodiversity the planet needs? What will we do about the fact that so many children do not know how to read? Museums need not steer completely clear of today's complex and difficult social issues. In fact, if they do, it will be to their peril. Through exhibits, programs, and community partnerships, museums can provoke discussion and actively participate in projects that strive to achieve goals related to literacy, cultural understanding, and sustaining our natural environment.

5. *The museum as catalyst.* To the extent that our programs are successful, others will build on them. As museums emerge as vital community learning centers, they will be among the institutions setting the agenda for their communities.

The museum as educator. The museum as forum. The museum as community center. The museum as provocateur. The museum as catalyst. To some, this vision for expanding the role of the museum may seem too far afield, too ambitious, too insane. However, to borrow another insight, "Though this be madness, yet there is method in't."[4] If we stay true to our convictions about our audiences and learning, our course is set. Through our creative and purposeful improvisation, it will be achieved.

I would like to thank Jennifer Eagleton for her invaluable assistance in preparing this essay.

NOTES

1. Mary Catherine Bateson, *Composing a Life* (New York: Penguin Books, 1991), pp. 1–2.

2. Ibid., pp. 2–3.

3. Ibid., p. 4.

4. William Shakespeare, *Hamlet,* act 2, sc. 2, line 222.

20

Mining the Museum:
An Installation Confronting History

Lisa G. Corrin

What is a museum anyway? Or a curator for that matter? And what is an "audience"? Do museums have the corner on historical "Truths"? *Mining the Museum*, an installation by Fred Wilson, provided an opportunity to reflect on these questions. Presented from April 2, 1992, to February 28, 1993, Wilson's installation was made possible through a unique collaboration between The Contemporary and the Maryland Historical Society (MHS), two Baltimore-based museums.

Founded in 1989, The Contemporary's mission is to explore the connections between the art of our time and the world we live in. The museum encourages interaction between artists and audiences and directly involves communities in the development, implementation, and evaluation of its programs. The Contemporary works out of a permanent administrative facility but presents exhibitions in temporary locations; its concept of a "collection" consists of placing art in community settings on long-term loan.

The MHS is a 150-year-old institution with an important collection housed in a permanent museum. Its fifty-plus staff members oversee many thousands of objects ranging from decorative arts, paintings, and sculpture to extensive archives and a library of Maryland history. It is in many ways typical of large, established state historical museums across the country.

In May 1991, The Contemporary opened its first international exhibition in the former Greyhound Service Terminal, located near the MHS. George Ciscle, The Contemporary's director, and I paid a social call on the society's director, Charles Lyle, to introduce ourselves. We talked at length about the differences between the ways our respective institutions operate. Lyle expressed his desire to have his insti-

Lisa G. Corrin is Deputy Director of Art/Curator of Modern and Contemporary Art at the Seattle Art Museum. She was co-curator of *Mining the Museum* while curator at The Contemporary in Baltimore, Maryland. "Mining the Museum: An Installation Confronting History" appeared in *Curator: The Museum Journal* (Vol. 36 No. 4 [October 1993], pp. 302–31). It is reprinted here by permission of AltaMira Press, Walnut Creek, Calif., a division of Rowman & Littlefield Publishers, Inc.

tution deal with current concerns and public interests and to develop an audience more representative of the community's cultural diversity.

Coincidentally, The Contemporary had been considering a project with Fred Wilson and had invited him to Baltimore to visit many of the city's museums to choose a permanent collection he would like to work with. Wilson's first choice was the MHS.

The Contemporary returned to the MHS with a suggestion: a three-way collaboration with Fred Wilson in which he would create an installation artwork during a one-year residency period. Our staffs would use the experience as an opportunity for a self-study to help us identify new approaches to interpreting collections, shaping future acquisition policies and programs, and expanding our audiences. Wilson would have access to the MHS collection as a "gold mine" of ideas and reinstall it from his own point of view. Then *Mining the Museum* began to take shape. We agreed that whatever objects Wilson chose would be made available to him for use in the installation.

The exhibition was designed to address problems we felt were of concern to many museums, regardless of their discipline. The aim would be to confront the difficulty of putting theories of diversity and historical revisionism into practice and to offer a model for change responsive to our particular community. The directors of the two organizations felt strongly that presenting the exhibition concurrently with the 1992 American Association of Museums annual conference in Baltimore might catalyze provocative dialogue within the profession.

ABOUT WILSON'S WORK

Fred Wilson is an installation artist of African-American and Carib descent. His entry into the museum world began with free-lance assignments in the education departments of a number of museums, including the American Museum of Natural History, The Metropolitan Museum of Art, the Whitney Museum of American Art, and the American Crafts Museum. More recently, he has been involved with arts organizations as a museum educator, a gallery director, and a practicing artist.

Until *Mining the Museum*, Wilson's installations had used re-productions and fabricated artifacts in "mock museums" that had drawn attention to the ways in which curatorial practices affect our interpretation and understanding of museum collections. Wilson's "museums" underscored the fact that history is an act of interpretation and that contemporary events are part of its flux. His work has provided a savvy and thought-provoking critique of the museum environment.

His insights first surfaced in *Rooms with a View: The Struggle Between Culture, Content and Context in Art*, a project he curated for the Bronx Council of the Arts in 1987. Three distinct spaces simulated different display environments: ethnographic and Victorian museums and a contemporary gallery. In each room, Wilson placed different works of art by thirty artists, surrounded by the accouterments appropriate to the space. The ethnography museum grouped objects according to type, with vague labels identifying the artistic medium but not the maker. The Victorian museum gave the objects a rarefied disposition, suggesting precious antique *objets d'art* through selective lighting and ornate pedestals. The "white cube" gallery gave the works the necessary cutting-edge mystique to certify them as works of contemporary art.

The new contexts so thoroughly transformed the audience perceptions of the artworks that Wilson decided to take on "the museum." Describing his reasons, Wilson said, "It is there that those of us who work toward alternative visions . . . get hot under the collar and decide to do something about it."

Visitors to *The Colonial Collection* (1991) at the Gracie Mansion Gallery (no longer in existence) viewed African masks blindfolded with the flags of their French and British colonizers and others labeled "Stolen from the Zonga tribe," highlighting how museum euphemisms whitewash the acquisition of such objects. These "spoils" were displayed in dramatically-colored spaces with theatrical lighting, sometimes animated with the addition of video special effects. This, according to Wilson, illustrated how a museum display "anesthetizes their historic importance . . . [it] certainly covers up the colonial history."

The proposed collaboration offered Wilson an opportunity to work with real museum objects and occupy the curatorial "hot seat," putting his theories into practice in the environment curators operate in every day and with similar limitations.

DEVELOPING THE EXHIBITION

Principals on the project from the two collaborating institutions were the directors, the chief curator and the director of education at the MHS, and the curator/educator and an intern at The Contemporary. The Contemporary raised the necessary funds ($25,000) and managed the budget. Public programming, public relations, and development of educational materials were implemented cooperatively. The Contemporary provided orientation to the topic of installation art and the process of creating it for MHS staff and docents.

Wilson made all artistic decisions and set the project's philosophical, aesthetic, and historical trajectory. He participated in all aspects of the project's development and implementation, including education. He visited the society frequently over a one-year period, and for two months prior to the opening, he remained on site. He came to know the collections and other resources as well as the society's curatorial, registrarial, educational, and governance practices.

Mining the Museum was not the first museum collaboration or the first time an artist "curated" a collection or created a museum-critical work for a specific institution. But a self-study process implicit in the installation made the project not only different as an exhibition but an intervention. Throughout the project, an ongoing evaluation of the collaborative process and the impact of the installation was carried on. It examined commonly-held definitions of "museum," "history," "exhibition," "curator," "artist," "audience," "community," and "collaboration." The curators created a "think sheet," a series of topics developed to measure changes in the way individuals saw themselves, the artist, and their institutions during the development of the installation. Wilson was assisted in his research by independent volunteers who had expertise in African-American local and state history, astronomy, and museum history. The curators gave Wilson entry into the less-well-known parts of the museum and shared historical information about the objects.

A WALK THROUGH THE EXHIBITION

The exhibition investigated both the African-American and Native-American experiences in Maryland, using art and artifacts from the MHS collection that either had never been seen before or had never been viewed in this context.

Personal history forms the basis of Wilson's engagement with the past. Objects, he believes, become "generic and lifeless" outside the context of personal experience. "I look at the relationship between what is on view and what is not on view." Wilson's fear of imposing a personal morality on others led him to use the questioning process as the organizing principle of his work.

To encourage visitors to begin questioning immediately, the curators created a handout that was posted in the elevator. It read:

What is it?
Where is it? Why?
What is it saying?
How is it used?
For whom was it created?
For whom does it exist?
Who is represented?
How are they represented?
Who is doing the telling? The hearing?
What do you see?
What do you hear?
What can you touch?
What do you feel?
What do you think?
Where are you?

Mining the Museum employed display techniques that are second nature to most curators: artifacts, labels, selective lighting, slide projections, and sound effects. But they were used to explore our "reading" of historical truth through sometimes startling juxtapositions of objects representing vastly different historical "facts," revealing stereotypes and contrasting power and powerlessness. (Highlights from the installation follow.)

The installation opened with the silver and gold "Truth Trophy Awarded Until 1922 for Truth in Advertising," surrounded by three white pedestals bearing white marble busts of historic personages and three empty black pedestals. It encapsuled the issues at the heart of the exhibition. Whose truth is on exhibit? Whose history is being told? Wilson thus established that *Mining the Museum* would explore not *what* objects mean but *how* meaning is made when they are "framed" by the museum environment and museum practices.

Those left out of the museum's historical narrative were literally given voice in a room where nineteenth-century paintings were on display. When a viewer stepped toward the dimly lit works of art, spotlights and hidden sound effects were triggered to highlight the African-American children represented. A boy asked, "Am I your brother?" "Am I your friend?" And, alluding to his metal collar, "Am I your pet?" The names of slaves depicted in a rare painting of workers in the fields were added to the label after the plantation owner's inventory book listing them along with other household items and animals was found in the archives.

Examples of how the museum classification system inadvertently represses the layered and complex history behind objects was illustrated in "Modes of Transport," "Metalwork," and "Cabinet-making, 1820–1960." The first of these examined who traveled in colonial Maryland—why and how. A model of a slave ship was shown alongside a once-elegant sedan chair; a painting depicting a similar chair highlighted who carried whom. A Ku Klux Klan hood replaced the customary linens in an antique pram; nearby was a photograph of black "nannies" pushing similar carriages. The suggestion that children absorb their parents' racial stereotypes early on was clear. Disproportionate sizes of objects displayed together conveyed a sense of power or the lack of it. On display in a space focusing on runaway slaves were decoy ducks and a toy figure of a running black soldier "targeted" by a large punt gun used in hunting the birds in Chesapeake Bay. In "the rebellion room," Wilson inverted this relationship. Miniature white figures in a doll house were dwarfed by a black doll dominating them. A diary on display revealed panic on the part of white landowners of a "Negro uprising," reflecting the source of this nightmarish vision.

Some objects were brought into the light here for the first time. A rocking chair, a basket, and a jug made by enslaved African Americans were displayed along with objects made by Africans in the colony for freed slaves in Liberia. Only the jug, made by "Melinda," had been exhibited; few had seen the Liberian objects. Found in storage, a wooden tourist box with its ticket of passage to Africa led to the identification of the "new" objects. The box had been given to the MHS in the mid-nineteenth century by a member of the Colonization Society. At the end of the corridor hung a painting, "Maryland in Liberia," by John H. B. Latrobe, founder of the MHS and an active member of the Colonization Society.

The final section focused on the aspirations, dreams, and achievements of African Americans. The focal point was a journal kept by the astronomer and mathematician Benjamin Banneker (1731–1806). Software that could generate images of the night sky as Banneker saw it was loaded into an IBM computer. (The computer was labeled.) Drawings from the journal were projected on the wall. Banneker was hired by Thomas Jefferson to help survey the area that became Washington, DC, and the two men corresponded. The journal contains an article that Banneker sent to Jefferson urging him to abolish slavery and saying: "Sir I freely and Chearfully acknowledge that I am of the African race." The book tells the story of a free black who was no less immune to the oppression of the slavery system than his enslaved brothers and sisters.

The installation ended with a globe used in Banneker's time; by formally and metaphorically echoing the opening Truth Trophy, the installation came full circle.

EDUCATIONAL PROGRAMS AND OUTREACH

The museum educators reconsidered their usual approaches to interpretation and public programming. Their aim would be to stimulate debate and encourage active audience engagement with the material.

An educational handout was produced after the exhibition opened. "Do you have questions about *Mining the Museum?*" was based on questions most frequently asked of and reported by guards, docents, receptionists, and gallery-store staff. Visitors received it at the end of the installation, so that the active questioning process of their experience would not be lost. It provided background information on such topics as the lives of historical personages, information about some of the objects, and an explanation of installation art.

Programs for the public took place at the MHS. Open studio visits were held weekly just prior to the opening so that the public could gain first-hand experience of Wilson's working process and have a chance to speak with him. Workshops for the docents on contemporary art focused on the installation medium and how artists today often address social and political issues in their work. They also included tours of the MHS with the artist. Discussions about the exhibition as a work of contemporary art were conducted by nine area artist/docents each Saturday. Other public lectures included: "Contemporary Artists and Cultural Identity," "African-American Women in Maryland 1750–1860," and "Free at Last," a dramatic reading of primary documents related to slavery and abolition in Maryland.

"Exhibiting Cultures," a continuing studies course at the Johns Hopkins University, was based on the book *Exhibiting Cultures: The Poetics and Politics of Museum Display* (Karp and Lavine, 1991). Lectures took a critical look at the challenges curators of all disciplines face when exhibiting artifacts from cultures other than (and including) their own. The final class brought together scholars in the fields of art history, anthropology, and African-American history, including Ivan Karp, to present papers on the issues raised by the installation. The artist/docents were given scholar-ships to attend the course.

AUDIENCE RESPONSE

A community exhibit, on view for the final month of the exhibition, chronicled audience participation in the project, including drawings, essays, creative writing by children and art students as well as responses to a questionnaire asking for reactions. Visitors had been requested to hang them on the bulletin board to create a dialogue among members of the audience.

Almost every evaluation received remarked on the emotional impact of the installation. The subtleties of Wilson's work were not lost on the young.

> *When I go to a museum, I hope to say "Wow" but today I was thinking "Wow!" in a different way.*
>
> *I like that he asks questions and doesn't answer them.*

And from adults:

> *You always have to question information presented because even if presented as "truth" it is always from a specific cultural point of view. (Attorney)*
>
> *It interested me in seeing Maryland History in terms of an African American although I am white. I've never been interested in seeing this museum before this show.*
>
> *I want a sense of understanding history as good or bad in order to repeat it or to discard it so as not to repeat it. (Retired police officer)*
>
> *I found my history in this exhibition. My ancestors were never slave owners . . . but as a Caucasian American, I share some responsibility for the continuing state of racial strife today. (Immigrant economist)*
>
> *Can you force all of Baltimore to see this? (Unemployed white male)*
>
> *Never have I witnessed any form of artwork that has had such an emotional effect on me. (College student)*

Not all responses were positive.

> *Mining the Museum has the ability to promote racism and hate in young Blacks and was offensive to me. (Retired dentist)*
>
> *I found Mining the Museum "artsy" and pretentious. It was a waste of space that could be used to better purpose. A museum should answer questions not raise questions unrelated to the subject. (Engineer)*

It snookered me.

I liked the pedestals without statues least because they were visually boring and emptiness is decidedly uninteresting, period. (Curator)

DISCUSSION AND CONCLUSION

Mining the Museum examined how the MHS had defined itself and how this self-definition determines whose history has been included or excluded. It also spoke to how those excluded have come to see the museum. It was about the power of objects to speak when museum practices are expanded and the artificial boundaries museums build are removed. It was about how deconstructing the museum apparatus can transform the museum into a space for ongoing cultural debate.

It stimulated so much enthusiasm within the profession that children's museums, natural history museums, science centers, and art museums suddenly wanted "Fred Wilsons" of their own; they were encouraged to look at their own collections with a renewed sense of purpose and possibility. Two Wilson installations based on permanent collections have taken place since the installation at the MHS: *The Spiral of Art History* at the Indianapolis Museum of Art and *Museums: Mixed Metaphors* at the Seattle Art Museum. A condensed version of *Mining the Museum* is currently being developed as a permanent display at the MHS, using objects from the original installation.

Throughout the course of the collaboration, both institutions and the artist have had to deal with problems that arose because of assumptions we had about one another and our expectations for the project. One of the greatest difficulties for the participants was learning to adapt to one another's working style. As one staff member stated, "We occasionally speak a somewhat different language." Gradually, staff and docents began to realize that the way their jobs had been previously defined did not always apply to the role they had to assume for the installation. Wrote one staff member, "The insistence on secrecy and preserving the mystery of the work of art until the last possible moment made it difficult to plan and, indeed, to schedule normal pre-exhibition activities, such as the movement of artworks from storage to the installation space. It took a great leap of faith."

All project evaluations are being utilized to generate short- and long-term goals concerning policies, practices, and future programming at both The Contemporary and the MHS. We continue to reflect on our respective missions and on the role a museum can play in a rapidly changing world. The project offered our staffs a practical way to explore different methodologies and professional points of view and to exchange ideas valuable for future collaborations. The docents are considering how their experiences might become useful in giving tours in other parts of the museum. *Mining the Museum* also generated a critical exchange of ideas between local artists, area cultural institutions, and our community.

Finally, Wilson's installation demonstrated dramatically that current issues are as legitimate a concern for history museums as the distant past. Our audiences told us that they want to be challenged and feel it is appropriate that cultural institutions provide a forum to discuss issues of a controversial nature. Moreover, they cautioned us that if museums are to be truly diverse, they must allow for questioning and be responsive to the questions they hear. Most important, we realized that the project would have been impossible without Fred Wilson's residency. For, as one educator stated, "only with the perspective and creative resources of an outsider could . . . [any museum] undertake as self-critical and creative a project as *Mining the Museum*."

ACKNOWLEDGMENTS

Thanks for the support of the project go to the Andy Warhol Foundation for the Visual Arts, the Maryland Humanities Council, the Maryland State Arts Council, and the Puffin Foundation and the Mid-Atlantic Arts Foundation (M-AAF). Parts of this report are adapted from *Arts Ink*, the M-AAF journal (Fall, 1992). Thanks also go to the volunteers and docents who were largely responsible for the successful interpretation of the installation, and to the directors, George Ciscle and Charles Lyle, to Jennifer Goldsborough, chief curator at the MHS, and Judy Van Dyke, director of education at the MHS. For further information about the project, see Corrin, Lisa G. (Ed.) (in press). *Mining the Museum*. Baltimore, MD: New Press. The book includes contributions by Lisa G. Corrin, Ira Berlin, Fred Wilson, and Leslie King-Hammond.

REFERENCE

Karp, Ivan, and Lavine, Stephen D. (Eds.) (1991). *Exhibiting Cultures: The Poetics and Politics of Museum Display*. Washington, DC: Smithsonian Institution Press.

21

Evaluating the Ethics and Consciences of Museums

Robert Sullivan

In this essay, I make two arguments. First, I argue that museums are moral educators and must speak with confidence and competence on such ethical issues as gender and race equity.[1] As educational institutions, we are necessarily agents of change, not only changing the knowledge, beliefs, attitudes, and feelings of our individual visitors but also affecting the moral ecology of the communities that we serve. The pattern of our decision making in our governance policies, hiring practices, and collection and interpretation programs sends value-laden messages to our communities about what we consider to be worthwhile and just.

Second, based on the extent to which one race and/or gender dominates museums' governance, policies, practices, and programs, I argue that museums are generally racist and sexist institutions. I do not contend that as institutions museums overall are maliciously racist and sexist, although I believe that there have been incidents of overt racism or sexism. I believe, however, that we are thoughtlessly racist and sexist institutions. It is not that we do not care but that we lack systematic ways to assess and to evaluate our flaws in order to direct cumulative change in our activities.

Museums tend to be what I call "episodic institutions," having episodes of success but having difficulty sustaining longitudinal change. With this in mind, rather than merely describing the problem, I propose criteria for systematically assessing sex equity issues in permanent exhibits. I hope that these criteria may assist us in developing professional standards that might lead to longitudinal change in our institutions and ultimately in societal behaviors.[2]

THE MUSEUM AS MORAL EDUCATOR

Museums are ritual places in which societies make visible what they value. Through the selection and preservation of artifacts, specimens, and documents, museums

Robert Sullivan is Associate Director of Public Programs at the National Museum of Natural History at the Smithsonian Institution. "Evaluating the Ethics and Consciences of Museums" first appeared in *Gender Perspectives: Essays on Women in Museums*, edited by Jane R. Glaser and Artemis A. Zenetou, and published in 1994 by the Smithsonian Institution Press. It is reprinted here by permission of the Press.

begin to define for their societies what is consequential, valuable, and suitable as evidence of the past. Through their presentation and interpretation of this evidence, museums define not only what is memorable but also how it is to be remembered. Museums are thus unavoidably linked with their cultural settings. They are a collective self-reflection culminating in the maintenance, sustenance, and presentation of a cultural identity, as well as the embodiment of cultural values and attitudes believed to be important. Museums thus reveal their own moral nature, competence, and maturity in their decisions about what and how to transmit social values and ideas. While museums often claim to be value-neutral, nonmoral, and nonpolitical in intent, in their actual practice and behavior, they are moralizing institutions, reflecting as well as shaping their communities' moral ecology.

The core of museums' moral dimension is located in the decisions and the choices that they must make and then visibly enact: What do they choose to collect and not to collect? What themes and materials are exhibited and under what interpretive conditions? What audience or audiences are courted and welcomed in the museum, and what audience or audiences are ignored? Who is given comfortable psychological, intellectual, and physical access to the museum and its resources? What programmatic themes are addressed? How is the museum governed? Who is on the board? Who is on the staff? These choices are value laden and, combined, establish a pattern of policies, procedures, and public programs that define and communicate the museum's norms, ethics, and moral identity—its compelling sense of self. This contention that museums, because of their educational and social intent and institutional choices, cannot be value-neutral or nonmoral in their actions and behaviors, suggests that the question to be addressed is not *should* museums be moral educators but *how* museums should be involved in moral education. How can museums develop a conscious moral purpose based on appropriate aims, concepts, and content? If the goal of museums as educators is to assist in developing the whole person—his or her knowledge, attitudes, beliefs, and feelings—then how should a museum develop the intellectual, aesthetic, and moral judgments of its visitors and communities? What *ought* a museum do?

SEX EQUITY AND THE PERMANENT EXHIBIT

Permanent exhibitions at the New York State Museum are those that are expected to remain in place, relatively unchanged, for forty years. It is not accidental that such exhibits last for about one generation, before their style and content are declared old-fashioned, irrelevant, or even unethical. As assumptions and attitudes toward what is valuable in history or the natural environment change, exhibits are no longer in touch with their community's expectations.

In 1976 the New York State Museum began its ongoing efforts of planning, designing, and installing 120,000 square feet of new permanent exhibitions in its new home in the Cultural Education Center. Determining the overarching theme that would drive the exhibitions' aims and content was critical, since this point of view would define what themes would be excluded in the exhibits as well as those that would be included. The museum decided to abandon the traditional, discipline-based approach that treats human history and natural history as separate subjects. A more integrated, holistic style was chosen to address the central questions: How do human activity and the natural environment interact, and what are the consequences of one on the other?

Of particular concern was the issue of fair representation of race and gender in New York State's development. To address this issue, a sex equity committee was formed to examine exhibit themes, linguistics, and design. This committee was voluntary and composed of equal numbers of men and women. Formation of this internal advisory group resulted from a growing awareness of patterns of bias that had minimized the visibility of women and minorities in educational materials, including museum exhibits. Its draft report identified six forms of gender bias:

Invisibility

Certain groups are underrepresented in exhibits and other instructional materials. The omission of women and minority groups is very damaging because it implies that these groups are of less value and significance in our society.

Stereotyping

By assigning traditional and rigid roles or attributes to a group, exhibits and instructional materials stereotype and limit the abilities and potential of that group. Stereotyping denies students a knowledge of the diversity, complexity, and variation of any group of individuals. Children who see themselves portrayed only in stereotypical ways may internalize these stereotypes and fail to develop their own unique abilities, interests, and full potential.

Imbalance/Selectivity

Exhibits and instructional materials perpetuate bias by presenting only one interpretation of an issue, situation, or a group of people. This imbalanced account restricts students' knowledge about the varied perspectives that might apply to a particular situation. Through selective presentation, instructional materials frequently present an unrealistic portrayal of our history and our contemporary life experience. Controversial topics are glossed over, and discussions of discrimination and prejudice are avoided. This unrealistic coverage denies children the information they need to recognize, to understand, and perhaps some day to conquer the problems that plague our society.

Fragmentation/Isolation

By separating issues related to minorities and women from the main body of the text, exhibits and instructional materials imply that these issues are less important and not a part of the cultural mainstream.

Linguistic Bias

Curricular materials reflect the discriminatory nature of our language. Masculine terms and pronouns, ranging from "our forefathers" to the generic "he," subtly ignore references to the participation of women in our society. Further, occupations such as "mailman" are given masculine labels that deny the legitimacy of women working in these fields. Imbalance of word order and lack of parallel terms that refer to females and males are also forms of linguistic bias.

The internal advisory group recommended the following criteria for evaluating museum exhibits, programs, and publications for gender equity:

Invisibility

1. Are equally meaningful roles given to both men and women? What effort has been made to represent men and women as having equal status: professional, social, economic, etc.?
2. Do the visible credits on the exhibit, film, or program reflect the broad range of individuals who contributed to the product?
3. Are men and women both equally represented by the artifacts? By people? By voice?
4. Are quotes and anecdotes from women in history and from important living women used as frequently as those from men?
5. If men and women have different roles, are these separate roles shown as being equally important to the overall development of culture?
6. Have opportunities been missed to present sex-fair images?

Stereotyping

1. When people are presented visually in roles, is an effort made to avoid stereotyping their behaviors and aspirations? For example, are women always presented as nurturers and men as builders or persons involved in technology?
2. Are opportunities taken to give examples of both men and women in significant roles that do not contradict historical fact?
3. Unless there is a specific reason for not doing so (i.e., historical example), are both sexes portrayed from similar attitudinal perspectives (e.g., humor, satire, respect, etc.)?
4. Is an effort made to avoid using only pastel colors and fuzzy line definition to illustrate females and only strong colors and bold lines to portray males?
5. Do graphs and charts use other than stereotypical stick figures?
6. Do the materials indicate mutual respect among the characters through their posture, clothing, and gestures?
7. Are physical and emotional stereotypes avoided? Is an effort made to avoid showing men only as vigorous and powerful and women only as delicate and fragile?

8. Do illustrations include other than young, attractive, and preferred body types?

Imbalance/Selectivity

1. Do artifacts reflect varieties of populations and subcultures whenever possible?
2. If artifactual evidence is not available, how are unrepresented populations accounted for?
3. How is the planning staff of the exhibit, program, or film balanced for gender and other constituent group representation to provide a variety of experiences and perspectives?
4. Are experts such as sociologists brought in at appropriate times so that the full spectrum of peoples contributing to our society's evolution is reflected in all aspects on the museum?
5. Does the material presented reflect other value systems besides that of the majority white male culture?
6. If historical bias exists, how does the exhibit, film, or program, acknowledge this limitation? (E.g., in the past women couldn't attach their names to literature, music, inventions, etc.)

Unreality

1. What effort is made to discuss, to exhibit, and/or to encourage programs on controversial topics such as discrimination and prejudice?
2. When a historically biased situation is cited or represented, how is it qualified as past values that are no longer acceptable?

Fragmentation

1. Have certain issues that are gender-related been separated from the main body of materials, implying that these issues are less important?

Linguistic Bias

1. Is the generic "she" used where the antecedent is stereotypically female (e.g., "the housekeeper . . . she")?
2. Is the generic "he" used to include both males and females when gender is unspecified?
3. Does the material use sex-fair language initially and then slip into the use of the generic "he" (e.g., "A worker can have union dues deducted from his pay.")?
4. Are women identified by their own names rather than their husband's names (e.g., Madame Pierre Curie, Mrs. F. D. Roosevelt)?
5. Are nonparallel terms used in referring to males and females (e.g., Dr. Jones and his secretary, Ellen; Senator Kennedy and Mrs. Ghandi)?
6. When referring to both sexes, does the male term consistently precede the female (e.g., he and she, boys and girls)?

7. Are occupational titles used with -man as the suffix (e.g., chairman, business-man)?

8. When an individual holds a nontraditional job, is there unnecessary focus on the person's sex (e.g., the woman doctor, the male nurse)?

9. Are women described in terms of their appearance or marital and familial status, while men are described in terms of accomplishments or titles (e.g., Senator Kennedy and Golda Meir, mother of two)?

10. Is the text consistent with the illustrations in terms of sex fairness?

The New York State Museum is now in the process of applying these criteria to its existing exhibits and programs, as well as to those in progress. Already, the linguistics of the museum has changed. The portrayal of the division of labor and women's role in prehistoric Native American cultures has been refined for our upcoming life groups. The posture, gestures, and attitudes of figures in these life groups have been more consciously considered. A heightened awareness exists among staff of the unconscious, or at least preconscious, prejudices and stereotyping that can be packaged into every aspect of exhibit scripting and design.

Identifying what is intolerable to us and combating it is a hopeful beginning. We agree that sexism, racism, and inequity are intolerable to us, but the other half of this concluding strategy is "acting against" them. According to Susan B. Anthony,

> Cautious, careful, people, always casting about to preserve their reputation and social standing never can bring about a reform. Those who must be really in earnest must be willing to be anything or nothing in the world's estimation, and publicly and privately, in season and out, avow their sympathy with despised and persecuted ideas and their advocates, and bear the consequences.[3]

In the belief that Anthony is fundamentally correct, that reform of institutions comes from committed, passionate, risk-taking behavior by individual staff members. I suggest a list of individual acts that we can follow in order to initiate change:

1. Write a critique of one exhibition and submit it to your supervisor.

2. Refuse to distribute—especially to teachers and children—learning materials, brochures, and any literature that uses sexist or racist language.

3. Form a voluntary equity committee.

4. Fight for pay equity for undervalued staff and categories of staff (such as clerical staff and instructors); and refuse raises until pay equity is reached.

5. Write and submit a report and recommendations on specific equity issues in your institution.

6. Confront positively all sexist and racist remarks.
7. Remove office materials that are sexist or racist.
8. Announce that you are a feminist (especially if you are a man).

NOTES

1. I join these two issues only because they are generally interrelated in this society and are essentially moral issues with related principles and concepts of equity, justice, and empathy.

2. As an aside, I think it is self-evident that complete societal change, which is preceded by institutional change, is precipitated by the insistent moral commitment of key individuals within those institutions. We now clearly understand the need to address racism and sexism in our economic, judicial, and educational institutions, but relatively little attention has been paid to our cultural institutions. Sadly, this is probably because neither museum professionals nor the society in general take museums seriously as agents of change. Museums have enormous potential as "thermostatic" institutions that counteract dangerously prevalent and dominating ways the society transmits and receives information and experience—but this is the topic for another essay.

3. Ida Husted Harper, *The Life and Work of Susan B. Anthony, Including Public Addresses, Her Own Letter . . . during Fifty Years* (Indianapolis: Hollenbeck Press, 1898), 1:197.

Additional Recommended Reading

Collins, Zipporah W., ed. *Museums, Adults, and the Humanities: A Guide for Educational Programming.* Washington, DC: American Association of Museums, 1981.

"Formalizing Exhibition Development." *Exhibitionist* 21, no. 1 (Spring 2002).

Hirsch, Joanne S., and Lois Silverman, eds. *Transforming Practice: Selections from the Journal of Museum Education, 1992–1999.* Washington, DC: Museum Education Roundtable, 2000.

Karp, Ivan, and Steven D. Lavine, eds. *Exhibiting Cultures: The Poetics and Politics of Museum Display.* Washington, DC: Smithsonian Institution Press, 1991.

"Making Meaning in Exhibits." *Exhibitionist* 18, no. 2 (Fall 1999).

McLean, Kathleen. *Planning for People in Museum Exhibitions.* Washington, DC: Association of Science-Technology Centers, 1996.

Newsom, Barbara Y., and Adele Z. Silver, eds. *The Art Museum as Educator.* Berkeley: University of California Press, 1978.

Pitman, Bonnie, ed. *Presence of Mind: Museums and the Spirit of Learning.* Washington, DC: American Association of Museums, 1999.

Roberts, Lisa C. *From Knowledge to Narrative: Educators and the Changing Museum.* Washington, DC: Smithsonian Institution Press, 1997.

Serrell, Beverly. *Exhibit Labels: An Interpretive Approach.* Walnut Creek, CA: AltaMira, 1996.

THE ROLE OF THE OBJECT: THE OBLIGATION OF STEWARDSHIP AND CULTURAL RESPONSIBILITY

What has traditionally set museums apart from other educational and cultural institutions is that they hold or use objects to further their public service mission. The range of collections is vast and may include the tiniest of scientific specimens to locomotives to live animals to entire villages of buildings connected to a specific period of time. Many museums house archives in addition to their collections, while others have archives as the centerpiece of the institution and its interpretation. Botanical gardens not only care for and present living specimens but may be actively involved in propagating new species. Aquariums and zoos care for living creatures, from whales and starfish to elephants and lemurs. The care of collections, whether a fine piece of art or a living thing, has evolved into a science of documentation, standards, conservation and preservation, ethics, cultural property rights, and more. The acceptance of an object or living thing into a collection comes with a myriad of responsibilities, legal and financial, as well as moral and ethical. The transformation of the world of collecting has been dramatic and complex, and intimidating at times. At the beginning of the twenty-first century, the management of collections requires attorneys; content specialists or scientists; collection managers; and astute, informed leadership at the head of the museum, aquarium, or zoo.

Before deciding the role of its collections, any museum must first be clear about its mission and its overarching goals in service to the public. Supporting that may or may not be the desire to amass collections. Many museums today have opted to feature exhibitions or borrow collections for display but to forfeit the cost and challenges of long-term responsibility for a collection. For those who have always had collections or for those museums choosing to collect, there are, at the very least, a range of core issues to be resolved at the outset. What is the scope of our collecting effort? How will the proper care, documentation, and use of these collections be assured and monitored? What policies and procedures will support our aims and protect the collections for generations to come? Is it our place to collect these items? What are the ethical or cultural considerations associated with these collections?

What are the associated costs of collecting, including storage, computer support and software, staffing, preservation and conservation, research requests, and so on?

As the cost of caring for collections has increased, so, too, have the voices from community groups and activists. For those collecting living specimens, the challenges of the environment present matters of extinction and whether or not to actively engage in species propagation. Many zoos, aquariums, and botanical gardens have entire departments devoted to husbandry and issues around the survival and future of particular animals or plants. Such landmark legislation as the Native American Graves Protection and Repatriation Act (NAGPRA) brought two diametrically opposed worlds to the table to resolve questions about whose right and responsibility it was to care for Native American collections and who were the rightful owners of these collections. Native American leaders and museum leaders worked through a myriad of issues resulting in a law that upheld the respect and value represented by both viewpoints with a clear understanding of the nature of responsibility of each. In addition, legal challenges over the provenance of national treasures such as the Elgian Marbles provoke the question "Whose treasures are they?" To say that the stewardship of collections has changed is to oversimplify. Rather, cultural awareness, environmental responsibility, and issues greater than the agenda of a single museum have yielded a new set of criteria and perspectives for those leading museums. Nations, cultural groups, activists, and the public now better understand their rights with respect to caring for the treasures of their own heritage and the environment.

Given such complexities, Elaine Heumann Gurian, a senior museum consultant to government-run museum projects around the world and the former deputy director of the National Holocaust Museum, launches this part's discussion with her dissection of the role of the object. In "What Is the Object of This Exercise?" Gurian elucidates the range of roles held by the object and its diverse and dynamic value to the museum and to the public.

Stephen Weil, a longtime presenter and participant in the American Legal Institute/American Bar Association annual conferences on emerging legal issues that concern museums, has historically helped museums understand the spectrum of legal issues affecting collections and institutional responsibilities to the public. Weil shares his perspective on the changing arena of collecting and its implications for those ultimately responsible for collections in "Collecting Then, Collecting Today," published in 2002.

James Gardner and Elizabeth Merritt, in their 2002 article "Collection Planning: Pinning Down a Strategy," emphasize the necessity of collection planning. They argue that such activity is no longer a choice but is key to assuring the ongoing responsible care of the collections in order to make informed decisions for the future development of the collection and its ultimate beneficiary, the public.

Next, Carole Milner, the head of conservation and collection care at the Museums & Galleries Commission in London, lifts the oft-neglected topic of conservation into the main dialogue of museum decision making in "Who Cares? Conservation in a Contemporary Context," published in 1999. She argues that the proper conservation of collections is a shared responsibility for all involved in running a museum, not just the collections manager and conservator. Not to observe proper conservation standards and procedures at all levels of the museum would be at cross purposes with the public service mission of museums—to share and celebrate the stories objects represent and their place in our understanding of the cultural and natural world.

"A Philosophical Perspective on the Ethics and Resolution of Cultural Properties Issues," written in 1999 by Karen Warren, a professor of philosophy at Macalaster College in St. Paul, dissects the layers and issues at play with cultural objects, including the emotional stage of ethics, rights, and responsibilities. Her detailed treatise provides an entry point into the complexities surrounding cultural objects, enabling the reader to gain a depth of understanding about the opposing perspectives on cultural property.

Complementing Warren's article with a specific example, "Deft Deliberations" explains one of the most significant pieces of legislation to affect museums in the United States in recent times: NAGPRA of 1990. Authors Dan Monroe, the executive director and CEO of Peabody Essex Museum, and Walter Echo-Hawk, a staff attorney for the Native American Rights Fund in Boulder, Colorado, document the historic process of merging the perspectives of U.S. museums and Native American tribal leaders into a law devoted to the respectful care and stewardship of Native American human remains and sacred objects. NAGPRA represents two divergent perspectives, and the resulting legislation has forever changed the relationship between museums and Native Americans.

Wrapping up Part IV is the 1991 article "Deaccessioning: The American Perspective" by Marie Malaro, an attorney and professor emeritus of the George Washington University, as well as the author of the benchmark book, *A Legal Primer on Managing Museum Collections*. Malaro discusses the process of honing collection holdings through deaccessioning—the legal removal of an object from a museum collection. Handled with forethought and sensitivity to donors and the public, deaccessioning can be an effective strategy for strengthening the focus and depth of collection holdings for museums, but the need to exercise care, prudence, and deliberation cannot be stressed enough.

Today, the issues surrounding collections are some of the most daunting and complex aspects of museum operations, yet the interpretation and use of collections is the very experience that sets museums apart from the rest of today's cultural and educational experiences. The effort to care for the real thing must involve due diligence, unparalleled commitment to ethical standards, and adept management to assure the long-term care of the cultural and natural heritage of any nation or group on behalf of greater society.

22

What Is the Object of This Exercise?
A Meandering Exploration of the Many
Meanings of Objects in Museums

Elaine Heumann Gurian

"Why did the Serbs and Croats shell each other's historic sites when they had so little ammunition and these were not military targets?" I routinely ask my museum-studies graduate students this question when I lecture. "To break their spirit," is always the instantaneous answer. Museums, historic sites, and other institutions of memory, I would contend, are the tangible evidence of the spirit of a civilized society. And while the proponents of museums have long asserted that museums add to the quality of life, they have not understood (as the graduate students did when confronted by the example of war) how profound and even central that "quality" was.

Similar examples reveal the relationship between museums and "spirit" in sharp detail. Why did the Russians proclaim, one day after the Russian revolution had succeeded, that all historic monuments were to be protected even though they most often represented the hated czar and the church? Why did Hitler and Stalin establish lists of acceptable and unacceptable art and then install shows in museums to proclaim them while sending the formerly acclaimed, now forbidden, art to storage? Why did the Nazis stockpile Jewish material and force interned curators to catalog and accession it, intending to create a museum to the eradicated Jews? Why, when I was in the rural mountains of the Philippines, was I taken to hidden closets that served as museums, curated by tribal members, holding the material of the tribe's immediate past, secreted from the dealers who were offering great sums for the same material?

In adversity it is understood, by antagonists and protagonists alike, that the evidence of history has something central to do with the spirit, will, pride, identity, and civility of people, and that destroying such material may lead to forgetting, broken

Elaine Heumann Gurian is a senior museum consultant specializing in international museum projects and former deputy director for the National Holocaust Museum in Washington, D.C. She is the founder and president of The Museum Group. "What Is the Object of This Exercise?" was written for inclusion in the special issue of *Daedalus* devoted to museums and contemporary issues. It is reprinted here by permission of *Daedalus*, Journal of the American Academy of Arts and Sciences, from the issue entitled "America's Museums," Summer 1999, Vol. 128, No. 3.

spirits, and docility. This same understanding is what motivates cultural and ethnic communities to create their own museums in order to tell their stories, in their own way, to themselves and to others.

Yet neither the museum profession nor its sibling workers in the other store-houses of collective memory (archives, libraries, concert halls, and so forth), makes (nor, I would contend, understands) the case clearly about its institution's connect-edness to the soul of civic life. In cities under duress you can hear the case being made better by mayors and governors. Dennis Archer, the mayor of Detroit, said re-cently while being interviewed on the radio, "Detroit, in order to be a great city, needs to protect its great art museum, the Detroit Institute of Art." It was Archer and his predecessor, Coleman Young, who championed and underwrote the latest in-carnation of Detroit's Museum of African American History. And it was Teddy Ko-lik, the fabled former mayor of Jerusalem, who was the chief proponent of the creation of the Israel Museum (and who placed one of his two offices within the building). Mayors know why museums are important. Citizens, implicitly, do too. A recent survey in Detroit asked people to rate the importance of institutions to their city and then tell which they had visited. The Museum of African American History was listed very high on the important list and much lower on the "I have visited" list. People do not have to use the museum in order to assert its importance or feel that their tax dollars are being well spent in its support.

The people who work in museums have collectively struggled over the proper definition and role of their institutions. Their struggle has been, in part, to differ-entiate museums from other near relatives—the other storehouses of collective memory. The resulting definitions have often centered on things—on objects and their permissible uses. I believe the debate has missed the essential meaning (the soul, if you will) of the institution that is the museum.

OBJECTS ARE NOT THE HEART OF THE MUSEUM

The following discussion will attempt to capture that soul by throwing light on the shifting role of museum objects over time. It will show how elusive objects are, even as they remain the central element embedded within all definitions of museums. This essay will also postulate that the definition of a "museum object" and the asso-ciated practices of acquisition, preservation, care, display, study, and interpretation have always been fluid and have become more so recently. Objects did not provide the definitional bedrock in the past, although museum staffs thought they did. I will show that museums may not need them any longer to justify their work.

But if the essence of a museum is not to be found in its objects, then where? I propose that the answer is in being *a place* that stores memories and presents and organizes meaning in some sensory form. It is both the physicality of a place and the memories and stories told therein that are important. Further, I propose that these two essential ingredients—place and remembrances—are not exclusive to museums. And, finally, I contend that the blurring of the distinctions between these institutions of memory and other seemingly separate institutions (like shopping malls and attractions) is a positive, rather than negative, development.

Not meaning to denigrate the immense importance of museum objects and their care, I am postulating that they, like props in a brilliant play, are necessary but alone are not sufficient. This essay points out something that we have always known intuitively: that the larger issues revolve around the stories museums tell and the way they tell them. When parsed carefully, the objects, in their tangibility, provide a variety of stakeholders with an opportunity to debate the meaning and control of their memories. It is the ownership of the story, rather than the object itself, that the dispute has been all about.

This essay suggests what museums are not (or not exactly) and, therefore, continues the dialogue about what museums are and what makes them important, so important that people in extremis fight over them.

WHAT IS AN OBJECT?

"Ah, but we have the real thing," museum professionals used to say when touting the uniqueness of their occupation. When I began in museum work, in the late 1960s and early 1970s, the definition of museums always contained reference to the object as the pivot around which we justified our other activities.[1] Although there were always other parts of the definition, our security nonetheless lay in owning objects. With it came our privileged responsibility for the attendant acquisition, its preservation, safety, display, study, and interpretation. We were like priests and the museums our reliquaries.

The definition of objects was easy. They were the *real* stuff. Words were used like "unique," "authentic," "original," "genuine," "actual." The things that were collected had significance and were within the natural, cultural, or aesthetic history of the known world.

Of course, *real* had more than one meaning. It often meant "one of kind," but it also meant "an example of." Thus, artworks were one-of-a-kind, but eighteenth-century farm implements may have been examples. Things made by hand were unique, but manufactured items became examples. In the natural history world, almost all specimens were examples but had specificity as to location found. Yet some could also be unique—the last passenger pigeon or the last dodo bird. Objects from both categories, unique and example, were accessioned into the collections. Museums owned the objects and took on the responsibility of preserving, studying, and displaying them.

Yet even within these seemingly easy categories there were variations. In asserting uniqueness (as in made-by-hand), specific authorship was associated with some objects, such as paintings, but not with others, most especially utilitarian works whose makers were often unknown. Some unique works were thought of as "art" and some as "craft"; with some notable exceptions, art was individualized as to maker but craft was not. This practice, which is now changing, made it possible to do research and mount shows of the work of particular artists in some, but not all, cultures.

WHAT ARE COLLECTIONS?

In the early 1970s the American Association of Museums (AAM) established an Accreditation Commission. As its members deliberated, they discussed whether groups of living things could be called collections and whether institutions that so "collected" should be classified as museums. Heretofore, "museums" were conserving things that had never been, or now were no longer, alive. The field debated if the living things in botanical gardens, fish in aquaria, or animals in zoos were "collections"; if so, were those institutions, *de facto*, museums? It was decided that, yes, at least for funding and accreditation purposes, they *were* museums, and the living things they cared for were likewise to be regarded as collections, and hence objects.[2]

Yet there were other institutional repositories that cared for, protected, preserved, and taught about "objects" but were not called museums nor necessarily treated by museums as siblings. Archives and libraries, especially rare-book collections, were considered related but not siblings even though some museum collections contain the identical materials. There were also commercial galleries and private and corporate collections that were considered by museum professionals to be different and outside the field, separated supposedly by an underlying purpose. A legal distinction of "not-for-profit" was considered an essential part of the definition of a museum. It was clear that while objects formed the *necessary* foundation upon which the definition of a museum might rest, they were not *sufficient* in themselves.

CAN NONCOLLECTING INSTITUTIONS BE MUSEUMS?

The Accreditation Commission of the AAM next sought to determine if places that resembled collections-based museums but did not hold collections (i.e., places like not-for-profit galleries and cultural centers) were, for purposes of accreditation, also museums. In 1978, they decided that, in some instances, galleries could be considered museums because, like museums, they cared for, displayed, and preserved objects even though they did not own them. Ownership, therefore, in some instances, no longer defined museums.

There was also the conundrum brought to the profession by science centers and children's museums, mostly of the mid-twentieth century. Earlier in the century, these places had collected and displayed objects, but by mid-century children's museums and science centers were proliferating and creating new public experiences, using exhibition material that was built specifically for the purpose and omitting collections objects altogether. How were these "purpose-built" objects to be considered? They were three-dimensional, often unique, many times extremely well made, but they had no cognates in the outside world. Much of this exhibit material was built to demonstrate the activity and function of the "real" (and now inactive) machinery sitting beside it.

The Adler Planetarium, applying to the AAM for accreditation, also caused the AAM to reconsider the definition of a museum. The planetarium's object was a machine that projected stars onto a ceiling. If institutions relied on such "objects," were these places museums? Had the profession in advertently crafted a definition of objects that was restricted to those things that were created elsewhere and were then transported to museums? That was not the case in art museums that commissioned site-specific work. Certainly the murals of the depression period applied directly to museum walls were accessionable works of art—an easy call! Portability, then, did not define objects.

In 1978, the Accreditation Commission of the AAM, citing these three different types of noncollections-based institutions (art centers, science and technology centers, and planetariums), wrote specific language for each type of museum and, by amending its definition of collections for each group, declared these types of organizations to be . . . museums! They elaborated: "The existence of collections and supporting exhibitions is considered desirable, but their absence is not disabling . . ."[3] In response, many museums set about creating more than one set of rules—one for accessioned objects, and another for exhibitions material—and began to understand that the handleable material they used in their classes (their teaching collections) should be governed by a different set of criteria as well.

Nevertheless, there were often no easy distinctions between the handleablity of teaching collections' objects and those others deserving preservation. The Boston Children's Museum loan boxes, for example, created in the 1960s, contained easy-to-obtain material about Northeast Native Americans. But by the 1980s, the remaining material was retired from the loan boxes and accessioned into the collections because it was no longer obtainable and had become rare and valuable.

Even purpose-built "environments" have, in cases such as the synagogue models in the Museum of the Diaspora in Tel Aviv, become so intriguing or are of such craftsmanship that they, decades later, become collections' objects themselves. So, too, have the exhibitions created by distinguished artists, such as parts of Charles and Ray Eames's exhibit *Mathematica: A World of Numbers and Beyond.*

Dioramas were often built for a museum exhibition hall in order to put objects (mostly animals) in context. These display techniques, which were considered a craft at the time they were created, were occasionally of such beauty, and displayed artistic conventions of realism (and seeming realism) so special, that today the original dioramas themselves have become "objects," and many are subject to preservation, accession, and special display. The definition of objects suitable for collections has, therefore, expanded to include, in special cases, material built for the museum itself.

WHAT IS REAL? IS THE EXPERIENCE THE OBJECT?

In the nineteenth century, some museums had and displayed sculptural plaster cast-ings and studies. The Louvre and other museums had rooms devoted to copies of famous sculptures that the museum did not own. The originals either remained in situ or were held by others. People came to see, study, and paint these reproduc-tions. They were treated with the respect accorded the real thing. For a long time, museums and their publics have felt that though there were differences between the "original" and reproductions, both had a place within their walls.

Similarly, reconstructed skeletons of dinosaurs have long appeared in museums. They usually are a combination of the bones of the species owned by the museums plus the casting of the missing bones from the same species owned by someone else. Sometimes museums point out which part is real and which is cast, but often they do not. "Real," therefore, takes on new meaning. Curators recognize that the expe-rience of seeing the whole skeleton is more "real," and certainly more informative, than seeing only the authentic, unattached bones that do not add up to a complete or understandable image.

Likewise, multiples or limited editions were always considered "real" as long as the intention of the artist was respected. Thus, the fact that Rodin and many others authorized the multiple production of some pieces did not seem to make each one any less real or less unique. The creation of additional, though still limited, copies, using the same etching plates, but after the death of the artist, caused more prob-lems. But often, while acknowledging the facts of the edition, such works also hung in museums and, if the quality was good, were accessioned into their collections.

IS THE IMAGE THE OBJECT?

The twentieth century's invention of new technologies has made multiples the norm and made determining what is real and what that means much more difficult. While original prints of movies, for example, exist, it is the moving image that the public thinks of as the object rather than the master print of film. Questions of au-thenticity revolve around subsequent manipulation of the image (e.g., colorization, cutting, or cropping) rather than the contents of any particular canister.

Printed editions with identical multiples are considered originals, and become more valuable, if signed; unsigned editions are considered less "real" and certainly less valuable. In such cases one could say that the signature, rather than the image, becomes the object. Photographs printed by the photographer may be considered more real than those using the same negative but printed by someone else. With the invention of digital technology, many identical images can be reproduced at will without recourse to any negative at all. So the notion of authenticity (meaning sin-gularity or uniqueness) becomes problematic as images indistinguishable from those in museums are easily available outside the museum. It is the artist's sensibil-ity that produced the image. It is the image itself, therefore, that is the object.

IS THE STORY THE OBJECT?

Of the utilitarian objects of the twentieth century, most are manufactured in huge quantities and therefore could be termed "examples." Which of these objects to collect often then depends not upon the object itself but on an associated story that may render one of them unique or important.

The objects present in the death camps of the Holocaust were, in the main, created for use elsewhere. There is nothing unique in the physicality of a bowl that comes from Auschwitz-Birkenau. These bowls could have been purchased in shops that sold cheap tableware all over Germany at the time. However, when the visitor reads the label that says the bowl comes from Auschwitz, the viewer, knowing something about the Holocaust, transfers meaning to the object. Since there is nothing aside from the label that makes the bowl distinctive, it is not the bowl itself but its associated history that forms importance for the visitor.

DOES THE CULTURAL CONTEXT MAKE THE OBJECT?

As Foucault and many others have written, objects lose their meaning without the viewer's knowledge and acceptance of underlying aesthetic or cultural values. Without such knowledge, an object's reification even within its own society cannot be understood. Often the discomfort of novice visitors to art museums has to do with their lack of understanding of the cultural aesthetics that the art on display either challenges or affirms.

By accessioning or displaying objects, the creators of museum exhibitions are creating or enhancing these objects' value. Further, society's acceptance of the value of museums themselves likewise transfers value to their objects. When museums receive gifts or bequests from a major donor's holdings, they are inheriting—and then passing on—a set of value judgments from someone who is essentially hidden from the visitor's view. A particular aesthetic pervades such museums because of the collections they house and the collectors who gave the objects in the first place.

This issue of values determining choice comes into sharper focus when museums begin acquiring or presenting collections from cultures whose aesthetic might be different. When installing a show of African material in an American art museum, should the curator show pieces based on the values inherent in the producing culture (i.e., focusing on the objects that attain special aesthetic value within that culture), or should the curator pick objects that appeal more to the aesthetic of his or her own culture? This question, the source of much debate, arises when museums attempt to diversify their holdings to include works created by a foreign (or even an assimilated) culture quite different from that which produced the majority of their holdings. For example, the selection of which African or Latino art to accession or show has to do not with authenticity but with quality. The notion of quality has been sharply debated between the scholar within the museum and the peoples representing the culture of the maker. So the question becomes: who selects the objects and by what criteria?

In material created by indigenous artists, the native community itself sometimes disagrees internally as to whether the material is native or belongs to a modern tradition that crosses cultural boundary lines. Some within the native population also argue about the birthright of the artist; blood quantum, traditional upbringing, and knowledge of the language sometimes have considerable bearing on whether artists and their creations are considered native. In such cases, the decision about what is quality work that should be housed in a museum may have little to do with the object itself and more to do with the genealogy of the producer.

WHAT IF YOUR STORY HAS NO OBJECTS OR DOES NOT NEED THEM? IS THE ABSENCE OF OBJECTS THE OBJECT?

Most collections were created by wealthy people who acquired things of interest and value to themselves. The everyday objects of nonvalued or subjugated peoples were usually not collected. Often the people in the lowest economic strata could hardly wait to exchange their objects for those that were more valued, giving no thought, at the time, to the preservation of the discarded material. So it goes for most peoples during their most impoverished historical periods. Accordingly, their museums must choose among a narrow band of choices—do not tell that part of their history, recreate the artifacts and environments, or use interpretative techniques that do not rely on material evidence.

The Museum of the Diaspora in Israel, struggling with this issue more than twenty-five years ago, decided to tell the complete story of five thousand years of Jewish migration without using a single authentic artifact. It elected to create tableaux that reproduced physical surroundings in an illustrative manner based on scholarly research into pictorial and written documentation of all kinds. The museum did so because its collection could not accurately or comprehensively tell the story, and a presentation of settings that appeared "like new" honored the history of Jewish migration more than an assortment of haphazard authentic artifacts showing their age and wear. The experience, wholly fabricated but three-dimensional, became the object. It presented a good public experience, many argued, but still did not qualify as a "museum." Ultimately, this total re-creation was accepted as a highly distinguished museum. The Museum of the Diaspora also presented movies, photos, and recordings in a publicly accessible form, arguing that a comprehensive presentation required material that was non-artifactual.

The U.S. African-American and Native American communities have suggested, in the same vein, that their primary cultural transmission is accomplished through oral language, dance, and song—vehicles that are ephemeral. Their central artifacts, or objects, if you will, are not dimensional at all, and museums that wish to transmit the accuracy of such cultures, or display historical periods for which material evidence is not available, must learn to employ more diverse material. It may be the performance that is the object, for example. And the performance space might need to be indistinguishable from the exhibit hall. As museums struggle to do this, one begins to see videos of ceremonies and hear audio chanting. Such techniques, formerly thought of as augmentation rather than core interpretation, have increasingly taken on the role and function previously played by collection objects.

Even in museums like Cleveland's Rock and Roll Hall of Fame or the soon-to-be-opened Experience Music Project, it is the sound and performance of the artists that is the artifact much more than the stationary guitar that, say, Jimi Hendrix once used. Indeed, musical instrument archives at the Boston Museum of Fine Arts and other places have long struggled with the proper presentation of their "artifacts." "Silent musical instruments" approaches an oxymoron.

HOW IS THE OBJECT TO BE PRESERVED? IS THE OBJECT TO BE USED?

The museum, in accepting an object for its collection, takes on the responsibility for its care. In doing so, collections managers follow rules organized for the safety and long-term preservation of the objects. Climate control, access restrictions, and security systems are all issues of concern to those who care for objects. Institutions devoted to music or performance transform the notion of collections and certainly the notion of preservation, because while it is true that most things are preserved better when left alone, some musical instruments are not among them. They are preserved better if played, and so, for example at the Smithsonian's Museum of American History, they are.

Likewise, many native people have successfully argued that accessioned material should be used in the continuance of ceremony and tradition. Artifacts, rather than being relinquished to isolated preservation (and losing their usefulness), are stored in trust waiting for the time when they must again be used. In the 1980s, when native people from a specific clan or group asked for an object to be loaned for a short-term use, this was a radical notion for most natural history museums. That request now is more common and often accommodated. For example, at the end of the 1980s, the Dog Soldiers of the Northern Cheyenne requested their pipe, which the Smithsonian's National Museum of Natural History holds, and used it in their ceremonies, after which it was returned to the museum.

Now, native museums and, less commonly, some general museums that hold native material accept objects into their collections with the express understanding that they will be loaned out and used when needed. The notion of a museum as a storehouse in perpetuity has, in these instances, evolved into the museum as a revolving loan warehouse. A long-standing and easily understood example predates this relatively new development. The Crown Jewels of the British monarchy, which are displayed in the Tower of London, are worn by the monarch when he or she is crowned. And so it has been for many centuries.

WHOSE RULES ARE USED FOR OBJECT CARE?

There are other fundamental rules of collections care that are successfully being challenged worldwide by native people's involvement. Collections care has been predicated on the basic notion that objects are inanimate. Though some objects were once alive, they now are no longer, and most had never been alive. Thus, collections-care policies proceeded from the assumption that objects should be preserved in the best manner possible, avoiding decay from elements, exposure, and use. Protective coverings and storage cases were designed to do just that. Extremes in the exposure to light and temperature, and all manner of pest infestation, were to be avoided. But when the museum was recognized to be neither the only nor the absolute arbiter of its material holdings, accommodation to the beliefs of the producers of the materials or their descendants became necessary.

These beliefs often included a lack of distinction between animate and inanimate. Thus, spirits, "mana," fields of power, and life sources could live within an object regardless of the material from which it was made. And that being so, the care for these living things, it was argued, is, and should be, quite different from the care of dead or never alive things. So, for example, bubble wrap, while an excellent protector of objects, does not allow for breathing or "singing and dancing at night." Those working with native populations in good faith have come to respect native understanding of their own objects and now provide for the appropriate life of the object. Some objects need to be fed, some need to be protected from their enemies, some need to be isolated from menstruating women. Collections are no longer under the absolute province of the professional caregivers. Storage facilities that accommodate the native understanding of their objects require new architectural designs that allow for ceremony for some and isolation from the curious for others.

WHO OWNS THE COLLECTIONS?

This change in collections use and care alters the notion of the museum as owner of its collections and opens the door to multiple definitions of ownership. These new definitions have far-reaching implications. If tribal communities can determine the use, presentation, and care of objects "owned" by museums, can the descendants of an artist? Can the victims or perpetrators of a war event? In the recent Smithsonian National Museum of Air and Space *Enola Gay* exhibition controversy, it was the veterans who flew the plane and their World War II associates who ultimately controlled the access to, presentation of, and interpretation of the object. Ownership or legal title to an object does not convey the simple, more absolute meaning it did when I began in the museum field.

The notion that if you buy something from a person who controlled it in the past, then it is yours to do with as you wish is clearly under redefinition in a number of fields. What constitutes clear title? Under what rules does stolen material need to be returned? What is stolen, in any case? Do the Holocaust victims' paintings and the Elgin Marbles have anything in common? The issue is so complex and varied that countries forge treaties to try to determine which items of their patrimony should be returned. Similarly, museums in countries like New Zealand, Canada, and Australia have developed accords that, in some cases, give dual ownership to collections. Museums and the native populations then jointly control the presentation, care, and even return of the objects, or museums give ownership to the native populations, who, in turn, allow the museum to hold the objects in trust. Ownership has developed a complex meaning.

IF I OWN IT CAN I HAVE IT BACK, PLEASE?

Some of this blurring of ownership began with native people maintaining that some items should not be in the hands of museums regardless of their history. That this would be claimed for human remains held in collections was easy to understand. Almost all cultures do something ceremonial and intentional with the remains of their people, which, in almost all instances, does not include leaving bodies for study in boxes on shelves. So when native people started to call for the return of their ancestors' remains, there was an intuitive understanding of the problem in most circles. This, however, did not make it any easier for the paleontologists and forensic curators whose life work had centered on the access to these bones, nor for the museumgoer whose favorite museum memories had to do with shrunken heads, mummies, or prehistoric human remains. The arguments that emanated from both sides were understandable and difficult to reconcile. It was a clear clash of world views and belief systems. To the curators it seemed that removal of human remains within museum collections would result in the unwarranted triumph of cultural tradition and emotionalism over scientific objectivity and the advancement of knowledge.

As it turned out, the Native American Grave Protection and Repatriation Act (NAGPRA)[4] made clear that Native American tribes had rights to the return of their sacred material and to their ancestors' remains and associated grave goods, regardless of the method by which museums had acquired the material. However, the emptying of collections into native communities, as predicted by the most fearful, did not happen. Rather, museums and native communities, working together in good faith, moved into an easier and more collegial relationship, as between equals. In most cases, the objects returned are carefully chosen and returned with due solemnity. Some tribes have chosen to allow some forensic samples to be saved, or studied prior to reburial, and some have reinterred their ancestors in ways that could allow for future study should the native community wish it.

NAGPRA struck a new balance between the world view of most museums and their staff (which endorsed a rational and scientific model of discourse and allowed for access to as much information as could be gathered) and the spiritual interests of traditional native peoples. A variety of museum practices were broadened, and visitors began to see the interpretation of exhibitions changed to include multiple side-by-side explanations of the same objects. For example, *Wolves*, an exhibition created by the Science Museum of Minnesota, presented scientific data, native stories, conservation and hunting controversies, and physiological information together in an evenhanded way. An argument for multiple interpretations began to be heard in natural history museums whose comfort level in the past had not permitted the inclusion of spiritual information in formats other than anthropological myth.

HOW OLD IS AN OBJECT?

The scientific dating of artifacts used in religious practices often holds little relevance to the believers. When an object such as the Shroud of Turin, for example, is carbon dated and shown to be insufficiently old, the problem of writing its museum label becomes complex. An object held in TePapa, the Museum of New Zealand, was returned to an iwi (tribe) that requested it, with all the solemnity and ceremony appropriate. So too went records of its age and material composition, at variance with beliefs held by the Maori people. But if, as the Maori believe, spirit or mana migrates from one piece to its replacement (rendering the successor indistinguishable from its more ancient equivalent), then what relevance is the fact that dates or materials are at variance? The object's cultural essence is as old as they say.

Similarly, when restoration of landmarks includes the replacement of their elements (as is routinely the case in Japanese shrines), the landmark is said to be dated from its inception even though no material part of it remains from that time. That does not upset us. So even something so seemingly rational and historical as dating is up for interpretation.

THE OBJECT IS OFF-LIMITS. IT IS NONE OF YOUR BUSINESS

Museums, even in their earliest incarnations as cabinets of curiosities, were available to all interested eyes or at least to those allowed to have access by the owners of the cabinets. In fact, part and parcel of conquest and subjugation was the access to interesting bits of the subjugated. This assumption that everything was fair game held currency for a long time. Though the notion of secret and sacred was also understood (for example, no one but the faithful could enter Mecca), this concept did not attach to museums nor to the holdings thereof. If a museum owned it, the visitors could see it if the curator/staff wished them to.

So it came as a surprise to some curators that contemporary native peoples began to make demands on museums to return not only human remains but material that was sacred and once secret. Accommodations negotiated between the museums and the native people sometimes led to agreements to leave the material in the museum but to limit viewing access. The notion that one people, the museum curators, would voluntarily limit their own and others' access to material owned by museums came initially as a shock to the museum system. But under the leadership of sympathetic museum and native people and, further, under the force of NAGPRA, museums began to understand that all material was not to be made available to all interested parties.

It was the beginning of the "It is none of your business" concept of museum objects. It held that the people most intimately concerned with and related to the material could determine the access to that material. In many cultures sacred ceremonies are open to all, and the objects in use are available for view in museum settings, but that too may change. For example, in Jewish tradition, Torahs once desecrated are supposed to be disposed of by burial in a prescribed manner. Yet some of these are available for view, most notably at the United States Holocaust Memorial Museum. There may come a time when such artifacts are petitioned to be removed for burial even though the statement they make is powerful.

WHO SAYS ALL OBJECTS NEED TO BE PRESERVED?

Ownership is not always an issue; sometimes it is the preservation of the object itself that needs examination. Museums have felt their most fundamental responsibility extended to the preservation of the object, yet in returning human remains to the earth, artifacts are being intentionally destroyed. That was difficult to reconcile for those trained in preservation. Even more difficult was the belief that not all things made by hand were intended to be preserved; perhaps some should be allowed to be destroyed. The Zuni war gods preserved by museums were returned to the Zuni tribe when it was successfully proven that these could only have been stolen from grave sites. But even more difficult was the Zuni's assertion that these objects were created to accompany the dead, and that preservation of them was therefore anathema. The war gods were returned to the Zuni, who watched over the gradual decay of these objects as they returned to the earth. In effect, the Zuni were entitled to destroy the objects that the museums had so carefully preserved.

The notion of preservation has, therefore, also been blurred. Museum personnel began to wrestle with the notion that all people do not hold preservation of all objects as a universal good. The Tibetan Lamas who create exquisite sand paintings only to destroy them later would certainly understand this.

THE OBJECT SPEAKS

I would be remiss if I did not also acknowledge the power of some objects to speak directly to the visitor, for example, in the sensual pleasure brought about by viewing unique original objects of spectacular beauty. But the notion that objects, per se, can communicate directly and meaningfully is under much scrutiny. The academicians of material culture, anthropology, history, and other fields are engaged in parsing the ways in which humans decode objects in order to figure out what information is intrinsic to the object itself, what requires associated knowledge gleaned from another source, and what is embedded in cultural tradition.

In some ways, it is because of this parallel contemporary inquiry into the "vo-cabulary" of objects that I can inquire into the object's changing role in the defini-tion of museums.

WHAT ARE MUSEUMS IF THEY ARE LESS OBJECT-BASED?

Museum staff intuitively understand that museums are important—an under-standing that the public shares. However, especially for the public, this understand-ing does not always revolve around the objects, though objects are, like props, essential to most museums' purposes: making an implicit thesis visible and tangi-ble. The nature of the thesis can range from explanation of the past to advocacy for a contemporary viewpoint to indication of possible future directions—in each case through a medium that presents a story in sensory form.

Museums will remain responsible for the care of the objects they house and col-lect, but the notion of responsibility will be, and has already been, broadened to in-clude shared ownership, appropriate use, and, potentially, removal and return.

The foundational definition of museums will, in the long run, I believe, arise not from objects, but from "place" and "storytelling in tangible sensory form," where cit-izenry can congregate in a spirit of cross-generational inclusivity and inquiry into the memory of our past, a forum for our present, and aspirations for our future.

Coming back to definitions, the current definition of museums used by the Ac-creditation Program of the AAM encompasses all museums and no longer separates them by categories. Museums, in this definition, ". . . present regularly scheduled programs and exhibits that use and interpret objects for the public according to ac-cepted standards; have a formal and appropriate program of documentation, care, and use of collections and/or tangible objects. . . ."[5]

For the visitor, it is the experience of simultaneously being in a social and often celebratory space while focusing on a multisensory experience that makes a mu-seum effective. Virtual experiences in the privacy of one's home may be enlighten-ing but, I think, are not part of the civilizing experience that museums provide. It is the very materiality of the building, the importance of the architecture, and the prominence that cities give to museum location that together make for the august place that museums hold. Congregant space will, I believe, remain a necessary in-gredient of the museum's work.

The objects that today's museums responsibly care for, protect, and cherish will remain central to their presentations. But the definition of "objectness" will be broad and allow for every possible method of storymaking. These more broadly de-fined objects range from hard evidence to mere props and ephemera. I hope I have shown that objects are certainly not exclusively real nor even necessarily "tangible" (even though the AAM uses that word). For it is the story told, the message given, and the ability of social groups to experience it together that provide the essential ingredients of making a museum important.

Museums *are* social-service providers (not always by doing direct social-service work, though many do that), because they are spaces belonging to the citizenry at large, expounding on ideas that inform and stir the population to contemplate and occasionally to act.

Museums are not unique in their work. Rather, they share a common purpose with a host of other institutions. We need museums and their siblings because we need collective history set in congregant locations in order to remain civilized. Societies build these institutions because they authenticate the social contract. They are collective evidence that we were here.

NOTES

1. "For the purposes of the accreditation program of the AAM, a museum is defined as an organized and permanent non-profit institution, essentially educational or aesthetic in purpose, with professional staff, which owns and utilizes tangible objects, cares for them, and exhibits them to the public on some regular schedule." American Association of Museums, *Museum Accreditation: Professional Standards* (Washington, D.C.: American Association of Museums, 1973), 8.

2. ". . . owns and utilizes tangible things animate and inanimate." Ibid., 9.

3. An art center "utilizes borrowed art objects, cares for them and maintains responsibility to their owners . . . [its] primary function is to plan and carry out exhibitions." Ibid., 12. A science and technology center ". . . maintains and utilizes exhibits and/or objects for the presentation and interpretation of scientific and technological knowledge. . . . These serve primarily as tools for communicating what is known of the subject matter . . ." Ibid., 12. A planetarium's ". . . principal function is to provide educational information on astronomy and related sciences through lectures and demonstrations." Ibid., 11.

4. Native American Grave Protection and Repatriation Act (25 U.S.C. 3002).

5. American Association of Museums, *A Higher Standard: The Museum Accreditation Handbook* (Washington, D.C.: American Association of Museums, 1997), 20.

23

Collecting Then, Collecting Today: What's the Difference?

Stephen E. Weil

It is astonishing to me to realize how great a gulf has opened up during the past twenty-five years or so between private collecting by individuals and institutional collecting by museums. Private collecting today is pretty much as it has always been. Although every collector has a distinctive style, all of those styles still combine a unique mix of passion, instinct, and impulse, on the one hand, and caution, deliberation, and calculating connoisseurship on the other. In sharp contrast, the nature of institutional collecting has changed almost completely during the years that I've been involved with museums.

Three factors, I think, primarily account for that change: First, it was only since the 1960s and with the introduction of more modern management methods that museums began to recognize the exponential rate at which their collections were tending to grow and the enormous economic burden represented by those collections, at least to the extent that they included indiscriminately acquired objects in quantities vastly greater than the institutions responsible for their care might ever conceivably use. Second, during this same period, the legal rules applicable to a variety of objects—particularly objects of foreign origin—proliferated enormously. Virtually all of these new rules had the effect of limiting the lawful import of such objects into the United States. Third, and most important, the very nature of museums themselves underwent an almost complete transformation, in which their focus changed from an inward concentration on their collections to a newly articulated outward concentration on the various publics and communities that they served.

Perhaps the earliest systematic effort to calculate the rate at which museum collections tend to grow was a study in the mid-1970s at the Smithsonian's dozen-plus

Stephen E. Weil is senior scholar emeritus at the Center for Museum Studies, Smithsonian Institution. "Collecting Then, Collecting Today: What's the Difference?" was originally delivered at the conference "Collecting the Twentieth Century—Tiffany to Pokeman," held in Cooperstown, New York, in October 2000 and was included in a collection of his essays entitled *Making Museums Matter*, published by the Smithsonian Institution Press in 2002. It is reprinted here by permission of the Press.

museums. Although not definitive, it did suggest an average growth rate of between 1 and 2 percent annually. Offering some confirmation of that figure was a subsequent study of sixty-one British museums conducted by Gail and Barry Lord and their associate John Nicks (*The Cost of Collecting*) in 1988–1989. Their average figure was about the same: 1.5 percent.

Although 1.5 percent may sound like a relatively benign figure, it becomes less so when calculated as a compound rate, meaning that a collection's size could double every fifty years and increase fourfold over a century, and considering that the expense of storing, guarding, and caring for collections, in the aggregate and over time, comes to a great deal more than even the most sophisticated of museum workers generally realize.

The pioneering work on collection-storage costs was done by the architect George Hartman of the Washington-based firm Hartman-Cox. In 1983, building on some work done several years earlier at the Institute of Archaeology and Anthropology at the University of South Carolina, Hartman developed a series of formulas that sought to take into account the "specific costs of such elements as accessioning, cataloguing, periodic inventory, maintaining accessible records, environmental and pest control, storage hardware, security, conservation, insurance, and general overhead including management and building expense."

In its May–June 1988 issue, *Museum News* applied Hartman's formulas to a hypothetical 100,000-square-foot (9,000-square-meter) museum building with an annual operating budget of $3 million. The results were startling. The annual operating cost allocable to an object kept in storage came—in 1988 dollars—to $30 per square foot (78 square centimeters). Hartman's numbers indicated that the average stored museum object—an average made up of coins, locomotives, beetles, and elephants—required not just 1 but 2 square feet (1.5 square meters) of storage, so the total cost per object was $60 per year. Using the consumer price index to adjust for the intervening inflation, that would translate into slightly more than $86 per object per year in today's dollars. For a stored collection of 1,000 objects, you might be looking at $86,000 of annual expense attributable to storage; for 10,000 objects, $860,000. From 11,600 objects upward, the annual cost of storage can average $1 million or more. Note, too, that those are only operating expenses and don't take into account the original capital expended to construct such storage in the first place.

Using a different methodology, the Lord and Nicks study arrived at a similar cost for British museums. They also found that close to two-thirds of all museum operating expenses were attributable directly or indirectly to the cost of managing and caring for collections, those on public display as well as those maintained in storage.

What has been the impact as museums have come to a better understanding of those numbers? In some instances, institutions have responded by becoming far more selective about what they will acquire, particularly as gifts. In others they have even resolved not to accept gifts—especially gifts of large groups of objects—unless such gifts are accompanied by sufficient funds to endow their future care. Finally, in some museums—primarily in the United States, not in Europe—systematic deaccessioning programs have been established as a routine aspect of collections management. Many feel that collections, no less than forests or herds of elk, can benefit from periodic thinning. For most institutional collectors, whatever their approach, collecting has become a far more deliberate and purposive activity than it was in the past.

Compounding this new deliberateness are many of the changes in the legal—and also the ethical—climate in which museums operate. The most dramatic of these relate to objects originating in other countries. Until the early 1970s, the prevailing rule in American law had been that it was not illegal per se to import an object into the United States solely because it had been illegally exported either from its country of origin or some intermediate jurisdiction. In practice this meant that museums were basically free to acquire anything that appeared on the market in this country after satisfying themselves, at a minimum, that their potential acquisitions had not been smuggled into the country, that is, that they had entered the United States under a lawful declaration of their origin and value. Buying things outside the country was a little trickier, to the extent that there might be complications pertaining to their export.

The first crack in this rule came in 1970 when the United States and Mexico signed a treaty providing for the recovery and return of stolen archaeological, historical, and cultural properties. Just two years later, similar protection was extended to a larger geographic area when Congress passed a statute regulating the import of pre-Columbian monumental and architectural sculptures and murals from (alphabetically) Bolivia, British Honduras (now Belize), Honduras, Costa Rica, the Dominican Republic, El Salvador, Guatemala, Mexico, Panama, Peru, and Venezuela.

What was eventually to prove the most significant event of the early 1970s was the U.S. ratification in 1972 of the UNESCO 1970 Convention on the Means of Prohibiting and Preventing the Illicit Import, Export, and Transfer of Ownership of Cultural Property. I say "eventually" because the convention was not self-executing. Implementing legislation was required to give it domestic force within the United States, and eleven more years passed before the Reagan administration was finally able to push such legislation through Congress in the form of the Convention on Cultural Property Implementation Act. Only now, nearly twenty years later, is the full force of that act beginning to be felt.

The Cultural Property Implementation Act (CPIA) was originally administered by the U.S. Information Agency, now a part of the U.S. Department of State. It is a massive and complex piece of legislation—suffice it to say that it provides in several ways for the imposition of import restrictions on various categories of cultural property originating from other state parties to the UNESCO convention. The state parties whose patrimonies are in one degree or another subject to an import restriction under the CPIA include Bolivia, Cambodia, Canada, Cyprus, El Salvador, Guatemala, Italy, Mali, Nicaragua, and Peru.

To understand the impact of the CPIA on museum collecting, consider the case of Peru. In an effort to prevent any further looting of the newly discovered and much-publicized Mocha tombs in its Sipan region, Peru successfully requested that the United States impose an import restriction on pre-Columbian archaeological materials originating from that area. Such a restriction, initially imposed by executive order, became effective on May 7, 1990. It provided that no such material could enter the United States unless either there was proof that it had been exported from Peru before the effective date or it was otherwise accompanied by documents indicating that its export from Peru had been in compliance with Peruvian law. In June 1997 that protection was folded into a more comprehensive regulatory scheme. Under a bilateral agreement between the United States and Peru, dated June 11, 1997, restrictions were extended to cover all pre-Columbian archaeological materials from Peru, wherever found, as well as colonial-era ethnographic materials, particularly those taken from churches.

Faced with the possible acquisition of a Peruvian-originated object—a Mocha gold ornament, say, or a carved wooden Santos figure—a museum in the United States may act at its peril unless it can establish on what date and, in some cases, under what circumstances the object left Peru. Failure to do so may result in the object's seizure and return to its country of origin.

While Congress and the State Department were following this UNESCO-based approach, the U.S. Department of Justice and the Customs Service were developing an alternative one of their own. Underpinning their approach is a four-step argument. First, they argue that the patrimony-protecting legislation of countries around the world actually operates to vest the legal title to protected patrimonial objects in the governments of those countries. Second, they argue that to remove such objects from those countries without the approval of their governmental owners would thus be tantamount to theft. Third, they argue that, consequently, any such object so removed might rightly be characterized as stolen property. Fourth and finally, they argue that any effort to bring such stolen property into the United States would render it subject to seizure under the customs laws. Worse still, anybody found dealing with such an object might be subject to criminal prosecution under the National Stolen Property Act.

The Justice Department first unveiled this theory in the late 1970s in *United States v. McClain*, a case that involved smuggled Mexican antiquities. Following a rigorous examination of the pertinent Mexican statutes, to determine whether these truly vested ownership of all such antiquities in the Mexican government, the federal Fifth Circuit Court of Appeals upheld the smugglers' convictions. The theory surfaced again in the widely discussed Steinhardt case—*United States v. An Antique*

Platter of Gold—involving a fourth-century-B.C. antiquity that New York collector Michael Steinhardt had purchased in 1991 for some $1.2 million and which, following a request from the government of Italy, the Customs Service seized from Steinhardt's Fifth Avenue apartment in 1995. In the district court case that followed, the presiding federal judge ruled that, under a 1939 Italian cultural patrimony law, the platter was ostensibly the property of Italy and, accordingly, an object of "stolen property" for purposes of applying U.S. domestic criminal law. Although the Court of Appeals for the Second Circuit subsequently affirmed the lower court's decision upholding this seizure in July 1999, it did so on a different ground—the case also involved a false customs declaration.

Meanwhile, the museum community—which had filed an amicus brief on Steinhardt's behalf—was left with the frightening possibility that, under this legal theory, other antiquities taken out of Italy since 1939 might also be deemed someday to have been stolen and could become subject to seizure and/or the basis for a criminal prosecution. Any museum collecting Italian antiquities today will certainly do so in a very different and far more circumspect manner than it might have done in earlier years.

Beyond legal restrictions with respect to collecting foreign-source objects, some museums have also subjected themselves to voluntary ethical constraints. The Smithsonian Institution is one example. The Smithsonian has had a rule in place since 1973—roughly the time that the United States approved the UNESCO convention— that forbids any of its museums to acquire, by gift or purchase, any material that was unlawfully removed from its country of origin after the date on which that rule went into effect.

Another area of collecting in which legal and ethical considerations come into play involves "Nazi-era" objects: in general, works of art and other artifacts that were created before 1945 and acquired after 1933. In reviewing their collections, most major art museums are engaged in an effort, through Web-site postings or otherwise, to track down whatever provenance information for that period they may be missing. Beyond that, both the AAM and the AAMD have issued detailed guidelines for the use of their memberships. These not only apply to their existing collections and material borrowed for exhibitions but refer to future acquisitions as well. These guidelines provide broad coverage. Issued late in 1999, the AAM's apply not only to objects that may have been unlawfully appropriated during the period 1933–1945, as a result of actions in furtherance of the Holocaust or taken by the Nazis or their collaborators, but also to "objects that were acquired through theft, confiscation, coercive transfer, or other methods of wrongful expropriation." Museums are urged by these guidelines not only to resolve the Nazi-era provenance status of objects before acquiring them but also—if credible evidence of unlawful appropriation without subsequent restitution should be discovered—to notify the donor or seller and all other interested parties of any such findings. Whatever merit "Don't ask; don't tell" may have in other spheres of life, it is emphatically not the rule with respect to Nazi-era objects.

For other kinds of objects, still other rules apply. Museums that collect Native American materials must, of course, be mindful of NAGPRA—the Native American Graves and Repatriation Act, under which objects they acquire may be subject to claims for repatriation. Museums that collect firearms—automatic ones, particularly—may have to be mindful of the federal Bureau of Alcohol, Tobacco and Firearms regulations concerning their ownership and/or interstate shipment. Museums that collect objects that include parts of animals—ivory chess sets or feather headdresses—must be aware of endangered species legislation and make sure that they are in compliance. Although private collectors are subject to many of these same rules—from those covering imports to those dealing with animal parts—they neither operate in the same kind of public fishbowl as do museums nor live under the perpetual threat that any perception of wrongdoing may jeopardize their funding.

Copyright can also present an increasingly tricky hurdle, particularly for art museums. Collage and "appropriation art"—to the extent that these may incorporate original work by others—can be especially troublesome. Both the Whitney Museum of American Art in New York City and the Museum of Contemporary Art in Los Angeles are defendants in a lawsuit involving an untitled 1990 artwork by the well-known feminist collage artist Barbara Kruger. The work—copies of which are in both of their collections and which both museums have frequently reproduced—depicts a young woman peering through a magnifying glass. Emblazoned across the image is the slogan IT'S A SMALL WORLD BUT NOT IF YOU HAVE TO CLEAN IT. The plaintiffs are a photographer, who claims to own the image—he alleges that Kruger copied it out of a 1960 German photography magazine without his permission—and who is suing for infringement, and the young woman depicted in the photograph, who is suing for invasion of privacy. This case involves only a single image. For museums that collect in the area of media—the Museum of the Moving Image in Queens, the Museum of Television and Radio with its branches both in New York and Los Angeles, or the Experience Music Project in Seattle—problems such as this may be compounded a thousand times over.

Ultimately, the most important change in the nature of institutional collecting is rooted in the changing nature of the museum itself from a focus on collection to a focus on public service. This decentering of the collection as the museum's raison d'être has by no means been uniform from one institution to another.

In a large number of instances, that change has meant that a museum's collections—which might once have been thought of as its "end"—can now be seen as a "means," as an instrument for the achievement of a larger end and simply one among a number of resources that the museum can employ to carry out its service obligations to the public. It is precisely at this point, at which the collection is no longer an end but a means, that institutional collecting is at its greatest distance from individual collecting. For a museum today, the question that hovers over every potential acquisition is not the one that a private collector might well have asked in the past and still asks today: "Is this a truly remarkable and intrinsically desirable object?" The question for the institutional collector is, instead, a question of utility: "How might this object be useful to the museum in carrying out its institutional mission?"

If that distinction needs an underline, it can be found in the AAM's *Handbook for Accreditation Visiting Committees* (2000). In listing the principal characteristics of an accreditable museum, the handbook notes that a museum's collections "are appropriate to the mission." Strongly implied is the proposition that—in a mature and functioning museum—it is the mission that shapes the collection and not the converse: that the collection can forever be accumulated willy-nilly and the mission subsequently reshaped from time to time to somehow fit around it.

That the latter alternative—to shape a mission around an existing collection, no matter how oddly formed or misshapen that collection might initially be—might well be the formula for a dysfunctional museum is not simply theoretical. In two notable and curiously parallel instances, both rooted in the late 1960s but played out in the 1990s, we have been able to witness the actual consequences of such an approach. One case involved Canadian lawyer Eric Harvie's entirely eccentric collection of more than a million objects, nearly another million photographs, and twenty-four thousand works of art; the other, the Eastman Kodak heiress Margaret Woodbury Strong's almost equally eccentric accumulation of some three hundred thousand artifacts including twenty-seven thousand dolls. In both cases it was assumed that a very large private collection could be readily converted into an effective museum collection. In both instances as well, the museums that were thus created—the Glenbow Museum in Calgary and the Strong Museum in Rochester—eventually found it necessary to reconceptualize themselves, and these massive collections were subordinated to a larger vision of the museum's role in the community. In the case of the Strong Museum, this involved turning itself into an entirely different kind of institution—a family and children's museum instead of the history museum that it started out to be.

My personal participation in the reshaping of a private collection for the use of a public institution happened during my years at the Hirshhorn Museum and Sculpture Garden, from its opening in 1974 to my retirement in 1995. Although Joseph H. Hirshhorn gave the museum some twelve thousand works of art—roughly half during his lifetime and the balance at his death—it was understood from the very beginning of his conversations with the Smithsonian in the 1960s that the museum was not to serve as a memorial to Hirshhorn's personal predilections as a collector—the Smithsonian had already been "burned" once by agreeing to that in the case of Charles Lang Freer. Instead, it would function as an educationally oriented institution, intended to develop a broader public understanding and appreciation of modern and contemporary art.

The reshaping of the Hirshhorn collection involved pruning away, primarily by disposition at auction, the excesses of Hirshhorn's sometimes glaring ebullience—he had collected more than fifty paintings by Milton Avery, more than eighty sculptures by Henry Moore, and more than four hundred paintings by Louis Eilshemius—and using the proceeds from those dispositions to begin to fill the equally glaring gaps in the collection—major movements in twentieth-century art in which he had little or no interest. It also involved the transfer to other museums within the Smithsonian of entire subcollections—Benin bronzes, Eskimo carvings, Middle Eastern antiquities—that had nothing to do with modern and contemporary art. Twenty years after Hirshhorn's death, this process of pruning and gap filling continues. My own guess is that it may take another twenty or thirty years to complete.

The museum has always tried to make clear that this reshaping process should in no possible way be interpreted as critical or disrespectful of Hirshhorn's activities as a private collector. He did what the private collector has always done and remains uniquely and gloriously privileged to continue to do: He collected not only for his own deep pleasure but also—as Francis Henry Taylor once pointed out with respect to individual collectors in general—"as a complex and irrepressible expression of the inner individual" that he was. Hirshhorn the mighty hunter and Hirshhorn the proud possessor were both wonderfully reflected in the collection he amassed.

If once upon a time museums—or at least museum directors or senior curators acting on their behalf—could collect in such a passionate, vital, and self-expressive way, collect with that same bravado and zest that typifies the private collector in hot pursuit of his or her quest, such a time has long since gone. Museum collecting today, for all these reasons—the burden of caring for collections, the necessity to negotiate a labyrinth of legal considerations, and the need for acquisitions to be carefully related to mission—has become something else. Still exciting, still rewarding, but—to a great degree—it is stately, sober, and deliberate as well. It is said that blondes have more fun. So too, I think—and it's a rueful thought—do private collectors.

24

Collections Planning:
Pinning Down a Strategy

James B. Gardner and Elizabeth Merritt

Collecting is central to the mission of most museums. Museums devote significant resources to the acquisition and maintenance of collections. It is surprising then that collections planning is among the rarest of museum activities. It is surely one of the most critically needed.

As financial and other resources become scarce and competition for them grows more intense, exerting greater control over the content and size of a museum's collection has become an issue for all institutions, large and small. All across the country, museums are discovering that they cannot afford to care for every object that they might acquire, even if it is directly related to institutional mission. As a result, some tough choices have to be made about what to collect, what not to collect, and what to remove from the collections. Even when financial resources are not a limiting factor, collecting decisions made by individuals, however knowledgeable, do not automatically result in a coherent, well-rounded collection that best serves the needs of the institution. What is needed is a carefully prepared collections plan—one that has earned the support of the director, the board, and the senior staff.

The lack of collections planning is not limited to small and mid-size museums. Even a large institution such as the Smithsonian faces the same challenges. One might assume that, as the nation's history museum, the National Museum of American History (NMAH) would have a relatively clear collecting mandate—to preserve and interpret American history and culture. But in fact, its staff acquire objects without clearly articulated institutional parameters or vision. Though the curatorial units nominally have collecting plans, these mostly are, as one staff member described them, little more than "shelf inventories." Self-directed curators build on

James B. Gardner is Associate Director for Curatorial Affairs at the National Museum of American History, Behring Center, Smithsonian Institution, and Elizabeth Merritt is director, Museum Advancement & Excellence at the American Association of Museums in Washington, D.C. "Collections Planning: Pinning Down a Strategy" is reprinted here with permission from *Museum News*, July/August 2002. Copyright 2002, the American Association of Museums. All rights reserved.

their predecessors' interests and work, adding depth and new topics, but often operating in isolation from other staff and other units. As a result, while the museum's collections are exceptional in terms of their quality and depth, they are also rather idiosyncratic; the parts don't add up to a whole. There is no substitute for a serious, institutionally coordinated attempt at collections planning.

NMAH is far from alone; museums around the country face the same problem, perhaps different in scale but similar in kind. Museums often believe their collections policies constitute collecting plans, but they rarely do. Collections policies list conditions that must be met for an object to be acquired—for example, good provenance, high quality, relevant to mission—and generally outline the scope of the collection. Such "Scope of the Collection" statements draw broad boundaries—for example, geographic origin, time period, subject matter—around what might be acquired and summarize what is already in the collection. However, these statements usually provide only the most basic guidance for determining what types of items might be acquired. And the description of the collection sometimes includes material that the museum owns but does not want to retain. Policies cannot replace a current, ongoing, institutionally supported planning process.

What many institutions need is better focused and more disciplined collections planning. Planning is an inclusive effort, one that brings together staff from across departmental boundaries and may also reach out to external stakeholders. The planning process may lead board and staff to reexamine basic assumptions about the museum's mission and its role in the community. The process also may challenge assumptions about traditional staff roles and areas of authority. At NMAH, for example, a culture of autonomous curators working in relatively isolated collecting units presents a particularly daunting organizational challenge. Unless all those units buy in to a new collecting plan, it is doomed to fail. In other words, the human aspects of planning require at least as much care and thought as the physical, financial, and administrative aspects. It is one thing to write a plan; it is quite another to implement it. And the work doesn't end with implementation. Collections planning must be an ongoing process, not fossilized in a document that sits on the shelf, overlooked by the curators.

Data from AAM's Accreditation Program suggest that collections planning is a concern throughout the field. The Accreditation Program recognizes museums that are committed to the highest standards of operation and public service. Nationally about 750 museums are accredited, and about 25 more apply to the program each year. Each year about 100 museums are reviewed by the nine-member Accreditation Commission, either as first-time applicants for accreditation or as part of the process for subsequent accreditation. According to the Commission, a lack of collections planning is a major impediment to the success of many of the institutions that they review. These museums commit significant time and resources to achieving excellence while also submitting to a detailed, systematic review by peers. As such, they may serve as an early-warning system for issues in the field at large.

The Accreditation Commission has identified a pattern of recurring problems connected to collections stewardship and institutional planning: insufficient resources to support collections; collections unrelated to the institution's mission; and a lack of integration between planning for collections, interpretation, and facilities. These issues interfere in concrete ways with the museum's ability to succeed: the collections may suffer from poor care; limited resources may be spent on acquiring material that is unrelated to institutional mission; and the institution may perform ineffectively because its collections, exhibits, and educational activities are neither connected to each other nor supported by a financial plan. The Commission believes that these issues can be addressed through a collections-planning process that is strategic, audience-centered, visionary, tied to resource allocation, and encompasses all collections and all functional areas of the institution.

DEFINITIONS

(adapted from glossaries used by AAM's Museum Assessment and Accreditation programs):

COLLECTING PLAN: A plan guiding the content of the collections that leads the staff in a coordinated and uniform direction over a period of years to refine and expand the value of the collections in a predetermined way. By creating a plan, a museum seeks to gain intellectual control over collections.

COLLECTIONS PLANNING: The integrated, institution-wide process of creating a collecting plan.

COLLECTIONS MANAGEMENT POLICY OR COLLECTIONS POLICY: a written document, accepted by the governing body, that specifies the museum's policies concerning all collections related issues including accessioning, documentation, storage, and disposition. Often includes a Scope of Collections Statement.

SCOPE OF COLLECTIONS STATEMENT: defines the purpose of the collection, and sets agreed upon limits such as subject, geographical location, and time period to which each collection must relate. The statement also may consider the uses of a collection and state the types of objects that will be acquired to fulfill the purposes of that collection. These statements tend to be very broad and often describe what is in the collection now rather than focus on plans for the future.

Recently AAM and NMAH issued a call for sample collecting plans from museums of all types, sizes, and geographic locations. These plans vary greatly in style and content, but they do have certain similarities. Although there is no field-wide "template" for a collecting plan, many museums have discovered independently that certain components are useful and necessary. After a preliminary examination, it is clear that most collecting plans:

1) **Identify the museum's audience(s) and how their needs will be served by the collections.** Selecting the "right stuff" can be done only in the context of the intended use of the collections. A collection intended to support in-depth, scholarly research will be very different from one meant to provide the public with a general survey of a topic. This "needs assessment" also may encompass the museum's plans for exhibits and educational programs—in what ways does the collection need to grow to support those activities? In other words, an effective collecting plan must be tied to the institution's strategic planning.

2) **Review the strengths and weaknesses of the existing collections.** All curators have an understanding of their collections, but rarely put this information down on paper or share it with their colleagues throughout the museum. In an institution as large as NMAH, for example, things sometimes fall between the cracks without notice or discussion—from the little-used collections that sit unnoticed in large curatorial units to the collecting opportunities that remain unaddressed simply because they fall outside existing specializations or interests.

3) **Include a "gap analysis" contrasting the real and the ideal collection.** NMAH has taken the first step by developing a central theme—"What has it meant to be an American?"—as well as sub-themes that provide the context for assessing the existing collection and envisioning "the ideal."

4) **Set priorities for acquisition and deaccessioning based on the needs assessment and gap analysis.** This is the key to the planning process, since setting priorities can drive change and focus efforts. Prioritizing acquisitions is a way to show donors that the material you seek is key to your success. Deaccessioning is sometimes a controversial activity that museums often avoid due to concerns about bad publicity. A good collections-planning process can explain to the public that the museum is making responsible and appropriate choices about deaccessioning that will best serve its audience(s).

5) **Identify "complementary collections" held by other museums or organizations that may affect the museum's collections choices.** In a world of rapidly constricting resources, museums are turning to partnerships and cooperative agreements with other institutions. Many museums consciously choose not to collect in areas that are strongly represented in other museums, particularly if those museums serve the same audience. Some institutions have begun to cooperate by building mutually supportive, complementary collections that can be used as joint resources. Others proactively identify other museums that may be suitable recipients for donations they wish to route away from their own organizations.

6) **Take into account existing or needed resources.** A powerful collecting plan is one that ties its objectives to a concrete analysis of the financial, human, and physical resources needed to support the collection. Building a compelling vision of the future can help leverage funds and support. On the other hand, failing to plan for the necessary resources for new acquisitions can render the museum unable to fulfill its collections stewardship responsibilities.

Admittedly, NMAH's goal in partnering with AAM in this initiative is a self-serving one—the museum expects to gain not only a useful understanding of best practices but also a new collecting plan, a clearly articulated vision of how its collections should be shaped and developed. The museum takes pride in the collections that it has built, but it also recognizes that it cannot assume that its current collecting approach will meet its future responsibilities. Its staff must continue to make tough choices about what to collect. But those choices have to be better informed and made within the context of NMAH's larger role as the nation's history museum.

But there is a bonus to taking this project on: the opportunity to help AAM lead the larger museum community in a critically needed discussion about collections planning. We hope that ultimately other museums of all sizes and type, in all regions across the country, will be able to benefit from what we learn. After all, this is planning that gets at the heart of what so many of us are all about—collecting and collections.

25

Who Cares? Conservation in a Contemporary Context

Carole Milner

The United Kingdom (England, Scotland, Wales and Northern Ireland) has a population of almost 60 million. Spread across the country are its 2,500 museums and galleries. These range from the nineteen large nationals, such as London's National Galleries and Victoria and Albert Museum (with its budget of £29 million and a staff of 800), to city museums like Glasgow and Bristol, and to small community museums with possibly no permanent staff and budgets of just a few hundred pounds. Collections contain everything from fine art to beetles and battleships. Objects can be as small as historic cave fauna which can only be identified through microscopes or as large as the largest object of all—the building itself which houses the collection.

The first national museum in the world, the British Museum, was founded in 1753 but there were no public art galleries in England until the nineteenth century. The Museums Act of 1845 enabled town councils to establish public museums of art and science and a further Act of 1850 stipulated that such museums should be free. These museums and galleries provided a sense of identity and became emblems of great civic pride. They were intended to delight and improve the visitor's mind and those with the desire for self-improvement flocked to them, sometimes travelling long distances to do so.

Today they perform a multiplicity of roles. Some are temples of art and culture. Others preserve all that remains of our industrial heritage—textile mills, coal and tin mines—and what was once the day-to-day life and cultural identity of a whole region, town or street. Others are more like heritage centres with their 'living experiences,' automats and interactives. What they all have in common are their primary aims: to care for and make accessible their collections for the enjoyment, education

Carole Milner is Head of Conservation and Collection Care at the Museums & Galleries Commission in London. "Who Cares? Conservation in a Contemporary Context" appeared in *Museum International* (Vol. 51, No. 1 [1999], pp. 22–27). It is reprinted here by permission of Blackwell Publishing.

and inspiration of the public. That is the context in which conservation operates to-day in the United Kingdom.

CONSERVATION AND ACCESS—BALANCED PRIORITIES

This context implies, by definition, a balancing act. On the one hand, all objects are subject to decay and deterioration, depending on their constituent nature, the environment they are kept in, the treatment they receive and the use that is made of them. Materially, they need to be looked after and given proper treatment. They belong to the nation and we have a collective 'duty of care' to ensure they are preserved for posterity.

On the other hand, our museums and galleries are part of the growing leisure industry. In the United Kingdom, especially since the advent of weekend opening in 1995, they are in competition with leisure centres, theme parks, shopping malls and sports complexes. They have to compete for their markets and that competition is increasingly fierce. The buzz words at all levels for museums in the United Kingdom are: access, information technology, entertainment, education, enjoyment. In the current climate of restrictions, it is easy to forget that some degree of balance has to be kept between the resources being ploughed into front-of-house activities to attract the public into museums and those required for the behind-the-scenes care which sustains the collections for their longer-term use.

Conservation should not be perceived as a competing priority but one which underpins so many other museum activities. It is not an end in itself but a means to an end. That end is ensuring that we can continue to use and enjoy our heritage not only today but for generations to come. Our museums attract around 75 million visits a year and 60 percent of overseas tourists visit the United Kingdom precisely because of the lure of its museums and galleries. Cultural tourism is of growing economic importance but our heritage is a non-renewable resource and is under increasing threat. A simple 'good housekeeping' adage says it all: 'If you want to keep it, look after it!' Access and care go hand-in-hand as balanced priorities at every level: in museums, historic buildings and heritage sites, nationally and internationally. That is the route to managed sustainability.

RIGHTS AND RESPONSIBILITIES

So who is responsible for making sure this happens? Whose job is it to care about our collections and to care for them? At one end of the spectrum we have the bench conservator working on his or her object in the conservation laboratory, state or private. Further up the chain we have the person at the other end who pushes the button which sets this process off and enables it to happen.

The planning process is where it all starts. Overall needs, of which conservation is only one, have to be assessed in the light of the museum's mission statement, its aims and objectives and forward plan. Priorities must be established, decisions made and funding allocated accordingly. Only then can the rest of the work begin. The duty of caring for collections is a collective one but the statutory responsibility lies ultimately with those who are legally responsible for the collections—directors, chief executives, boards, owners or trustees who may or may not be the active decision-makers. The next layer of responsibility lies with the planners and those who take the decisions—directors, managers and administrators, curators, keepers and collections managers.

Once the decisions are made and the funding allocated, the responsibility for actual care and treatment passes down the line to those with the specific expertise: conservation professionals, specialists in the care of collections, conservation teachers and scientists. They do some of the work and are likely to supervise the work of others to whom tasks are allotted under supervision, such as conservation technicians, students and volunteers. When the objects are back on display or in use there are those whose day-to-day vigilance can ensure that potential threats are identified and alarm bells set ringing—the guardians and warders, volunteers, cleaners, security guards and even museum visitors themselves. Key actors on a par with the rest are all who are involved with the construction, renovation and maintenance of the buildings in which the collections are housed—engineers, architects, buildings maintenance teams and so on.

Finally, outside the museum building with its administrative, professional and technical personnel, are the national, regional and local policy-makers. Their decisions to cut grants, reduce budgets, promote the heritage, close or open more museums, establish regional or national preservation plans such as the Delta Plan (in the Netherlands) will, of course, set the stage for all other decisions, weakening or strengthening them.

When they work in synergy, these responsibilities link together and form an effective chain. However, the chain can break at any point—a leaking roof, an unidentified pest infestation, improperly trained conservators, unsupervised helpers, a lack of long-term vision or leadership, inadequate forward planning. That is when, sooner or later, the objects and collections will fall victim to someone's dereliction of duty along the way.

Why do such breakdowns occur? It is usually because the right connections are not being made. The fact that integrated conservation is a collective responsibility throws up the need for effective communication at all levels. This means good teamwork within institutions, better networking outside them and a concerted effort to promote greater understanding and appreciation of conservation by the general public and all other stakeholders.

In the United Kingdom we are fortunate in having networks and structures in place which facilitate reasonable two-way communications—bottom up as well as top down! Government departments fund the work of national advisory and standard-setting bodies such as the Museums & Galleries Commission (MGC). This, in turn, supports the activities of a network of ten regional organizations (Area Museum Councils) and their 2,500 member museums and associated organizations. Close links are maintained with training centres and with key representative bodies such as the Museums Association and the Conservation Forum (an umbrella body which represents the eleven main conservation professional bodies). By getting actively involved in their work, constructive relationships have also been forged with international organizations such as ICCROM (International Centre for the Study of the Preservation and Restoration of Cultural Property) and the Getty Conservation Institute.

ISSUES AND IMPLICATIONS

With all this in mind, what are the needs of conservation today and what implications are there for the way we manage our responsibilities and seek to organize the care we give to our museum collections at institutional, national, European and international levels?

In order to care for their collections and to manage that process effectively and efficiently, museums need, first and foremost, to know what they have got and where it is. They need to know what condition their collections are in and what the priorities are for their use, as this will determine the level of care and treatment given. Then, in practical terms, they need:

- support with conservation planning and management—models and tools for assessing needs and measuring progress in raising standards, as well as hard, contextualized information on needs and provision to help argue the case for funding convincingly;
- reliable information and advice on how to care for their collections;
- access to competent, qualified conservation professionals who meet the necessary technical, professional and ethical standards;
- guidance on establishing constructive contractual relationships and consensus over the standards to be met and what constitutes 'value for money';
- access to training for all those who are in any way engaged in caring for collections;
- help in raising awareness and promoting the work they do to look after their collections.

Underpinning all this, they need the support at every level for the principle that care and access go hand-in-hand as balanced priorities within museums, and that this is the way to the sustainability of our cultural heritage.

The United Kingdom with its structured network of support and information services has made good progress in many of these areas. However, because of the great number of museums and decreasing levels of revenue funding, there is a danger of serious backlogs building up. Statistics show, for instance, that only 3 percent of museums estimate they have enough storage space for expansion of their collections; only 12 percent have air conditioning and more than half evaluate their environmental data less than once a year, if ever!

The impact of the contract culture has made itself felt in every sector of the country. Patterns of conservation need and provision have altered and the boundaries between public and private sectors have blurred. There are few ivory towers left, funding is ever tighter and, public or private sector, we all now function in a competitive market. The need for standards and for organizations which set and monitor them has become self-evident. The Museum Registration Scheme run by the MGC sets institutional standards for all areas of museum activity including conservation, and the Digest of Museum Statistics (DOMUS) database provides overview information on progress towards meeting those standards. The MGC's database of conservation practices, the Conservation Register, provides information to British museums, heritage organizations and the public on 700 independent conservation practices which meet consensus standards. Finally, the conservation profession is taking increasing control of professional standards and, through the Conservation Forum, a more unified approach to the regulation of these standards through systems of accreditation.

To do a little crystal-ball gazing, there are issues in the United Kingdom which will inevitably impact on the way conservation evolves into the millennium. Can we go on opening new museums and collecting when we already can't look after what we've got? Should a new acquisition be made dependent on the availability of resources for the long-term care of the object? Do we need to prioritize both our collections and the objects in them for long-term preservation? Should we reassess our policies on use and accept that certain objects will be used and ultimately lost? In a world of theme parks, Disneyland and back-through-time experiences how important is 'the real thing' going to be in fifty years' time—will the 'virtual museum' take over, replacing direct contact with the objects and what implications will that have for conservation?

There is currently in Europe a tangible rise in the level of mutual concern over threats to the preservation of our common cultural heritage. This has been reflected in the momentum for change that has been building up since the beginning of 1997. The main concerns of the conservation professionals and decision-makers appear to be standards in training and education, conditions for research, and the qualifications, competence and responsibilities of those who can, if improperly prepared, pose the most direct threat to the objects and collections—the conservator-restorers themselves.

These issues have all been picked up in a series of meetings which have taken place over the last year. The first was the 'Centres of Excellence' workshops which took place in Amsterdam in May 1997. This was followed by the ECCO (European Confederation of Conservator-Restorers' Organizations) conference, held in Florence. Finally, in October 1997, a European Summit held in Pavia, Italy, produced a number of key recommendations for future action which have now been transmitted to the European Union and other key national and international decision-making bodies.[1]

Communication, which is always linguistically awkward on these occasions, is not helped by the fact that concepts which form the basis of work being undertaken in one country may not even exist in another or have no simple one-to-one translation. Ultimately, however, the important thing is not that we should all agree on everything but that we should be talking constructively to each other. Despite the difficulties, over the last year European conservation professionals in the movable heritage sector have succeeded in presenting their concerns and possible ways forward in a cohesive manner to the powers that be and this is now bearing fruit: 'United we bargain, divided we beg!'

Finally, setting the context for us all, are the wider international concerns for the long-term preservation of our cultural heritage, both movable and immovable. These appear to centre around issues of sustainability, the impact of cultural tourism and the role of conservation as a key stabilization factor and as a conduit for economic and social development. Efforts are being made in some countries to gather statistical information on conservation needs and provision and to quantify the economic impact of conservation and the cost/benefits of long-term strategies for preservation. Many countries want access to more conservation management and planning tools in order to empower them in the decision-making process whilst others are still overridingly concerned with the need for further technical assistance and training. A number of these issues have been gradually moving up the agenda for ICCROM and, at the General Assembly of ICCROM's ninety-four member states in December 1997, they were voted into the new biennial programme as core areas for development.

ACCENTUATE THE POSITIVE . . .

Conservation in the United Kingdom, as elsewhere, has evolved: from heritage skills and crafts, to repair and reconstruction, to restoration, conservation, care and maintenance, preservation and rescue. Priorities, perceptions, patterns of employment and funding are all changing rapidly. We have to rise to these new challenges and become ever more effective advocates for conservation at every level: public, professional and political.

Who cares? We all do. But it is only by pulling together, pooling resources and expertise, looking outwards rather than inwards and building on what we have in common that we will be able to ensure a safe future for our collective past.

NOTE

1. See Gaël de Guichen, 'The Pavia Document: Towards a European Profile of the Conservator-Restorer', *Museum International*, No. 199—Ed.

26

A Philosophical Perspective
on the Ethics and Resolution
of Cultural Properties Issues

Karen J. Warren

INTRODUCTION

Who, if anyone, owns the past? Who has the right or responsibility to preserve cultural remains of the past? When, if ever, should preservational or educational considerations override national sovereignty in determining the disposition of cultural materials? What should be declared illegal or illicit trade in cultural properties? What values are at stake in conflicts over cultural properties, and how should these conflicts be resolved?

Questions such as these are at the heart of the debate over so-called "cultural properties." These questions raise important philosophical issues about the past (e.g., what constitutes the past; who, if anyone, may be said to own the past; who may have access to the past and to the information derived from it; what controls may be exercised over remains of the past). They also bring to the fore both the diversity of values associated with the preservation of cultural properties (e.g., aesthetic, educational, scholarly, cultural, and economic values) and the conflicts of interests of the various parties to the dispute (e.g., governments or nations, private citizens, collectors, art and antiquities dealers, museums and museum curators, suppliers or sellers, customs agents, indigenous peoples, present and future generations of humans).

It is easy to get lost in this cacophony of voices over cultural properties. These voices raise very different, often competing, perspectives on the nature and resolution of cultural properties issues. What is needed to help guide one through the morass is a philosophical framework for understanding and assessing the variety of claims and perspectives in the debate over cultural properties.

The primary purpose of this essay is to provide such a framework. I begin by presenting an overview of what I take to be the main arguments and issues in the debate

Karen J. Warren is professor of philosophy at Macalaster College in St. Paul, Minnesota. "A Philosophical Perspective on the Ethics and Resolution of Cultural Properties Issues" is the introduction to *The Ethics of Collecting Cultural Property: Whose Culture? Whose Ethics?* edited by Phyllis Mauch Messenger and published in 1999 by the University of New Mexico Press. It is reprinted here by permission of the Press.

over cultural properties. This section is intended to be reportive of what I understand to be the central arguments in the debate and suggestive of some of the key philosophical issues raised by that debate. I then suggest that what is at stake philosophically in the debate over cultural properties is much deeper and richer than a critique of any particular argument would show; what is at stake is the very way in which one conceives the dispute, and, hence, the way in which one attempts to resolve that dispute. I do this by showing how the current debate over cultural properties reflects what I call "the dominant perspective" in the Western philosophical tradition, and by suggesting some respects in which that perspective is itself problematic as a conceptual framework for identifying and resolving so-called cultural properties issues. I conclude by suggesting that what is needed is a rethinking of the debate in terms which preserve the strengths of a dominant perspective while making a central place for considerations often overlooked or undervalued from that perspective. This is the promise of "an integrative perspective" on cultural heritage issues.

PHILOSOPHICAL OVERVIEW: THE 3 R'S

One way to organize the various claims which surface in the dispute over cultural properties is in terms of what I call "The 3 R's." The 3 R's are claims concerning the restitution of cultural properties to their countries of origin, the restriction of imports and exports of cultural properties, and the rights (e.g., rights of ownership, rights of access, rights of inheritance) retained by relevant parties.

Claims to the 3 R's are offered by the various parties to the disputes and represent a wide range of relevant values. Typically, these claims conceive the debate over "cultural properties" as a debate over ownership of the past, where "the past" is understood not only as the physical remains of the past (e.g., artifacts, places, monuments, archaeological sites) but also the "perceptions of the past itself" (e.g., information, myths, and stories used in reconstructing and transmitting the past).[1]

Some of the arguments in support of the claims concerning the 3 R's are mutually compatible; others are not. Many of these arguments turn on how one answers the question "Who owns the past?" Three sorts of alternative and competing answers are given: (1) "Everyone owns the past," since the past is the common heritage of all; it is "humanity's past;" (2) "Some specific group (e.g., indigenous peoples, scholars, collectors, museums, nations) owns the past," since that group speaks for or represents the important values that are at stake in the debate over cultural properties; and (3) "No one owns the past," since the past is not really the sort of thing that is ownable. As will be shown, these three sorts of answers reflect competing philosophical positions about the ownership of "cultural property," understood here in the widest sense to include both physical remains of the past and "perceptions of the past itself."

In this section I identify what I take to be the main sorts of arguments for, and the main sorts of arguments against, claims to the 3 R's by countries of origin,[2] and the basic philosophical issues raised by each. I treat each argument like the basic plot line of a story: The argument's plot line is the basic focus or issue addressed. While a change in cast of characters and circumstantial details provides different, often more complex, versions of the story, the plot line of the story remains basically unchanged by these variations on a theme.

Six Arguments Against Claims to the 3 R's by Countries of Origin

1. *The Rescue Argument* Many of the sorts of cultural properties at issue would have been destroyed (e.g., by natural elements, war, looters) if they had not been rescued by those foreigners or foreign countries with the skills and resources to preserve them. Those who rescued them now have a valid claim (right, interest, entitlement) to them, whether or not they had such a claim prior to their rescue and preservation by foreigners. Hence, the rescue of these cultural properties by foreigners and foreign countries justifies their retention by foreign parties or countries. Any efforts toward repatriation of these properties by countries of origin, on whatever basis, is unjustified.

The Rescue Argument raises two basic, interrelated issues about the practice of rescuing or saving cultural properties. The first issue is whether that practice is justified; the second is, if justified, whether that practice gives foreign countries (including individual foreigners) a valid claim to the rescued properties.

Three grounds for justification of the rescue of cultural properties are typically offered: first, the values preserved and interests served justify the rescue as a practice, whatever the costs or benefits of the rescue in a particular case; second, the benefits gained in a particular case justify the rescue in that case; and, third, those who rescue cultural properties have a right (e.g., right of ownership) to those properties, which right is passed on to genuine beneficiaries.[3]

Notice that, taken together, these three different grounds offered for the justification of rescuing cultural properties draw upon the whole range of issues about values, rights, and utility (e.g., cost-benefit) considerations which are addressed by the remaining five arguments given below. As such, whether or not the Rescue Argument is sound will turn, in part, on the strengths and weaknesses of these other arguments.

2. *The Foreign Ownership Argument* The removal of many cultural properties by foreign countries (or foreigners) was undertaken legally (e.g., by permit); they were neither stolen nor illegally imported.[4] Since they were legally removed, those who removed them (or their genuine beneficiaries), and not the countries of origin, own them and are legally entitled to keep them. Therefore, no claims to restitution, restriction, or rights of ownership of countries of origin against such foreign countries or foreigners are valid.

The main issue raised by the Foreign Ownership Argument is what constitutes "legality" with regard to the removal of cultural properties. How one answers that question will affect how one answers the secondary question of the legality of claims to the 3 R's—restitution, restriction, and rights—by countries of origin.

Considerations of legality are not, as they might first appear, straightforward questions of fact. To determine legality one must ask a host of other questions as well: According to whom was the cultural property legally removed? According to which laws was the removal deemed legal? What is illicit or illegal under the existing law of the country of origin? Was the country of origin under foreign rule at the time the property was removed? What are taken to be the relevant facts bearing on the issue of legality? Are the facts intersubjectively and interculturally verifiable and agreed upon as facts?

Such questions make visible important issues about what counts as a fact and whether agreement about facts is sufficient to ensure agreement about the legality of the removal of cultural properties. For even when alleged questions of fact are resolved, there may still be important ethical disagreement about how to value the facts, for example, about what valuational attitude to take toward the facts. This ethical disagreement in attitude may persist even when agreement in belief is reached about the facts or about the legality of the removal of cultural properties. Until agreement in attitude on the relevant ethical issues is also reached (e.g., agreement on how to value the facts, or whether what is legal ought to be legal), disagreement on whether such practices should be declared illicit or illegal will persist.

Attempts to answer these definitional, empirical, and valuational questions reveal the respects in which the resolution of many legal issues presupposes the resolution of many nonlegal issues (e.g., about what one takes as fact and how to value the facts). Determining the soundness of the Foreign Ownership Argument, then, will involve determining the correctness of a whole range of other commitments (explicit or implicit) on other-than-strictly legal issues; in fact, it will turn on just such issues as are raised by the other five arguments against claims to the 3 R's by countries of origin.

3. *The Humanity Ownership Argument* Many cultural properties have artistic, scholarly, and educational value which constitutes the cultural heritage of human society. But the cultural heritage of human society belongs to a common humanity. Hence, these cultural properties belong to a common humanity: they are not and cannot be owned by any one country, and no one country has a right to them. Since countries of origin do not own or have a right to them, blanket declarations of ownership by countries of origin are not binding and ought not be upheld by foreign courts.

The general issue raised by the Humanity Ownership Argument is whether one can speak meaningfully of the past being owned by "everyone, and no one in particular." If so, then any claims to ownership by any specific group (whether a foreign country or country of origin, whether a collector, art dealer, or museum curator) are moot.

Certainly there is precedent in law and ethics to speak of rights which hold against "the world at large"—so called *in rem* rights, in contrast with *in personam* rights. "No trespassing rights" are frequently cited as examples of in rem rights. But whether any such rights talk, including talk of a "common humanity" as rightful owner of cultural properties, is properly construed as talk of ownership is a controversial issue. That issue would have to be resolved in the affirmative in order for the Humanity Ownership Argument to be plausible. Furthermore, there would need to be agreement that there is a relevant common humanity. Marxists or feminists might challenge just such a claim as presupposing a mistaken, ahistorical notion of what it is to be human. For traditional Marxists, humans are always historically and materially located; "human nature" is always a response to the prevailing mode of economic production in a society or culture. On this view, there is no such thing as a "human nature" or "common humanity," if by that, one means a transcendental ahistorical, asocial "essence" which all humans have, independent of their particular concrete and historical location. Similarly, many feminists have argued that in contemporary culture, thoroughly structured by such factors as sex/gender, race, and class, there is no such thing as a *human simpliciter* all humans are humans of some sex/gender, race/ethnicity, class, affectional preference, marital status, etc.[5] Such feminists argue against "abstract individualism," that is, the view that humans can meaningfully be said to exist independent of and abstracted from any social, historical circumstances. If the "common humanity" referred to by the Humanity Ownership Argument refers to some notion of an ahistorical essence or abstract individualism, the argument will be rejected by these classical Marxists and feminists.

4. *The Means-End Argument* The practice of selling or exporting cultural properties has materially aided the promotion of many important values: the preservation of priceless artifacts; the enrichment of aesthetic sensibilities; the advancement of education and scholarship; the breakdown of parochialism; the encouragement of cultural pluralism; the role of art as a good will ambassador. Not only is the promotion of these values both desirable and justified; its continuance requires the "free flow" of at least some cultural properties. Hence, the practice of selling or exporting cultural properties is both desirable and justified, and restrictions on such practices are undesirable and unjustified.

The Means-End Argument is a utilitarian argument against regulations of imports and exports in terms of the multifarious benefits of import/export practices. The philosophically interesting issues it raises are many: When do such utilitarian considerations outweigh nonconsequentialist (deontological) considerations[6]— such as ones based on alleged claims of rights, claims to restitution, or claims to compensatory justice (e.g., by repatriation of stolen or taken cultural properties) by countries of origin? What is the scope of such utilitarian claims? Are only some practices of selling or exporting some cultural properties undesirable and unjustified, and hence only some restrictions desirable and justified on utilitarian grounds?

Or is the scope wider than this? And even if the utilitarian benefits of (some) unrestricted export/import practices is established, where should the cultural properties stay? Claims to restitution by countries of origin are not automatically ruled out by the Means-End Argument.

The Means-End Argument is a very popular kind of argument against claims to the 3 R's by countries of origin. This is because the Means-End Argument makes a fundamental place not only for the full range of values at issue in the debate over cultural properties, but also for those parties to the debate who support the export/import of cultural properties on the basis of the benefits and advantages gained by such practices for themselves and others. However, the Means-End Argument leaves totally open the question about *how* to control the international trade in cultural properties in order both to prevent theft and looting and to ensure the protection and preservation of those properties. Should one do so through physical protection, economic incentives and sanctions, embargos, screening and licensing systems, or import/export regulation?[7] If the use of export-import regulations is desirable and justified, one must state exactly which ones are, which cultural properties are/should be regulated by them, and how appeal to them preserves the relevant values at stake. It is on just these points of substance and detail that advocates of the Means-End Argument differ drastically. To resolve those issues, more is needed than the Means-End Argument itself (as given here) provides.

5. *The Scholarly Access Argument* In order to preserve cultural properties, those whose primary responsibility or role is to promote and transmit cultural information and knowledge (e.g., scholars, educators, museum curators) must have scholarly access to cultural properties. Restitution to or retention by countries of origin of cultural properties will prevent such persons from having scholarly access to cultural properties. Hence, such restitution and retention is unjustified.

If scholarly access to cultural properties is viewed primarily as a necessary means to a desired end (viz. the preservation of cultural properties), then the Scholarly Access Argument is a version of the Means-End Argument and can be treated as such. If, however, scholarly access to cultural properties is viewed as a right or responsibility of persons properly authorized to preserve cultural properties, then the Scholarly Access Argument is a separate argument in its own right. Understood as the latter, it is grounded on the assumptions that there is a responsibility to preserve cultural properties, and that fulfillment of that responsibility is the right or duty of properly authorized persons—typically authorized because of the official powers, roles (offices, positions), or institutions (e.g., museums) such persons have, occupy, or represent.

On either interpretation of the Scholarly Access Argument, then, the main issues raised are the same: What is the nature and ground of a responsibility to preserve cultural properties, and whose responsibility, or even right, is it to do so? If it is the right or responsibility of some specific group (e.g., scholars, collectors, museum officials), then those arguments which locate that right elsewhere (e.g., in "everyone" or in "no one"), or which do not see the preservation of cultural properties as an issue of rights at all (e.g., the Means-End Argument), are seriously problematic, if not simply unsound.

6. *The Encouragement of Illegality Argument* The practice of restricting the selling or export of cultural properties encourages illegal activity (e.g., the looting of archaeological sites, black market trade). Since such illegal activity ought not be encouraged, such practices are unjustified.

The Encouragement of Illegality Argument raises an important issue about the practice of restricting the "free flow of art": Is such restriction part of the problem or part of the solution (or both)? A variation on the argument is expressed by such sentiments as "If I don't buy (sell) it, someone else will" and "It's no good for one country to stop buying or trading cultural properties if everyone else continues to do so."[8] This is more than just a worry about the consequences of export/import regulation; it is a worry about the justification of the practices themselves, and whether those practices serve the ends they are intended by design (and not simply by consequences) to serve. As such, the Encouragement of Illegality Argument raises just the sort and range of philosophical issues that the traditional utilitarian-deontological controversy in ethics raises: Do the net costs of the consequences of the practices render the practices themselves unjustified? Or are there other, nonutilitarian considerations (e.g., rights of courts, customs offices, bona fide owners) which justifiably trumps utilitarian considerations in cases of illegal practices? Resolving this question will call into play the same sorts of complex and controversial considerations that surface in traditional utilitarian-deontological disputes.

To summarize, the six arguments (or, properly speaking, argument-types) discussed here are a rendering of what I understand to be the main sorts of arguments given against claims to the 3 R's by countries of origin, and some of the main philosophical issues raised by each. Consider now the sorts of arguments given in support of claims to the 3 R's by countries of origin.[9]

Three Arguments for Claims to the 3 R's by Countries of Origin
1. *The Cultural Heritage Argument* All peoples have a right to those cultural properties which form an integral part of their cultural heritage and identity (i.e., their "national patrimony"). The practices of permitting foreign countries to import cultural properties and to retain those currently housed on foreign soil deprive indigenous peoples and countries of origin of their right to their cultural heritage. Hence, such practices are unjustified. These practices should be stopped and cultural properties presently displaced in foreign countries should be returned to their countries of origin.

The Cultural Heritage Argument raises the vital issue of the relevance and legitimacy of claims to cultural property based on considerations of national patrimony, that is, those aspects of a country which are of special historical, ethnic, religious, or other cultural significance and which are unique in exemplifying and transmitting a country's culture. The Cultural Heritage Argument assumes that countries have a legitimate claim to preserve, foster, and enrich those aspects of their culture that represent their national identity. What it leaves open is which cultural properties those are, which import/export practices must be stopped, how many cultural properties must be returned, and whether "cultural patrimony" must stay permanently in the country of origin.

It is what is left open, and not the main assumption about a country's right or claim to its cultural patrimony, which makes the Cultural Heritage Argument especially controversial. Unless it is clear which cultural properties constitute a country's national patrimony and which regulations are supported by claims to a country's cultural heritage, the argument loses its critical bite. Foreign countries could use the same sort of argument to defend claims to the retention of cultural property that has been in the country so long that it now constitutes part of *their* cultural heritage. Foreign countries also could reject the argument by rejecting the remedies proposed (e.g., import/export restrictions), without rejecting the main assumption on which the argument is based, viz. that countries of origin have a legitimate claim to protect and preserve their cultural heritage. Since both uses of the Cultural Heritage Argument by foreign countries would be unacceptable to its advocates, the Cultural Heritage Argument must provide answers which rule out such usurpations of the argument.

2. *The Country of Origin Ownership Argument* The past, as expressed in cultural property, is owned by the property's country of origin. Since the countries of origin own them, they have a right to have their cultural property returned to them or, if already located in the country, to keep it there.

This argument repudiates claims to ownership of cultural property that locate that ownership elsewhere than in countries of origin. Hence, it constitutes a rejection of both the Foreign Ownership and the Humanity Ownership Arguments. Nonetheless, like those arguments, it construes the main issue concerning cultural properties as one of ownership: it assumes that the question "Who owns the past?" is legitimate; it simply provides a different answer. Whether any of these arguments is plausible, then, will depend on the strength of the position that the past—both the material remains and the "perceptions of the past"—is properly described in terms of ownership and property.

3. *The Scholarly and Aesthetic Integrity Argument* The practices of collecting and importing cultural properties contribute to the breakdown in the scholarly value of those properties and their aesthetic integrity as an artistic complex (e.g., by mutilating large monuments, disrupting a series of interconnected panels, "thinning" intricately carved stelae, destroying the complex system of hieroglyphic inscriptions necessary for identifying artifacts).[10] Since it is important to preserve the

educational value and aesthetic integrity of cultural properties, such practices are unjustified. Restriction on the import/export of such cultural properties is therefore required and justified.

There are two main issues here, one which is relatively uncontroversial and a related one which is quite controversial. The relatively uncontroversial issue is whether the practices which destroy or jeopardize the scholarly or aesthetic integrity are wrong. Nearly everyone agrees that they are, even though there is disagreement about just what constitutes the practice, whether an individual activity genuinely "falls under this (rather than some other) practice," and whether the practice may be justified in a particular (though not all) case. The main question, then, is whether restrictions on the import/export of particular cultural properties falling under those practices, or of restitution to countries of origin of other cultural properties (i.e., those collected or imported without jeopardizing their scholarly or aesthetic integrity), should be permitted or required. This question remains even if the practices which violate the scholarly or aesthetic integrity of cultural properties are wrong and ought to be restricted.

RETHINKING THE DEBATE

The preceeding overview of the debate over cultural properties has been organized in terms of nine main kinds of arguments concerning claims to the 3 R's by countries of origin, noting the key philosophical issues raised by each. In the remainder of this chapter I take a different approach. I look at the debate taken as a whole, and offer reasons for supposing that the traditional categories and concepts used in the debate, as given by these arguments concerning the 3 R's, are inadequate as is to provide a theoretical framework for addressing and resolving conflicts concerning the disposition of cultural remains of the past. To do that, I discuss four issues: the nature and importance of conceptual frameworks; the language used to discuss cultural properties; ways of correcting bias in a theory or perspective; and alternative models of conflict resolution. Taken together, I show how acknowledgment of the importance of these four issues can help in the attempts to resolve the debate over cultural properties.

The Nature and Importance of Conceptual Frameworks

Whether we know it or not, each of us operates out of a socially constructed world view or conceptual framework. A conceptual framework is a set of basic beliefs, values, attitudes, and assumptions that shapes, reflects, and explains our view (perception, description, appraisal) of ourselves and our world.[11] It is the lens through which "we" (whoever we are) conceive ourselves and our world. As a social construction, a conceptual framework is affected by such factors as sex—sex/gender, race/ethnicity, class, age, affectional preference, religion, and national background.

Some conceptual frameworks are oppressive.[12] An oppressive conceptual framework is one which functions to justify or maintain dominant-subordinate relations, or subordination of one group by another. As I use the term, an oppressive conceptual framework is characterized by three features: (1) Value, hierarchical or "Up-Down" thinking—an organization of diversity by a spatial metaphor ("Up-Down") that attributes greater value, prestige, or status to that which is "Up" or higher than to what is "Down" or lower.[13] (2) Value dualisms—disjunctive pairs in which the disjuncts are presented as exclusive (rather than inclusive) and oppositional (rather than complementary), and where greater value, prestige, or status is attributed to one disjunct than the other. (3) A logic of domination—a structure of argumentation or reasoning which justified subordination, typically on the grounds that whatever is "Up" has some property that whatever is "Down" lacks and in virtue of which what is "Up" is superior to that which is "Down." The unstated assumption is that the superiority of what is "Up" justifies the subordination or unequal treatment of what is "Down."

When an oppressive conceptual framework is Western and patriarchal, traditionally Western male-identified beliefs, values, attitudes, and assumptions are taken as the only, or the standard, or the more highly valued ones. In a Western and patriarchal conceptual framework, inappropriate or harmful Up-Down thinking is/has been used to justify the inferior treatment of women and Third World peoples on the grounds that the claims (beliefs, values, attitudes, assumptions) of these groups are less significant, less cultivated, or otherwise inferior to those of the dominant Up-group and its claims. In a Western patriarchal conceptual framework, inappropriate value dualisms conceptually separate as opposites aspects of reality that are in fact inseparable or complementary, for example, treating as ontologically or metaphysically separate and opposed what is human to what is nonhuman, mind to body, reason to emotion.

Current conceptions of the debate over cultural properties in terms of arguments for and against claims to the 3 R's by countries of origin in many important ways reflects a Western and patriarchal conceptual framework. It also (and not incidentally or accidentally) reflects a familiar perspective—what I call the "dominant perspective" in the Western philosophical tradition. What I want to show now is one way this tradition and the sort of Western and patriarchal conceptual framework which houses it contribute to a particular and not altogether satisfying way of construing the so-called debate over cultural properties. I do so by discussing a favored approach, what I call a "rights/rules approach," to talking about humans, ethics, and ethical conflict resolution in what I refer to as the "dominant tradition" in Western philosophy.

A rights/rules approach to discussions of humans, ethics, and ethical conflict resolution is an ethical framework for assessing what is morally right, wrong, or obligatory in terms of either alleged rights or duties (legal or moral) of relevant parties (e.g., individuals, groups of individuals, nations) or governing legal or moral rules which warrant as justified or morally permissible the action or practice in question. Typically these rules are utility-based or duty-conferring rules; that is, they specify the net utility of performing or not performing a given act or kind of act, or of acting in accordance with a given rule, or the duties persons have in virtue of the governing rules (respectively). A rights/rules ethical framework views moral conflict as essentially a conflict among rights and duties of individuals or groups of individuals, and/or a conflict of relevant rules. Typically, a rights-rules approach adjudicates moral conflicts by appeal to the most basic right, duty, or rule in a value-hierarchical way, for example, where the "authority" of a right, duty, or rule is given from the top of a hierarchy and is appealed to in order to settle the conflicts or dispute.

In the dominant tradition, the inappropriate or harmful use of a rights/rules ethic occurs when all moral situations are mistakenly or misleadingly construed as adequately captured by talk either of who has what rights or duties, or which rules prevail. In the dominant tradition, rights are assumed to be *prima facie rights* which hold "other things being equal," and the relevant moral rules are assumed to be objective, universal, impartial, and cross-culturally binding.

In recent discussion of ethics, feminists have begun to challenge this hierarchical rights/rules approach to ethics in the Western philosophical tradition. For example, in her book *In A Different Voice*, psychologist Carol Gilligan contrasts this Western philosophical highly individualistic, hierarchical, rights/rules ethic with an essentially contextual, holistic, and web-like ethic of care and responsibility in relationships.[14] Gilligan argues that these two ethical orientations have thematic and gender significance: they reflect important differences in moral reasoning between men and women on such basic issues as how one conceives the self, morality, and conflict resolution.[15] According to Gilligan, the moral imperative in the rights/rules ethic tradition is an injunction to protect the rights of others against interference, to do what is fair, and to do one's duty. In the ethic of care, the moral imperative is an injunction to care and avoid hurt, to discern and relieve the "real and recognizable suffering" of this world, to express compassion.[16] The contrasting images of hierarchy and web convey different ways both of structuring relationships and of viewing the self, morality, and conflict resolution.[17] According to Gilligan, the image of a hierarchy emphasizes an exclusive realm of individual rights, a morality of noninterference, and a conception of the self in separation or isolation, while the image of a web provides a nonhierarchical vision of human connection, an inclusive morality of care and responsibility, and a contextual conception of the self in community or in relationships.[18]

Philosopher Kathryn Pyne Addelson makes a related point in her article, "Moral Revolution." Addelson argues that there is a bias in the dominant world view which results from the near exclusion of women from the domain of intellectual pursuits. That bias conceives of ethical problems "from the top of the hierarchy," and assumes that the authority of that position represents the "official" or "correct" or "legiti-mate" point of view.[19] Addelson offers as her paradigmatic example of such bias the rights/rules ethic of the Western philosophical tradition.[20] According to Addelson, the dominant tradition perpetuates the sort of dominant-subordinate structures which create inequality, in part by not noticing that the point of view at the top of the hierarchy is not, as the tradition assumes, a value-neutral objective, universal, and impartial point of view. According to Addelson, the perceptions and power of subordinate groups (e.g., women, Third World peoples) are necessary to create new social structures and world views which do not have such a bias.[21]

This is not the place to discuss the strengths and weaknesses of the Gilligan and Addelson accounts. They are offered merely to show the respects in which "the dominant tradition" has come under attack recently by feminists who view it as bi-ased in key respects (e.g., by sex/gender, by race/ethnicity, by class/privilege). Con-sider, now, how an understanding of this sort of criticism of the dominant perspective applies to the "debate over cultural properties."

Language and Conceptual Frameworks

The language we use and the questions we ask reflect our conceptual framework or world view. In the debate over cultural properties, the language we use reflects our conception of the main issues in that debate and sets into place the sorts of remedies that are taken to be relevant to resolving that debate. To illustrate this, con-sider the title of this book, *The Ethics of Collecting Cultural Property: Whose Culture? Whose Property?*

First, the language used in the title reflects the by now familiar conception of the debate as essentially a debate about property. As such, the language grows out of and reflects a conceptual framework which takes as fundamental and most important (most highly valued) considerations of property and ownership. But such talk is un-packed in terms of the rights and duties of relevant parties. The debate therefore presupposes the legitimacy and efficacy of construing the debate over cultural prop-erties in terms of both properties which properly can be said to be owned, and a rights/rules framework for stating and resolving what are taken to be the most im-portant ethical issues addressed in the debate: Who owns what cultural properties? To which cultures (countries) does the cultural property properly belong? Who has a right to collect or own cultural properties? Who has what duties with regard to cultural properties? Which rules prevail in the disposition of cultural properties— ones expressing utilitarian considerations, or ones expressing deontological, nonu-tilitarian considerations?

The nine specific sorts of arguments for/against claims to the 3 R's—restitution, restriction (or regulation), and rights—are couched in the same sort of language. The assumption underlying them is not simply that the question "who owns the past?" is a meaningful and important question; it is typically the main or focus question. Several arguments are explicitly so construed (i.e., the Rescue, Foreign Ownership, Humanity Ownership, Cultural Heritage, and Country of Origin Ownership Arguments). The other arguments (i.e., the Means-End, Scholarly Access, Encouragement of Illegality, and Scholarly and Aesthetic Integrity Arguments) implicitly or covertly appeal to a rules ethical framework for justifying serious consideration of values and interests not explicitly unpacked in terms of property and rights. Thus, all of the specific sorts of arguments given are presented within some sort of rights/rules framework.

Second, the language used to conduct the debate over cultural properties is often male gender-biased. Interchangeable talk of cultural properties and national patrimony goes unnoticed as a gender-biased category of analysis. Since "one way a tradition conceals data is through the concepts and categories it uses,"[22] use of the concept or category national patrimony to discuss an entire society's cultural heritage is at least misleading. Surely it is at least an open question whether the concept national patrimony, like the concepts of property, ownership, utility, and rights, properly captures the relevant information about the relationship of all people to their cultural history. For persons in a cultural context where "the past" is not viewed as property, perhaps not even as "past" (e.g., some Native American cultures), or where talk of property, ownership, utility, and rights do not capture important conceptions of the past (e.g., communal kinship with the "living past") or where one's cultural heritage and relationship to that heritage is not captured in the male-biased language of patrimony, what one takes to be the relevant issues—in fact, what one takes to be the debate itself—will not be captured by the current conception of the debate in terms of the dominant perspective on cultural properties. These concerns about the adequacy of the very language in which the debate is couched affect many of those cultures/countries from which the relevant cultural properties originate. Parties to the debate must take enormous care not to see as inferior, irrelevant, or of less significance the sorts of concerns that indigenous peoples, for example, may raise about both how their cultural heritage is talked about and how it is treated if they are to avoid conducting the debate over cultural artifacts from within an oppressive, Western, and patriarchal conceptual framework.

What all of this suggests is that it is important to recognize and appreciate the nature and power of conceptual frameworks and of the language by which they are given concrete expression. By conceiving the dispute over cultural heritage issues as a dispute over properties, and by focusing the debate over cultural properties on the question of rights and rules governing ownership of or access to the past, the dominant perspective keeps in place a value-hierarchical, dualistic, rights/rules ethical framework for identifying what counts as a worthwhile value or claim, for assessing competing claims, and for resolving the conflicts among competing claims. Where such a framework is problematic or inadequate, what can be done to remedy the inadequacy?

Correcting Bias in the Dominant Tradition

If there is a bias in a theory, it may be that reforming the theory by making internal changes—redefining key terms, changing assumptions, extending its application in a new or different way—will remedy the bias. But if the bias is within the theory itself, rather than with its application, then that bias will not be remedied simply by reforming the application of the theory, altering a few of its assumptions, or revising the arguments given within the theory.[23] In such a case, more radical ways of construing and resolving the debate will be needed.

Is there a kind of bias in the debate over cultural properties, one which has been introduced by the near exclusive reliance on a value-hierarchical, value-dualistic, and rights/rules ethic, which subordinates the interests or claims of those in subordinate positions relevant to the dispute? If so, is it a bias that reforming from within that conceptual framework will remedy, or is it the sort of bias that requires reconceiving the very terms of the debate itself?

I already have suggested that there is such a bias, and that it enters into the debate in two ways.[24] The first way bias is introduced is by construing the dispute as basically a dispute about ownership, property, and rights. Since several of the main arguments concerning the 3 R's are explicitly couched in such terms (viz. the Rescue, Foreign Ownership, Humanity Ownership, Cultural Heritage, and Country of Origin Ownership Arguments), they overtly contribute to that bias. To the extent that at least some cultural properties issues really are issues of property, and to the extent that others are not, tinkering from within will be appropriate in some cases and not in others.

The second way bias is introduced relates to the first: Casting the dispute as a dispute about ownership, property, rights and rules at least encourages a resolution of conflicts over cultural properties from a value-hierarchical, win-lose perspective. Such a strategy of conflict resolution will be appropriate to the extent that the issues of the controversy genuinely fit a hierarchical model of conflict resolution (discussed below); to the extent that they do not, it biases the issues to treat the resolution of all cultural heritage issues from the perspective of a hierarchical model. Since all of the arguments given concerning the 3 R's are presented from within a hierarchical rights-rules model, the question of bias arises for each of them.[25]

In order to eliminate whatever bias there is in the conception of the debate over cultural properties from within the dominant tradition, it is necessary to identify those issues which can, and those issues which cannot, be adequately addressed and resolved from within that perspective. While it is outside the scope of this essay to do that critical work here, what I have said so far suffices to show how the issue of the adequacy of the dominant conceptual framework arises, why it is such an important issue, and what would need to be shown to decide the issue one way or the other.

Any workable remedy to bias probably lies somewhere in between the extremes of reform and revolution. Some of the biases are correctible by reform; others are not. In order to know which sorts of remedies apply in which sorts of cases, it is important to recognize alternative models of conflict resolution. It is to that issue that I now turn.

Models of Conflict Resolution: 3 Alternatives

Three alternative models of conflict resolution are what I refer to as the hierarchical, compromise, and consensus models. On the hierarchical model, one chooses between competing rights, claims, interests, and values by selecting the most basic, most important, or otherwise most stringent one. This model presupposes a pyramidal or hierarchical, Up-Down organization of the relevant variables, and appeals to some basic rule (principle, standard, criterion), value, or right to justify selection of the relevant variable as most stringent. If, for example, a claim to right of ownership of a foreign country conflicts with a claim to right of ownership of a country of origin, on a hierarchical model one would decide which right is more stringent or valid by appeal to some governing rule (principle, standard). The hierarchical model is particularly useful in a litigious approach to conflict resolution.

The hierarchical model is an adversarial, win-lose model which presupposes that one not only can organize diverse claims in terms of hierarchies, but that one can provide some way of rank ordering them. First, conflicting rights, claims, interests, and values do not always neatly form hierarchies, especially when the variables are of different types. For example, how should one hierarchically order the scholarly value of collecting cultural artifacts with the right of a country of origin to restrict their distribution? Second, there are problems with providing objective rankings or weighting for selecting among these competing considerations: What is the appropriate weighting and ranking of rights vis-à-vis scholarly values? Furthermore, underlying the hierarchical model is the assumption that it is possible and appropriate to resolve (all) conflicts by providing a value-hierarchical ranking. But this assumption is controversial. As has been suggested, value hierarchical rankings often maintain inequalities or misdescribe reality by perceiving diversity in terms of value dualisms and Up-Down orderings (e.g., of dominate-subordinate relationships). And those values which do not neatly fit into a value-hierarchical ranking (e.g., web-like values of care, friendship, or kinship) or do not translate neatly into a rights/rules framework without misdescribing the situation (e.g., as a situation of rights rather than as one of compassion and care), seem to get lost in the model.[26] Lastly, the model dictates a winner and loser in the resolution of the conflict. But not all conflict must have a winner and a loser. That is a limitation of the model, not necessarily a limitation of the controversy, the values or claims at issue, or the parties to the dispute. To see that this is so, consider two alternative models.

A compromise model is designed to provide something, though not everything, for all parties to the dispute, or to provide some of each of the relevant values, rather than realizing any one value to the exclusion of others. Some claims or values are traded-off in order to realize others. Underlying this model is the presumption that values can be realized in degrees. Its successful use requires that parties to a dispute are willing to compromise.

A third model is the consensus model: all parties voluntarily engage in a process of reaching mutually agreed upon goals, typically with the help of a third party facilitator or mediator perceived to be a neutral party to the dispute. Consensus-building is process oriented. Typically it begins with people putting their values and attitudes on the table, and uses empowerment strategies and techniques to have people collectively, voluntarily, and cooperatively decide what the problem is, how they will resolve it, and what will count as a resolution of the conflict. Since this model involves voluntary cooperation in a non-binding decision making process, it takes time, good will, and cooperation. It fails when mutually acceptable agreement is not reached.

There may be some situations in which the hierarchical model is the most, or the only, appropriate model. For example, in the context of cultural properties, it may be useful to litigate conflicting legal claims by parties to the dispute. Nonetheless, exclusive reliance on this model contributes to the problem, not the solution, by promoting an adversarial, value-hierarchical, win-lose approach to the resolution of all conflicts over "cultural properties." It is particularly inappropriate and inapplicable if one reconceives at least part of the debate in terms other than those of property or rights. To illustrate this, consider a tenth, different sort of argument than the nine we have already considered concerning the 3 R's.

"The Non-Renewable Resource Argument"

So-called cultural properties are like environmentally endangered species. First, they are non-renewable resources; once exhausted or destroyed, they cannot be replenished or replaced. Second, they are not anyone's property and no one can properly be said to own them. Our relationship to them is more like that of a steward, custodian, guardian, conservator, or trustee than that of a property owner. Since these cultural properties ought to be preserved yet are no one's property, no one has a right to them. Hence, no one has a claim to their restitution or restriction based on an alleged right (e.g., right of ownership) to them. Their protection and preservation is a collective responsibility of all of us as stewards: it must acknowledge our important connection with the past, be conducted with care and a sense of responsibility for peoples and their cultural heritages, and respect for the context in which cultural remains are found.

There are at least four related main issues raised by the Non-Renewable Resource Argument: (1) How much are at least some cultural properties like environmentally endangered species? (2) To what extent are humans like stewards, custodians, guardians, conservators, or trustees of cultural heritages? (3) Exactly whose responsibility is it to preserve cultural heritages? And, (4) Is a responsibility to preserve cultural heritages based on or grounded in a web-like ethic of care? If the analogy between environmentally endangered species and cultural heritages is strong, then at least some talk of cultural property is a misnomer. We should speak instead of endangered cultural heritages, endangered cultural pasts, or even, more simply, endangered cultures. If those who have responsibility to preserve cultural heritages are conceived as stewards of that heritage, then talk of property rights and ownership of that heritage is inappropriate and misguided. If this responsibility is grounded in web-like considerations of care and contextual appropriateness, then the dominant tradition's rights/rules ethic also is either inappropriate, limited, or seriously inadequate as a framework for capturing all or perhaps even the most important relevant ethical considerations.

The linguistic changes in how one speaks about cultural heritage issues which are suggested by the Non-Renewable Resource Argument are significant: they challenge not only how one conceives the debate over so-called "cultural properties" but also how one solves that debate. If at least some aspects of a culture's heritage or past are not the sort of thing that properly can be talked about in terms of property, ownership, and rights, then, the construal of the debate in such terms is inappropriate.

Furthermore, a hierarchical model of conflict resolution simply is the wrong tool for the job if what one is trying to do is resolve competing claims about who has what communal responsibilities of care regarding the preservation of cultural heritages. That issue is complex, not simple, and requires that we complexify both our thinking about and our remedies to the issue of endangered cultures in ways that resist simple constructions of the debate in terms of rights or rules.

In summary, by construing the debate over cultural heritages as a debate over cultural properties, and by viewing conflicts in that debate as conflicts among competing claims concerning restitution, restriction, and rights (i.e., the 3 R's), the debate is conceived from a perspective characterized by value-hierarchical, normatively dualistic, rights/rules thinking and a model of conflict resolution that is a win-lose model. Given that there are alternative ways to conceive the debate and to resolve the conflicts over cultural heritage issues, the dominant perspective seems inadequate by itself as a theoretical framework for understanding and resolving so-called cultural properties issues.

RETHINKING THE DEBATE: AN INTEGRATIVE PERSPECTIVE

In this chapter I have attempted both to provide an overview of the main arguments and issues involved in the current debate over cultural properties and to suggest why it is important to rethink the terms of that dispute from a nonhierarchical, nonadversarial (win-lose) perspective. I have also attempted to suggest why an adequate solution to the dispute will involve more than simply refining arguments from within the dominant perspective on cultural properties. It will require what I call an integrative perspective to the understanding and resolution of cultural heritage issues.

An integrative perspective is intended to preserve the strengths and overcome the limitations of the dominant perspective's approach to cultural heritage issues. It does so by making a central place for considerations typically lost or overlooked in that approach: (1) It takes seriously cultural heritage issues which are not properly viewed as concerns about property, ownership, and rights (e.g., concerns of indigenous peoples who do not see land or cultural artifacts as possessions one owns); (2) It emphasizes preservation as a primary value and recognizes the respects in which cultural heritages are like endangered species; (3) It encourages talk of stewardship, custodianship, guardianship, or trusteeship of the past, especially for those aspects of the past—both the physical remains of the past (artifacts, places, sites, monuments) and the perceptions of the past (information, stories, myths)—which are not owned or ownable; (4) It acknowledges and preserves the importance of the diversity of values and perspectives involved in the resolution of cultural heritage issues. This means it is flexible in when and how it is appropriate to apply considerations of rights, property and ownership, and when it is not, and it recognizes the variety of available strategies and solutions for resolving conflicts over cultural heritage issues; (5) It involves the meaningful use of compromise and consensus models for resolving disputes over cultural heritage claims. One way it does this is by encouraging nonlitigious, voluntary, reciprocal, and mediated solutions to conflicts and the sharing of cultural artifacts (e.g., through museum collection sharing programs; loans; jointly undertaken studies, restorations, publications, and exhibitions); (6) It involves the restitution of legitimate "cultural heritage" to countries of origin and the use of restrictions to eliminate illicit traffic in cultural artifacts.

The first step to implementing an integrative perspective to cultural heritage issues is to make visible the conceptual framework in which the debate over cultural properties is currently conducted. This will require abandoning language which biases the terms of the dispute in favor of the dominant perspective (e.g., replacing inappropriate talk of cultural properties and cultural patrimony with talk of cultural heritage issues or endangered cultural heritages). It also will require recognition of nonhierarchical models of conflict resolution. By making visible the nature and function of the dominant conceptual framework, one is in a position to envision alternatives for how one conceives and resolves the debate over cultural heritages.

The second step to implementing an integrative perspective is to make context central to how one understands cultural heritage issues. Most of the physical remains of the past are at best fragments. All cultural properties, like the cultural heritage that constitutes the past, come with a context. Objects without a context (i.e., without provenance) are dispossessed of the very sorts of information that are essential to their constituting a cultural heritage. An integrative perspective to cultural heritage issues would make context central to any adequate account or resolution of cultural heritage issues. Once the twin goals of making visible the conceptual framework of the dominant perspective and incorporating contextual considerations into the discussion of cultural heritage issues are realized, an integrative perspective can begin to implement specific changes in the way the debate over "cultural properties" is conceived and conducted (e.g., changes suggested at 1–6 directly above).

An integrative perspective on cultural heritage issues encourages all of us to rethink the dispute as one of preservation (not, or not simply, one of ownership) of the past, and to rethink the resolution of the cultural properties conflict from a compromise or consensus model of conflict resolution, rather than from a value-hierarchical, normatively dualistic, win-lose model. An adequate resolution of cultural heritage issues—that is, one which uses appropriate language, concepts, and categories, captures the diversity of values, claims, and interests of various parties to the dispute, and provides flexibility in the resolution of conflicts—requires that we rethink the terms of the dispute. That is what an integrative perspective on cultural heritage issues promises.

NOTES

1. For a discussion of these two different foci of ownership of the past, see Isabel McBryde's "Introduction" in *Who Owns the Past?*, ed. by Isabel McBryde (London: Oxford University Press, 1985) and Cha. 5, "Whose Past?" in Karl E. Meyer's *The Plundered Past* (New York: Atheneum Press, 1977).

2. I treat these as arguments for and against claims to the 3 R's which are advanced by countries of origin, rather than as claims organized around a typology of relevant values (e.g., aesthetic, educational, religious or economic values) or as claims advanced by other groups (e.g., specific individuals, such as curators, collectors, scholars); foreign countries (i.e., countries which have or would like to have cultural property but are not the country of origin of that property); humanity as a whole. The rationale for identifying the arguments in terms of claims to the 3 R's by countries of origin is that this provides an organizational schema which accommodates all the values and parties to the dispute, while accurately highlighting how issues concerning cultural properties arise (viz. because the traffic in cultural property is basically traffic from countries of origin outward; whatever values and interests are at stake are so ultimately because of this traffic outward). Hence, this typology appropriately leaves open the question whether foreigners or foreign countries do or might support some of the claims to the 3 R's by countries of origin (e.g., by arguing on behalf of the relevant values and interests of indigenous peoples to their cultural heritage).

3. In the case of what is owed, a "genuine beneficiary" is one who has a legitimate or valid claim (i.e., a right) to what is owed, while a "mere beneficiary" is one who stands to benefit from the performance of an owed act but does not have a legitimate or valid claim (i.e., a right) to what is owed. This distinction is particularly important in the case of inheritances, e.g., the inheritance of possessions or properties owned by benefactors. If those who rescued cultural properties have a right to them, and their descendants (whether individuals or countries) are acknowledged as "genuine beneficiaries," then those descendants also have a right to them.

4. In his book *The International Trade in Art* (Chicago: The University of Chicago Press, 1982), Paul M. Bator discusses what counts as "illegality" in the international art trade under existing law. Since not all illegal export is theft (or some other form of illegal taking) and not all illegal exports are cases of illegal import, the structure of illegal trade consists of four factors: export regulations, theft, importing illegally exported cultural properties, and importing stolen cultural properties (pp. 9–13). According to Bator, in the United States, the only case of illegal export that constitutes illegal import is the 1972 statute "Importation of Pre-Columbian Monumental or Architectural Sculptor or Murals," which bars the import of illegally exported "pre-Columbian monumental or architectural sculpture or mural" (cited in Bator, p. 11, n. 32).

5. See, e.g., the position of Alison Jaggar, *Feminist Politics and Human Nature* (Totowa, N.J.: Rowman and Allanheld, 1983); Naomi Scheman, "Individualism and The Objects of Psychology," in *Discovering Reality: Feminist Perspectives on Epistemology, Metaphysics, Methodology, and The Philosophy of Science*, eds. Sandra Harding and Merrill B. Hintikka (Netherlands: D. Reidel Publishing Company, 1983): 225–244.

6. Utilitarian and deontological theories of ethics are both normative theories of moral obligation. They provide theoretical answers to the question "What acts, or kinds of acts, or human conduct is right, wrong, or obligatory?" Utilitarian theories are "consequentialist theories," i.e., they assess the rightness, wrongness, or obligatoriness of human conduct solely in terms of the consequences of such conduct. Specifically, according to utilitarianism, performing a given act (or kind of act), or following a certain rule, is justified if and only if no alternative act (kind of act, rule) provides a higher net balance of good over evil (typically understood in terms of pleasure over pain). Jeremy Bentham and John Stuart Mill are the historical figures most frequently associated with utilitarianism. Deontological theories are nonconsequentialist, i.e., they assess the rightness, wrongness, or obligatoriness of human conduct in terms other than the consequences of such conduct. Aristotle and Immanuel Kant are among the prominent historical figures identified with deontological ethical theories.

7. For a clear and thorough survey of the options available for controlling the international trade in art (including cultural properties), and the author's view of which ones are desirable and why, see Paul M. Bator, ibid., Cha. III.

8. See Karl E. Meyer, ibid., pp. 190–191.

9. These three arguments are not simply rebuttals of the six arguments already given. They involve additional claims about the claims of countries of origin against foreign countries and others.

10. See Paul M. Bator, ibid., Chas. I and II.

11. Recent feminist theory in all academic disciplines has focused attention on describing and critiquing what I call here a "world view" or "conceptual framework." This is especially so in philosophy and ethics. See, e.g., Kathryn Addelson's "Moral Revolution" and Joyce Trebilcot's "Conceiving Women: Notes on the Logic of Feminism," in *Women and Values: Readings in Recent Feminist Philosophy*, ed. by Marilyn Pearsall (Belmont, Ca.: Wadsworth Publishing Co., 1986: 291–309 and 358–363, respectively; Elizabeth Dodson Gray's *Patriarchy As A Conceptual Trap* (Wellesley, Mass.: Rountable Press, 1982); Alison Jaggar, ibid.

12. For a discussion of oppressive, especially patriarchal, conceptual frameworks, see my "Feminism and Ecology: Making Connections," *Environmental Ethics* (Spring, 1986): 3–20.

13. For a discussion of value-hierarchical thinking in what she calls "patriarchal conceptual frameworks," see Elizabeth Dodson Gray. *Green Paradise Lost* (Wellesley, Mass.: Rountable Press, 1981), p. 20. See also my discussion of patriarchal conceptual frameworks in "Feminism and Ecology: Making Connections," *Environmental Ethics* (Winter, 1987).

14. Carol Gilligan. *In A Different Voice* (Cambridge, Mass.: Harvard University Press, 1982).

15. Gilligan writes that "the different voice" she describes is "characterized not by gender but by theme. Its association with women is an empirical observation, and it is primarily through women's voices that I trace its development. But this association is not absolute . . ." (ibid., p. 2.) Gilligan uses "the male voice" and "the female voice" to highlight a distinction between two modes of thought and two different ways of conceiving the self, morality, and conflict resolution. It is this aspect of what Gilligan says that I am interested in conveying here.

16. E.g., ibid., pp. 73, 90, 100, 164–165.

17. Ibid., p. 62.

18. Ibid. Note that Gilligan does not argue for the superiority of one view over the other. Rather, she argues for a convergence of the two perspectives (i.e., an "ethic of justice" or a rights/rule ethic and an "ethic of care"). See pp. 151–174.

19. Ibid., p. 307.

20. Addelson calls this dominant tradition in ethics "the Thomson tradition," named after Judith Jarvis Thomson's approach to doing ethics, and contrasts it with a minority tradition, what she calls "the Jane tradition," named after a group of politically active women in Chicago who formed an organization called Jane.

21. Ibid., p. 306.

22. Addelson, ibid., p. 305.

23. This is the main point expressed by Kathryn Addelson in her article, "Moral Revolution," ibid.

24. While I do not explicitly argue for the claim that there is a bias in the dominant tradition's construal of the debate over cultural properties, what I have said about world views, the dominant tradition and its associated "patriarchal world view" is sufficient to show what such a defense would involve.

25. Notice that those arguments which focus either on the values or the practices associated with collecting "cultural properties" and are presented in connection with utilitarian considerations (e.g., the Means-End, Scholarly Access, Encouragement of Illegality, and Scholarly and Aesthetic Integrity Arguments) implicitly introduce the first sort of bias by relying on an objective and universalizable "rules" approach to resolving cultural property issues. They also encourage the second sort of bias, since they presuppose a resolution of cultural properties conflicts from within a value-hierarchical win-lose model.

26. Although I do not argue explicitly for these claims here, the arguments given earlier by Gilligan and Addelson are among the sorts of arguments which have been given in support of these claims.

27

Deft Deliberations

Dan L. Monroe and Walter Echo-Hawk

The Native American Grave Protection and Repatriation Act of 1990 might be the most important human rights legislation ever passed by Congress for Native Americans. It also represents landmark legislation for museum people.

Repatriation legislation is important for native people because it provides them equal rights regarding their dead. It recognizes that scientific rights of inquiry do not automatically take precedence over religious and cultural beliefs: it provides a mechanism for return of objects that were not acquired with the consent of rightful owners; and it creates an opportunity for Native Americans and museum people to work in partnership together.

Federal repatriation legislation is important for museums because it establishes a new ethical outlook for them in their relationships not only with native people but with all racial and cultural minorities. Museums are leaders, not followers, in creating a society that respects and celebrates cultural pluralism. The recent legislation creates the basis for a new partnership between museums and native people that may enhance knowledge of collections and create a new and richer form of public education through exhibits, programs, and publications. Rich as these benefits may be, the greatest benefit to museums is likely to be the increased maturity that comes of a commitment to truth and moral courage born out of the repatriation debate.

Museums and Native Americans debated and discussed repatriation for years inside and outside Congress. Museum people were among the first to recognize the value of Native American art and culture. They collected and preserved millions of Native American cultural items to prevent their loss or dispersal. They documented and recorded Native American culture to preserve traditional knowledge for future generations of natives and non-natives alike. And they interpreted and presented

Dan L. Monroe is Executive Director and CEO of the Peabody Essex Museum in Salem, Massachusetts, and Walter Echo-Hawk is staff attorney for the Native American Rights Fund in Boulder, Colorado. "Deft Deliberations" is reprinted here with permission from *Museum News*, July/August 1991. Copyright 1991, the American Association of Museums. All rights reserved.

Native American culture to millions of people worldwide in a substantial education effort.

Yet when Native Americans first asked museums to return Native American dead or sacred objects, many museum people felt threatened: What would happen to museum collections if objects were repatriated? Who would assure preservation of repatriated objects? How would museums carry out their educational or scientific missions if collections were gutted through repatriation claims?

Before detailing some of the ramifications of the new federal legislation established to address these questions, it is useful to review the debate that preceded Congressional action.

VIOLATION OF RIGHTS

From the point of view of Native Americans, one of the many "trails of tears" in American Indian history is the fact that U.S. museums and universities hold staggering numbers of dead native people who provide mute testimony to the pervasive violation of Native American rights.

Respect for the dead is deeply ingrained in U.S. society and jurisprudence. Yet legal safeguards taken for granted by most citizens did not protect the graves and dead of Native Americans. American law and social policy wholly failed to protect the sanctity of the Native American dead (as Chief Seattle said in 1855, "To us, the ashes of our ancestors are sacred, and their resting place is hallowed ground") or the sensibilities of the living. As a result, tribal communities suffered painful human rights violations. Repatriation is one means of redress.

Historians documented the troubling means by which many of the dead were collected. Samuel Morton, an early American physical anthropologist, collected large numbers of Indian crania in the 1840s. His "finding" that native people were racially inferior to white people and therefore bound for extinction provided ample "scientific" justification for taking land from Indians, relocating them, and committing cultural genocide through government policies. In 1868, the U.S. Surgeon General issued an order directing Army personnel to obtain as many Indian crania as possible; thus those killed in battles were decapitated and their heads sent East for scientific study.

The policy of treating Native American dead unlike white Americans was translated into law in 1906 when Congress passed the Antiquities Act. This law, intended to protect archaeological resources, defined dead Indians located on federal lands as archaeological resources and converted them to federal property. Consequently, governments—and many museums and universities—treated dead Native Americans not as human beings but as "historical property," "pathological materials," "scientific data," or "scientific specimens."

This treatment stemmed, in part, from lack of access to U.S. courts by native people. Disputes between Native Americans and U.S. citizens usually were settled on the battlefield, not in courtrooms. Even when Indians managed to get into the courts, they had little hope of a fair hearing given the prevailing racial views of most white Americans. It was not until 1879 that federal courts recognized an Indian as a person within the meaning of law; citizenship was granted by Congress in 1924.

Thus state and federal law failed to recognize native American burial practices and religious beliefs. No consideration was given during the development of U.S. common law to the effect of forced displacement of native people from their homelands and traditional burial grounds.

THE POWER OF SOCIAL MYTH

Social myths shaped the views of most U.S. citizens—including museum people—in their interactions with Native Americans. Until recently, U.S. schools taught that Europeans "discovered" America. Students learned that their ancestors came seeking religious and political freedom: they brought law, order, and civilization to a great and untamed wilderness; and they created a new nation dedicated to liberty and freedom for all. No mention was made of the facts that early settlers took land from Native Americans by force and chicanery; that they dismembered native cultures; and that surviving natives subsequently were placed on reservations considered unfit for any other purpose. It was within this context that museums collected cultural materials and Native American dead.

Acting on the assumption that native people were destined for extinction or cultural assimilation, museums began collecting Native American materials in an effort to preserve them before they disappeared. And competition was keen to build collections, especially between 1875 and 1929. Some museum people robbed graves or participated in other forms of theft or deceit to acquire objects, although it also is true that the majority of acquisitions were made legally and ethically.

In retrospect, museum collecting continued long after the initial rationale had disappeared, and Native American material by the 1940s was upgraded to the status of art. Collecting gathered momentum, and museums acquired objects for their own purposes—sometimes including objects needed to continue traditional Native American religious practices or tribal or clan identities. The greatest jeopardy many objects faced was the potential of acquisition by other collectors. Museum interest in collecting sometimes superseded the needs and interests of the people who made the objects or their culture.

Museums, however, used their collections to create a new and widespread awareness of Native American people and culture in the U.S. and abroad. Since 1960, museums have produced a host of exceptional traveling exhibitions on Native American art and culture seen by millions of people: museums also produced high-quality publications. This increased visibility has helped native people advance many causes, including repatriation.

THE REPATRIATION LAW

Following intense negotiations, the Native American Grave Protection and Repatriation Act was signed on November 23, 1990, and codified as 25 USC 3001. This law and its accompanying legislative history—which further clarifies its provisions—should be studied closely both by museums and Indian tribes. We believe that implementation will be easier and more harmonious when all parties are fully informed about the duties and opportunities afforded by the law.

The law does four things:

1. It increases protection for Native American graves located on federal and tribal lands and provides for disposition of cultural items found there in the future.
2. It prohibits traffic in Native American human remains.
3. It requires federal agencies and federally funded museums to inventory their collections of Native American human remains and associated funerary objects in five years and repatriate them, if requested, to culturally affiliated tribes or native groups.
4. It requires federal agencies and federally funded museums to summarize their collections of Native American sacred objects, objects of cultural patrimony, and unassociated funerary objects in three years and repatriate items to specified native claimants when the agency or museum does not have a right of possession.

Many sections of the law spell out definitions, standards, and procedures for accomplishing these objectives. Separate procedures are given for the treatment of human remains and associated funerary objects and all other cultural items covered by the law (sacred objects, objects of cultural patrimony, and unassociated funerary objects). Each of these items is defined in the law, and the legislative history gives more clarification.

- *Human remains and associated funerary objects.* Museums must inventory these in five years. The inventory must be done in consultation with tribal government and Native American religious leaders. The required inventory must be a simple itemized list; new studies and research are not required. If necessary, museums may request an extension from the Secretary of the Interior.

  If culturally affiliated tribes request return of human remains or associated funerary objects, museums are required to comply with the request expeditiously. There is a provision for delay if a scientific study of national importance is being conducted on the remains or objects, in which case return must be accomplished 90 days after completion of the study.
- *Cultural items.* Museums are required to summarize their Native American cultural items and notify appropriate tribes within three years. The procedure for handling requests for return of sacred objects, objects of cultural patrimony, or

unassociated funerary objects involves a four-step process. Native people must show that the requested items fall within the definitions given for sacred objects, objects of cultural patrimony, or unassociated funerary objects. Native people must next establish their cultural affiliation to the object in question or show prior ownership.

If the foregoing steps are met, then native people must present a *prima facie* case showing the federal agency or museum does not have a right of possession to the item. The law spells out the criteria for a right of possession based on relevant common and property laws and principles. The federal agency or museum then may present its case for right of possession. Finally, the institution must make a decision, based on the preponderance of the evidence, regarding disposition of the object.

If Native Americans are unsatisfied with the decision, they may submit the matter to a Federal Review Committee comprised of Native American and museum representatives. The review committee may issue findings that are not judicially binding but may help resolve the matter. The issue may also be submitted to a court of competent jurisdiction for resolution.

The relationship between museums and Native Americans has been complex and impossible to characterize as good or bad. The passage of the Native American Grave Protection and Repatriation Act of 1990 recognizes the necessity for change, and the change in attitudes, values, and mutual understanding that underlie the new law create an opportunity for museums and native people to work together.

As the result of input from AAM and its new repatriation task force, we are confident that museums and native people will succeed in resolving questions regarding collections and enriching the interpretation of Native American life and culture. We also look forward to seeing tribes and museums move into the future as partners.

Here Are Answers to Common Questions about the Congressional Action

Many museum professionals have questions about the new Native American Grave Protection and Repatriation Act of 1990. Here are answers to some of the most common:

1. *How will museum and Native American costs be met?* The act authorizes Congress to appropriate funds for implementation. AAM and native groups are pressing Congress for such appropriations: Museum and federal responsibilities for compliance, however, must be met with or without federal appropriations.
2. *How can museums satisfy requirements to consult with native people?* Consultation with native leaders is desirable. Tribal governments are easy to locate and contact. AAM is establishing a special task force consisting of native and museum representatives to assist museums in this and other aspects of the new law.

3. *Should museums expect large numbers of repatriation requests for cultural items?*
   The repatriation process for cultural items requires careful research and preparation. Requests, then, are likely to focus on a comparatively small number of objects of paramount importance to native people.

4. *What happens if museums fail to comply with the law?* Monetary civil penalties
   can be assessed against museums by the Secretary of the Interior. In addition,
   federal courts can hear actions brought by parties claiming a violation of the law.

5. *How will museums know what objects are sacred objects or objects of cultural patrimony?* In many cases, museums will not know. The purpose of the notification
   of tribes and the narrative summary of a museum's collections is to establish the
   basis for dialogue regarding a museum's collections.

6. *What should a museum do if it questions the integrity of a repatriation request?* The
   law emphasizes the importance of working with tribal governments and traditional Native American leaders. It is in the best interest of the museum and native people to ascertain together that repatriation requests have merit.

7. *How can museums obtain further clarification of key definitions of the new law?*
   House and Senate reports and floor statements elaborate on the definitions, so
   consult these sources first; AAM can help museums obtain these reports (contact
   the Government Affairs department, AAM, 1225 Eye St. N.W., Suite 200, Washington, D.C. 20005, (202) 289-9125). The Secretary of the Interior will issue regulations to carry out parts of the law. Tribal groups and traditional Native
   American religious leaders will be able to assist, and the AAM task force might
   also be of assistance. Finally, consult with legal counsel as necessary.

28

Deaccessioning: The American Perspective

Marie C. Malaro

Perhaps I should begin by pointing out that I have never been able to find the word "deaccession" in my dictionary. The fact that those who bless new words have never seen fit to recognize the term does not seem to bother many in the United States. We have been engaged in "deaccessioning" for years, and if there has been debate—and there has been—it has not been over terminology but over the practice which the term describes.[1]

First, let me define what I mean by deaccessioning: "It is the permanent removal of an object that was once accessioned into museum collection." Accordingly, the term does not apply when an object is placed on loan by a museum (there is no permanent removal) nor does it apply if the object in question was never accessioned. For example, if a museum acquires an object but never accessions it because it is not deemed of collection quality, the disposal of that object is not a deaccession. There was never an intellectual judgment made that the object in question was worthy of indefinite preservation and therefore, the removal of that object raises less formidable hurdles. Also, I use the term "deaccession" to cover the entire process of removal. In other words, for me, deaccessioning encompasses two major questions:

- Should this object be removed?
- If so, what is the appropriate method of disposal?

I make this clarification merely because some limit the term to just the first issue—the decision to remove—and consider the method of disposal an administrative detail. From my experience it is more prudent to consider all aspects of a proposed removal before any decisions are made. Sometimes the method of disposal can raise more difficult questions than the issue of whether the object should go.

Marie C. Malaro is professor emerita at George Washington University and the author of *A Legal Primer on Managing Museum Collections*. "Deaccessioning: The American Perspective" originally appeared in *Management and Curatorship* (Vol. 10, No. 3, 1991, pp. 273–279). It is reprinted here with permission from Elsevier.

One more prefatory comment is in order. When discussing deaccessioning we must bear in mind both legal and ethical standards.

- *Legal standard*—What I can and cannot do.
- *Ethical standard*—What I should or should not do.

It is important to understand the difference because each standard serves a specific purpose, and when we confuse the two, intelligent discourse is all but impossible. The law sets the lower standard. It tells us how we must act if we want to avoid civil or criminal liability. We find the law in statutes or by reading decided cases—what the lawyer calls precedent. *The law is not designed to make us honorable—only bearable—* and therefore we often can engage in some highly questionable conduct and yet stay within the law. The law, however does have clout. If you are found guilty of violating the law you must pay fines or you may go to jail.

Ethics are a different matter. A code of ethics sets forth conduct deemed necessary by a profession to uphold the integrity of the profession. It sets a higher standard because it is based on principles of personal accountability and service to others. A code of ethics, however, frequently has no enforcement power. It is effective only if there is personal commitment and informed peer pressure. This distinction between law and ethics is very important to bear in mind when we look at the history of deaccessioning in the United States. We have very little law in the United States that inhibits deaccessioning, and we have a tremendous variety of museums that are governed mainly by independent boards composed of private citizens. Accordingly, we have had all sorts of museums experimenting with deaccessioning under a wide variety of circumstances. And we have everyone commenting on the ethics of each particular situation with little law defining what is actually enforceable. You name it, we have probably done it in the United States, so it is worthwhile to take a closer look at how we have fared.

Most museums in the United States are not controlled by the government. They are what we call nonprofit organizations—organizations incorporated to serve a public purpose but run by boards of private citizens. Support comes through private donations, grants, and some revenue-producing activities. It is estimated that well over 90 percent of the objects in United States museums have been donated. The nonprofit sector is deeply rooted in the American tradition, and one of the reasons we sustain this sector is to provide diversity. Anyone in the United States can start a museum for any purpose as long as the purpose falls within our broad definition of "service to the public." We have museums in this nonprofit sector of every size and shape. For example, the Smithsonian Institution is not a government agency. It owes its existence to the bequest of an Englishman, James Smithson, who left his fortune to start, in the United States, an institution "for the increase and diffusion of knowledge." The Smithsonian is chartered as a nonprofit organization and is governed by an independent board of regents. The Metropolitan Museum in New York is an independently managed nonprofit organization, as are the majority of the almost 7,000 museums listed in our professional directory.

Under our laws a nonprofit organization has a broad range of powers, and one of them is the ability to dispose of its assets under the supervision of its governing board. Thus any museum organized as a nonprofit has an inherent right to deaccession material unless its charter specifically limits this right. It is possible for the creator of a museum to restrict the ability to remove objects as, for example, the Freer Gallery of Art in Washington or the Gardner Museum in Boston. Here under the terms of the donors' gifts no objects can be removed from those collections, but these instructions reflect the wishes of private parties, they do not reflect public policy. What all this means is that whether a museum in the United States engages in deaccessioning is pretty much left to its governing board, acting in light of its own particular circumstances.

Added to this is the factor that the United States, with very limited exception, has never seen fit to restrict the movement of cultural objects located within its borders.[2] In fact, cultural objects can leave the country more freely than they can enter. What we have then is no centralized policy regarding collecting our collections and a government that plays no discernible role in shaping a national cultural policy. What is collected and what is disposed of is usually left in the hands of those who are interested in a particular museum. But all is not *laissez-faire*. Perhaps to fill a void, the museum profession in the United States talks a lot about ethics and public accountability. Several of our major professional organizations promulgate codes of ethics and each code has something to say about deaccessioning. The codes recognize deaccessioning as a valid practice, but set down guidelines for implementation. For example, the code promulgated by the American Association of Museums makes the following points:

1. Every museum should have a public statement regarding its policy on deaccessioning.
2. When considering disposal, the museum must weigh carefully the interests of the public that it serves.
3. When disposing of an object due consideration should be given to the museum community in general as well as the wishes and financial needs of the institution itself.
4. While the governing board bears the ultimate responsibility for a deaccession decision, great weight should be given to the recommendation of the curatorial staff regarding the pertinence of the object to the mission of the museum.[3]

The code promulgated by the Association of Art Museum Directors stresses the following points:

1. Deaccessioning should be related to policy not to the exigencies of the moment.
2. Procedures for deaccessioning should be at least as rigorous as for the purchase of major works of art.
3. While final decisions rest with the governing board of the museum, full justification for a disposal should be provided by the director and the responsible curator.
4. Funds obtained through disposal must be used to replenish the collection.[4]

A careful reading of each code shows that both professional organizations require a museum to have a policy regarding deaccessioning, both place final decision-making responsibility with the governing board (as the case law in the United States requires) and both require that the board pay attention to curatorial opinion, but in other respects there are different emphases. The Association of Art Museum Directors addresses the use of proceeds from deaccessions and insists that these proceeds be used to replenish the collections. The American Association of Museums, which represents all types of museums, has (at the time of writing) nothing in its code about use of proceeds from deaccessions. Instead, it speaks of considering the needs of the museums community generally when one is contemplating deaccessioning. In other words, there is less focus on dollar return, with more emphasis on trying to place the unwanted object with another collecting organization. These differences in the codes of ethics themselves highlight the fact that even in a country where deaccessioning is generally accepted there are differing views on its implementation, and differences frequently can be associated with discipline. For example, art museums are quite comfortable with sales in the marketplace but there is great pressure to require that sale proceeds be used only to replenish the collections. History museums seemed more concerned with finding an appropriate new home for a piece, and less stress is put on the matter of what is done with any proceeds that may accrue. Anthropology museums and natural science museums tend to favor only exchanges with other collecting organizations. These differences can be explained in part by the fact that up until recently only art brought substantial prices in the marketplace. With this factor changing, because now there seems to be a market for almost anything, and with the very high sale prices we have seen over the last few years, history museums as well as natural science museums are being forced to grapple with the lure of the marketplace.

If I were listing recent developments in the United States that are affecting deaccessioning this might be the first one:

Development 1. The very active and lucrative market for not only art but other collectibles has put added pressure not only on art museums but on all types of museums.

There are other developments that have been equally if not more responsible for renewed attention to deaccessioning. One is the fact that in 1986 a new tax reform act was passed in the United States, which makes it less attractive at times for individuals to donate objects to museum collections. As I mentioned earlier, museums in the United States depend almost exclusively on donations to form their collections. With donations down this means that collections will not grow unless museums can buy in the marketplace—buy, in many cases, the very works that would-be donors are now selling. But where is the money to come from, especially with prices escalating? A logical solution for many is to look for objects to deaccession and sell in order to raise purchase money.

The second development then is:

Development 2. The change in the United States tax law that discourages donations of objects to museums and forces museums to consider buying.

But there have been more profound and pervasive developments. Over the last decade or so the museum community in the United States has begun to examine itself more carefully, and this has been brought about by several factors. One is that there is more public interest in museums. As people become more educated and more affluent they are demanding more from museums and they are questioning the quality of governance in museums. At the same time we are seeing more professionally trained people attracted to museum work. In an effort to respond to the greater demands on museums these people are examining in a comprehensive way how their museums operate. Too often what they find are: disorganized collections, poor documentation, and horrendous storage conditions. A natural response is to re-examine the collecting practices of a museum so that there is some assurance the museum will collect wisely and that objects, once acquired, can be maintained, conserved, and used effectively. Accordingly we have a growing number of museums in the United States that have refocused their collecting activity and are seriously concerned about proper maintenance and conservation of their collections. Because of this, I can add to my list two other developments that are affecting deaccession activity. These are developments not usually highlighted by the press when a deaccession story makes the newspapers, but they are of fundamental importance.

Development 3. Many museums have more carefully focused their collecting and now find themselves with objects that are extraneous to their missions.

Development 4. Because of heightened concern for quality storage and conservation, museums are questioning the validity of retaining objects that are not clearly furthering the goals of their museums.

Because of all the above-described developments we are seeing more deaccessioning activity in the United States and, as might be expected, renewed debate concerning the practice. Most of the newspaper stories and magazine articles feature major art museum deaccessions because these are always more dramatic and often involve the disposal of a work or works in order to acquire immediately a preferred replacement. This allows everyone the opportunity to play critic on the merits of the particular exchange and some, in their zeal, call for the outlawing of all deaccessioning. I do not believe it likely that the United States in the foreseeable future will consider seriously any legislation that would ban deaccessioning. Such a move would be at odds with our concept of a museum and with our whole tradition of leaving cultural development in the hands of the people rather than the government.

On the first point—our concept of a museum—we view museums essentially as educational organizations with responsibilities to collect wisely, maintain prudently and encourage public use and enjoyment. Collecting in an educational organization is not a mechanical process. It is a combination of intelligent selection and periodic re-evaluation. What serious educator would ever take the position that what is deemed "right" today should never be subject to review? But this attitude is inherent in a general prohibition against deaccessioning. How can a museum present itself as an educational organization and yet relinquish a continuing responsibility to review critically its progress in achieving its particular goals? Accordingly, in the United States, the prevailing view is that if museums want to be considered educational organizations they must be free to deaccession.

The second reason for arguing that the United States would never seriously consider outlawing deaccessioning is our tradition of leaving cultural development in the hands of the people—as evidenced by our nonprofit sector. This system, which encourages great diversity, has served us rather well. We have museums that never dispose of anything, others that are free-wheeling, and every shade in between. Each can survive as long as enough people are willing to support it. By encouraging diversity we encourage the direct participation of many in shaping a cultural heritage. A ban on deaccessioning, which would seriously inhibit the present system, just does not make sense.

While I would argue that the last thing the United States needs or wants is any legislation inhibiting deaccessioning, I will readily admit that our museum community is not without fault in this area. The weak spot is not the general rules we have developed for deaccessioning, it is a failure to promulgate these rules as aggressively as we should. If more time and effort were to be spent educating the profession with regard to these general rules, the few problems we have with deaccessioning would probably disappear.

Our general rules are all drawn from our major codes of ethics, and they reflect our very American view that each museum is responsible for its own destiny. Our rules give wide discretion to those in authority within a museum, but they also require that those in authority answer directly to the people they serve and on whom they depend for support. The general rules on deaccessioning are essentially these:

1. Deaccessioning should never be addressed in isolation. It is dependent on a clear articulation of a museum's collecting goals and prudent acquisition procedures. In other words, deaccessioning is not a method for curing sloppiness in accessioning. A first consideration, therefore, is to have strict acquisition guidelines in place.
2. Collections should be reviewed periodically for relevance, condition and quality. When this is done routinely more objective opinions result, and with no urgency to remove, there is time to reflect on initial judgments.
3. There should be written policies and procedures on deaccessioning. These should stress thoughtful review, clear delegation of responsibility, careful record-keeping and public disclosure. The policies and procedures should address:
   a. reasons that may justify removal;
   b. the importance of clarifying the museum's unrestricted title to an object before it is considered for removal;
   c. the role of professional staff in the process;
   d. when outside opinions are to be sought;
   e. appropriate methods of disposal that may be considered;
   f. who has final responsibility for deciding whether an object is to be removed;
   g. who has final responsibility for deciding the method of disposal;
   h. who is responsible for keeping records of the process;
   i. who is responsible for providing information to the public on a planned disposal;
   j. when and how notification of deaccessioning is given to donors of objects;
   k. the importance of avoiding even apparent conflicts of interest in the deaccessioning process.

A museum that has such written policies and procedures—and follows them carefully when deaccession situations arise—will probably make sound decisions and will maintain public confidence. This is so because in the very process of preparing its deaccession policies and procedures the museum will have re-examined its mission, clarified its collecting goals and pondered the long-term effects of its actions. Also, it will be acutely aware that the burden of justifying deaccessioning decisions rests with it. After all this preparation, the museum is truly ready to take on individual cases, and as decisions are made the museum will be able to convey a sense of purpose and thoughtful adherence to previously articulated goals. This is the essence of good governance.

However, I must mention that I am always rather perplexed by the amount of controversy we see on the subject of deaccessioning as compared with the general apathy concerning the issues of mindless collecting or collecting with negligible documentation. Is the public better served by an undisciplined or poorly documented collection? I would suggest that if there is persistent agonizing over deaccessioning the museum profession should look more deeply. Those who cannot come to terms with deaccessioning may be avoiding taking decisions in other areas of collections management. When you look at the total collection management picture within a museum, and demand that all facets be reviewed and controlled in light of the museum's mission, the matter of deaccessioning falls into perspective. It becomes a small part of an integrated plan and, as such, it can be handled with confidence and in a way that inspires confidence.

In conclusion, if there are lessons to be learned from studying deaccessioning in the United States they are these:

a. In order to justify deaccessioning you must first be able to demonstrate that the museum has control over its collections. Control means that there is a collecting plan which is in accord with the mission of the museum, and the plan is religiously followed.
b. You must be able to demonstrate that your collections are periodically and objectively reviewed for adherence to collecting goals.
c. You must have written procedures for considering proposed deaccessions, and these procedures should stress full discussion, clear delegation of decision-making authority and complete record-keeping.

If these lessons are followed one does not have to worry about deaccessioning being used as a quick and shallow solution to immediate problems. By the time a museum has taken all the required steps and is at a point where deaccessioning can be considered it will have educated itself. What decisions are then made should be relatively thoughtful, supported by clearly articulated policies. This approach offers the public the greatest protection because it demands that the museum profession understand and practice the full scope of its responsibilities.

NOTES

1. Some claim the word merely demonstrates ignorance of Latin. *Ad cedere* is the Latin for "to cede to" or "accession." *Decedere* is the Latin for "to cede from" or, logically, "decession." Somehow we "deaccession" or "cede from to."

2. The exceptions are mainly archaeological objects removed from federal or Indian lands. Federal statutes control the use of these objects. States may have similar statutes regarding such materials found on state property.

3. *Museum Ethics* (American Association of Museums, 1978).

4. *Professional Practices in Art Museums* (Association of Art Museum Directors, 1981).

Additional Recommended Reading

American Association of Museums. *Caring for Collections: Strategies for Conservation, Maintenance, and Documentation/A Report on an American Association of Museums Project.* Washington, DC: Author, 1984.

Ames, Michael M. *Cannibal Tours and Glass Boxes: The Anthropology of Museums.* Vancouver: University of British Columbia Press, 1992.

Buck, Rebecca A., and Jean Allman Gilmore, eds. *The New Museum Registration Methods.* Washington, DC: American Association of Museums, 1998.

Case, Mary, ed. *Registrars on Record: Essays on Museum Collections Management.* Washington, DC: Registrars Committee of the American Association of Museums, 1988.

Csikszentmihalyi, Mihaly. *The Meaning of Things: Domestic Symbols and the Self.* New York: Cambridge University Press, 1981.

"Designing for Conservation." *Exhibitionist* 20, no. 2 (Fall 2001).

Keene, Suzanne. *Managing Conservation in Museums.* Boston: Butterworth-Heinemann, 1996.

Malaro, Marie C. *A Legal Primer on Managing Museum Collections.* Washington, DC: Smithsonian Institution Press, 1998.

Messenger, Phyllis M., ed. *The Ethics of Collecting Cultural Property: Whose Culture? Whose Ethics?* Albuquerque: University of New Mexico Press, 1999.

Weil, Stephen, ed. *A Deaccession Reader.* Washington, DC: American Association of Museums, 1997.

THE ROLE OF LEADERSHIP:
THE ESSENTIAL INGREDIENT

The best intentions, the most innovative exhibits, and the most coveted piece of art quite literally cannot by themselves make the difference in the future of a museum—it is the vision and the quality of the leadership that make the difference. Over the past century, museum leaders—executive directors and trustees—have had to add new elements and challenges to the complex juggling act of managing and governing museums. Challenges include increasing legislation, burgeoning technologies, and new tools for disseminating and managing information to a public that is more sophisticated in its expectations. Market savvy, audience development, Internet access, and NAGPRA are just four elements completely unimaginable a century ago—even twenty years ago. Pressures from the external environment continue to grow and change as the standards and ethics of the museum industry have become more explicit and more refined. Thus, strategic planning for a museum in today's world is dependent on informed and insightful leadership—leadership that can balance the external challenges while effectively guiding the internal needs, staff, and resources in support of the mission.

Without a doubt, the partnership between the board of trustees and the CEO must be strong and balanced with an ongoing commitment to planning, fiscal responsibility, mission-based decision making, and the upholding of museum standards, practices, and ethics. An effective board is paramount to an effective operation in the eyes of the director and staff, and the director's empowerment can energize the leadership on the board. This interrelatedness requires that board and staff remain well informed and operate at a professional level. A lack of professional behavior on the part of either can dramatically hinder progress for a museum or even jeopardize its future. Museums with astute leaders committed to sustainability and a wise marshalling of resources in support of the institution's mission stand a better chance of survival. Yet, it should be said that leadership can be exercised at all levels, whether trustee, director, staff, or volunteer.

Introducing this part is Stephen Weil's 1995 essay "Creampuffs or Hardball: Are You Really Worth What You Cost or Just Merely Worthwhile?" Fearless and direct, Weil lays out the facts about survival for museums today, jarring those "asleep at the wheel" into an alert state of consciousness and hopefully leading museum leaders to abandon long-held assumptions about what is adequate and appropriate and to move toward developing meaningful measurements of value. In the next article, Weil partners with Earl Cheit to codify the qualifications of "The Well-Managed Museum." They offer a checklist of the hallmarks of the well-run museum. Just like Judy Rand's "Visitor's Bill of Rights" in Part II, this list should be widely distributed among trustees and staff as a constant reminder of the essential ingredients for to-day's museum.

In 1991, Willard Boyd, an attorney and the former longtime director of the Field Museum, wrote a primer on the rules of the game in "Museum Accountability: Laws, Rules, Ethics, and Accreditation." This article is a classic and stands as an elo-quent clarification of the distinction between each of these formal guidelines in museum management.

John Carver, a well-known spokesperson and author on the topic of trusteeship, tackles issues in governance in an excerpt from his 1997 book *Boards That Make a Difference: A New Design for Leadership in Nonprofit and Public Organizations.* In the excerpt, "Toward a New Governance," he provides a list of expectations for trustees within his governance model. His writing presents a complex topic in a compelling and accessible manner, providing an inspirational framework for those desiring to shift the nature of their governance structure.

Will Philips, a seasoned consultant in both the for-profit and nonprofit worlds, tackles the barriers to institutional change and the nature of change itself in his ar-ticle "Institution-wide Change in Museums," written in 2000.

And, closing out this part and this volume is an excerpt entitled "Persistent Para-doxes" from Robert Janes's book, *Museums and the Paradox of Change: A Case Study in Urgent Adaptation.* In this open dialogue with the museum profession, Janes, the former director of the Glenbow Museum in Calgary, Canada, poses profound and poignant questions for the industry to ponder—questions that linger in the midst of museums' efforts to achieve new levels of effectiveness and innovation. At the heart of his discourse is the tension between the traditions of museums and the quest of museums to learn and adapt in appropriate ways for survival.

29

Creampuffs and Hardball: Are You Really Worth What You Cost or Just Merely Worthwhile?

Stephen E. Weil

The questions about their field that museum workers serve up to one another at their periodic gatherings (national, regional, and local) are generally creampuffs. Although shaped and flavored in a variety of ways, these questions can almost invariably be reduced to the single one of whether the museum, in essence, is truly a worthwhile institution. With almost equal invariability, those attending these gatherings conclude that it is. To those who work in them, it appears all but self-evident that, notwithstanding their temporary shortcomings, museums do make an important contribution to society. They preserve and transmit our natural and cultural heritage, they add to the world's store of knowledge, and they provide their publics with expanded opportunities for learning, personal growth, and enjoyment.

As crunch time approaches, however, and as the demands that are made on the public and private resources available to the nonprofit sector continue to grow at a faster rate than those resources themselves, virtually every museum may find itself faced with several much tougher questions—not creampuffs this time but hardball. Without disputing the museum's claim to worthiness, what these questions will address instead is its *relative* worthiness. Is what the museum contributes to society really commensurate with the annual cost of its operation? Could some other organization (not necessarily a museum) make a similar or even greater contribution at a lesser cost? What would be the consequence—how much lost? how much gained?—if the same expenditure were to be devoted to some other activity entirely? We currently spend billions of dollars each year on the operation of our museums. We have yet to determine, however, in what measure that expenditure

Stephen E. Weil is senior scholar emeritus at the Center of Museum Studies, Smithsonian Institution. "Creampuffs and Hardball: Are You Really Worth What You Cost or Just Merely Worthwhile?" is one of the essays in his 1995 collection entitled *Cabinet of Curiosities: Inquiries into Museums and Their Prospects*. It is reprinted here with permission from *Museum News*, September/October 1994. Copyright 1994, the American Association of Museums. All rights reserved.

represents a wise and informed public policy choice and in what measure it may simply be the hangover of some old and still-to-be-fully-examined habit.

Underpinning these hardball questions is a profound and ongoing shift in the way that nonprofit organizations are being evaluated by those who provide them with resources. This shift, which appears to have started with social service and health care agencies and worked its way through higher education, can now be sensed as spreading across the entire nonprofit sector. It involves a newly heightened concentration on "outcomes" rather than either "inputs" or "outputs" as the principal basis on which to judge a charitable organization's public programs.

Little more than a generation ago, a museum was still measured largely by the resources (i.e., the inputs) that it had available: How good was its collection? How well trained and respected was its staff? How adequate and in what condition were its facilities? How solid was its attendance? How large was its endowment? Good numbers equated with a good museum.

In the years that followed—in the 1970s and well into the 1980s—the principal focus shifted from inputs to outputs. No longer judged so much by the measurable resources that they had available, museums tended to be judged instead by the programmatic use to which they put those resources. "Better utilization of collections" was a key phrase, and peer review became a principal means of evaluation. Who better could judge the skill with which a museum staff deployed the limited resources at its disposal than its colleagues in other museums who daily faced the same challenge? Output analysis goes still a step farther. It examines the impact of those programs rather than simply their quality.

In the United Kingdom, a remarkably direct phrase has emerged to describe the expectation of those responsible for providing public funds. What they expect is "value for money." Typical of its use are recent remarks by the Right Honorable Peter Brooke, who, as the United Kingdom's Secretary of State for National Heritage, oversees the funding of the United Kingdom's major museums. Noting that publicly supported cultural organizations will be expected to carry out their day-to-day operations "within an overall framework of priorities and public policies determined by Government," Brooke emphasized that they must also "assure value for money for the taxpayer in pursuit of those aims."

What this all involves in essence is a new accountability in which organizations will be required to demonstrate not only (a) that they can account for the resources entrusted to them and (b) that they used those resources efficiently but, above all, (c) that they also used those resources *effectively*—that they used them to produce a positive outcome in the community intended to be served. The museum that seeks to meet the standards of this new accountability must be prepared to show in what positive ways its target community has benefited from its programs. This need not be a narrow constraint. That the museum continues to preserve a community's otherwise endangered heritage might certainly be one such beneficial outcome. Other beneficial outcomes might relate to the transmission of knowledge and/or skills, to the modification of behavior, or simply to the provision of enjoyment or recreation. The only required constant is that the benefits described be in response to what some have called the ultimate "so what?" questions. So what difference did it make that your museum was there? So what would have been the difference had it not been?

Implicit also in this new accountability is the question of limits. How are those allocating funds to determine the boundaries of an applicant's need? Is the outcome that an organization seeks infinite in scope (with the inference that the organization's need for additional resources will consequently be insatiable) or is there a point at which the organization may be considered as accomplishing its goals? Is there such a thing as an adequately funded museum, or is nothing ever enough? Richard F. Larkin, the Technical Director for the Not-for-Profit Industry Services Group at Price Waterhouse, has observed that this is a problem endemic to almost all charitable organizations. Their goals are generally formulated in open-ended terms ("to encourage an understanding and appreciation of contemporary art" or "to improve the health services available to the indigent members of our community") with little to indicate what would constitute actual success or assist an observer seeking to determine whether it was being achieved. This is in sharp contrast to the for-profit organization in which success or failure can be determined by comparing some bottom line "outcome" figure with one or another of the organization's inputs.

Without a definition of success, of course, museums also lack a definition of failure. Might this be the reason that so few museums ever seem to fail? Dance companies dissolve, symphony orchestras collapse, and literary magazines disappear with regularity. Most museums, though—held in place perhaps by their collections—seem to survive indefinitely. They may shrink, they may lose or fail to earn accreditation, but rarely do they expire. Short of outright insolvency, the museum field seems to have few ways to identify those institutions whose chronic inability to achieve any demonstrably beneficial outcome cannot possibly justify the ongoing expense of their maintenance.

The museum seeking to articulate the ways in which it intends to have an effect on its target community would be wise to observe one caution: that it concentrate on those object-related outcomes that are most distinct to museums and not inadvertently undermine its unique importance by describing outcomes that might as easily be achieved by some other organization. Put another way, a museum may only be considered essential so long as its impact is perceived to be both valuable *and* incomparable. Consider, to use a wicked example, the museum improvident enough to base its case for public support on an economic impact study that quantifies its value to the community in terms of tourism, jobs, and purchasing power. What will justify the continuing public investment in such an institution when some other entity (a sports team, a theme park, a rock concert amphitheater) can demonstrate that—for a similar public investment—an even greater economic impact might be achieved? If museums cannot assert their importance *as* museums, then museums may not be perceived to be important at all.

More troubling in this respect is the extent to which some museums have begun to stress general educational objectives as the principal outcome for which they ought be valued. By doing so, they may ultimately leave themselves vulnerable to the claims of more traditional educational institutions that these latter could, with a only little inexpensive tinkering, deliver a comparable value at a fraction of the cost. The recent emergence of so-called single-subject museums—story-centered rather than object-centered and relying on what the designer Ralph Applebaum (a leading practitioner of the form) describes as "theatrical constructs" instead of what he calls a "giant cabinet-of-curiosities approach"—may pose a similar problem. The experiential outcome at which these museums aim may eventually (as soon, perhaps, as the widespread advent of virtual reality) be accomplishable by other and, again, less costly means. When incomparability is no longer an issue, then such cost comparisons may validly become the single criterion by which an institution is judged. The museum that casts its aspirations in such nontraditional terms cannot complain of "apples and oranges" when it finds itself unexpectedly measured against organizations of other kinds that can provide a comparable value at a far lower cost.

Beyond making the case for continued support, the ability of a preponderance of museums to define their intended outcomes and to specify what they would consider a successful level of achievement might have an important side effect. It could help lay to rest the perception that museums sometimes operate as what Philip M. Nowlen, Director of the Museum Management Institute, has called "federations of self-interest." In a field so largely self-initiated, the images that Nowlen conjures are all too familiar: the museum whose governing board believes—notwithstanding the clear language of its charter or its current mission statement—that organizational survival is the institution's driving and highest purpose, the museum in which the staff channels a disproportionate effort into its own professional development, the museum summoned into being for no better reason than to house a privately gathered collection that might otherwise have had to be dispersed, the museum that survives primarily to serve as a social focus for those who support and take turns governing it. Future funding prospects may be dimmest for those museums that appear to be little more than sites for self-indulgence, brightest for those that can most adequately answer the question "To what ongoing public need is this institution a response?"

It will be argued by those who resist these impending hardball questions—those who find them crude, insensitive to cultural values, too money-minded, or too result-oriented—that they constitute nothing more than an inappropriate effort to apply a clumsy cost-benefit analysis to an activity that belongs in some different sphere altogether. Although there may certainly be institutions (e.g., the family, public schools, religious orders) as to which such a cost-benefit analysis seems inappropriate, nowhere is it written (nor may it be any more than wishful thinking) that museums necessarily will or ought be exempt from such scrutiny. That museums were once described as "temples of the human spirit" is no guarantee that they will be forever considered sacred. Nor is the fact that they have been well supported in the past a guarantee that they will always be thought to have such an entitlement.

If this analysis still seems far-fetched, consider health care. The time is fast approaching when, in allocating health care resources, public policy–based decisions will have to be made about the value of providing care to one patient in comparison to another, about the value of, literally, saving one life rather than another. That the lives involved may all be worthwhile will be beside the point. Not every human being can be saved, and hateful as we may find the thought, medical care must ultimately be rationed by public decision, just as it has hitherto been rationed by the less visible forces of the marketplace. Might one reasonably expect something more clement for museums?

In summary, when (not if, but only when) the anticipated crunch in public and private funding materializes, worthiness alone may not justify the continued support of every museum or similar institution. The question that each museum may have to answer are just these hardball ones: Are you really worth what you cost or just merely worthwhile? Could somebody else do as much or more than you do for less? Are you truly able to accomplish anything that makes a difference, or are you simply an old habit, or possibly even a kind of indulgence? Beyond doubt, the great majority of museums will be able to develop positive and solidly convincing responses to these indisputably difficult questions. It is by no means too soon, however, for a museum's governing authority and senior staff to begin to consider just how that might best be done. Hardball is nigh.

30

The Well-Managed Museum

Stephen E. Weil and Earl F. Cheit

Summarizing his twenty-nine-year tenure (1908–37) as director of Cambridge University's Fitzwilliam Museum, the late S. C. Cockerell said, "I found it a pig sty; I turned it into a palace." If we assume that Cockerell meant to describe something more than just positive changes in the Fitzwilliam's physical facilities—that he referred as well to improvements in its collections, staff, finances, governance, records, and public image—then his remark might serve as a neat shorthand summary of good management. Good management is to move an organization from the "here" of a less well managed condition to the "there" of a better managed one—from being something near a pig sty toward being something like a palace. The aim of good management is to have a well-managed museum.

What do we mean by a well-managed museum? The clearest indications that a museum is well managed might be its ability to demonstrate that it makes the most efficient and effective use possible of the resources which it has available. In day-to-day practice, however, it is only rarely that a museum can be measured on so all-encompassing a scale. Most frequently, the degree to which a museum is well managed—or could, at least, be better managed—can only be determined by examining a number of more detailed and specific factors that relate to its programs, planning capability, governance, staff, finances, facilities, collections, records, and outside relationships.

What, then, might some of these factors be? What are some of the attributes of a well-managed museum? The following nonprioritized list (on which a number of entries may overlap) is intended to be suggestive rather than exhaustive:

Stephen E. Weil is senior scholar emeritus at the Center for Museum Studies, Smithsonian Institution, and Earl F. Cheit is the Edgar F. Kaiser Professor of Business and Public Policy Emeritus and Dean Emeritus at the Haas Business Public Policy Group, University of California, Berkeley. "The Well-Managed Museum" is © The J. Paul Getty Trust 1989. Excerpted from *Curriculum Statement*, 2d revised edition, prepared for the Museum Management Institute Advisory Committee, March 29, 1989. It is reprinted here with permission of the Getty Leadership Institute, an operating program of the J. Paul Getty Trust.

- a clearly defined mission and set of shared long-term goals and underlying values;
- the ability to formulate and to pursue such strategies as may be necessary to acquire, process, and expend the resources that it needs to fulfill its mission together with an array of ongoing and successive programs that readily relate to—and demonstrably further—that mission;
- the ability to formulate and to adhere to long-term and short-term budgets, timetables, and other operational plans consistent with its various strategies;
- a structure of governance that provides for wise oversight, a long-range institutional view, and access to the varied resources that may be necessary to produce its programs;
- a commitment to develop the managerial and vocational skills and knowledge of its staff;
- a competent, loyal, stable, mutually respectful, well-motivated and well-led staff that is able to work with relative independence in pursuit of a series of agreed-upon and well-understood goals;
- appropriate physical facilities that are maintained in good repair and provide adequate space for the production of its various programs;
- a system for implementing each of its functions such as, for example:
  - closely followed policies for the acquisition and management of its collections that assure their proper physical care; that provide for the maintenance of appropriate records as to their identification, location, condition, and provenance; and that assure their maximum public accessibility consistent with their care;
  - information management systems that permit the swift, accurate retrieval of the data necessary to manage its resources and to produce its various programs;
  - financial systems that operate to keep the expenditures of resources within budgeted targets, that keep management accurately advised as to the museum's current status, and that serve as the basis for providing timely reports to various outside individuals and authorities;
- a capacity to resolve issues related to the diversity of its present and potential staff and markets by continually renewing and, where necessary, modifying its practices and programs;
- a sensitivity to the needs and wishes of its existing and potential patrons and markets sufficiently acute that it can make considered decisions about the extent, if any, to which its programs will be shaped to meet those needs and wishes;
- the maintenance of a positive public image through which the actions of the institution and its staff are consistently and broadly perceived as related to the pursuit of the institution's mission and goals rather than any undisclosed or self-serving agenda; and
- the maintenance of a favorable legal status pursuant to which the institution will continue to be exempt from federal, state, and local income taxes, donors will

continue to be able to claim charitable deductions for their contributions, and the museum will continue to enjoy whatever other privileges may be extended by its locality to not-for-profit organizations.

No claim is made that the presence of any or most or even all of these attributes would in itself be sufficient to make a museum an excellent institution. Management, even at its best, is only a single dimension of a museum's overall operation. Excellence in a museum must depend as well on the quality of its educational and other programs, the importance of its purpose and the disciplinary value of its collection. Nonetheless, it is difficult to conceive that a poorly managed museum would ever be able to achieve and to sustain a level of excellence for any extended time. Good management may not be the measure of a good museum but, in the long run, it would most certainly appear to be one of its critical prerequisites.

31

Museum Accountability: Laws, Rules, Ethics, and Accreditation

Willard L. Boyd

"Museums . . . hold their possessions in trust for mankind and for the future welfare of the [human] race. Their value is in direct proportion to the service they render the emotional and intellectual life of the people."

(AAM Code of Ethics for Museum Workers, 1925)

The American Association of Museums (AAM), as early as 1925, adopted a code of ethics affirming the responsibility of museums to the public. Now AAM has adopted a new Code of Ethics which resolutely confirms "the ethic of public service as the foundation of [museum] actions and their contribution to society."[1]

This commitment to public service and responsibility is remarkable, since most museums in the United States are organized as private not-for-profit corporations. Private museums do not think of themselves as public institutions. In fact, they are *quasi-public institutions* because, in America, private organizations are used to accomplish public objectives in lieu of governmental agencies. Unlike other countries, we channel a substantial amount of social and economic effort through our private not-for-profit organizations. To encourage private action, nonprofits are given special tax status and frequently receive some governmental funding. The "not-for-profit" sector is a hybrid between private business and government. As a hybrid, it has a quasi-public character. In that sense, every museum has a mission of public service.

Since museums are institutions of public service, it follows that they are accountable to the public. In an era of more public accountability for government and business, there is a rising demand for accountability by nonprofits. Public accountability is institutionalized through regulations. Accordingly, museums are

Willard L. Boyd is an attorney and former director of the Field Museum in Chicago. "Museum Accountability: Laws, Rules, Ethics, and Accreditation" appeared in *Curator: The Museum Journal* (Vol. 34, No. 3, [July 1991], pp. 165–177). It is reprinted here by permission of AltaMira Press, a division of Rowman & Littlefield Publishers, Inc.

increasingly subjected to government-imposed, self-imposed, and peer-imposed regulations. While the increase in museum regulations is certain, still not clear are: who is accountable? for what? and to whom?

Who Is Accountable?

Most often, the museum itself is said to be accountable. Yet museums are people and, therefore, individuals are accountable for the actions they take in the museum's name—historically, the board, administration, and curators but increasingly education, library, and collection management staffs. To be a professional in any field is to be accountable for a generally accepted standard of performance.

Accountable for What?

Museums are accountable for the acquisition, conservation, management, and deaccession of collections. Museums are also accountable for the content, nature, and quality of their scholarship, exhibits, and programs.

Museums are accountable for endowment accumulation, preservation—or loss—and expansion of income sources. Museums are accountable, of course, for budget deficits.

In operating its auxiliary enterprises, museums are accountable to ensure that these enterprises are related to the museum's central mission. For example, publications and stores must be educationally oriented, and food services must be aimed at visitors.

Finally, museums are accountable for drafting personnel policies and practices that comply with legal requirements for both paid and volunteer staff. For instance, museums are accountable for implementing safety procedures that comply with state and local legal requirements.

Accountable to Whom?

Museums owe this accountability to the public. The public is comprised of various individuals, groups, and organizations: visitors to the museum; donors; peers; other museums; regulators, including the state attorney general, the legislature, and the IRS; cultural groups; employees; and the community at large.

There must be a generally acceptable standard of conduct for all museums since the actions of a few can affect all. For example, some contend that museums in concert with donors abused the deduction of gifts in kind by overvaluing objects. That abuse was partially responsible for federal restrictions on the deductibility of gifts of appreciated objects, which are the lifeblood of museums. Following a series of articles concerning donor and curatorial activities involving the Smithsonian gem collection, *The Washington Post* on March 30, 1983, editorialized that the tax deduction for gifts of objects should be eliminated to stop this abuse.[2]

Year by year, museums, their boards, and staff members are being subjected to greater accountability. That accountability is emanating from three sources: the public law, the museum's own regulations, and the peer community standards.

GOVERNMENT-IMPOSED REGULATIONS

Governmental laws and regulations are contained in common law (customary law developed by judicial interpretation) and statutory law. Laws are prescribing more and higher standards of operational conduct for museums.

STATUTORY LAW

All levels of government are regulating not-for-profits. Federal, state, and local governments are enacting laws and promulgating rules to carry out these laws.

The principal form of federal regulation of museums is through taxation. Museums seek income-tax-exempt status that will free their income from taxation and assure tax deductions for their donors. The Internal Revenue Code specifies the basis for exemption and the nature of deductions. In addition, granting agencies such as the National Endowments for the Arts and Humanities, the Institute for Museum Services, and the National Science Foundation (NSF) assure compliance with grant restrictions through financial audits and program reports.

Recent NSF audits of university and research museums concerning indirect and direct costs are vivid examples of government oversight. On January 10, 1990, the *Los Angeles Times* reported that 19 museums were being audited by NSF in a rigorous manner comparable to university audits.[3]

Federal regulatory legislation also affects how museums conduct business. The major federal safety, health, and environmental laws apply to museums—the Occupational, Safety and Health Act (OSHA), including the latest Laboratory Standard, and the Resources Conservation and Recovery Act (RCRA) on hazardous waste management. The new Americans with Disabilities Act (ADA) requires reasonable accommodations for disabled employees. In addition, the Civil Rights Act of 1964 (Title VII) and the Americans with Disabilities Act impact on a museum's employment practices.

Local government reporting requirements are increasing for museums receiving local government support—requirements concerning both requests for and administration of funds. In addition, museums and other nonprofits have to be concerned about local property and sales-tax exemptions. In the past, these exemptions have been granted to charities and educational institutions. But as local governments aggressively seek tax revenue, nonprofit local tax exemptions are questioned. In 1983, an unsuccessful attempt was made to withdraw the Asia Society's real-estate tax exemption on the grounds it ". . . failed to meet the definition of an educational institution by the New York state property tax law."[4]

Local governments are also asserting that the mounting "commercial activities" of nonprofits make them ineligible as charities for real-estate and sales-tax exemption. This is particularly true in the hospital arena, where nonprofit and profit hospitals compete and local real-estate-tax exemptions are being withdrawn to provide a level playing field for all commercial enterprises.[5]

Most museums are organized under state nonprofit laws. They file annual reports with the secretary of state, setting forth their compliance with the laws under which they were created.

The state attorney general monitors the activities of the state's not-for-profit organizations. Museums must file annual reports concerning their conduct in general and, in particular, their solicitation and administration of funds secured from the general public. The National Association of Attorney Generals promotes legislation designed to protect the public from unscrupulous fund-raising practices. For example, there is increasing public concern over telephone solicitations for seemingly worthy causes where most of the funds collected have gone to pay for the soliciting. The approach of the attorney generals is to require solicitors to disclose how much goes to the worthy cause.

COMMON LAW

Under common law, museum accountability traditionally centers on the fiduciary responsibility of its board, principal administrative officers, and curators. Museums, like for-profit corporations, are now also responsible for wrongful acts committed by employees in the course of their duties.[6] Injured parties can seek compensation from those employees, their supervisors, board members, and the museum.

Common and statutory fiduciary duties are divided into two general categories: the duty of loyalty and the duty of care.

The Duty of Loyalty

The duty of loyalty addresses conflicts of interest—where an individual's interest conflicts with that of the institution, and the possibility exists that the individual will put his or her self-interest ahead of the institution's. The conflicts are of two types:

1. Self-dealing that involves a transaction between the individual and the institution. Self-dealing occurs when a staff or board member sells an object to the museum for its collection or provides legal services for compensation. Self-dealing also occurs in the case of an employee who has a separate business that sells exhibit products or consulting service to the museum.
2. Self-dealing that involves taking an opportunity for individual gain, an opportunity that the individual became aware of because of the museum connection and

an opportunity in which the museum also may have an interest. The classic case is the curator or board member who collects in the same general area as the museum and learns about an opportunity through his or her museum association. Without disclosing the opportunity to the museum, the employee or board member acquires the object for his or her individual collection.

Conflicts of interest are not per se improper or prohibited. While avoiding them is preferable, they can—and must—be managed so that they avoid unfairness to the museum. Proper management requires a full disclosure of both the conflict and the opportunity to disinterested museum persons in authority. In addition, the common law ordinarily provides that the person with the conflict cannot be a crucial participant in making the decision affecting the conflict. A board member who wishes to purchase an object from the museum or to sell an object or a service to the museum can be at the board meeting and can be counted in determining a quorum but cannot be counted toward the majority needed for action. The common law does not require the higher standards the public is coming to expect.

With increasing public concern about "conflicts of interest," it is good practice for the board member to be absent from the board meeting and to refrain from discussing the issue with the other members of the board, together or separately. We live in a time when ethics statutes that require disclosure and sometimes avoidance of conflict of interest are being enacted. For example, the 1990 reauthorization legislation for the National Endowment for the Arts prohibits a representative of an applicant from serving on a panel that reviews the application.

In all circumstances, it is good practice to follow the highest conflict-of-interest standards whenever there is dealing between the museum and its board members, officers, and employees. Museums should strive to avoid even the appearance of impropriety. A museum should annually require disclosures from board members, officers, and staff of their potential conflicts of interest with the museum.

The Duty of Care

The duty of care requires regular and responsible action with respect to the museum's affairs, action which is taken in good faith and which is prudent under the circumstances. "Good faith" means an honest belief that the action is the right thing for the museum. That alone is not enough. The duty is also to exercise sound judgment. The action must be sensible in light of the museum's mission and needs.[7]

Due care as well as good faith must be exercised in the operation of a museum. What do a prudent board and staff do when the museum is operating at a deficit and the building and collection are deteriorating? Do they sell a part of the collection in order to save the museum? It depends on all of the circumstances. There is no simple answer.

The highest fiduciary duties apply to the collections, which are the *sine qua non* of museums. The collections are intended to be a permanent asset and are not intended to be acquired or disposed of for profit. On the other hand, in the case of the museum store, the purpose is to buy and sell. In between the collections and the store is the endowment. It needs to be conserved, but it needs to be invested so that it will grow to offset inflation. It is not prudent to freeze the endowment principal.[8]

Since the exercise of the duty of care is evaluated after the fact, careful recording of all deliberations of the board, administrators, curators, and staff is imperative. Board meetings, reflected in the minutes, should focus on the pros and cons of major actions to be taken so that subsequent examination will reveal a reasonable basis for them. Board members must participate and will be considered to have acquiesced in the action unless they registered their dissent.

Assuming that there is a breach of the duty of loyalty or care or both, who can sue and when? Historically, the attorney general of the state in which the museum is incorporated represents the public in bringing actions. The decision to sue or not to sue is discretionary but may be influenced by other issues, such as media pressure. After a series of articles in the *Chicago Tribune*, the Illinois Attorney General commenced an action against the Harding Museum directors for breach of fiduciary duties resulting from alleged improper deaccessions, investments, self-dealing, salaries, and failure to open the museum to the public after it had moved to new quarters. Although the litigation covered some 15 years, the appellate opinions on the case did not produce any holdings or dicta that are instructive on the subject of fiduciary duties. However, the public interest aroused by the case led to a report by the Illinois Legislative Investigative Commission causing many Illinois museums to adopt formal deaccession policies.

The major lesson of the *Harding* case, like other newsworthy cases, is that fiduciary duties of museum board members and staff are fashioned by public inquiries and reports as well as by cases and statutes. On the negative side of public scrutiny is the possible overreaction to isolated cases resulting in unrealistic and unnecessary demands on board members and staff. On the positive side is the impetus for codes of ethics and sound practices and procedures for museums.

It is the primary responsibility of the museum's board to assure that the museum staff and board members discharge their fiduciary duties of loyalty and care. It is possible for board members to bring an action against one or more co-board members. It is also possible for successive board members to sue previous board members.

Unlike board members, founders, donors, visitors, and the public generally have not been permitted to enforce fiduciary duties. This is to prevent undue litigation and harassment of not-for-profit board members.

It is unclear whether museum members can sue. If members have no voting rights and are merely "friends groups," they usually do not have standing to sue.

Recent state and federal legislation provide that Native Americans have the right to request return of human remains and certain other objects where the petitioners have cultural affinity or similar connection with remains or objects claimed.[9] Museums are beginning to adopt formal repatriation policies dealing with Native American remains and objects and, in the case of the Field Museum, other cultural groups as well. Based on internal museum policies, several museums have returned to the Zuni tribe of New Mexico specific "War Gods." In deaccessioning patrimonial collections, museum board members must be mindful of their legal duties under the law of the state in which the museum is incorporated so that the fiduciary duty of care with respect to collections is properly discharged.

Assuming that there is standing to sue, the attorney general and others can bring an action immediately to enjoin a questionable action of the museum. When the act has occurred, the appropriate parties can sue to recover the money damages sustained as a result of the breach of fiduciary duty. If there is no monetary damage, there is no basis for a suit.

In addition to the common law, fiduciary duties are also created by statute. For instance, the Revised Model Nonprofit Corporation Act (Section 8.32) provides: "A corporation may not lend money to or guarantee the obligation of a director or officer of the corporation."

On the other hand, there is a growing statutory movement to protect unpaid nonprofit board members and officers for breach of the duty of care. These volunteers are liable only for willful and wanton conduct. Such volunteer-protection statutes could be argued to relieve volunteer directors of their duty to act prudently if they have acted in good faith.

As an added protection, most nonprofit codes permit the museum to indemnify board members for judgments and legal costs assessed against them where the members acted in good faith and in a manner which was believed by them to be in the best interests of the museum.

SELF-IMPOSED REGULATIONS

Self-imposed museum policies and procedures are expanding because the public, the museum profession, and museum board and staff want them. The museum may adopt regulations affecting its own conduct either because of government mandate or because the peer community deems them appropriate. For instance, a museum might adopt its own affirmative action policy to implement a government policy or adopt its own code of ethics in order to comply with the 1991 [the most recent] AAM Ethics Code.

Museum regulations ordinarily cover the conduct of all members, paid and volunteer. These policies may refer to equal-opportunity employment, termination, sexual harassment, and overtime. Usually initiated by staff, the governing board adopts policies. Administering them is a staff function.

As self-imposed regulations expand, the nature of the staff relationship to the museum may change. Under common law, most staff members are employees at will and serve at the pleasure of the museum's board or administration; they can be terminated immediately with or without cause. However, courts are beginning to hold that some personnel policies and practices may restrict the employer's right to terminate.

Of course, an employer is not free to terminate a person for an illegal cause, such as one involving a discriminatory motive based on an employee's race, age, sex, or religion. In the absence of legislative restrictions, the more specific the promise to an employee by the employer, the more likely it is that a promise or policy may be construed as an implied-in-fact contract of ongoing employment that is not freely terminable. For example, courts have held that specific representations made in employment handbooks and policy manuals may constitute terms of a binding employment contract. Even codes of ethics may soon give rise to rights that are enforceable in the courts by museum staff members. The more that is said about the duty of a museum to staff, the more likely it is that a court may infer the terms of contract of employment.

Generally speaking, self-imposed rules and regulations should apply equally and consistently to all employees. The existence of a well-articulated grievance procedure for registration of staff complaints is good personnel practice. A museum may provide for a grievance committee of staff members to review disciplinary actions and make recommendations to the museum director or president. If the staff member is not satisfied, he or she may have a right to appeal the action externally, first to a governmental agency and then possibly to the courts. The courts will generally be reluctant to interfere if a museum has an established procedure that the courts consider to be binding upon the museum and that appears to have been followed in a consistent and fair manner. Other judicial and administrative forums of redress are also available to employees in disputes involving discrimination, unemployment compensation, and worker's compensation.

PEER-IMPOSED REGULATIONS

These usually take two forms: codes of professional ethics and institutional accreditation. Ethics codes may apply to individuals or institutions or both. Accreditation is usually institutional. The peer group may be an umbrella group, such as the AAM, or a specialized group, such as the Association of Art Museum Directors and the American Institute for Conservation of Historic and Artistic Works.

Ethical Codes

Ethics are the rules of conduct adopted by a profession for serving its clientele and for regulating relationships among the professionals themselves. First developed in law and medicine, ethics are the means by which self-employed professionals police themselves. Ethics are now also beginning to deal with the relationship of professionals to institutions. Imposed by the profession or by the institution itself, ethics are ordinarily higher than the legal standards of conduct. For example, while a board member with a conflict of interest can legally be present when the board addresses the conflict, the museum's ethical code may prohibit it.

Ethics statements are not always precise. What is ethical is often in the eye of the beholder. Ethics really involve putting the public—the constituency—ahead of the institution, ahead of the profession. Failure to do so has led to national concern about ethical conduct. The country is awash in charges of ethical abuses. Every day, the newspapers carry stories about government officials, business leaders, professionals, and even museums that have taken advantage of the public to further their own objectives.

Ethics courses are springing up in all "professional curricula." Frequently they focus on specific cases—how to shave it closely, as in the case of collecting by museum staff and board members. Seldom is there an emphasis on the underlying thesis of ethics. We need always to remember the fundamental basis for ethics so that we avoid close encounters. Ethics go to the essence of our beliefs and reflect how we feel and care for others. A code of ethics inhibits our freedom to act solely for our own gain and demands a sense of responsibility to others.

In the not-for-profit field, there is a unique condition not found in the for-profit area. A cadre of specialists often controls the central service performed by the nonprofit organization. College and university faculties, hospital medical staff, and museum curatorial staff are accorded great latitude in their performance because they are the most knowledgeable about their subject matter. They have broad discretion and privileges within the institutions, but that broad discretion carries with it professional, and institutional duties and responsibilities. These professionals, recognizing their power, adopt peer ethics codes to assure that their conduct is in the public interest. However, the public is usually not invited to participate in the drafting and enforcing of these professional codes.

According to the 1991 AAM Code: "In submitting to this code, museums assume responsibility for the actions of the members of the governing authority, employees, and volunteers in the performance of museum-related duties." The proposed code affords a broad framework in which each museum can develop its own code. It admonishes the governing authority to ensure the museum's ethical conduct— and properly so because legally the governing board *is* the museum and is ultimately responsible for the adoption and enforcement of an ethics code. Although the Museum Trustee Association understandably felt left out of drafting the 1991 code, museums now look to their trustees to take the initiative with their museum administrations to enlist staffs to draft individual museum codes based on public service. The time has come for our trustees and museum staffs to set aside their differences in favor of the public interest.

Accreditation

Institutional evaluation is designed for public protection. The public needs this protection because it cannot determine the quality of the museum's services as easily as it can judge that of consumer goods. Accreditation is a means by which a group of similar institutions seeks to standardize institutional quality without casting all institutions into the same mold.

The accreditation process is basically a dialogue between peers in and outside the museum. It centers on a self-study designed to encourage systematic planning that leads to clearer goals and more effective action to achieve them. The AAM handbook states that accreditation promotes "the achievement of the highest standards" and "increased awareness of these standards among all museums." The standards are general in order to encourage diversity. The AAM accreditation manual states that there are two questions to be addressed in the process:

1. How well does the museum achieve its stated mission and goals?
2. How well does the museum's performance meet standards and practices as they are generally understood in the museum field at large?[10]

The handbook further states:

> There is no list of the specific requirements for museum accreditation. The entire program is predicated on recognition that standards in museums continually evolve and that the needs and resources of individual museums vary significantly.[11]

This seems almost circular in its logic and elusive in its enforceability. Fortunately, by focusing accreditation on the self-study, the institution sets its own mission and goals and then is judged by its peers as to how well it is achieving those goals.

There is no sanction for failing to be accredited. AAM membership is not predicated on accreditation. Nor does a lack of accreditation preclude a museum from securing federal funds, unlike the case of colleges and universities.

Like other accrediting agencies, AAM states that the data involved and the decisions made are confidential. Among post-secondary educational institutions, there is a trend to disclose information about the accreditation of a particular institution. Journalism schools make all accrediting information available to the public. Nevertheless, there is concern that too much disclosure will inhibit gathering information and making forthright recommendations. Because nonprofit accreditation is based on protecting the public, it can be argued that some accreditation records and proceedings should be open to the public.

The AAM's accreditation program was initiated in 1970 to help the public and various private and public agencies "identify those museums that meet accepted professional standards of cultural and educational service to the public." Presently, there are 685 accredited museums out of a total of 6,500 museums listed in the *AAM Official Museum Directory*. Museum accreditation is in its early stages compared to that of schools, colleges, and hospitals. Nevertheless, museum accreditation is exceptionally well formulated; and the self-study components such as governance, collections, and exhibitions are clearly articulated.

CONCLUSION

The 1991 AAM code of ethics rightfully stresses that museums exist to serve the public. As public servants, museums are accountable to the public through government-, self-, and peer-imposed regulations. The more we try to be accountable, the more our constituencies will hold us accountable.

The governing board, as the legal persona of the museum, is responsible for assuring that board and staff members comply with the regulations. The board should not administer, but it must monitor, the museum's compliance with these external and internal regulations. In the final analysis, the board is the body accountable for the museum. To assure this accountability, the board might well establish a regulatory compliance audit committee comparable to, but separate from, the financial audit committee. More and more for-profit organizations are developing compliance mechanisms like this. However structured, the board must assure that its oversight role is regularly and vigorously exercised.

We have moved beyond the rhetoric and have entered the reality of accountability. Museum regulations must be followed every day by everyone. Self-regulated compliance is the essence of accountability.

NOTES

1. American Association of Museums Code of Ethics for Museums (second draft, February 1991) page 4. In 1978, the AAM adopted a second code of ethics. *Museum Ethics*, AAM 1978. The AAM has also published elaborations on ethically related issues through seminal monographs such as *Museum Trusteeship* (1981) by Alan and Patricia Ullberg, and *Of Mutual Respect and Other Things* (1989) by Helmuth Naumer.

2. See also "The King of Gems" by Ted Gup. *Washington Post* (3/27–30/83).

3. "U.S. Clamps Down on Museum Grants" by Alan Pericini. *Los Angeles Times* (1/10/90).

4. "Should Museums Be Exempt From Taxes?" by John Russell. *New York Times* (3/20/83).

5. See Utah County v. Intermountain Health Care, Inc. 709 P. 2d 265 (Utah, 1985).

6. See, e.g., Brown and Boyd. The Program Fraud Civil Remedies Act: The Administrative Adjudication of Fraud Against the Government, 50 Federal Contracts Report 691, 695–96 (1988).

7. See Marsh, "Governance of Non-Profit Organizations: An Appropriate Standard of Conduct for Trustees and Directors of Museums and Other Cultural Institutions," 85 Dickinson Law Review 607 (1981). *See also* Section 8.30, Revised Model Nonprofit Corporation Act, adopted by The Subcommittee on the Model Nonprofit Corporation Law of the Business Law Section, American Bar Association, Summer, 1987, Prentice Hall Law and Business (1988).

8. See, e.g., Stern v. Lucy Webb Hayes National Training School for Deaconesses and Missionaries, 381 F. Supp 1003 (D.D.C. 1974).

9. Native American Graves Protection and Repatriation Act Pub. L. No. 101-601, 14-Stat 3048 (Nov. 16, 1990). See also Boyd, Disputes Regarding the Possession of Native American Religious and Cultural Objects and Human Remains: A Discussion of the Applicable Law and Proposed Legislation, by Thomas H. Boyd, 55 Missouri Law Review, 883, 901–907 (1990).

10. *Museum Accreditation: A Handbook for the Institution*, 1990. Washington, DC: American Association of Museums, p. 25.

11. Ibid.

32

Toward a New Governance

John Carver

A model of governance is a framework within which to organize the thoughts, activities, structure, and relationships of governing boards. A designed model yields a new nature of governance, quite unlike a collection of even wise responses to specific governance problems. What should we expect from a model? What conditions should be better if there were a better framework within which to build governance actions? I think we have a right to expect a good model of governance to

1. *"Cradle" vision:* A useful framework for governance must hold and support vision in the primary position. Administrative systems cause us to devote great attention to the specifics. Such rigor, itself commendable, can overshadow the broader matter of purpose. There must be systematic encouragement to think the unthinkable and to dream.
2. *Explicitly address fundamental values:* The governing board is a guardian of organizational values. The framework must ensure that the board focuses on values. Endless decisions about events cannot substitute for deliberations and explicit pronouncements on values.
3. *Force an external focus:* Because organizations tend to focus inward, a governance model must intervene to guarantee a marketlike, external responsiveness. A board would thus be more concerned with needs and markets than with the internal issues of organizational mechanics.
4. *Enable an outcome-driven organizing system:* All functions and decisions are to be rigorously weighed against the standard of purpose. A powerful model would have the board not only establish a mission in terms of an outcome, but procedurally enforce a mission as the central organizing focus.

John Carver is a consultant on board leadership and has written extensively on the subject of governance and nonprofit boards. "Toward a New Governance" is an excerpt from his book *Boards That Make a Difference: A New Design for Leadership in Nonprofit and Public Organizations.* Copyright © 1997 Jossey-Bass. This material is used by permission of John Wiley & Sons, Inc.

5. *Separate large issues from small ones:* Board members usually agree that large issues deserve first claim on their time, but they have no common way to discern a big item. A model should help differentiate sizes of issues.

6. *Force forward thinking:* A governance scheme should help a board thrust the majority of its thinking into the future. Strategic leadership demands the long-term viewpoint.

7. *Enable proactivity:* So that boards do not merely preside over momentum, a model of governance should press boards toward leading and away from reacting. Such a model would engage boards more in *creating* than in *approving.*

8. *Facilitate diversity and unity:* It is important to optimize the richness of diversity in board composition and opinion, yet still assimilate the variety into one voice. A model must address the need to speak with one voice without squelching dissent or feigning unanimity.

9. *Describe relationships to relevant constituencies:* In either a legal or a moral sense, boards are usually trustees. They are also, to some extent, accountable to consumers, neighbors, and staff. A model of governance should define where these various constituencies fit into the scheme.

10. *Define a common basis for discipline:* Boards have a tough time sticking to a job description, being decisive without being impulsive, and keeping discussion to the point. A model of governance should provide a rational basis for a board's self-discipline.

11. *Delineate the board's role in common topics:* A model of governance should enable a board to articulate roles without isolating roles from each other, so the board's specific contribution on any topic is clear.

12. *Determine what information is needed:* A model of governance would introduce more precise distinctions about the nature of information needed to govern, avoiding too much, too little, too late, and simply wrong information.

13. *Balance overcontrol and undercontrol:* It is easy to control too much or too little and, ironically, to do both at the same time. The same board can simultaneously be a "rubber-stamper" and a "meddler." A model of governance would clarify those aspects of management that need tight versus loose control.

14. *Use board time efficiently:* Members of nonprofit and public boards receive token pay or none in exchange for their time. Though they willingly make this contribution, few have time to waste. By sorting out what really needs to be done, a model should enable boards to use the precious gift of time more productively.

A conceptually coherent way to approach governance would be strong medicine for nonprofit and public organizations. It would also apply in business corporations. In fact, McConkey (1975, p. 1) foreshadowed a business breakthrough originating in the nonprofit sector when he predicted that "the next major breakthrough in management will not occur . . . in the world of business. The breakthrough will, and must, take place in the so-called nonprofit sector."

Whether, as he indicates, the breakthrough "must" take place, it certainly *should* take place, given the serious flaws that exist. The most significant management breakthrough that could occur would be in the highest-leverage element of organization—the governing board. Both the leverage and the room for improvement scream urgently for attention.

But boards have been around so long that it is hard to see that the emperor has no clothes. We have grown accustomed to mediocrity in nonprofit and public board process, in the empty rituals and often meaningless words of conventional practice. We have watched intelligent people tied up in trivia so long that neither we nor they notice the discrepancy. We have observed the ostensible strategic leaders consumed by the exigencies of next month. Mindful people regularly carry out mindless activity and appear to be, as Phillip T. Jenkins of Bryn Mawr Associates in Birmingham, Michigan, put it, "the well intentioned in full pursuit of the irrelevant" (personal communication). Inexplicably, effective people have a different standard of excellence for public and nonprofit boards than for other pursuits, "often [tossing] aside the principles of good management, and sometimes even common sense, when they put on trustee hats" (Chait and Taylor, 1989). The forum in which *vision* could be the chief order of business is mired so chronically in details that, growing weary, we come to see nothing amiss. Boards, after all, will be boards!

We need strong boards and we need strong executives as well. "One of the key problems," observed Robert Gale, "is that many boards are either too weak to accomplish anything or so strong they wind up managing the organization" (personal communication, 1989). When increased strength is dysfunctional, the solution is not, of course, to weaken the strong. It is better that the blessing of a strong engine be augmented by an improved chassis, not "solved" by shorting out a few spark plugs. When their strength causes boards not to do their job better but to intrude into the jobs of others, something is awry in the design. We must take a fresh look at governance concepts and the board-management partnership. The stark truth of Gale's comment is reason enough for a new model of governance.

It need not bespeak paranoia to observe along with Louden (1975, p. 117) that "if we do not concern ourselves with how we can rule organizations, the organizations will rule us." But the paradigm with which we traditionally "rule" is worthy neither of the people who give their time and talent nor of the missions they serve. Governance is overdue for a rebirth. Though much has been written over the past several decades about governing boards, with rare exceptions the efforts offer incremental improvement to an inadequate vehicle via new paint and tires. The purpose of this book is not to indict previous efforts or current performance so much as to prescribe a better way. Its message is that strategic leadership is exciting and accessible.

REFERENCES

Chait, R. P., and Taylor, B. E. "Charting the territory of nonprofit boards." *Harvard Business Review* 129 (1989): 44–54.

Louden, J. K. *The effective director in action.* New York: AMACOM, 1975.

McConkey, D. *MBO for nonprofit organizations.* New York: AMACOM, 1975.

33

Institution-wide Change in Museums

Will Phillips

Change agents have been a part of human society since prehistoric times; they have been called prophets, wizards, shamans, and seers. But these labels and the roles they embody fell into disuse and disrepute with the age of science and the Industrial Revolution. In turn, during the 1950s the organizations created during the Industrial Revolution were challenged to change in ways that stretched their own internal capabilities. New models and new tools for change were needed, and so the modern wizard was born—the organizational consultant. I use this term to describe the outsider who views an organization holistically and works to bring it to a new state of health that allows it to thrive in the current and future world. This article will briefly outline some tools of the organizational consultant that seem appropriate for museums to consider at this point in their history. Reading about them, of course, is only the first step. You must learn how to put them into practice in your museum.

TOOL 1: UNDERSTANDING THE EXTERNAL FORCES OF CHANGE

The forces that began challenging the organizations in the 1950s have accelerated and boomed in the 1990s, and they are now shaping our future in dramatic ways. They are the forces that broke up of some of the largest and most significant organizations of this century—IBM, General Motors, Sears, and the Soviet Union—and they threaten museums of all sizes. They include globalized competition, demographic shifts, electronic technology, audience fragmentation, and the democratization of museum support. I will highlight these for their special impact on museums. For more information read *The Popcorn Report* and *Megatrends 2000.*[1]

Will Phillips is president of QM2 and is a consultant to for-profit and nonprofit organizations. "Institution-wide Change in Museums" appeared in the *Journal of Museum Education* (Vol. 18, No. 3, Fall 1993, pp. 18–21). It is reprinted here with permission of Museum Education Roundtable, all rights reserved. For more information contact: Museum Education Roundtable, 621 Pennsylvania Ave., SE, Washington, DC, 20003; or www.mer-online.org or email info@mer-online.org.

Globalized Competition

The economy of the world's richest seven nations is on the skids, and there is no clear prospect of recovery. To a large extent this decline is due to a new brutally competitive world economic order that is emerging with the demise of the cold war. The forces that are propelling this new order will persist for years and promise to make life tougher for almost everyone. To the extent you raise the standard of living of developing countries, you must have a corresponding drop in the living standard in the West.[2] As a result, the inflation-adjusted income in the United States has been declining since the 1970s.

Demographic Shifts

The demographic profiles of your audiences and your donors have changed. For example, many large communities in the southwestern states now have a majority of Spanish-speaking residents. Even Green Bay, Wisconsin, has a significant and growing Southeast Asian population, and New York City's Puerto Rican population is an increasing force. These new populations have yet to find proportionate representation on the staff or boards or in the programs of the museums in their respective areas. We talk about diversity; we have not yet done it.

Are you up to date on demographic changes? If not, demographic changes are creeping up on you. Most community planning boards have specific local data on these trends. Get it. Understand it. Share it. And finally, use it in building your staff, board, and audience.

Electronic Technology

Recent advances in electronic technology are having and will have a dramatic impact on how we handle information and how we do our work. Some current capabilities include:

- instant access to data
- simultaneous availability of data
- expert systems that enable generalists to become experts
- replacement of photography with digital images.

Organizations that are not exploring and using technology in these ways will move more and more slowly at higher and higher operating costs.

Audience Fragmentation

More choices are competing for the discretionary time and dollars of potential museum visitors and donors. Many leisure time options are doing a better job than museums of targeting and serving growing populations. If a museum remains passive in this environment, it will be passed up. The challenge is to create new ways to carry out your basic mission and still compete with video, sports, Disney, and 500-channel interactive television.

The Democratization of Museum Support

Museums were founded and financially supported by the aristocracies of their nations. But the aristocracies of our society are no longer willing and able to be the exclusive supporters of museums. Museums have been very slow to adapt to this change and serve new audiences. After an interim stage when aristocratic persuasion led to public monies being assigned to museums for the "public good," the public has begun to seriously question the value of the "good" supposedly delivered by museums.

Most museum professionals will find little new information in the above summary of trends. But they need to be addressed. These are the questions to ask:

- Have staff leaders in your museum discussed these external trends and agreed on the critical few that are most likely to affect your museum?
- Have these top trends been clearly stated and communicated to all staff and board?
- Is there an ongoing effort to better understand the specific local manifestation of the trends?
- Have you assigned someone to investigate how other museums are addressing these trends? Do you have data on what has or has not worked for them?
- Have you explored the impact the top trends will have on your museum if they continue at their present rate? What if the trends accelerate?
- Do you have plans in place and actions under way to respond to the trends in a way that truly addresses the causes rather than simply providing symptomatic relief? Are you making sufficient progress to keep up with each critical trend?

When a museum can answer each of the above questions positively, it is thinking strategically and managing for the future. By addressing and responding to these questions a museum can convert anxiety to action. Then it can mobilize the necessary energy and creativity to succeed. When the answers are "unsure" or "no," the museum has failed to take full responsibility and is building its future on the hope that the external trends will change and become more supportive.

TOOL 2: UNDERSTANDING THE INTERNAL BARRIERS TO CHANGE

Forces naturally grow inside any institution that reduce its ability to respond positively to change. These internal forces gain momentum so slowly that they are not readily noticed. They even take on a life of their own and become revered as ends in themselves. Some of the major internal barriers are described below. Assess the strength of these internal forces in your museum by having staff rate them on a scale of 1 to 10.

Mental Aging of the Board, Director, and Key Staff

Mental aging is characterized by a shift from accepting risks in order to grow to avoiding risks in order to preserve the status quo. There are two remedies for mental aging. The first one is a whack on the side of the head to wake up the leadership. This usually happens when the crisis really hits. Before the real crisis, however, there are usually many smaller crises that trigger short-term financial solutions, but they rarely get to the root causes of the crisis.

The second remedy is a proactive whack on the side of the head by a skilled organizational consultant (or *in*sultant). It takes more courage to be proactive, but the benefit is that the museum is in control of the change process instead of change being in control of the museum.

Plateau Market Share

When the tried-and-true mechanisms for attracting audience, volunteers, and donors reach a point of diminishing returns, the museum's market share plateaus. At this plateau there is a feeling of accomplishment ("We've done it; let's relax.") or a feeling of hopelessness ("What more can we do to attract them?"). Museums have great difficulty understanding their potential new markets and are often unwilling to learn about them. This irresolution represents a lack of respect for the diversity and differences in an expanded market.

Museums can open up huge new audience and donor markets if they are willing to do the hard work of understanding demographic shifts and learning about these potential new markets aggressively and respectfully. Then they must make changes to better serve the needs of their expanded markets.

Silosclerosis

As a museum matures, its functional structure begins to harden in place and the walls between functional departments grow. Curators vs. educators vs. administrators vs. developers—each staff person develops allegiance to his or her functional specialties and professional associations and journals rather than to the institution or the field as a whole. It's as if each department is willing to have the museum weaken as long as its own function remains strong.

These barriers between specialties can create a climate of disrespect, dramatically increase the time it takes to complete complex projects, and add enormous cost to the bottom line. They breed waste, rework, duplication, and poor coordination between departments. Radical redesign of the organizational structure may be needed to break down the walls that form between the silos of individual departments.

Cross-functional teams are powerful ways to reduce the costs of these silos and deliver on your museum's mission.

TOOL 3: A MODEL FOR CREATING CHANGE

Change seems to occur in a three-step process. Since the change itself only occurs in the last step, it is easy to neglect the first two steps, but each is a necessary part of the process.

1. *awareness* of the reasons why a change is necessary
2. *acceptance* of the awareness and the need for change
3. *action* to make the change.

Awareness

People are most willing to change when they are aware of the reason for the change. When everyone is busy at work and someone runs in and announces a desired change, few will change unless the reason is clear to them.

Unfortunately, many museums seek to change by announcing the solution without clarifying and agreeing on the problem. By aborting step 1, museum administrators fail to inform and involve the staff and volunteers. One of the most powerful ways of making change happen is to clarify and define the threats facing your museum in a way that encourages participation.

Acceptance

In some situations no change occurs even though the threat has been clarified and the tiger is at the door. Skeptics say, "It's only a paper tiger; don't let it scare you." The natural human reaction at this point is to jump up and down and accuse the skeptics of being blind, stupid, or negative. Of course, such accusations do not lead to change.

When the tiger or threat has been clearly identified and is still not accepted, resistance is usually the reason. Those who are resistant usually harbor a personal fear of change. There may be some hidden issues that are not yet on the table.

An initial attempt to surface this hidden resistance will always fail, unless each individual feels it is safe to put his or her agenda on the table. Once these agendas begin to be revealed, they must be totally respected. Laughing, discounting, and joking will scare these revelations away. Respecting what is revealed might sound like, "Ah, now I see why you are so concerned about making a change. The way you explain it, it makes sense to avoid the change. Thank you for sharing that with me."

Once the dialogue has gone through several cycles of surfacing and respecting, the resistance will no longer be hidden. Then it is possible to explore the resistance with those who are resisting. This process of exploration almost invariably leads to a solution that better integrates the organization's need for change with the individual's need for safety.

Here are some ideas for building acceptance of the tiger's reality:

1. Learn about resistance and how to bring it to the surface and respect it. The principles for dealing with resistance to change while building acceptance are:
   - Surface the resistance.
   - Respect the resistance.
   - Explore the resistance so you better understand it.
   - Explore ways of responding to the desired change and respecting the real fears of the resister.
2. Start talking regularly and openly in staff meeting about changes in the world that are having an impact on your museum. Avoiding such discussions encourages denial.

Action

Only when the individual or organization is fully aware and accepting of the reasons for change can action begin. Once awareness and acceptance have occurred, action is fairly easy and straightforward. Without awareness and acceptance, a great deal of effort is often spent trying to sell, push, or force the action. In spite of the effort put into the details of implementing the change, no real change occurs.

In trying to achieve change, we must keep our goals in sight and be flexible with our methods. Once a director or senior staff person decides that a change is needed, he or she often jumps to push for action immediately without building awareness or acceptance. If met with any resistance or reluctance to change, the initiator pushes harder for change, thereby increasing resistance to it. When this happens, the initiator has lost the fight because he or she has not laid the foundation for change by building awareness and acceptance. To allow for these first two steps, it is necessary to back off from the push for change to build a foundation of awareness and acceptance.

An experiment illustrates the point. Hungry chickens were placed on one side of a fence and their food on the other. The chickens tried to go directly through the fence to get to their food and failed. In subsequent experiments, the fence was shortened so that they could easily run around the end of the fence and reach the food. Although the fence got as short as three feet, the chickens could not back off far enough to see the possibility of an end run to achieve the goal. Similarly, those wishing their organization would change sometimes behave like hungry chickens.

Change is paradoxical. A direct effort to cause change will often fail; an indirect effort will often succeed.

TOOL 4: CREATING A CLIMATE FOR ORGANIZATIONAL LEARNING

All significant learning changes the learner. In today's fast-changing museum environment, it is no longer adequate to have a director or a few key staff members who can change. What is needed is an entire institution that can learn and change collectively. The director, staff, board, and volunteers will have to redesign the museum together. Your institutional learning quotient will determine how well and how fast this is accomplished. If the internal learning environment is weak, it will limit change and block attempts to connect with new and diverse audiences. The primary condition for such internal learning is a psychological environment that fosters learning between and among people.

Four elements are needed in a learning environment:

1. *Open, honest, and proactive communication.* Museum staff and volunteers tend to favor courtesy and pleasantries, often avoiding issues until they explode or go underground.
2. *Mutual respect of one another's experience.* Respect requires accepting the other person's view as truth and then working to understand how it could be truth rather than disagreeing, discounting, or explaining it away. Many museums focus on respecting the diversity of their potential audiences but fail to build internal respect among, for example, the curator and educator and security guard. Until museums learn to respect the diversity within their staff and volunteer corps, they will have an especially difficult challenge grappling with the diversity in their communities.
3. *Willingness to explore and experiment with new ideas and methods.* To create a climate for organizational learning, it is particularly important to consider new ways of structuring and operating the museum.
4. *Taking responsibility for what is happening instead of blaming or becoming a victim.* It is helpful to describe outside forces as "opporthreats." These events or trends are in themselves neither opportunities nor threats; it is the museum's response that determines what they become. This view encourages the museum to take responsibility for the outcome instead of being a passive victim.

EDUCATION, TRADITION, LEARNING, AND CHANGE

Educators have an interest in learning, but there are two very different aspects of learning that must not be confused. The first is learning about the past. This traditional kind of learning dominates classroom education. It is based on memorizing correct answers that authorities have given.

The second type of learning is learning how to change in order to be successful in the future. This nontraditional type of learning requires significant creative input and risk. It involves reframing the questions and letting go of the past in order to move into the future. Good museums do this when they present objects and leave learners free to interpret their own meaning and discover their own answers.

Museum educators often find themselves in the position of leading internal change. They must become comfortable with this role by learning as much about change as about tradition. The tools presented in this article were selected to help educators help their museums start learning about themselves as institutions. Only then can they successfully change and adapt to the new forces that are challenging museums.

NOTES

1. Faith Popcorn, *The Popcorn Report* (New York: Harper and Co., 1992); John Naisbitt and Patricia Auburdene, *Megatrends 2000* (New York: Morrow, 1990).

2. Christopher Farrell and Michael J. Manvel, "What's Wrong?" *Business Week*, August 2, 1993, p. 54.

34

Persistent Paradoxes

Robert Janes

I am not sure that there is a more incisive statement than this of the effort required to ensure that museums continue to be valued as social institutions in our society. We have good reason to worry about this, or even to despair. Despite the many efforts at change currently underway in Canadian museums, however modest, there remains little or no indication that they will ensure a desirable future for museums as we know them. This is not a matter of being optimistic or pessimistic by nature. For me, it is a reflection of several persistent questions which may, in fact, not be answerable but which must be acknowledged. These questions are paradoxical, meaning that they are simultaneously contradictory, unbelievable, absurd, true or false in their meaning and implications.

Charles Handy (1994: 12–13), who has given up his cherished belief in a perfect world and "A Theory of Everything," observes that the more turbulent and complex the world, the more paradoxes there are. He notes that paradoxes are like the weather—"something to be lived with, not solved, the worst aspects mitigated, the best enjoyed and used as clues to the way forward." Coping with paradoxes also means accepting the fact that even understanding does not always mean resolution. Indeed, it is perhaps those intellectual and creative problems that we will never resolve which claim the lion's share of our energies (Conroy 1988:70). What follows is an attempt to look at a sample of paradoxical questions which already dominate the museum landscape, with a view to uncovering any clues to understanding the future that they might contain.

IS THE CUSTOMER ALWAYS RIGHT?

All sectors of society, be it government, industry or arts and culture, are inundated with the dictum to serve the customer. This language of customer service is a relatively

---

Robert Janes is a museum consultant and the former director of the Glenbow Museum in Calgary, Canada. "Persistent Paradoxes" is a chapter from his book, *Museums and the Paradox of Change: A Case Study in Urgent Adaptation*. Glenbow Museum and University of Calgary Press, 1997. Used by permission of University of Calgary Press.

new one to museums, and has been met with a predictable amount of hostility—not only because of its newness, but also because of its association with the coarse goings-on of the marketplace. This cool reception must be acknowledged, as even the private sector is now admitting that the customer is not always right, and that superior service is no guarantee of future success (Evans 1991, Shapiro 1995). As has been noted on numerous occasions, the customer did not demand the compact disc player or ABS braking systems—these were developed through the creative efforts of highly trained and motivated engineers, working in an environment which allowed the free expression of their abilities. Furthermore, will we ever be able to entice an unlimited number of what our culture calls the typical consumer, recognizing that professional museums currently occupy a niche market which appeals primarily to well-educated, curious people? Can museums ever become broadly popular, recognizing that they are knowledge-based, and irrespective of the multi-media technology used, will always require people to read and think in order to derive benefit and pleasure from their visit? These are all questions which the customer service rhetoric in museums ignores.

Although these are legitimate questions, they are not sufficient cause to dismiss customer service as yet another management fad or popular panacea. Museums, to a greater or lesser extent, have always engaged in some sort of service, from school programs to answering telephone calls about the collections. What the late twentieth century is demanding is a redefinition of what service means. For museums, it will mean going beyond the self-interest which governs much of what we do, and assuming more accountability for the museum and its relationship to the broader society. This is not meant to imply that this sense of greater responsibility was missing in the past. It was there, albeit unevenly, but most museums were simply not internally aligned to allow its full expression. Making a commitment to service requires that an organization achieve a balance of power where people can act on their own choices, help to define purpose and meaning, and are rewarded equitably (Block 1993:xxxxi). As discussed earlier, many museums are only now beginning to address these issues, which are all about governance and management. How we govern and manage will either inhibit or promote our collective ability to commit to something outside of ourselves, and it is increasingly clear that organizational compliance and control will not get us to where we need to be.

Herein lie the paradoxes. At a time when museum work is becoming more complex and more time-consuming because of multidisciplinary collaboration in the absence of traditional, functional departments, we must insist that there may be greater public involvement in our work. At a time when we are told that the customer is king, we are rediscovering our potential to show leadership as brokers of complex relationships and societal issues, none of which are value-free and all of which demand engagement, not passivity. At a time of diminishing resources, we must provide new and creative ways of serving a growing and diverse clientele. At a time when we are placing renewed emphasis on our unique role as knowledge workers, we are advising staff that there may not be time for them to spend an hour answering a curatorial inquiry. There are no lasting solutions to these contradictory tensions. Our only hope is for committed staff who will accept and cope with them, and perhaps even make sense of them over time.

ARE MUSEUMS SUSTAINABLE WITHOUT SIGNIFICANT CONTRIBUTIONS OF PUBLIC MONEY?

Although hindsight will be the judge of this, I believe that the answer to this question is possibly yes, but that the path is virtually uncharted. I base this less than optimistic response on my limited experience at Glenbow, which continues to be one of Canada's most financially self-sufficient museums, considering its overall size. Of the top ten museums in the country, there are none which approach Glenbow's 1994/95 operating budget of 52% self-generated revenues and 48% of provincial and federal revenues. Admittedly, our efforts at self-sufficiency are made much easier because of our relative autonomy from government—an advantage that few of the other museums in the top ten category share.

Despite this autonomy and unprecedented level of commitment to moneymaking activities at Glenbow, our revenue projections for 1995/96 reflect only modest increases. These projections are even more modest if you exclude the increased income from our endowment funds. Why only modest revenue increases in an organization with a clear track record of self-sufficiency? To begin with, our private sector fundraising projections are mostly flat. With government providing less money to health and education, the intense competition for funding among non-profits is almost comic. And this at a time when there is simply less money to go around, if we believe what we are told by the private sector. Museums must also realize that fundraising is intensely competitive on the personal level, and requires aggressive, sustained action on the part of individual board members. It is easy to lose ground in this work when a board and staff are preoccupied with organizational change, but such neglect cannot be allowed to persist for long.

Another hindrance is the fact that commercial activities, a new and potentially important source of revenue for us, require a more gradual build-up than we had anticipated. Despite a booming facility rentals business, which hosts weddings and dinner parties in gallery spaces, it takes time to build up a client base. It also takes time to identify commercial partnerships, such as the one we have developed with a long-distance telephone wholesaler. By signing up our members, volunteers and staff, we are able to share in a percentage of the wholesaler's profits on a monthly basis. Convincing staff that their professional knowledge is saleable has also been difficult, and we are still struggling to normalize this revenue stream within an overall attempt to levy fees for a variety of museum services which have always been free.

In short, despite a diversified revenue base and numerous innovative initiatives to further diversify this base, the idea of complete self-sufficiency with no public money is currently unachievable for Glenbow, given our current sense of self-reference. It is possible, however, given the following two strategies. The first strategy would be to cut back all operations to a point where public monies are no longer required. The risk here is the beginning of a vicious cycle, whereby less money means diminished visibility, which in turn leads to greater indifference among the museum's constituencies, followed by less financial support and so on.

It might also be possible to reduce the scope of operations as part of this strategy, without risking the vicious cycle described above, by rethinking what is actually required to fulfill the purpose of a museum. We must pose the question—if we did not exist, would we reinvent ourselves and what would we look like (Handy 1994:58)? All medium and large museums in Canada have tremendous overhead costs, due in large part to the tradition of employing a wide variety of specialists and technicians on a year-round basis, coupled with the tradition of working in virtual isolation from even closely related institutions. Perhaps it's time to disassemble some of the country's larger museums, and reduce them to a core of say 25 to 75 knowledge specialists, who would then purchase all the additional services they require from a host of professional and technical people outside of the organization. This is the true meaning of the shamrock organization, and might possibly enhance effectiveness and reduce expenditures simultaneously.

In addition, museums could position themselves to benefit from more support and interaction with like-minded organizations—universities for example. The Museum of Anthropology (MOA) at the University of British Columbia in Vancouver is the finest example of this model in North America. This museum currently has a core of about 18 professional museum staff, several of whom have academic cross-appointments. They, in turn, are supported by up to 80 students who work for MOA in a variety of capacities as they pursue their undergraduate and graduate degrees.

The second strategy for achieving economic self-sufficiency represents a pronounced departure from the core business of museums. It would require becoming very aggressive about generating revenue, and creating opportunities which have little or nothing to do with the core activities as we know them. It might mean purchasing a high profile, fast-food franchise or assuming a partnership in an oil and gas venture. There are plenty of opportunities for making money, if one is willing to set aside a commitment to self-reference. Juggling these two extremes may be quite possible, although there is plenty of evidence from the business world that engaging in alien business ventures can result in costly failure. Museums may be forced to consider such unholy alliances if public funding continues to evaporate, and it is not as unusual as it may appear at first glance. The growing presence of IMAX and Omni-Max theatres at museums and science centres is a relevant example of broadening the revenue base in a more familiar manner than opening a McDonald's on the other side of town. Sending tax money to Revenue Canada might be the kind of problem museums would like to have. If one is serious about reconciling opposites as discussed earlier, we must remain open to the possibility of balancing the core purpose of a knowledge-based organization with one or more businesses which might be considered completely unrelated from a traditional perspective. Doing this would require a firm sense of purpose, the necessary expertise to operate the commercial activities, and unswerving commitment to the notion that the business ventures exist to serve the museum and its needs, not the other way around. There would have to be a clear separation of church and state, so to speak.

The real difficulty at this point in time is that most, if not all, museums have virtually no discretionary money with which to experiment with new approaches to sustainability. At Glenbow, for example, our operating budget is so tight that nearly all revenues must go to fund operating costs. We have no money to set aside for the research and development which is ultimately required to identify, pilot and assess new ways of achieving financial stability. And I am not referring to blockbuster exhibitions here, as they are mostly more of the same with greater and greater costs and risks. Strategic partnerships with business are obviously one alternative, and numerous discussions are underway across the country between museums and agents of the Information Highway (such as Digital Corporation), to determine if alliances are feasible. The thinking is that museums would supply the content in the form of images and artifacts, and the corporations would supply the technology—all for the purpose of making money, of course. But whose money, how much, and what are people paying for? Herein lies the paradox. At a time when a concerted effort must be made to identify new ways of enhancing the sustainability of museums, it is all most museums can do to keep the wolf from the door. Experimenting, improvising, designing, testing and implementing new forms of sustainability all cost money, which underscores the adage that it takes money to make money. Partnerships with the private sector are a real possibility.

Many museums have not yet confronted this paradox of having to learn and grow without additional resources, but it is only a matter of time. This paradox, too, will also have to be managed by reconciling opposites, if we are to continue to shape the "second curve." Handy (1994:58–67) uses the sigmoid curve to illustrate how organizations start slowly, wax and wane. A new future, rather than demise, is achievable if a second or new curve is started before the first one dies out. Starting the new curve means challenging all assumptions and devising alternatives, including everything from new ways of operating to meaningful public service. This is difficult to achieve because so many museum people want to prolong the old ways indefinitely, yet enhancing sustainability in the face of decreasing public money is part of the second curve that all museums must acknowledge. My only fear is that we might have left it too late, because of the current lack of resources to test, evaluate and implement new approaches to sustainability. We are fortunate, however, that asking questions and generating new possibilities do not cost money. It is essential that this questioning become an urgent task for all museums, if we are to find a path through this paradox of sustainability before events overtake us. There is some comfort in knowing that there will never be any flawless solutions to any of this. For the traditionalists who decry the entrepreneurial museum, I am afraid there will be little solace in the years to come.

ARE THERE TOO MANY MUSEUMS?

In short, yes there are. I have already referred to an overbuilt situation in Alberta, but this condition extends far beyond this province. Perhaps it is not that there are too many museums in the country, but that there are too many museums with undifferentiated resources (Hatton 1992:32–35). That is, the public may not see the difference between one museum or another as being all that critical, because they have neither the inclination nor knowledge to differentiate on the basis of the breadth and depth of the collections, in the way that museum professionals do. If museum collections are largely undifferentiated in the mind of the public, then I suppose to a great extent, all museums are in competition with each other. We know that we are competing for both people's time and their disposable income, but it is not all that clear what competitive business we actually see ourselves in. Is it heritage, education, preservation, leisure, tourism, entertainment or knowledge production (Hatton 1992:34–35)? Is it all of these? Although few museums are explicit about this, it appears that nearly two-thirds of Glenbow's annual expenditures are spent directly or indirectly on the care of the permanent collections. Does this mean that we are basically in the warehouse business? If so, do we need an unknown number of museums spending a great deal of time and money warehousing the same objects? We always tell ourselves that it is our collections which make us unique, but are they sufficient to give us an advantage in the race for people's leisure time and attention? There are many more related questions, some of which border on tautology, and none of which have received sufficient attention as we pursue the *status quo* with ever-increasing fervour.

One solution, albeit a painful one, may lie in reducing the number of museums. As Weil (1994:2) has observed, "museum people have a gut sense that all museums are not of equal quality, that some museums are better than others." Through the application of performance measures, assessment and accreditation, decisions could be made about which museums merit public support. Such assessments would have to recognize the extraordinary variability among museums in terms of origin, funding, governance and collections, and herein lies the rub. The application of some universal accreditation scheme would undoubtedly ride roughshod over the concept of local autonomy—that all manner of work should be done at the most local level where it can be done well. If museums, however small or undifferentiated, can successfully compete for grants, function with a volunteer staff or close their doors on a seasonal basis to conserve resources, then so be it. Their adaptive skills would appear to be in order.

The difficulties and the potential solutions are more the purview of the larger, so-called professional museums and galleries. I use the word professional primarily to indicate the presence of trained staff who adhere to a recognized body of museological method and theory, have advanced education and share common values. These institutions have it in their power to rethink their interrelationships, especially within a geographical or political jurisdiction, with a view to funding the right mix of critical resources among themselves. This could be the basis of defining competitive advantages among museums, which up until now probably appear to be largely undifferentiated in the public's view. Any attempt to challenge the insularity and fierce independence characteristic of museums would have to be a gradual process.

It must begin, however, with both federal and provincial governments agreeing to a moratorium on the construction of any new museum or gallery facilities for at least the next five to ten years, as the Canadian Museums Association recently recommended. The only exceptions would be those new initiatives which can demonstrate absolutely no need for public money. This may sound harsh, but the consequences of not doing so are worse. It is no longer reasonable for museums to be built on political whim, as highways and hospitals have been. In Alberta, in 1995, there is yet another multi-million dollar heritage facility currently under construction, funded in large part by public money. The ongoing operating costs have not been publicly discussed, except to observe that admission revenues will carry the day. This notion of self-sufficiency through gate receipts is one of the newest red herrings to appear on the Alberta museum scene, and in other places as well, I suspect. It diverts attention from the real issue of sustainability, as I know of no professional museum in Canada where admission fees even come close to paying the operating costs. This is simply not feasible at this time, no matter how fervently we wish it to be so.

The next step, after a construction moratorium, requires seriously assessing the feasibility of consolidating collections, with a view to eliminating redundancy and enhancing quality. Why does Glenbow need to keep one of the best mineralogical collections in North America, when we are a human history museum and have no curator of mineralogy? It once made sense, when we operated a mineralogy department. Now, we rationalize keeping the collection on the basis that the minerals continue to draw visitors. There is obvious truth in this, but perhaps this valuable exhibition space might be more effectively used in other ways more germane to our mandate. The double standard which emanates from the force of tradition is intriguing. It's professionally acceptable to retain and exhibit collections for which there is no in-house curatorial expertise, but it is still largely unacceptable in Canadian museums to present exhibitions, often of a topical nature, which have no basis in the permanent collections. It is more sensible to send the minerals to the Provincial Museum in Edmonton which, as a human and natural history museum, already has an outstanding mineralogical collection. The addition of our material would make theirs superlative. In the interests of further differentiating our resources, I suggest that, in return, the Provincial Museum augment our internationally renown Northern Plains ethnology collections by making available through gift, loan or trade, the relevant material in their collections. This transaction, subject to whatever conditions are mutually acceptable, would assist each of our institutions in doing better what we already do well. It means making a choice between having a little bit of everything, or consolidating and refining our unique strengths to the point where they are critical masses of highly visible resources.

There is an excellent example of critical resources in the Royal Tyrrell Museum, located in a tiny town in southeastern Alberta. There you will find a palaeontology museum, second to none in the world, which draws hundreds of thousands of visitors from all over the world. Admittedly, dinosaurs rank right up there with mummies and shrunken heads for their popular appeal, but the Royal Tyrrell has raised this appeal to new heights with its single-minded focus. The Royal Tyrrell's approach may, in fact, represent a new form of elitism, something which Michael Ames (1992: personal correspondence) advises that museums should never abandon. The task, in his view, is to retain quality *and* make that more accessible, rather than making museum presentations more "popular," simply to attract crowds. Ames points to holy shrines as elite in a religious sense, and yet thoroughly popular in terms of attendance. Similarly, the Royal Tyrrell combines first-rate public presentation with leading-edge research.

Perhaps the single largest obstacle to this idea of strategic sharing and consolidation comes from the highly developed proprietary interests so characteristic of museums. By proprietary, I mean the strong sense of ownership that we claim over everything we do and have. It is still sufficiently strong to prevent or discourage any real collaboration, as exemplified by my earlier example of our failing to launch a regional arts and heritage magazine. Julian Spalding (1993) lamented these proprietary instincts in another form, when he observed that the curator must be removed from the possession of the object. In his view, curators must be encouraged to love and study objects but not possess them, as it is this possession which creates so much undue worrying and conflict. It is curious that one thing we have in common with the business world is proprietorship, and it is rapidly becoming a liability. Overcoming the resistance it engenders will require a conceptual model and a great deal of will.

The question, when considering the number and variety of museums within a particular province or region, is how to combine autonomy with cooperation. There needs to be some model or mechanism with which to overcome the tyranny of institutional and individual territoriality, although tyranny may be too strong a word. There is presumably no malice in the persuasive tendency for most specialists, including senior government officials, to insulate themselves from broader concerns. Nevertheless, the result has been less than adequate communication between museums as organizations, which in turn contributes to a seeming inability to devise fresh, lateral perspectives on a variety of issues and concerns.

Perhaps it is time to consider the concept of a federal organization and whether or not it would be useful in the conduct of museum affairs, whether locally, provincially or nationally. Federalism implies a variety of individual groups allied together under a common flag with some shared identity (Handy 1989:117). Federalism seeks to make it big by keeping it small, or at least independent, combining autonomy with cooperation. Federalism is an old idea, but an appropriate one at this time, because it matches paradox with paradox. The potential of this federal model of organization for addressing the paradoxes confronting museums is sufficiently impressive to merit a more detailed look at its characteristics. In doing this, my role is not that of an originator, but as a transmitter of the ideas of Charles Handy (1989:117–140; 1994:109–113, 135–139).

Federalism is not the same as decentralization, as the latter implies that the centre delegates certain tasks while remaining in overall control. The centre still initiates, delegates and directs. In federalism, the centre's powers are given to it by the outlying groups. As a result, the centre coordinates, advises, suggests and influences, with the initiative, drive and the energy coming mostly from the parts. Nor is federalism the same thing as confederation, which is an alliance of interested parties who agree to do some things together. They are "organizations of expediency, not of common purpose" (Handy 1994:112), and hence are not going anywhere because there is no structure or mechanism to decide what direction to take.

Other salient characteristics of federalism include:

- Being big in some things and small in others
- Centralized in some respects and decentralized in others. The individual parts or members turn over some of their powers to the centre, because they believe that the centre can do some things better collectively. The powers of the centre are negotiated jointly
- Local in its appeal, but national and global in scope
- Maximize independence, while ensuring interdependence
- Encourage difference while maintaining a strong centre
- Led from the centre but managed by its parts.

The role of the centre, more specifically, is to be responsible for developing and orchestrating the strategic vision, as well as developing the shared administrative and organizational infrastructure. This infrastructure might include everything from legal services to human resources to communications. Although those in the centre have a view of the whole, it should be sufficiently small not to allow them to run the organization. The information age has now made federalism possible in Handy's (1994:138) view, because the centre can be well-informed but small, and strong, but dispersed. In summary, the federal idea acknowledges what has already been a recurring theme throughout this book. No individual, executive group or single organization in the museum world is sufficiently all-knowing and competent to balance all the opposites and manage all the paradoxes.

This concept of federalism is equally as applicable to a group of like-minded organizations, as it is to the internal workings of a single organization. Consider, for example, the possibility of a federal model linking a number of major institutions in western Canada, ranging from the Royal British Columbia Museum to the Manitoba Museum of Man and Nature. A joint purpose could be developed, with common standards and common aspirations, followed by negotiations leading to a formal constitution. The constitution would specify the power of the centre. The centre would then have to be designed and staffed with the appropriate executives, who would be largely concerned with the future—plans, possibilities, scenarios and options. The principle would be to leave power as close to the action as possible, while at the same time forging these local and separate institutions into one whole, served by a common centre. Federalism is about managing the paradox, and there would be some restriction on local independence, if it helps the larger whole. This will only work if there is confidence in the central function, coupled with a sense of belonging to the larger whole. A federation with sufficient critical mass might also foster the development of professional and technical service companies, staffed by former museum employees who have lost their permanent jobs. A federation of museums could provide a sufficient level of work to these companies to justify their start-up, and to ensure their continuance.

Clearly this flies in the face of Canadian museum tradition, with its emphasis on government-controlled museums which operate singularly and mostly in isolation, whether on a national, provincial or local level. In a time of scarce resources, we continue to increase our costs and dissipate our declining funds, *ad nauseam*, by publishing separate magazines, developing our own information systems, purchasing materials and supplies separately, and so on. We have few resources, as a result, to invest in the research and development that is required to ensure that we remain skeptical, curious and inventive. Perhaps the federal model would permit some creative efforts in this direction, as it is clear that nearly all museums, perhaps with the exception of the largest ones in Canada (the former National Museums, the Royal Ontario Museum and the Art Gallery of Ontario), are increasingly incapable of doing this work on their own.

I am not proposing the rebirth of the defunct National Museums Corporation (NMC) in a provincial or regional setting, under the guise of a federal model. The NMC was a command and control bureaucracy in the traditional sense, which failed to negotiate a mutual understanding of the power of the centre and the autonomy of the parts. Achieving workable federalism is not magic, but the hard work of forging a common purpose which holds the parts together. This is the leadership of ideas and consensus, not personalities (Handy 1989:124).

The weight of tradition will not be the only obstacle to experimenting with the federal idea. A more formidable obstacle will be the whole notion of power, as federalism is an exercise in the balancing of power. The hard truth is that we are always reluctant to give up power unless we have to (Handy 1994:111), especially to an idea whose outcome is unpredictable, very different, perhaps messy and a far cry from what we are doing today. In the final analysis, the best reason for considering the federal idea is simply because the *status quo* is losing ground to the mounting complexities in contemporary museum work. If there are other alternatives, we should consider those as well.

Yes, there are the paradoxes again. At a time when the public money available for museums diminishes annually, various governments continue to build heritage facilities in the name of economic development or political expediency. At a time when far too many museums are preoccupied with their survival, it is imperative that we accomplish our purpose. In a not-for-profit organization, survival does not necessarily equate with success (Weil 1994:4). At a time when expansive organizational networks are vital to renewal, we stumble under the twin burdens of insularity and myopic professional pride in our own achievements. At a time when the future is rife with possibilities such as federalism, we are constrained by provincial domination of the museum sector, which is based on the belief that if you want to control it, own it (Handy 1989:239). Or conversely, if you want to own it, control it. Either way, will provincial cultural ministries embrace the notion of federalism, with all its implications for the loss of power in the centre? Perhaps not, especially when one considers that various people in positions of power have been there for up to two decades. Longevity on the job tends to foster contempt, or at least discomfort, with reframing one's understanding of things. This is part of the sense of infallibility which inevitably develops from past success. These obstacles, however onerous they may appear, should not dissuade us from pursuing these and other opportunities. This effort of will must be accompanied by a genuine effort to change the way we think about what is possible. The current need for cooperation, group expertise and diversity represents such a major psychological and philosophical change in how we do things, that one writer has called it a shift in human consciousness (von Sass 1993:25). Federalism may not be the answer to the problem of too many museums, but it might very well help us to cope with this new reality in unprecedented and creative ways.

CAN MUSEUMS FULFILL THEIR POTENTIAL?

Put another way, is an adaptive museum an oxymoron? If adaptability means the ability to adjust to new or changed circumstances, the answer to this question requires some serious reflection. There are many hindrances to adaptation in the museum world, some self-imposed and others not, beginning with the very purpose of a good museum. There is more to achieving purpose in museums, however, than answering the question—what does it mean to be a human being? A good museum must also be an argument with its society, and direct attention to what is difficult and even painful to think about (Postman 1990:58). Fulfilling this purpose, and hence remaining adaptive, must therefore proceed without any assurances that what is being done will be appreciated. Many boards of directors and many more colleagues are quick to judge and cast doubts on different, and perhaps untested, ways of achieving purpose and meaning under changing circumstances. In the end, the only escape from this inherent conservatism is through conviction and tenacity. There will certainly be mistakes in charting new directions and some, hopefully not too many, will go nowhere. Better this than the paralysis which comes from fear of disapproval. Although working individually or organizationally with minimal reinforcement under stressful conditions is no one's idea of rewarding work, this might also be viewed as the peculiar fate of good museums who admit to never being certain and never being done.

We must also contend with a societal stereotype which seems as firmly planted in people's minds as eating turkey on Thanksgiving Day. Museums, in this stereotypical view, are dusty, stodgy and essentially frozen in time in both content and approach. There is a story from Vancouver which is a priceless confirmation of this image of museums (Ames 1992: personal communication). A production company working in Vancouver was in need of a curator's office for a film they were shooting. They were shown a curatorial office at the Museum of Anthropology, which they rejected because it was of contemporary design, clean and well-lit, had no jumble of books, papers and artifacts, and furthermore, was equipped with a computer and all the associated hardware! The film company decided to create their own curator's office, instead, which conformed to their stereotype of the curatorial inner sanctum. My imagination sees it as cluttered, eccentric, old-fashioned, and tacitly irrelevant to the demands of everyday life.

The Canadian Museums Association's recent statistics on increasing museum visitation demonstrate that this museum stereotype is just that—a hackneyed notion, totally lacking in critical judgement. Nonetheless, we in the museum business must assume some ownership for this stereotype, because where there's smoke there is bound to be something burning. We have much to do to enhance our appeal, from ensuring that there is a full range of visitor amenities in our buildings, to overcoming the urge to keep the light levels in galleries so low that visitors become angry and alienated. None of these admonishments are new, but all of them require constant attention. It is simply not acceptable to indicate that an artifact on exhibition was removed for treatment in 1981, when the year is 1994! Nor is it necessary to go through the agony of creating the definitive scholarly text panel, which leaves most readers cold, with information so dense that little, if any, communication occurs. Museums must abandon their self-imposed task of being the authority, and replace this stubborn tradition with alternative views and rigorous insights which are designed to promote thought and feeling, not compliance. Many museums are making significant progress in this respect, but potential for museums to serve as brokers of societal complexity remains largely unfilled.

Maybe our inherent difficulty to treat the future and our relationship to it is in our bones. Perhaps the museum's very preoccupation with things that have survived the long passage of time makes us skeptical about the undefined future. After all, what is the impact of the next three to five years, if one is absorbed with objects and knowledge which are centuries and millennia old? It is not surprising that skepticism should greet the arrival of yet another prognostication about where we are headed as individuals and as organizations. As social institutions, however, museums cannot permit themselves this intellectual isolation, no matter how sensible it may seem from a long-term perspective. Exclusive commitment to change through time, or conversely, to the short-term without historical antecedents—both are maladaptive. Both these perspectives must exist simultaneously in our thinking and in our work. I cannot help but think of the world-renowned thinker and futurist, Buckminster Fuller. Although he was the inventor of the geodesic dome and the dymaxion car, as well as the author of *Operating Manual for Spaceship Earth* (1969), he apparently spent a good deal of time on an island off the coast of Maine living in a rustic house with no electricity or running water. Just thinking about this sort of contradiction is useful, as it parallels the oppositional forces with which museums must contend.

You can actually view this paradox of old and new from a different perspective, and conclude that museums are the only contemporary institutions with the privilege of bringing to bear the perspective of time on the elucidation of old and new societal issues. Government embodies the archetypal, short-term perspective, as a consequence of both unquestioned tradition and obvious self-interest. Industry is also a master of this, with its preoccupation on next quarter's performance to appease increasingly militant shareholders. In fairness, this is not universally true, as many corporations are increasingly aware of the need to invest in knowledge-building for the long-term. Nevertheless, the private sector as we know it has little interest or capability in addressing the questions which confound us as a species. Nor do institutions of advanced education, for they mostly exist to convey knowledge and meaning to a limited audience—their students. Although major efforts are underway through cooperative programs and continuing education, for example, to forge new relationships between colleges, universities and the broader community, this still requires a formal commitment on the part of each participant to enroll, pay a fee and dedicate their time. The museum, in contrast, exists as an institution of learning in that ambiguous realm which straddles education and entertainment, and is in a position to provide knowledge and meaning as a so-called leisure activity in a manner far more accessible than universities will ever be able to do.

It is not only a matter of museums adapting as organizations, but also whether they will fulfill their potential to enrich the evolution of our collective consciousness. Groundbreaking work in this direction is currently underway, such as in the realm of First Nations and sacred objects, but this is only the beginning. There are powerful urges to keep our distance as social institutions, whether they be our sensitivity to the fullness of time, so-called professional standards or the myths discussed earlier about the insularity of self-sacrificing cultural workers. None of these are insurmountable barriers to adaptation, if we are first willing to admit to them.

THE TYRANNY OF TRADITION

How does effective adaptation express itself in a business as idiosyncratic as that of museums? In museums which are conscious of their future, adaptation requires at least two related types of behaviour—freeing one's self from tradition and redistributing power and privilege. I will comment on each of these in turn. The idea of freedom from tradition engenders a certain hostility in the museum community because of the assumption that it means the erosion of professional standards and practice. Although professional practice is certainly part of this, freedom from tradition must also be seen more broadly.

The tyranny of tradition takes many forms from the mundane to the significant, and I will provide several examples of both to underscore the need for change. The permanent or semi-permanent exhibit, as it is euphemistically called, is the most pervasive expression of what a particular museum represents. These exhibitions are the most time-intensive and capital-intensive work we do, and remain in place from 15 years to a half century or more, despite the fact that they become dated, boring and shabby. The one defense they have is the legitimate notion that museums have certain concepts and facts that they wish to convey to all visitors, and permanent exhibitions are an effective way to do this. Implicit in this is the view that such information is more or less timeless, an assumption which is easily challenged. More importantly, the linear inertia which characterizes 99% of these installations has lost its appeal for many people, including most of today's youth. I am not suggesting that permanent exhibitions be replaced by instant gratification through multimedia technology—that's too easy. Instead, we must completely rethink the permanent exhibition concept.

Why not look at what works in people's private and social lives? In these contexts, there is always clearly defined space such as a living room or family room. Meaning comes from a variety of sources, including conversation and discussion grounded in memory and experience, the presence of numerous material objects which are valued for their personal, family, or social history, a variety of technological devices from televisions to VCRs, and in many cases, an eclectic selection of printed materials. All these things are arranged formally or informally, and are used intermittently or constantly, depending upon the changing needs and interests of the users.

If this crude description of how people build and sustain some of the meaning in their lives is even partially accurate, how can museums assume that a brightly-painted construction of wood and glass, incorporating 20,000 words of two-dimensional text in conjunction with objects that can only be visually examined, is necessarily effective in providing meaning and enjoyment? Or, how can we assume that a dazzling array of multi-media hardware is any more effective than the three-dimensional books we build called exhibits? Interactivity notwithstanding, there is still the fact that this approach, too, is unbalanced and too much of a good thing. It is time to fundamentally rethink the exhibition. I suggest that the next semi-permanent exhibition be a series of family rooms, modules or activity areas, call them what you wish, each devoted to a theme or topic based on sound research and topicality. There the visitor would be free to engage in the variety of behaviours outlined earlier, whether it is reading, watching or just sitting in a unique environment. The contents of these activity areas could change as required, without prohibitively expensive capital renovations. How well this would work is unknown. The point is that we must begin to truly experiment, at the expense of what has become an enslavement to an increasingly ineffective tradition.

Another area which requires rethinking is our inability to respond to issues, topics or crises which have broad interest, and come in off the street with little or no lead time. With our noses to the grindstones of habit and control, we rarely, if ever, are able to respond to these events, much less play a leadership role in initiating and creating such opportunities. The time has come to designate a team among staff who are ready and able to initiate and respond to broader issues and concerns which are unanticipated in typical museum planning processes. This team must have a budget, be multidisciplinary, with rotating membership in order to pass around the stress and the experience. An organizational capability to respond or initiate in a timely fashion could do much to enhance our adaptability, and perhaps diminish the view that doing something new in a museum is like turning a ship around in a bathtub. Many more museums should take the lead from the Royal British Columbia Museum.

A third consideration in enhancing our adaptive abilities is of a longer-term nature, but is no less dependent upon a reexamination of tradition. First, we must stop being so compulsive about the collections, especially with respect to conservation. It is erroneous to simply blame this behaviour on individual conservators, however, as they are responding to the requirements of their professional training. Access versus preservation is an age-old tension in museums, and the problem is that it continues, despite the best efforts of many conservators to reach daily compromises in the course of their work. The problem is obviously deeper than this and requires much closer communication between those who train conservators and those responsible for delivering public services. We, as institutions, are increasingly in need of generalist conservators, who are devoted to making objects "safely accessible," in Julian Spalding's (1993) words, not securing them for all time. The hapless victim of this lack of communication appears to be the contemporary conservator, who is tempted to fight rear guard actions or leave in frustration because professional training is not aligned with organizational imperatives. I know that awareness of this is increasing (Clavir 1993), but it does not seem to be happening fast enough. The internal struggles caused by this lack of alignment are responsible for a considerable waste of time and energy, not to mention ill-will among staff.

Related to rethinking professional training among conservators is the general need for continually raising the professional standards among museum knowledge workers in general. Advance training and continual learning are key ingredients in effective adaptation, both individual and organizationally, and review of the educational profile of Glenbow staff reveals some interesting information. Nearly 50% of the roughly 100 staff have undergraduate university degrees, with only four of the staff having no high school diploma. Of those with the university degrees, a dozen or so have advanced degrees such as a master's or doctorate. This is not a simplistic plea for advanced degrees as the solution to enhancing our effectiveness, but rather a recognition of the fact this trend is already established.

It is now virtually impossible to obtain an entry level position in any professional museum, without an undergraduate degree or some form of advanced training. Training on the job will continue to be essential, but it is no longer a sufficient basis for a career in a professional museum. Educational standards are rising substantially throughout North America, and museums cannot be exempted if they are to maintain their credibility. Learning must be continuous if we are to adapt effectively, especially for those who might have joined a museum staff before the trend for advanced degrees was well established. It is no longer possible to ignore this trend as being part of the ivory tower, and hence irrelevant to the "real" world of museums. Museums deal in knowledge, so anything that enhances the collection, creation or dissemination of this knowledge is adaptive. It wasn't that long ago when the director of a major Canadian museum prided himself on having only a high school diploma. I'm afraid that nowadays that director would be out of a job.

The last consideration in freeing ourselves from tradition is less tangible than the preceding discussion, and has more to do with attitude and perspective. Simply put, we in museums must grasp the fact that we don't need to tell people what they already know. For example, we do not need museums which dazzle us with electronic technology, and we do not need museums which celebrate that. North American culture is already providing us with a surfeit of this (Postman 1990:58). If we can start the argument with society and keep it going, through providing alternative views of complex things with frank discussion, museums can adapt and reinvent themselves for a new century. It is really up to us though, because society and our supporters will not make us do this. If we elect not to do this, society's disinterest will probably increase, and without the large injection of public money we had in the past, we may in fact finally suffer the fate of the unsuccessful in the marketplace. We will be put out of our misery because not enough people will wish to buy our programs and services. This is not an economic argument based on the almighty bottom line, but a surmise which hinges on whether or not museums are able to consistently offer some sense of reality which differs from current political, academic and advertising agency dogma. If we can do this, the support will be there.

REDISTRIBUTING POWER AND PRIVILEGE

In addition to the adaptive value of always casting a critical eye on tradition, the redistribution of power and privilege is another pathway to the future. This redistribution encompasses everything from reducing the number of managers to eliminating the absoluteness of functional departments. There are myriad other ways to achieve this redistribution, but the intent remains the same. That is to make each staff member responsible for the organization's culture, responsible for delivering meaning and value to our customers and supporters, and responsible for the quality of their own experiences (Block 1993:50).

Redistributing privilege is considerably more provocative for the executive director of a large museum than is defying professional traditions. In effect, we perpetuate work structures and management practices, born of our own societal traditions, which reinforce a class system. These practices keep ownership and responsibility focused at the top (Block 1993:51). The executive class has privileges which the other staff do not have, and we argue that such prerogatives come with the greater responsibility inherent in these positions. There is much truth in this, but there is still the nagging doubt that there might be a better way to do things. Does this mean that we have to reintegrate the managing and doing of work? As I look around Glenbow, this trend is established or well underway throughout the organization. Does this also mean that all executives should be doing their own typing and making their own travel arrangements, as one writer suggests (Block 1993:47)? At first glance, this seems nonsensical. At the same time, one cannot deny that our governance system, be it board or executive, is not necessarily a consistent route to the partnership with staff which we are seeking. There is still something missing. Are we talking about rank without privilege? What does this mean for museum executives who are already underpaid compared to positions of similar complexity in any other sector, not to mention the long hours? Is reducing the limited privileges among museum executives more palatable than it is in other sectors, because museum executives don't generate wealth and they don't save lives? Yet, many of society's most distinguished citizens flock to museums for the status and prestige they confer, often simply by association. We are inundated by paradox.

I know of at least one instance where these unanswered questions have not prevented a redistribution of power and privilege. This occurred recently in Glenbow's Library and Archives whereby the staff elect their own director from among themselves for a two-year term. Election to this position is normally accompanied by a substantial, albeit temporary, increase in salary. The staff of this work unit recently agreed, at their own initiative, and by keeping their own counsel, to substantially reduce this salary increase and to use the remaining monies to fund additional temporary staff within the Library and Archives to address a variety of work-related priorities. This was a quiet, but signal, rethinking of current practices about power and privilege which simply cannot be ignored. The implications of this decision are far from clear, but intentional or not, it has become a new template for considering power and privilege at Glenbow.

Such considerations are more than philosophical, as they also have implications for the design of adaptive organizations (Beer 1988:7). Research indicates that those organizations which have fewer distinctions in power and rewards, i.e., are more egalitarian, give people fewer things to lose. This apparently makes people more willing to accept the changes which inevitably occur as the work changes. Ultimately, the redistribution of power and privilege must be seen far beyond the organization—in the communities where we work. There is no doubt in my mind that meaningful community involvement in a museum's work is a direct reflection of the management style. Simply put, patriarchy and control foster isolation; while individual responsibility and stewardship nurture the web of community relationships.

Typically, paradoxes abound in this consideration of our ability to adapt to the future. Although seldom discussed, all good museums have an obligation to the dead and unborn, as well as to the paying customer. Yet, neither the dead nor the unborn vote or buy. This is apparently a conundrum which has defied the imaginations of nearly all politicians, as museums are increasingly judged by the number of bodies through the door. Another aspect of this paradox has to do with what one does to keep those numbers up. Can you compare an institution which rents an exhibit with contemporary appeal and thus serves as impresario, to an institution which serves the needs of internationally acclaimed researchers and writers? Of course you can't, because the same things are not being compared. But government officials and their political masters throughout the land have yet to concede that there is a difference which cannot be tabulated by visitor statistics alone.

Another profound paradox lies in the fact that, despite all the work devoted to designing for the future, no one will be able to assess the efficacy of this work until it is over. By then, it is too late, or just in time to start over. There are no answers and there are no guarantees. While this doesn't mean that organizational change and adaptation are a crap shoot, it does mean that we will never know the outcome until it happens, which means that the demand for prescient knowledge cannot be met and hence cannot be used as an excuse for inaction. Intimately related to this is the fact that leaders are liable for what happens in the future, rather than what is happening day to day (De Pree 1989:114). The emphasis on the duties and performance of leaders, including all senior executives, has to be on the future, and much of this performance cannot be reviewed until after the fact. Success or failure may only be apparent in the months or years to come.

Finally, organizations, including museums, are many things at once, none of us will ever know them completely (Morgan 1986:340–341). Irrespective of all the details in this case study, I claim only a partial understanding of Glenbow. We can only know organizations through our experience of them, which means there can be a huge difference between the rich reality of an organization and the knowledge we are able to gain about that organization. This continuous learning may help to explain the roller coaster ride which best describes organizational life in the 1990s. Ideally, what we learn from all these highs and lows will contribute to new mental maps (Senge 1990:239–240), as we must continually guide and shape our perceptions as museum staff and translate these changing perceptions into action. If we do not—if we continue to listen to the silent promptings of comfortable self-interest, if we continue to defer to culture critics whose main interest is the sanctity of their own opinions, and if we are seduced by the promise of government support in exchange for adherence to the lowest common denominator, then we must ask ourselves, as Peggy Lee did in her famous song—"Is that all there is?"

REFERENCES

Ames, Michael M. *Cannibal tours and glass boxes: the anthropology of museums.* Vancouver: UBC Press, 1992.

Beer, Michael A. "Leading change." *Harvard Business School Note 9-488-037.* Cambridge, Mass., Cambridge, 1988.

Block, Peter. *Stewardship.* San Francisco: Koehler Publishers Inc., 1993.

Clavir, Miriam. "Conceptual integrity of conservation in museums." Per Guldbeck Memorial Lecture at the 19th Annual International Institute of Conservation— Canadian Group Conference, Halifax, 1993.

Conroy, Frank. "Think about it—ways we know and don't." *Harper's Magazine* 277, no. 1662 (1988): 68–70.

De Pree, Max. *Leadership is an art.* New York: Bantam Doubleday Dell Publishing Group, 1989.

Evans, David. "The myth of customer service." *Canadian Business* (March 1991): 34–39.

Fuller, Buckminster. *Operating manual for spaceship earth.* New York: Pocket Books, Inc., 1969.

Handy, Charles. *The age of unreason.* Boston: Harvard Business School Press, 1989.

———. *The age of paradox.* Boston: Harvard Business School Press, 1994.

Hatton, Alf. "Museum planning and museum plans." *Museum Development* (January 1992): 32–39.

Morgan, Gareth. *Images of organization.* Newbury Park, California: SAGE Publications, Inc., 1986.

Postman, Neil. "Museum as dialogue." *Museum News* 69, no. 5 (1990): 55–58.

Senge, Peter M. *The fifth discipline.* New York: Bantam Doubleday Dell Publishing Group, Inc., 1990.

Shapiro, Eileen C. "Fad surfing in the boardroom." *The Globe and Mail Report on Business Magazine* (July 1995): 35–42.

Spalding, Julian. "Interpretation? No, communication." Keynote address to the Annual Conference of the Canadian Museums Association, Regina, Saskatchewan, 1993.

von Sass, Peter E. "The virtual corporation." *Business in Calgary* (March 1993): 25–34.

Weil, Stephen E. "Organization-wide quality assessments of museums: an immodest proposal." Paper presented at the International Council of Museums' International Committee on Management Meeting, London, September 1994a.

———. "Performance indicators for museums: progress report from Wintergreen." *The Journal of Arts Management, Law and Society* 23, no. 4 (1994b): 341–351.

Additional Recommended Reading

Anderson, Gail, ed. *Museum Mission Statements: Building a Distinct Identity.* Washington, DC: American Association of Museums, Technical Information Service, 1998.

Carver, John. *Boards That Make a Difference: A New Design for Leadership in Nonprofit and Public Organizations.* San Francisco: Jossey-Bass, 1997.

———. *Reinventing Your Board: A Step-by-Step Guide to Implementing Policy Governance.* San Francisco: Jossey-Bass, 1997.

Greenfield, James M. *Fund-raising Fundamentals: A Guide to Annual Giving for Professionals and Volunteers.* New York: Wiley, 1994.

Malaro, Marie C. *Museum Governance: Mission, Ethics, Policy.* Washington, DC: Smithsonian Institution Press, 1994.

Mathiasen, Karl, III. *Board Passages: Three Key Stages in a Nonprofit Board's Life Cycle.* Washington, DC: National Center for Nonprofit Boards, 1992.

Rutledge, Jennifer M. *Building Board Diversity.* Washington, DC: National Center for Nonprofit Boards, 1994.

Skramstad, Harold, and Susan Skramstad. *A Handbook for Trustees.* Washington, DC: American Association of Museums, 2003.

Texas Association of Museums. *Action Plan for Multicultural Initiatives in Texas Museums.* Austin: Author, 1995; available at www.io.com/~tam/multicultural/actionplan.html.

Weisz, Jackie, ed. *Codes of Ethics and Practice of Interest to Museums.* Washington, DC: American Association of Museums, Technical Information Service, 2000.

Wolf, Thomas. *Managing a Nonprofit Organization in the Twenty-first Century.* New York: Simon & Schuster, 1999.

Bibliography

Alexander, Edward P. *The Museum in America: Innovators and Pioneers.* Walnut Creek, CA: AltaMira, 1997.

———. *Museums in Motion: An Introduction to the History and Functions of Museums.* Walnut Creek, CA: AltaMira, 1996.

———. *Museum Masters: Their Museums and Their Influence.* Walnut Creek, CA: AltaMira, 1983.

American Academy of Arts and Sciences. *Daedalus: America's Museums.* Cambridge, MA: Author, 1999.

American Association of Museums. *America's Museums: The Belmont Report: A Report to the Federal Council on the Arts and the Humanities.* Washington, DC: American Association of Museums, 1968.

———. *Caring for Collections: Strategies for Conservation, Maintenance, and Documentation: A Report on an American Association of Museums Project.* Washington, DC: American Association of Museums, 1984.

———. *Excellence and Equity: Education and the Public Dimension of Museums: A Report from the American Association of Museums.* Washington, DC: American Association of Museums, 1992.

———. *Mastering Civic Engagement: A Challenge to Museums.* Washington, DC: American Association of Museums, 2002.

American Association of Museums Commission on Museums for a New Century. *Museums for a New Century: A Report of the Commission on Museums for a New Century.* Washington, DC: American Association of Museums, 1984.

Ames, Kenneth L., et al., eds. *Ideas and Images: Developing Interpretive History Exhibits* Walnut Creek, CA: AltaMira, 1992.

Ames, Michael M. *Cannibal Tours and Glass Boxes: The Anthropology of Museums.* Vancouver: University of British Columbia Press, 1992.

Anderson, Gail, ed. *Museum Mission Statements: Building a Distinct Identity.* Washington, DC: American Association of Museums, Technical Information Service, 1998.

Association of Art Museum Directors. *Different Voices: Social, Cultural, and Historical Framework for Change in the American Art Museum.* New York: Association of Art Museum Directors, 1992.

BoardSource. *New BoardSource Governance Series.* Washington, DC: BoardSource, 2002.

Buck, Rebecca A., and Jean Allman Gilmore, eds. *The New Museum Registration Methods.* Washington, DC: American Association of Museums, 1998.

Burcaw, George Ellis. *Introduction to Museum Work.* Walnut Creek, CA: AltaMira, 1997.

Carver, John. *Boards That Make a Difference: A New Design for Leadership in Nonprofit and Public Organizations.* San Francisco: Jossey-Bass, 1997.

———. *Reinventing Your Board: A Step-by-Step Guide to Implementing Policy Governance.* San Francisco: Jossey-Bass, 1997.

Case, Mary, ed. *Registrars on Record: Essays on Museum Collections Management.* Washington, DC: Registrars Committee of the American Association of Museums, 1988.

Collins, Zipporah, W., ed. *Museums, Adults, and the Humanities: A Guide for Educational Programming.* Washington, DC: American Association of Museums, 1981.

Commission on Museums for a New Century. *Museums for a New Century.* Washington, DC: American Association of Museums, 1984.

Council on Museums and Education in the Visual Arts. *The Art Museum as Educator: A Collection of Studies as Guides to Practice and Policy.* Berkeley: University of California Press, 1978.

Csikszentmihalyi, Mihaly. *The Meaning of Things: Domestic Symbols and the Self.* New York: Cambridge University Press, 1981.

"Designing for Conservation." *Exhibitionist* 20, no. 2 (Fall 2001).

Diamond, Judy. *Practical Evaluation Guide: Tools for Museums and Other Informal Educational Settings.* Walnut Creek, CA: AltaMira, 1999.

Falk, John H., and Lynn D. Dierking. *Learning from Museums: Visitor Experiences and the Making of Meaning.* Walnut Creek, CA: AltaMira, 2000.

———. *The Museum Experience.* Washington, DC: Whalesback, 1992.

Fischer, Daryl K. *Museums, Trustees, and Communities: Building Reciprocal Relationships.* Washington, DC: American Association of Museums, Technical Information Service, 1997.

Fischer, Daryl, and Barbara Booker. *The Leadership Partnership.* Washington, DC: Museum Trustee Association, 2002.

———. *Building Museum Boards: Templates for Museum Trustees.* Washington, DC: Museum Trustee Association, 2002.

"Formalizing Exhibition Development." *Exhibitionist* 21, no. 1 (Spring 2002).

Gardner, Howard. *Frames of Mind: The Theory of Multiple Intelligences.* New York: Basic Books, 1983.

Glaser, Jane R., and Artemis Zenetou, eds. *Gender Perspectives: Essays on Women in Museums.* Washington, DC: Smithsonian Institution, 1994.

Greenfield, James M. *Fund-raising Fundamentals: A Guide to Annual Giving for Professionals and Volunteers.* New York: Wiley, 1994.

Grinder, Alison L. *The Good Guide: A Sourcebook for Interpreters, Docents, and Tour Guides.* Scottsdale, AZ: Ironwood, 1985.

Gurian, Elaine Heumann, ed. *Institutional Trauma: Major Change in Museums and Its Effect on Staff.* Washington, DC: American Association of Museums, 1995.

Hein, George E. *Learning in the Museum.* New York: Routledge, 1998.

Hirsch, Joanne S., and Lois Silverman. *Transforming Practice: Selections from the* Journal of Museum Education, *1992–1999.* Washington, DC: Museum Education Roundtable, 2000.

Hudson, Kenneth. *Museums of Influence.* New York: Cambridge University Press, 1987.

Institute of Museum and Library Services. *True Needs, True Partners: Museums and Schools Transforming Education.* Washington, DC: Author, 1996.

Janes, Robert. *Museums and the Paradox of Change: A Case Study in Urgent Adaptation.* Calgary: University of Calgary Press and Glenbow Museum, 1997.

Karp, Ivan, Christine Mullen Kreamer, and Steven D. Lavine, eds. *Museums and Communities: The Politics of Public Culture.* Washington, DC: Smithsonian Institution Press, 1992.

Karp, Ivan, and Steven D. Lavine, eds. *Exhibiting Cultures: The Poetics and Politics of Museum Display.* Washington, DC: Smithsonian Institution Press, 1991.

Keene, Suzanne. *Managing Conservation in Museums.* Boston: Butterworth-Heinemann, 1996.

Kotler, Neil, and Philip Kotler. *Museum Strategy and Marketing: Designing Missions, Building Audiences, Generating Revenue and Resources.* San Francisco: Jossey-Bass, 1998.

Kurtz, Daniel. *Managing Conflicts of Interest.* Washington, DC: BoardSource, 2001.

Lord, Barry, and Gail Dexter Lord. *The Manual of Museum Management.* Walnut Creek, CA: AltaMira, 1997.

————, eds. *The Manual of Museum Exhibitions.* Walnut Creek, CA: AltaMira, 2002.

Lord, Gail Dexter, and Barry Lord, eds. *The Manual of Museum Planning,* 2d ed. Walnut Creek: CA, 1999.

Low, Theodore. *The Museum as a Social Instrument.* New York: Metropolitan Museum of Art, 1942.

Majewski, Janice. *Part of Your General Public Is Disabled: A Handbook for Guides in Museums, Zoos, and Historic Houses.* Washington, DC: Smithsonian Institution Press, 1987.

"Making Meaning in Exhibits." *Exhibitionist* 18, no. 2 (Fall 1999).

Malaro, Marie C. *Museum Governance: Mission, Ethics, Policy.* Washington, DC: Smithsonian Institution Press, 1994.

————. *A Legal Primer on Managing Museum Collections.* Washington, DC: Smithsonian Institution Press, 1998.

Mathiasen, Karl, III. *Board Passages: Three Key Stages in a Nonprofit Board's Life Cycle.* Washington, DC: National Center for Nonprofit Boards, 1992.

McLean, Kathleen. *Planning for People in Museum Exhibitions.* Washington, DC: Association of Science-Technology Centers, 1996.

Messenger, Phyllis M., ed. *The Ethics of Collecting Cultural Property: Whose Culture? Whose Ethics?* Albuquerque: University of New Mexico Press, 1999.

Museum Educators of the American Association of Museums. *The Visitor and the Museum.* Berkeley: University of California Press, 1977.

Newsom, Barbara Y., and Adele Z. Silver, eds. *The Art Museums as Educator.* Berkeley: University of California Press, 1978.

Peniston, William A., ed. *The New Museum: Selected Writings by John Cotton Dana.* Washington, DC: American Association of Museums, 1999.

Phelan, Marilyn E. *Museum Law: A Guide for Officers, Directors, and Counsel.* Evanston, IL: Kalos Kapp, 2001.

Pitman, Bonnie, ed. *Presence of Mind: Museums and the Spirit of Learning.* Washington, DC: American Association of Museums, 1999.

Price, Clement Alexander. *Many Voices, Many Opportunities: Cultural Pluralism and American Arts Policy.* New York: ACA Books, Allworth Press, 1993.

Ripley, S. Dillon. *The Sacred Grove: Essays on Museums.* New York: Simon & Schuster, 1969.

Roberts, Lisa C. *From Knowledge to Narrative: Educators and the Changing Museum.* Washington, DC: Smithsonian Institution Press, 1997.

Rutledge, Jennifer M. *Building Board Diversity.* Washington, DC: National Center for Nonprofit Boards, 1994.

Screven, C. G. "United States: A Science in the Making." *Museum International* 178 (Vol. XLV, no. 2, 1993). Paris: UNESCO.

Serrell, Beverly. *Exhibit Labels: An Interpretive Approach.* Walnut Creek, CA: AltaMira, 1996.

Skramstad, Harold, and Susan Skramstad. *A Handbook for Museum Trustees.* Washington, DC: American Association of Museums, 2003.

Smithsonian Institution Task Force on Latino Issues. *Willful Neglect: The Smithsonian Institution and U.S. Latinos.* Washington, DC: Smithsonian Institution, 1994.

Spiess, Philip D., II. "Toward a New Professionalism: American Museums in the 1920s and 1930s." *Museum News* (March/April 1996): 38–47.

Taylor, Samuel, ed. *Try It! Improving Exhibits through Formative Evaluation.* Washington, DC: Association of Science-Technology Centers, 1991.

Texas Association of Museums. *Action Plan for Multicultural Initiatives in Texas Museums.* Austin: Texas Association of Museums, 1995. Available online: www.io.com/~tam/multicultural/actionplan.html (accessed 26 August 2003)

Ullberg, Alan D. *Museum Trusteeship.* Washington, DC: American Association of Museums, 1981.

Warren, Karen J. "A Philosophical Perspective on the Ethics and Resolution of Cultural Properties Issues." In *The Ethics of Collecting Cultural Property: Whose Culture? Whose Ethics?* ed. Phyllis Mauch Messenger, 1–26. Albuquerque: University of New Mexico Press, 1999.

Washburn, Wilcomb E. "Education and the New Elite: American Museums in the 1980s and 1990s." *Museum News* (March/April 1996): 60–65.

Weil, Stephen E. *Beauty and the Beasts: On Museums, Art, the Law, and the Market.* Washington, DC: Smithsonian Institution Press, 1983.

———. *A Cabinet of Curiosities: Inquiries into Museums and Their Prospects.* Washington, DC: Smithsonian Institution Press, 1995.

———. *Making Museums Matter.* Washington, DC: Smithsonian Institution Press, 2002.

———. *Rethinking the Museum and Other Meditations.* Washington, DC: Smithsonian Institution Press, 1990.

———, ed. *A Deaccession Reader.* Washington DC: American Association of Museums, 1997.

Weisz, Jackie, ed. *Codes of Ethics and Practice of Interest to Museums.* Washington, DC: American Association of Museums, Technical Information Service, 2000.

Wittlin, Alma. "A Twelve Point Program for Museum Renewal." In *In Search of a Usable Future.* Boston: Massachusetts Institute of Technology Press, 1970.

Wolf, Thomas. *Managing a Nonprofit Organization in the Twenty-first Century.* New York: Simon & Schuster, 1999.

Zeller, Kerry. "From National Service to Social Protest: American Museums in the 1940s, '50s, '60s, and '70s." *Museum News* (March/April 1996): 48–59.

About the Editor

Gail Anderson has been active in the museum field for over twenty-six years. Today, she focuses her efforts on helping museum directors and trustees strategically position their institutions for growth and sustainability using the tools of strategic planning, organizational development, board development, and individual coaching. Prior to launching her own consulting business, Anderson was the deputy director of the Mexican Museum, vice president of Museum Management Consultants, chair of the Department of Museum Studies at John F. Kennedy University, assistant director at the Southwest Museum, and museum educator at the Museum of Northern Arizona. In 1996, she co-led a roundtable for museum directors to advise them about leading their institutions through change.

Throughout her museum career, Anderson has been active in professional organizations as a board member of the American Association of Museums (AAM), a member of the national committee that produced *Excellence & Equity: Education and the Public Dimension of Museums*, and as a longtime board member and past president of the Western Museums Association board of directors. She is a member of the national group of consultants, The Museum Group. She is the editor and contributing author of the AAM Technical Information Series publication *Museum Mission Statements: Building a Distinct Identity*. She is working on her next publication, an introductory text to complement this book, for AltaMira Press.